*Her critiques are
good (role of
observer ≥ only surface;
use of sci.?)
but they undermine her
own system too...*

CAMBRIDGE TEXTS IN THE
HISTORY OF PHILOSOPHY

———

MARGARET CAVENDISH,
DUCHESS OF NEWCASTLE
Observations upon Experimental Philosophy

2001!

invisible
4 - vs Hooke! (phil...)
9 - - say USE of sci ...
ie. what is reality?

48 . irony! Hooke's affirmation of
nature vs. art!
→ like Bodin! / encyclopedia –

138 If infinite parts of nature - why are
infinite use of instruments??

CAMBRIDGE TEXTS IN THE
HISTORY OF PHILOSOPHY

Series editors
KARL AMERIKS
Professor of Philosophy at the University of Notre Dame
DESMOND M. CLARKE
Professor of Philosophy at University College Cork

The main objective of Cambridge Texts in the History of Philosophy is to expand the range, variety and quality of texts in the history of philosophy which are available in English. The series includes texts by familiar names (such as Descartes and Kant) and also by less well-known authors. Wherever possible, texts are published in complete and unabridged form, and translations are specially commissioned for the series. Each volume contains a critical introduction together with a guide to further reading and any necessary glossaries and textual apparatus. The volumes are designed for student use at undergraduate and post-graduate level and will be of interest not only to students of philosophy, but also to a wider audience of readers in the history of science, the history of theology and the history of ideas.

For a list of titles published in the series, please see end of book.

MARGARET CAVENDISH, DUCHESS OF NEWCASTLE

Observations upon Experimental Philosophy

EDITED BY

EILEEN O'NEILL

University of Massachusetts, Amherst

CAMBRIDGE
UNIVERSITY PRESS

CAMBRIDGE UNIVERSITY PRESS
Cambridge, New York, Melbourne, Madrid, Cape Town,
Singapore, São Paulo, Delhi, Tokyo, Mexico City

Cambridge University Press
The Edinburgh Building, Cambridge CB2 8RU, UK

Published in the United States of America by
Cambridge University Press, New York

www.cambridge.org
Information on this title: www.cambridge.org/9780521776752

First published 2001

A catalogue record for this publication is available from the British Library

Library of Congress Cataloguing in Publication data
Newcastle, Margaret Cavendish, Duchess of, 1623?–1673.
Observations upon experimental philosophy/Margaret Cavendish, Duchess of
Newcastle: edited by Eileen O'Neill.
p. cm. – (Cambridge texts in the history of philosophy)
Includes bibliographical references (p. xlii) and index.
ISBN 0 521 77204 4 (hardback)
1. Philosophy of nature. I. O'Neill, Eileen. II. Title. III. Series.
B1299.N273 027 2001 192–dc21 00-050354

ISBN 978-0-521-77204-4 Hardback
ISBN 978-0-521-77675-2 Paperback

Contents

Acknowledgments

Desmond Clarke was not only the "proximate" cause that triggered my work on this edition, he was an "auxiliary" cause, aiding the "primary and sustaining" cause to the very end. I'm indebted to him for his sound advice and invaluable critical comments. I'd also like to thank Hilary Gaskin of Cambridge University Press for countless judicious suggestions. Peggy McKinnon did a remarkable job of swiftly and accurately keying in the unedited version of Cavendish's text. Edward Abrams provided research and computer assistance; Sylvia Howes handled numerous clerical and administrative matters. Few research projects can get off the ground without funding: for that I'm deeply grateful to Frederick Byron and Lee Edwards of the University of Massachusetts-Amherst. I've received valuable help from the librarians Richard Talbot, Jim Kelly, Susan Mathew, Mel Carlson, and MJ Canavan, the Interlibrary Loan Office and Microfilm Department of my home institution, the staff of the British Library, and the staffs of the rare book rooms at Harvard University, Smith College, Amherst College, the University of Pennsylvania, and the New York Public Library. Part of the Introduction was first presented at the 1997 conference on "Women Philosophers of the Seventeenth Century"; my colleagues Bob Sleigh and Vere Chappell were the moving forces behind that event. I thank them and my Department Chair, John Robison, for advice in regard to this edition and other research projects. Versions of the Introduction were also read at McGill University and the University of Pennsylvania. I'm especially grateful to Steven Gross, Alison Laywine, Eric Lewis, Susan Sauvé Meyer, and Tom Ricketts for feedback; to Allison Crapo, Gary Hatfield, Sarah Hutton, Christia Mercer, and Jim Ross for written comments; and to Stephen Menn for extensive written comments on the entire manuscript. While I have not been able to respond here to all of the issues these folks have raised, the edition has profited immensely from their help. Special thanks also go to Barbara Meyer for our conversations. Finally, Gary Ostertag read the entire manuscript and saved me from a number of stylistic, and more substantial, errors. I thank him for this, and for our ongoing dialogues on philosophy and poetry. I dedicate this edition to him.

Abbreviations

Cavendish's works

Poems	*Poems, and Fancies*, London, 1653; facsimile reprint Menston: Scolar Press, 1972; reprinted as *Poems, and Phancies*, Second Impression, London, 1664, and as *Poems, or Several Fancies in Verse: with the Animal Parliament, in Prose*, Third Edition, London, 1668.
Fancies	*Philosophicall Fancies*, London, 1653.
Opinions	*Philosophical and Physical Opinions*, London, 1655; Second Edition, London, 1663.
Olio	*The World's Olio*, London, 1655; Second Edition, London, 1671.
Pictures	*Nature's Pictures Drawn by Fancie's Pencil to the Life*, London, 1655/56; reprinted as *Natures Picture Drawn by Fancies Pencil to the Life*, Second Edition, London, 1671.
Plays	*Playes*, London, 1662; followed by *Plays, never before Printed*, London, 1668.
Orations	*Orations of Divers Sorts, Accomodated to Divers Places.* London, 1662/63; Second Edition, London, 1668.
Soc. Letters	*CCXI Sociable Letters*, London, 1664; facsimile reprint Menston: Scolar Press, 1969.
Phil. Letters	*Philosophical Letters: or, Modest Reflections Upon some Opinions in Natural Philosophy, maintained By several Famous and Learned Authors of this Age . . .*, London, 1664; letters on Descartes reprinted in Margaret

	Atherton (ed.), *Women Philosophers of the Early Modern Period*, Indiana: Hackett Publishing Co., 1994.
Observations	*Observations upon Experimental Philosophy, To which is added, The Description of a New Blazing World*, London, 1666; Second Edition, London, 1668; the added text reprinted in Kate Lilley (ed.), *The Blazing World and Other Writings*, London/New York: Penguin Books, 1992.
Life	*The Life of the Thrice Noble, High and Puissant Prince William Cavendishe, Duke, Marquess, and Earl of Newcastle* . . ., London, 1667; Second Edition, 1675; Latin translation by William Charleton as *De vita et rebus gestis . . . Guilielmi Ducis Novo-Castrensis* . . ., London, 1668; numerous reprintings.
Grounds	*Grounds of Natural Philosophy* . . ., London, 1668; facsimile reprint West Cornwall: Locust Hill Press, 1996.

Editions and translations of other works frequently cited

AT	*Œuvres de Descartes*, ed. Charles Adam & Paul Tannery, nouvelle présentation (Paris: CNRS/Vrin, 1964–74)
CSM	*The Philosophical Writings of Descartes*, ed. and tr. John Cottingham, Robert Stoothoff, Dugald Murdoch and Anthony Kenny, 3 vols. (Cambridge: Cambridge University Press, 1984–91)
CWA	*The Complete Works of Aristotle*, revised Oxford translation, ed. Jonathan Barnes, 2 vols. (Princeton: Princeton University Press, 1984)
EW	*The English Works of Thomas Hobbes of Malmesbury*, ed. Sir William Molesworth, 11 vols. (London, 1839–45; reprinted Germany: Scientia Aalen, 1962)
LP	*Letters and Poems in Honour of the Incomparable Princess, Margaret, Dutchess of Newcastle* (London, 1676)
WRB	*The Works of the Honourable Robert Boyle*, ed. Thomas Birch, Second Edition, 6 vols. (London, 1772)

Introduction

One of the main projects that seventeenth-century European philosophers undertook was that of providing a metaphysical framework for the new mechanical science – a scientific picture of nature that eventually replaced the Aristotelian world-view. In their attempt to achieve this end, they turned to the writings of the ancient Greek and Roman philosophers, which the Renaissance humanists had rediscovered and published. Thus, Pierre Gassendi (1592–1655) rehabilitated the philosophical doctrines of the ancient atomist Epicurus. Figures as diverse as René Descartes (1596–1650), Anne Conway (1631–79), Henry More (1614–87), and Mary Astell (1666–1731) drew on Platonic doctrines in the formation of their metaphysics.

But not all philosophers were willing to overthrow Aristotelianism. Kenelm Digby (1603–65) attempted to conserve many of the Aristotelian doctrines, and to make aspects of the mechanical science compatible with these doctrines. And there were many camps of anti-Aristotelian naturalists who rejected the picture of nature as a grand machine, and who endorsed various "vitalist" views of corporeal nature as self-moving, living, and knowing. Among these thinkers were the physicians and chemists, for example, Johannes Baptista Van Helmont (1579–1644), who followed in the tradition of the vitalist naturalist Paracelsus (1493–1541); while others included practitioners of natural magic, for example, Robert Fludd (1574–1637), who were part of the hermetic and occult traditions. Finally, Joseph Glanvill (1636–80), who despaired of producing the true system of nature, and who fully endorsed neither Aristotle nor the mechanists, rehabilitated arguments from the ancient sceptics.

These were the complex crosscurrents of philosophical and scientific thought in reaction to which Margaret Cavendish constructed her system of nature. Just as the mechanists had, she would reject the Aristotelianism of the schools; and as Van Helmont and other vitalists had, she would reject the view that mechanism provides the fundamental explanations of natural phenomena. Cavendish would draw on the doctrines of the ancient Stoics, and among her main philosophical contributions would be her Stoic-inspired attacks against the limitations of seventeenth-century mechanical philosophy.

While, as we have seen, the writing of natural philosophy was far from unusual in this period, the writing of it by a woman was. We now know that in the seventeenth century numerous women published philosophy, had translations of their work appear in print, and were discussed in the scholarly journals.[1] A few of these women were prolific writers of texts with philosophical content, for example, Antoinette Bourignon (1616–80), Madeleine de Scudéry (1607–1701), and Mary Astell. But very few published entire books on natural philosophy. There is Anne Conway's *The Principles of the Most Ancient and Modern Philosophy* (Latin, 1690; English, 1692) and Jeanne Dumée's *Entretien sur l'opinion de Copernic touchant la mobilité de la terre* [A Discussion of the opinion of Copernicus concerning the mobility of the earth] (n.d.; ms. *c.* 1680). Cavendish, on the other hand, is singular in having published some half dozen books in this area.

Nor was this all she wrote. Cavendish also published poetry, plays, orations, letters, fiction, an autobiographical sketch, and a biography of her husband. Of the almost six hundred and fifty books in English published between 1640 and 1700 by women, over a dozen were original works by Cavendish, subsequent editions of which raised her total number of publications to twenty-one. Hers was an extraordinary writing career, but it was eyed with suspicion by her contemporaries. For one thing, in an era in which anonymous authorship for women was standard, Cavendish adamantly published under her own name. In her autobiographical sketch she admitted that she was "very ambitious," not for wealth or power, but for fame. In her first publication she writes that man "hath a transcending desire to live in the world's memory, as long as

[1] See the groundbreaking Mary Ellen Waithe (ed.), *A History of Women Philosophers*, 4 vols. (Dordrecht: Kluwer Academic Publishers, 1987–95); and Eileen O'Neill, "Disappearing Ink: Early Modern Women Philosophers and Their Fate in History," in Janet Kourany (ed.), *Philosophy in a Feminist Voice* (Princeton: Princeton University Press, 1998).

the world lasts; that he might not die like a beast, and be forgotten; but that his works may beget another soul . . . which is fame" (*Poems*, p. 52).

However, unlike most of her male philosophical counterparts – and even a few women of the period, such as Anna Maria van Schurman (1607–78) who had studied philosophy, theology and ancient languages at the University of Utrecht – Cavendish had received no formal training in philosophy. And unlike some of the royal women, such as Princess Elisabeth of Bohemia (1618–80) and Queen Christina of Sweden (1626–89), she had not been privately tutored in languages and the sciences. (Indeed, despite years spent on the Continent, it appears that Cavendish never acquired the ability to read philosophical texts in any language other than English.) Further, Cavendish did not have a philosophical mentor in the way that Michel de Montaigne (1533–92) was a mentor to Marie le Jars de Gournay (1565–1645), and Henry More to Anne Conway; nor did she have a famous philosopher as interlocutor, in the way that Elisabeth could exchange ideas with Descartes, or Damaris Masham (1658–1708) with Gottfried Wilhelm Leibniz (1646–1716). These facts make her philosophical accomplishments all the more re-markable. In order to see how Cavendish gained access to the views of the ancient and modern philosophers, and what the influences on her own anti-Aristotelian, anti-mechanist natural philosophy were, we need to turn to some of the details of her life.

Margaret Lucas was the youngest of eight children born to Thomas Lucas and Elizabeth Leighton Lucas of St. John's near Colchester, Essex. The exact date of her birth is unknown, but is usually taken as 1623. Although her father was a gentleman of property, his death in 1625 left her in later years without a dowry. Her education was typical for girls of her rank: she was taught to read and write, and she studied singing, dancing, and music. Two important features of her psychology, which would incline her toward certain choices in life, especially her choice of career as a philosophical writer, were already apparent in her youth. First, she was painfully shy when speaking with anyone outside of her immediate family; second, she had a powerful desire to communicate her views to the world at large, and to receive recognition thereby. At an early age, she found that writing provided her with a painless vehicle for achieving her desire, and she filled numerous "baby books" with her thoughts.

In 1643, her desire for recognition dominated and led her to leaving home to become a maid of honor to Queen Henrietta Maria. Away from her family, and in the midst of the intrigues of the court at Oxford, her bashfulness soon overwhelmed her; she begged for permission to return home. However her mother feared that this move would irritate the Queen and disgrace her daughter; permission was denied. So in 1644, in response to increased danger from anti-royalist forces, she followed Queen Henrietta Maria into exile in Paris, where, in the following year, she met William Cavendish. After a largely epistolary romance, she left the service of the Queen, and married William, a widower thirty years her senior.

In addition to being one of the world's most skillful horse trainers, William Cavendish was also a patron of the arts, a writer of poetry and plays, and something of an amateur scholar. He owned telescopes and alchemical equipment, and was interested in the contemporary debates in philosophy. In England in the early 1630s, he and his mathematician brother, Charles Cavendish (1591–1654), had been given instruction in philosophy by Hobbes. The two brothers encouraged Margaret Cavendish's interest in philosophy, and helped to further her philosophical education. William Cavendish later defended his wife's writing of philosophy and praised it in print. In Paris from 1645 to 1648, the three gathered about them a group of exiled English philosophers influenced by the mechanical philosophy. This group, known as the "Newcastle Circle," included Hobbes, Digby, and Charleton among others. The circle also had contact with the continental mechanical philosophers Descartes, Gassendi, and Marin Mersenne (1588–1648). It is not clear how much philosophy Cavendish learned through her social encounters with these figures. Some of her published remarks suggest that she did not speak at all to Descartes, and that her dealings with Hobbes were minimal. Here her shy nature was an issue. Still, the excitement about atoms and corpuscles was contagious; it later inspired her first literary endeavor. And there is no question but that, of all the mechanists, Hobbes most strongly affected Cavendish's philosophical development. She would be one of the few seventeenth-century thinkers to dare to side with Hobbes in espousing a materialist philosophy that denied the existence of incorporeal souls in nature.

And for all that, her own system of nature would challenge the view that mechanical explanation could account for all natural phenomena. It is important, then, to see what early influences might have moved her in anti-Aristotle + anti-mechanist

Bacon's spirits

van Helmont

Stoicism

the direction of an alternative to mechanism that was nonetheless anti-Aristotelian. One possibility is the philosophy of Francis Bacon (1561–1626). In his earlier work (not published until 1653), Bacon had been sympathetic to the Democritean doctrine of the existence of unchanging atoms and the vacuum, but by the time he published his *Novum Organum* [New Organon] in 1620, he rejected these doctrines and now held that the properties and activities of all animate and inanimate bodies could be accounted for by various combinations of active spiritous matter with gross matter. Bacon's "spirits" or "pneumaticals" are invisible, rarefied bodies, endowed with appetition and perception, which interact with each other through non-mechanical processes, such as concoction. Bacon's mature theory bears a striking resemblance to Cavendish's treatment of matter in her early work, e.g., *Philosophicall Fancies*.

Another possible influence on Cavendish's anti-Aristotelian alternative to the mechanical philosophy is the work of the chemist Johannes Baptista Van Helmont. As we shall see, Cavendish would later criticize Van Helmont's vitalist natural philosophy, but in the early 1650s, his work may have inspired her to attempt to construct a system of nature that would rival that of the mechanists. The only material of Van Helmont's in print at this time were the three essays translated by Walter Charleton as *A Ternary of Paradoxes* in 1650.

A final early source of influence may have been Stoicism. As we shall see, Cavendish increasingly added Stoic doctrines to her developing system of nature. It is significant that when the Cavendishes were in Antwerp, they rented the house owned by the painter, Peter Paul Rubens, before his death. This famous baroque painter had been part of an important Neostoic circle. His brother had been a disciple of Justus Lipsius (1547–1606), who, with the publication of *De Constantia* [On Constancy] in 1584, had initiated the Neostoic movement. Among Lipsius' important contributions to seventeenth-century philosophy was the 1604 *Physiologia Stoicorum* [The Natural Philosophy of the Stoics]. In this milieu, Cavendish may have been exposed to Stoic doctrines.

When Cavendish returned to England in 1660, she began a serious course of study of the natural philosophy of her contemporaries. Her hope was that she could press this knowledge into the service of clarifying her own philosophy in future publications, by contrasting her views with those of recognized scholars. In addition to reading a number of works by Descartes and Hobbes, she also turned to the writings of Henry

More. She found that she needed to distinguish her own organicism, which admitted no incorporeals in nature, from the vitalism of More with its incorporeal "spirit of nature." It was also at this time that she read Van Helmont's treatise in chemical vitalism *Oriatrike, Or, Physick Refined* (1662). Cavendish's further studies included an examination of the views of the scientists Galileo Galilei (1564–1642) and William Harvey (1578–1657).

Between 1664 and 1666 Cavendish was engaged in two intellectual projects. The first was her critical reading of scholars working in dioptrics, meteorology, hydrostatics, thermochemistry, and magnetic theory. Besides the writings of Hobbes, Descartes, Digby, Van Helmont, and Charleton, she also examined the experimental science of the members of the Royal Society of London, especially the work of Robert Boyle (1627–91), Robert Hooke (1635–1703), and Henry Power (1623–68). Second, she attempted to master the natural philosophy of the ancients. Since she read no Greek or Latin, she turned to Thomas Stanley's *The History of Philosophy* (1655–62), which provides paraphrases of the source material for reconstructing the views of the various ancient sects. In her publications that followed this period of study, she criticized the views of Plato, Aristotle, Pythagoras, Epicurus, and the sceptics; but notably absent was any discussion of the Stoics. It is possible that Cavendish's silence here was fueled by the fear that her critics would charge her with a lack of originality, arguing that she had simply repeated the views of the Stoics. And if there was one thing Cavendish wanted as much as fame, it was to have views that were as singular as her dress and manners (against all of which her critics, including the diarist Samuel Pepys, tirelessly railed).

The publications in natural philosophy

Cavendish's first publication, *Poems, and Fancies* (1653), contained prose epistles arguing for women's suitability for writing poetry and apologizing for her own specific undertaking. While the poems deal with such themes as man's relation to animals, the passions, the comparison of animate and inanimate things, and fairies, it was the initial fifty pages of poems on atoms that set the stage for Cavendish's later foray into a more serious examination of natural philosophy. The numerous apologies for writing in verse and the Epicurean subject matter suggest that she was taking the *De Rerum Natura* [On the Nature of Things] of Lucretius (*c*. 94–*c*. 55 BC) as her model. Cavendish may well have been attracted by Lucretius' materialism, but this first book was not intended to give her considered views on natural philosophy. There she notes that "the reason why I write it in verse, is, because I thought errors might better pass there, than in prose; since poets write most fiction, and fiction is not given for truth, but pastime" ("To Naturall Philosophers," unpaginated). In subsequent writings she makes clear that "the opinion of atoms, is fitter for a poetical fancy, than for serious philosophy; and this is the reason I have waived it in my philosophical works" (*Observations*, p. 129). But the issue, fancifully handled in the poems, of the correct system of nature was to become the focus of her developing philosophical interest.

Three months after the publication of her first book, she published her largely prose composition, *Philosophicall Fancies* (1653). In this short, recondite text, Cavendish suggested, for the first time, an organicist alternative to the mechanical system of nature. Two years later, she republished this work as the first part of an expanded defense of her organicist materialism, *The Philosophical and Physical Opinions* (1655). Here she reveals that she has read Descartes' *Passions de l'âme* [Passions of the Soul] and Hobbes' *De Cive* [On the Citizen], and that she has learned the "terms of art, and the several opinions of the ancients" from her brother, husband and brother-in-law. But she argues at length for the originality of her philosophical views and even includes as frontispiece an engraving of herself in an empty study with the verse: "Her library on which She look's / It is her Head her Thoughts her Books . . ." By this point, Cavendish not only viewed her work in natural philosophy as her means of achieving literary fame, she began to harbor philosophical ambitions. This is especially clear in light of the further revisions of the work, and commentaries on it, that she would proceed to publish.

In 1663, a revised version of her treatise appeared, and in the following year she published a "commentary" on it: *Philosophical Letters* (1664). She now defended her system, and highlighted its originality and strengths, by pitting it against the mechanical materialism of Hobbes, Descartes' dualism, More's version of Platonism, and the chemical vitalism of Van Helmont. The genre she used this time was neither verse nor the treatise. She realized that there is no way to make opinions more intelligible "than by arguing and comparing other men's opinions with them" ("Preface," unpaginated). And since she had been unable to obtain critical responses to her previous publications from the acknowledged giants in the field, Cavendish now devised a pseudo-epistolary genre: she wrote "letters," to a presumably fictitious woman, in which she criticized the competing systems of nature, while expounding her own.

In 1666, she published another "commentary," *Observations upon Experimental Philosophy*. This work provided the most complete exposition of her system of nature, and did so by setting her views in relief against those of a range of "speculative" philosophers, "dioptrical and experimental" writers, and ancient philosophers.[2] It was followed in 1668 by the final revision of her philosophical opinions, the more concise and organized statement of her system *Grounds of Natural Philosophy*.[3] While this work summarized her considered views, it did not include the details of argumentation that appear in *Observations*.

It is clear, then, that beginning with her *Philosophicall Fancies*, Cavendish gradually developed an anti-Aristotelian alternative to the mechanical system of nature; this project runs throughout her subsequent publications on natural philosophy. Of this project she said, "I . . . [do] not persuade myself, that my philosophy being new, and but lately brought forth, will at first sight prove master of understanding, nay, it may be not in this age; but if God favour her, she may attain to it in after-times: And if she be slighted now and buried in silence, she may perhaps rise more gloriously hereafter . . ." (*Observations*, pp. 12–13). Cavendish's anticipations were more accurate than she might have wished; the scholarly response to her work was initially negligible.

The critical reception of these works

How did Cavendish's contemporaries respond to the fruits of her philosophical ambition? If we examine the collection of letters, published by her husband after her death, it emerges that she had not attained general recognition by the scholarly community. Kenelm Digby and Thomas Hobbes were polite, but they did not grace her natural philosophy with

---

[2] For evidence that Cavendish clearly took *Phil. Letters* and *Observations* to be commentaries, see *Observations*, pp. 11; 13.
[3] Cavendish is explicit that *Grounds* is the second, and much revised, edition of *Opinions*; see *Grounds*, "To All the Universities in Europe," unpaginated.

critical responses.[4] In 1667, her friend Walter Charleton, wrote her this backhanded compliment: "For your natural philosophy . . . may be, for ought I know, excellent: but give me leave, Madam, to confess, I have not yet been so happy as to discover much therein that's *apodictical*, or wherein I think myself much obliged to acquiesce . . . This Madam, can be no discredit to your philosophy in particular, because common to all others: and he is a bold man, who dares to exempt the physics of Aristotle himself, or of Democritus, or Epicurus, or any other hitherto known" (*LP*, p. 111). Henry More was harsher. In response to her *Philosophical Letters*, he confided to Anne Conway that Cavendish "may be secure from anyone giving her the trouble of a reply."[5] Aside from Charles Cavendish, the scholars who seem to have taken her natural philosophy most seriously were Constantijn Huygens, with whom she briefly corresponded on the phenomena of "exploding glasses," and Joseph Glanvill.[6] Glanvill carried on earnest debates with her about such views as the world soul, innate ideas, the pre-existence of human souls, evidence for the existence of immaterial spirits and their compatibility with the Scriptures.

If Cavendish was slighted and "buried in silence" in her own day, the response of some modern critics was hardly more sympathetic. In 1918, Henry Ten Eyck Perry published a detailed study of Cavendish's life and works in which he concluded that for her "lack of rational power she unconsciously substituted an overactive imagination." He referred to her publications as "so-called philosophical books."[7] In a similar vein, Virginia Woolf lamented that Cavendish "should have frittered her time away scribbling nonsense and plunging ever deeper into obscurity and folly."[8] Of course, Perry and Woolf were both literary critics, not scholars of early modern philosophy.

In 1966, the historian of science, Robert Kargon, argued that Caven-

---

[4] Hobbes did say that one of her books had "truer ideas of virtue and honour than any book of morality I have read . . ." (*LP*, p. 68).

[5] *The Conway Letters*, ed. Marjorie Nicholson, revised edition by Sarah Hutton (Oxford: Clarendon Press, 1992), p. 237.

[6] See Further Reading for the references for Huygens' and Glanvill's letters. On exploding glasses see R.[obert] Hooke, *Micrographia: or Some Physiological Descriptions of Minute Bodies Made by Magnifying Glasses, with Observations and Inquiries Thereupon* (London, 1665), "Observation VII: Of Some Phaenomena of Glass Drops."

[7] Henry Ten Eyck Perry, *The First Duchess of Newcastle and Her Husband as Figures in Literary History* (Boston/London: Ginn and Company, 1918), pp. 188; 197.

[8] Virginia Woolf, *A Room of One's Own* (New York: Harcourt, Brace and World, 1929), p. 65.

but possible
without
discourse?

dish's system is Epicurean atomism, and that she herself played "an interesting role in the establishment of atomism in England which has been largely overlooked." However, he noted that it has been overlooked "in part because it is difficult for the modern historian to take her seriously," for her atomism "was fanciful and of little use to the natural philosophers . . ."[9] In short, Kargon simultaneously gave her views a place in the history and philosophy of science, and put a damper on interest in them that lasted for more than a decade. It is important to note, however, that Kargon's treatment of Cavendish focused on her first book of poems, but, as we saw earlier, there is good reason not to count that work as providing her definitive philosophical position.

In the following decade, Carolyn Merchant decried "the almost total neglect by historians of philosophy of . . . a cluster of women who studied and contributed to philosophy, science, and educational literature of the seventeenth and eighteenth centuries."[10] In response to Merchant's work, and that of other revisionist historians, a number of more detailed studies of Cavendish's system began to appear. For example, Londa Schiebinger's examination of Cavendish's mature natural philosophy led her to characterize it as an eloquent statement of "the vitality of matter and the dignity of animals; and within contemporary discourse, these views were consistent with her anti-Cartesianism."[11] But Schiebinger admitted that it was still unclear why Cavendish endorsed vitalistic materialism over the stance of Cartesian dualism.

One recent account of Cavendish's system of nature has offered political reasons for her choice of vitalistic materialism. On this interpretation, the natural philosophy of her early works was a nonvitalist atomism. But between 1661 and 1663, for feminist political reasons, Cavendish allegedly attacked the authority of the "male-dominated" and "masculinist" mechanical science. An "underlying feminist ideology" moved her toward a "more organic and nurturing view of nature," such that her resulting system was an amalgam of "some of the basic axioms of the new science, for example the pervasiveness of matter in motion,

(ESS.)
FDM

---

[9] Robert Hugh Kargon, *Atomism in England from Hariot to Newton* (Oxford: Clarendon Press, 1966), pp. 73; 75.

[10] Carolyn Merchant, *The Death of Nature* (San Francisco: Harper and Row, 1980), p. 268.

[11] Londa Schiebinger, "Margaret Cavendish, Duchess of Newcastle," in Mary Ellen Waithe (ed.), *A History of Women Philosophers* (Dordrecht: Kluwer Academic Publishers, 1991), vol. 3, p. 9.

gendered knowledge

within an organic and vitalistic universe."[12] Attempts have been made to specify the "masculinist" feature of her early mechanical atomism in reaction to which Cavendish had formulated her mature "animist materialism." According to one scholar, "it is difficult to imagine anything but the most patriarchal conclusion derivable from Hobbes' ruthless, scientistic view of the priority of physical strength. Mechanism provided masculine dominance with a powerful organizational sanction, and . . . it was precisely the untenable nature of such conclusions that impelled Cavendish to distance herself from the mechanical explanation of natural change . . ."[13]

According to this account, Cavendish transformed her atomistic system of nature into an organicist one between 1661 and 1663 – the period culminating in the revised edition of the *Philosophical and Physical Opinions*. But that seems implausible, given the chronology of her writing. The original 1655 edition of the same work already contained a preface entitled "A Condemning Treatise of Atomes," and the book presented an "animistic materialist" system of nature. In addition, since the first section of the book is a reprint of the 1653 *Philosophicall Fancies*, her commitment to an animistic materialism dates from far earlier than 1661. A further difficulty which this account must face is that, in her publications, Cavendish did not explicitly discuss the political consequences of views in natural philosophy. But she did attempt philosophical justifications for her rejection of atomism and on behalf of her organicist materialism.

Quite recently scholars have begun to examine the details of these arguments and to compare them with those of Cavendish's contemporaries.[14] On the one hand, work is being done on the differences between her brand of anti-mechanism and the vitalism of seventeenth-century Platonists, for example Anne Conway. On the other hand, scholars are examining the influence of Hobbes' views on Cavendish's and analyzing the differences in their respective versions of materialism. Another recent project has been the reexamination of her position on atomism. One scholar has argued that her mature system was not a rejection of atomism as such, but only a rejection of *mechanical* atomism. According

[12] Lisa Sarasohn, "A Science Turned Upside Down: Feminism and the Natural Philosophy of Margaret Cavendish," *Huntington Library Quarterly* 47, 4 (1984): 299–307; see pp. 290; 295.
[13] John Rogers, *The Matter of Revolution: Science, Poetry and Politics in the Age of Reason* (Ithaca: Cornell University Press, 1996), p. 188.
[14] See the articles by Sarah Hutton and Susan James cited in Further Reading.

to this account, there is enough continuity between her atomistic concepts and those of Hobbes and Digby to term the views of all three
"particulate matter-theories."[15]

Cavendish's natural philosophy has, in a sense, been resurrected after
centuries of silence. Although it may not be a "glorious rising," and
although we still may not have entirely mastered an understanding of her
system, nonetheless, her work is now receiving the serious critical
attention that she had so passionately desired.

Cavendish's system of nature

In *Philosophicall Fancies*, Cavendish began outlining a materialist system
of nature in which body, rather than being inert and inanimate, is
self-moving, animate, sensitive and knowing. Furthermore, instead of
being atomic in structure, it is continuous. What accounts for these
features is the "spirits of nature or innate matter," an active material
principle which permeates gross matter. In speaking of these spirits,
Cavendish claims that "those figures they make by several, and subtle
motion, may differ variously, and infinitely. This innate matter is a kind
of God, or Gods to the dull part of matter, having power to form it, as it
please . . ." (*Fancies*, p. 12). She stresses that change in the configurations of matter, made by the self-moving spirits, gives rise to all natural
phenomena (*Fancies*, p. 20). She further claims that "whatsoever hath
motion hath sensitive spirits; and what is there on earth that is not
wrought, or made into figures, and then undone again by these spirits?
So that all matter is moving, or moved, by the movers; if so, all things
have sense, because all things have of these spirits in them; and if
sensitive spirits, why not rational spirits? For there is as much infinite of
every several degree of matter, as if there were but one matter: for there is
no quantity in infinite; for infinite is a continued thing" (*Fancies*, p. 54).

This vague picture of nature already has a number of affinities with the
ancient Stoic system.[16] Like the Stoics' *pneuma*, Cavendish's "rational
and sensitive spirits" are a unified corporeal principle which not only

---

[15] See the article by Stephen Clucas in Further Reading.
[16] My discussion of Stoic physics derives largely from A. A. Long and D. N. Sedley (eds.), *The
Hellenistic Philosophers*, 2 vols. (Cambridge: Cambridge University Press, 1987), S. Samburksy,
Physics of the Stoics (New York: Macmillan, 1959), Josiah B. Gould, *The Philosophy of Chrysippus*
(Albany: State University of New York Press, 1970) and Emile Bréhier, *Chrysippe et l'ancien
stoïcisme* (Paris: Press Universitaires de France, 1951).

binds the natural world into a single, continuous body, but also gives rise to all its physical qualities. The Stoics thought of this fiery breath or spirit, which they called "God," as the knowing and intelligent force that makes the whole of nature through which it extends a single living and intelligent organism. Thus, this force may be viewed as the soul of the world. Cavendish implicitly acknowledges the affinity between her "spirits or innate matter" and the Stoics' active principle in calling it "a kind of God . . . to dull part of matter"; and she explicitly agrees with the Stoics that "the innated matter, is the soul of nature. The dull part of matter, the body" (*Opinions* (1655), p. 30). What the Stoics have to say about the infinite can also help us to understand Cavendish's obscure remark that "there is no quantity in infinite; for infinite is a continued thing." When asked about the ultimate or least parts of nature, Chrysippus urged us "to think of each body as consisting neither of certain parts nor of some number of them, either infinite or finite."[17] Just as the Aristotelians did, the Stoics rejected the atomic theory, according to which bodies are composed of indivisible particles. Chrysippus' aim here was to show that since bodies are not aggregates of atoms, there is no point to the question of whether the body's atomic parts are finite or infinite in number. Rather, bodies are parts of the corporeal continuum, whose unity is brought about by the continuous tensional motions of the *pneuma*. It seems that, by 1653, Cavendish is already experimenting with the possibility that the structure of corporeal nature is continuous and held together by something subtle – which position the Stoics had urged in opposition to the Epicurean view. And she even stresses how the parts of this unified, continuous, animate nature are filled with sympathies and antipathies. The Stoics also had argued that the fiery spirit gives rise to the whole of nature being in sympathy with itself. That is, an occurrence in one part of nature has a non-mechanical effect upon all the other parts of the universe, analogously to the effect the condition of an organ has on the condition of the human body as a whole.

There are, of course, a number of anti–atomist Stoic views that are conspicuously absent in Cavendish's initial version of her materialist organicism, notably the doctrine of "blending" or "complete mixture," and the denial of the existence of an intracosmic vacuum. Since for both Cavendish and the Stoics, the presence of the active breath or spirit

[17] Plutarch, *De communibus notitiis contra Stoicos* [On Common Conceptions Against the Stoics] 1078E–1080E, in A. A. Long and D. N. Sedley (eds.), *The Hellenistic Philosophers*, 50C.

throughout the universe is what accounts for the "sympathy," by which the universe becomes a single body with a unified structure, they need a theory of how the active principle is everywhere mixed with matter. In her mature works, Cavendish will embrace a Stoic-like theory of complete blending, according to which the active spirits will so interpenetrate matter, that they will not simply be juxtaposed to matter by surface contact, but will be mutually coextended with matter, so that both the spirits and matter will be present in any part of the universe you pick, no matter how small. And in order to protect the unity of the sympathetic corporeal world, thoroughly blended with *pneuma*, the Stoics had argued: "In the cosmos there is no void as can be seen from the phenomena. For if the whole material world were not coalescent (*sumphues*) the cosmos would not be by nature coherent and ordered, neither could mutual interaction exist between its parts, nor could we, without one binding tension and without the all-permeating pneuma, be able to see and hear. For sense-perception would be impeded by the intervening empty spaces."[18] By 1655, Cavendish is still unsure how it will be possible to eliminate the vacuum. She writes in verse: "For what's unequall, cannot joyned be / So close, but there will be Vacuity" (*Opinions*, p. 4).[19] But in the 1660s, armed with a theory of complete blending, she will attack the doctrine of the void, arguing that its existence would produce causal chaos and unglue the unity of the corporeal continuum. This mature system of nature of the 1660s contains five major features:

(1) Materialism

Cavendish is a thoroughgoing materialist, with respect to the natural world. In opposition to the views of Descartes, More, Glanvill, and Van Helmont, she maintains that there are neither incorporeal substances nor incorporeal qualities in nature (*Observations*, p. 137). Still, she is at pains to make the thoroughgoing materialism of her natural philosophy consistent with certain Christian doctrines.[20] While holding the orthodox

---

[18] Cleomedes, *De motu circulari corporum caelestium* [On the Circular Motion of Celestial Bodies], 1, 1; the translation appears in Sambursky, *Physics of the Stoics*, p. 41.

[19] On this same page, Cavendish also offers considerations in favor of eliminating belief in the vacuum; she notes in the margin that "the readers may take either opinion."

[20] With respect to the human soul, which according to Christianity is immaterial and immortal, she writes that "the soul of man is part of the soul of nature, and the soul of nature is material: I mean

view that God is a "spiritual, supernatural and incomprehensible infinite,"[21] she nonetheless argues that God "being immovable, and beyond all natural motion, cannot actually move matter; neither is it religious, to say, God is the soul of nature; for God is no part of nature, as the soul is of the body . . ."[22] Instead she suggests that God made matter to be self-moving by a supernatural, general act of his "immutable will and all-powerful command."

For Cavendish, there is a single principle of all natural phenomena, namely matter, which comes in two "degrees" : "animate matter," which parallels the ancient Stoics' active principle, and "inanimate matter," which parallels the Stoics' inactive principle (*Observations*, p. 211). In an effort to underline her materialism, Cavendish has jettisoned the earlier ambiguous terminology of "spirits." She breaks from the Stoic tradition, however, in further specifying the functions of the active principle: animate matter is itself composed of "sensitive matter" and "rational matter." "Sensitive matter," whose motions, like a "labourer or workman," carry along the inanimate matter, gives rise to the variety of configurations in nature and makes nature a single living body filled with diverse bits of sensitive knowledge. "Rational matter," like an "architect, designer or surveyor," imbues parts of nature with a more general knowledge of the whole; when it moves within itself, it produces "fancies, thoughts, imaginations [and] conceptions," and when it moves in tandem with the motions of sensitive matter, it produces sense perception (*Observations*, pp. 150–65).

(2)   Complete mixture

As noted above, in her mature work Cavendish makes use of the Stoic theory of "blending" or "complete mixture" in her account of the

only the natural, not the divine soul of man, which I leave to the Church. And this natural soul, otherwise called reason, is nothing else but corporeal natural self-motion . . ." (*Observations*, p. 221). But sometimes Cavendish argues for a stronger thesis, namely, that no incorporeal entity – other than God himself – can exist: "An immaterial cannot, in my opinion, be naturally created; nor can I conceive how an immaterial can produce particular immaterial souls, spirits, and the like. Wherefore, an immaterial, in my opinion, must be some uncreated being; which can be no other than God alone. Wherefore, created spirits, and spiritual souls, are some other thing than immaterial . . ." (*Grounds*, p. 239.)

[21] *Observations*, p. 220; on God's immateriality, see *Observations*, II, ch. 9.

[22] *Observations*, p. 230. See also *Observations*, I, ch. 17, where Cavendish criticizes Descartes for conceiving of God as setting and conserving the world in motion analogously to the mechanical way a workman spins his lathe; see *Observations*, II, ch. 7 for her criticism of occasionalism.

relation of the two degrees of matter. She maintains that "there is such a commixture of animate and inanimate matter, that no particle in nature can be conceived or imagined, which is not composed of animate matter, as well as of inanimate" (*Observations*, p. 158). So the mixture of animate and inanimate matter is not simply a juxtaposition or meeting at a surface. For if we took a tiny portion of animate matter which so joined a tiny portion of inanimate matter, we could still find a tinier subsection of the former that was not in contact with any subsection of the latter. But complete blending requires that any particle you pick, no matter how small, will be composed of both types of matter. We should not think, however, that she has in mind some type of fusion. The two degrees of matter "do constitute but one body, because of their close and inseparable conjunction and commixture; nevertheless, they are several parts (for one part is not another part)" (*Observations*, p. 127). In other words, animate and inanimate matter, insofar as they are blended, have not lost their specific characters, rather they remain distinct "degrees" of matter, which nevertheless are found completely blended together throughout nature.

(3)   *Pan-organicism and pan-psychism*

Cavendish stresses that the blending with inanimate matter includes not just sensitive matter, but rational as well. She denies that rational matter, or mind, exists only in the brain or some other region of the human body. Rather, animate matter moves throughout nature with the result that nature is everywhere filled with "sensitive and rational knowledge" (*Observations*, p. 207). Pan-organicism and pan-psychism, then, follow directly from Cavendish's application of the theory of blending. She sums up this feature of the system of nature in this way: "As infinite nature has an infinite self-motion and self-knowledge; so every part and particle has a particular and finite self-motion and self-knowledge, by which it knows itself, and its own actions, and perceives also other parts and actions . . ." (*Observations*, p. 138).

(4)   *Continuum theory of matter*

We might think that, due to complete blending, there is pan-organicism and pan-psychism all the way down in nature to its least parts, or atoms.

Introduction

We might suppose that nature is the sum of the elaborate combinations of atoms, and, thus, that atoms are the first principles of natural phenomena. But this is not Cavendish's position.

Some of Cavendish's objections to atomism turn on conceiving of the atom as that which is conceptually indivisible. For example, Cavendish argues that since an atom is corporeal, and since what is corporeal is conceptually infinitely divisible, "there can be no atom, that is, an indivisible body in nature" (*Observations*, p. 125). A second piece of reasoning for denying the existence of atoms turns on her doctrine of complete blending. According to Cavendish, if we pick the smallest unit in nature, it would not be conceptually simple, it would be a composite blending of animate and inanimate matter. Thus, there cannot be atoms, which are by definition the *simples* out of which composite bodies are composed (*Observations*, I, ch. 31). Most of the seventeenth-century corpuscularians, however, denied that atoms are, like the mathematicians' points, conceptually indivisible; they are simply the least parts or *minima* of nature – the parts which are not found further divided in nature. Cavendish needs to offer further arguments against her contemporaries' atomic parts, and she does.

For example, she also makes use of a widely held attack against Epicurean atomism: it is highly improbable that the orderliness of the causal nexus of the universe is due to the random impact of "senseless" particles upon one another. Rather, it is more probable that the complexity, harmony and predictability of causal interactions is due to an animate intelligence ordering change in the universe (*Observations*, pp. 129; 169; 207–08). A special case of Cavendish's worry is how the random motion of inanimate smallest parts could give rise to sensitive, intelligent animate body (*Observations*, pp. 263–65).

Now if these three arguments against the existence of atoms constituted her complete arsenal, we might hold that the target of her attacks is simply a crude mechanical atomism. This would leave open the possibility that Cavendish herself is committed to providing structural explanations of all macro phenomena in terms of the self-moving smallest parts of "innated matter." In short, it would leave open the possibility that Cavendish is a vitalistic corpuscularian of sorts.

However she has further reasoning that would indicate that her target is not just mechanical atomism; rather she is attacking all particulate matter theories. For Cavendish, complete blending confers a unity on animate and inanimate matter, making of them a single, continuous self-subsistent organism. The parts of this continuous organism are not themselves self-subsistent, but depend for their existence and properties on their relation to each other and to the whole of nature: "[T]he head, although it has a whole and perfect figure, yet it is a part of the body, and could not subsist without it. The same may be said of all other particular and perfect figures: As for example, an animal, though it be a whole and perfect figure, yet it is but a part of earth, and some other elements, and parts of nature, and could not subsist without them . . . All which proves, that there are no single parts, nor . . . composition of loose atoms in nature . . . because nature is a body of a continued infiniteness . . ." (*Observations*, pp. 126–27). She further argues that if there were such self-subsistent parts, "nature would be like a beggar's coat full of lice: Neither would she be able to rule those wandering and straggling atoms, because they are not parts of her body, but each is a single body by itself, having no dependence upon each other. Wherefore, if there should be a composition of atoms, it would not be a body made of parts, but of so many whole and entire single bodies, meeting together as a swarm of bees" (p. 129). In other words, the sum of "single parts," or atoms related to each other solely through contact at a surface, could only constitute an aggregate or heap; but such a sum would not be unified, as the continuous body of nature is. Cavendish explains: "When I speak of the parts of nature, I do not understand, that those parts are like grains of corn or sand in one heap, all of one figure or magnitude, and separable from each other: but, I conceive nature to be an infinite body, bulk or magnitude, which by its own self-motion, is divided into infinite parts; not single or indivisible parts, but parts of one continued body, only discernible from each other by their proper figures, caused by the changes of particular motions . . ." (pp. 125–26). So while she can talk about portions of the continuous body of nature, and even distinguish one portion from another on the basis of the ratios of rational, sensitive, and inanimate matter, which give rise to perceivable configurations, this does not commit her to the atomic account of matter. That is, it does not commit her to the view that there are self-subsistent atoms, the sum of whose aggregates is corporeal nature.

And her examples show that her objections to atomism are not just to the mechanists' atoms. Even if the *minima* of nature were animate, like bees or lice, aggregations of such *minima* would not yield unified, middle-sized bodies. Nor could such vital atoms yield the continuous body of nature as a whole. Self-subsistent atoms (be they inanimate or animate) cannot be the items we refer to in our ultimate explanations of phenomena. Rather explanation, at the most fundamental level, works from the top down. Features of the continuous self-moving matter – such as its unity, or the changes in the speed or direction of its motion – explain the unity and change in its parts, i.e., in middle-sized objects. For Cavendish, self-sufficient atoms would be the "effects of matter, and not the principles of nature, or natural beings" (*Observations*, p. 231).[23]

Among the arguments Cavendish offers against the existence of vacua, the one upon which she places the greatest stress is one which underlines her commitment to the continuum theory of matter. She argues that since the orderliness of the causal nexus is due to the fact that a single, rational force (the sensitive and rational motions) unifies and brings about all the changes in the universe, vacua would sever the unified organism of nature. They would create parts of nature separated from each other spatially and causally. That is, they would give rise to the self-subsistent parts, which Cavendish has already attacked, and thereby engender causal chaos: "For, were there a vacuum, there would be no successive motions, nor no degrees of swiftness and slowness . . . The truth is, there would be such distances of several gaps and holes, that parts would never join, if once divided; insomuch, as a piece of the world would become a single particular world, not joining to any part besides itself; which would make a horrid confusion in nature . . ." (*Observations*, p. 129).

However there is an important difference between Cavendish's position on vacua and that of the ancient Stoics. For the same reasons that Cavendish gives, the Stoics had denied the existence of a void inside the cosmos, but they had also argued for an infinite void outside of the cosmos. Cavendish, on the other hand, takes nature to be quantitatively infinite in extension. On her view, there can be no space outside of the unified body of nature (*Observations*, pp. 130–31). Other worlds, should they exist, would just be parts of this single infinite body (*Grounds*, p. 256). So the Stoic reasoning against an intracosmic void becomes, for Cavendish, reasoning for denying any void.

[23] Cavendish sometimes makes use of structural explanation, as when she suggests that the figures of the particles of salt water are pointed, which accounts for such things as salt's penetrating quality (*Phil. Letters*, p. 118). But she holds that her occasional use of structural explanation in no way commits her to a particulate matter theory (*Phil. Letters*, pp. 117–21).

(5) Non-mechanical natural change

The mechanical philosophers explain natural change in terms of the impact of corporeal bodies on one another. Typically such explanation makes reference to the translation of motion or motive force. Cavendish argues, as Leibniz subsequently will, for the contentious view that a transfer model of causation underlies all such mechanical explanation. She has two main objections to this model. First, if motion is a mode of body, as many seventeenth-century mechanical philosophers held, then motion cannot travel outside of the bodily substance in which it inheres in the process of being transferred into another body (*Phil. Letters*, p. 98).[24] For, this would be to give motion the dubious status of the "real qualities" of the scholastics: things that are just properties, but nonetheless possessing the status of "complete things," rather than of modes. And mechanical philosophers, such as Descartes, denied the existence of real qualities. Second, since for Cavendish motion is inseparable from material body, if motion could be transferred, this would require that a portion of material body be transferred. Each translation of motion upon impact with another body would, then, diminish not only the motion in the agent of change, but also the agent's "substance and quantity" (*Phil. Letters*, pp. 77; 98).[25] Cavendish's point is not to deny that any diremptive actions take place in nature; rather her point is that the mechanical transfer of motion via impact does not underlie all natural change.

Cavendish offers the following account of changes in the quantity of motion in individual bodies, as an alternative to that of the mechanical philosophy:

> One body may either occasion, or imitate another's motion, but it can neither give nor take away what belongs to its own or another body's substance . . . Wherefore every creature being composed of this commixture of animate and inanimate matter, has also self-

---

[24] Cf. Thomas Hobbes, "[I]t is not to be thought that an accident goes out of one subject into another . . ." (*Elements of Philosophy*, II, ch. 8, § 21; *EW*. I, 117) and Gottfried Wilhelm Leibniz, *Monadologie* [Monadology], § 7.

[25] Walter Charleton, in *Physiologia Epicuro-Gassendo-Charltoniana, or a Fabrick of Science Natural Upon the Hypothesis of Atoms . . .* (London, 1654), discusses an argument, which he attributes to Alexander of Aphrodisias (fl. *c.* 200 AD), according to which "a continual efflux of substance must minorate the quantity of the most solid visible" (p. 140). One of Charleton's responses is that while bodies are continually losing minute parts of themselves in acts of natural change, these same bodies are also continual recipients of substantial effluvia from other agents of change.

motion, that is life and knowledge, sense and reason, so that no part hath need to give or receive motion to or from another part; although it may be an occasion of such a manner of motion to another part, and cause it to move thus or thus: as for example, a watchmaker doth not give the watch its motion, but he is only the occasion, that the watch moves after that manner, for the motion of the watch is the watch's own motion, inherent in those parts ever since that matter was . . . Wherefore one body may occasion another body to move so or so, but not give it any motion, but every body (though occasioned by another, to move in such a way) moves by its own natural motion; for self-motion is the very nature of animate matter . . . (*Phil. Letters*, pp. 98; 99–100).

First, we need to clarify Cavendish's understanding of an "occasion" and distinguish it from a "prime or principal cause" (*Phil. Letters*, p. 79). We also need to determine whether her commitment to an account of change in the quantity of motion in bodies in terms of occasional causes implies that the parts of nature are causally inefficacious with respect to each other. That is, does Cavendish deny transeunt causation?

Consider the following scholastic textbook characterization: an "occasion" is anything that aids, or is favorable to, the action of a principal cause such that: (1) the occasion has no intrinsic connection with the effect; (2) it is not necessary for the production of the effect; and (3) it has no direct influence on the production of the effect. The condition or circumstance of darkness, then, will count as an occasion of theft for the burglar. But the term "occasion" was also used by the scholastics to pick out things that were more than mere conditions favorable to the act of a prime cause. Take the example where bad company is an occasion for sin. The concept of an occasion operative here contains two further features: (4) an occasion has an indirect influence on the production of the effect by inducing the primary cause to act, and (5) insofar as it exerts this sort of influence, it counts as a partial efficient *moral* cause of the effect.[26]

As opposed to a "physical cause," a "moral cause" is one that indirectly produces its effect by applying or inducing the primary cause, via example, command, advice, solicitation, or even local motion, to produce this effect. For example, a general is the moral cause of the fighting that

[26] See St. Thomas Aquinas, *Summa theologiae*, II–II, q. 43, art. 1; see also the recent scholastic textbook of Peter Coffey, *Ontology or the General Theory of Being: An Introduction to General Metaphysics* (Gloucester, Mass.: Peter Smith, 1970), p. 359.

his troops do at his command. He is not simply a condition favorable to the activity of fighting; his command contributes to the efficient production of the fighting. But it is not his own physical causation that brings about the fighting; his physical causation reaches only to the troops who hear his command. To take another example, the arsonist is the moral, although not the physical, cause of the burning of a house. According to the scholastics, the arsonist himself does not physically have the causal power to incinerate a house; but he applies the fire which does have this power. So, the arsonist is the *physical* cause of his own motions in applying the fire; the fire is the *physical* cause of the incineration of the house; and the arsonist is the *moral* cause of the incineration of the house.[27]

So much for "occasions." What about Cavendish's "prime and principal causes"? Cavendish had at least second-hand knowledge of Cicero's rendering in *De Fato* of the Stoic distinction between "auxiliary and proximate" causes, as opposed to "perfect and principal" causes.[28] Consider the example of an auxiliary cause that Cicero cites: the push a person gives to a cylinder. Without the push, the cylinder will not roll at this time. There is a clear sense in which the person who gives an impulse to the cylinder aids in bringing about its motion. But is it the cause, in the strict sense, of the rolling motion? Surely the cylinder's nature is responsible for the rolling motion, just as the nature of a conically shaped object is responsible for its quite different motion. The auxiliary cause, the push, triggers the active force within the body. It is the cylinder's "own force and nature" which is the perfect and principal cause of the rolling motion. This internal, perfect cause not only accounts for why the cylinder has the motion it has, but also why it continues to roll after it has received the initial impulse. Finally, the auxiliary cause is dependent upon a perfect cause to bring about its effect. By itself the auxiliary cause does not necessitate the effect.

Notice the parallels between the Stoic account of this type of natural change and Cavendish's. She claims that "when a man . . . tosses a ball . . . the hand is only an occasion that the . . . ball moves thus and thus. I will not say, but that it may have some perception of the hand, according

[27] See Francisco Suárez, *Disputationes metaphysicae* [Metaphysical Disputations] (Salamanca, 1597), disp. 17, § 2, 6.

[28] Cicero, *De fato* [On Fate], XVIII, 41 ff. We know that Cavendish read Thomas Stanley, *The History of Philosophy*, 3 vols. (London, 1655–62), which gives the example of the cylinder (II, p. 432).

to the nature of its own figure; but it does not move by the hand's motion, but by its own" (*Observations*, p. 140). On her view, the hand – the occasion – is a kind of auxiliary and proximate, rather than principal, cause of the motion of the ball. It is the nature of the ball itself, and the force inherent in it, that is the principal and perfect cause of the ball's motion. And Cavendish appears to agree with the Stoics that the hand does efficiently contribute to the motion of the ball. She writes: "I do not say, that the motion of the hand doth not contribute to the motion of the bowl; for though the bowl hath its own natural motion in itself . . . nevertheless the motion of the bowl would not move by such an exterior local motion, did not the motion of the hand, or any other exterior moving body give it occasion to move that way; Wherefore the motion of the hand may very well be said to be the cause of that exterior local motion of the bowl, but not to be the same motion by which the bowl moves" (*Phil. Letters*, pp. 447–48).

Now if, on Cavendish's non-mechanical account of changes of motion in bodies, nothing is transferred from the occasional cause (e.g., the hand) to the body which changes (e.g., the ball), how does the occasion "influence" the primary cause to bring about change? The ancient Stoics held that the complete blending of the *pneuma* with matter made nature a unified organism, whose parts had mutual affinities and sympathies with each other. Similarly, Cavendish maintains that the blending of rational matter with both sensitive and inanimate matter gives rise to "agreeable combinations and connexions of parts in all productions" (*Observations*, p. 159). The pervasiveness in nature of rational matter accounts for how all the parts of nature know how to change their configurations on the occasion of changes in distinct parts of nature with which they share an affinity or sympathy. So Cavendish is attempting to replace a transfer model of change, where discrete parts of nature give and receive motion, with a model of the vital agreement and harmony in a unified organism. She understands this vital agreement in terms of the mutual "percep- tions" that the agent and patient of change have. With respect to "all the various changes of figures and parts, and of all the orderly productions, generations, transformations, dissolutions, and all other actions of nature; these cannot be performed without perception: for, all actions are know- ing and perceptive; and, were there no perception, there could not possibly be any such actions: for, how should parts agree, either in the generation, composition or dissolution of composed figures, if they had no

xxxii

knowledge or perception of each other?" (*Observations*, p. 167). Cavendish admits that there may be many types of perception that take place in nature, but the only one accessible to us humans is animal perception.

On her view of animal perception, the corporeal motions of external objects are the exemplar causes of the production of sensitive and rational motions by the principal and primary cause, namely the sentient body itself. The reason that an external object cannot be the principal cause is that Cavendish follows Hobbes' understanding of "primary cause," namely it is that which is both necessary and sufficient for the production of the effect. An external body cannot be necessary for the production of a perception since "the sensitive organs can make such like figurative actions, were there no object present" (*Grounds*, p. 56). Of course, they would not do so at this time, or precisely in this way: such determination requires an occasional cause. Neither is an external body sufficient for the production of a perception. Cavendish considers cases where we are mentally distracted such that, even though the object is present to our senses, we do not see it. Also when "the sensitive parts of the sensitive organs, are irregular, they will make false perceptions of present objects" (ibid.). So the sensitive body is the primary and principal cause of perceptions, and external objects are the occasional causes, i.e., the exemplar causes, which induce the body to imitate or "pattern out" one set of motions rather than another at a given time.[29]

Cavendish's account of perception would apply as follows in her non-mechanical explanation of change of motion in bodies. The hand does not transfer its motion to the ball upon impact. Rather, the rational matter in the ball, as part of the same organic body as the hand, has a sympathetic affinity with its matter; it "perceives" that the hand is about to so change its own configuration that it is about to diminish its motion by n degrees. The hand is the exemplar and efficient moral cause, which occasions the ball to "pattern out" n degrees of motion. The ball is the

---

[29] This account of the production of sense perception bears comparison with Descartes' in his *Notae in programma quoddam* [Comments on a Certain Broadsheet]. Descartes holds that external objects do not "transmit the ideas to our mind through the sense organs," rather their motion "gives the mind occasion to form these ideas by means of the faculty innate to it" (AT, viiiB, 359; CSM, I, 304). Descartes provides the following analogy: the workers are the primary cause and proximate cause, while the foreman is the remote and accidental, or occasional cause of the work done. By analogy, the external object (occasional cause) gives the innate mental faculty (primary cause) "occasion to produce its effect at one moment rather than another" (AT, viiiB, 360; CSM, I, 305). Cavendish's account is similar, but her organic materialism demands that the immaterial mind be substituted by the sentient, corporeal body.

principal and efficient physical cause of its n degrees of motion. Rather than the transference of motion, there has been a replication or imitation that does not violate the conservation of motion in the system of nature.

The question raised above was how an occasional cause (e.g., the hand) could induce the primary cause (e.g., the ball) to bring about change (e.g., to move). It may look as if Cavendish's explanation in terms of the perceptions of the sympathetic parts of nature just pushes the initial question back a stage. Now we can ask: how does an occasional cause induce the primary cause to have the perceptions that it does, if there is no direct physical causation at work between the occasion and the primary cause? Contemporaries, such as Leibniz, took the problem of how the harmony and agreement in nature works to be a formidable challenge that required significant efforts to meet. While Cavendish acknowledges that this is a fair question to raise, she appears to hold that this worry poses a greater threat to the competing systems of nature than to her own.[30] Perhaps her view is that our query is analogous to the question: how does the external push induce the cylinder to roll? She might reply that once we agree that the cylinder has by its own nature and force the power to roll, an explanation of the rolling is successfully given once we have cited the triggering occasional cause (the push), together with the causal power inherent in the nature of the cylinder. To ask, in addition, for an explanation of the cylinder's power to be able to roll, or for an explanation of the push's power to activate the cylinder's power, is to request what neither the scholastics, the mechanists, nor Cavendish can produce. Causal power is not explainable. For example, it is not reducible to the transfer of motion via impact, as the mechanists would have it. Rather, it is the bedrock of explanation. Similarly, the power that the ball has to "pattern out" or imitate certain perceptions, and the power that the hand has to trigger these perceptions are the bedrock of explanation of the ball's motion on the occasion of the action of the hand. We are now in a position to see that Cavendish's commitment to an account of change in the quantity of motion in bodies in terms of occasional causes does not imply that the parts of nature are causally inefficacious with respect to each other. It is true that occasional auxiliary causes are only moral, not physical, causes of the changes that the principal causes effect. But Cavendish does not deny that natural phe-

---

[30] For further discussion of this point, see the article by Susan James, listed in Further Reading.

nomena have physical causal powers with respect to other phenomena; she does not deny transeunt causation. Recall that the hand's physical causation extends to the surface of the ball, where it can effect changes in local motion. And while animal perception takes place by an internal "patterning out" of the external exemplar cause, which itself is a moral, not a physical, cause of the patterning, Cavendish maintains that it is unlikely that all perception in nature works in the way that animal perception does. So it might be that some perception in nature requires the transfer of corporeal parts. Thus her system of nature, while it bears some interesting similarities to Leibniz's, must be distinguished from his harmony of the perceptions of monads which "express" each other; Leibniz's system denies transeunt causation at the monadic level. Finally, Cavendish insists that transeunt causation takes place all the time in animal generation and in the varieties of "respiration." These cases of natural change require the emission of corporeal parts from one individual body to another body.

The significance of the text

Cavendish's books of natural philosophy may appropriately be viewed as published notebooks, in which the features of her system of nature unfold at the same time as she develops as a philosopher. But they are more than this. They are also a testament to her perseverance as a seventeenth-century woman attempting to make original contributions to a cutting-edge field of philosophical endeavor: natural philosophy in the age of scientific revolution. At a time when women largely wrote spiritual tracts, defenses of, and manuals for, the education of women, and discussions of the passions, Cavendish was experimenting with the genres in which to give voice to natural philosophy written by a woman. She continued to negotiate her relationship to the recognized ancient and modern natural philosophers in the hopes that her work would be seriously considered for a place within the tradition. Thus, the Cavendish of 1655 who rightly feared that critics would question whether her views were original and whether the writing was her own, boasted of having read little philosophy. But by 1664, numerous publications later, Cavendish would now acknowledge that she was the serious student of Hobbes, Descartes, More, and Van Helmont. Despite the charges of being bold, conceited, extravagant, ridiculous, and mad, Cavendish kept

il. ALIGNMENT

admirable expose (6)

doing natural philosophy: studying the work of others, and honing her own reasoning. The publication of *Observations* showcases her system of nature by setting it in relief against the doctrines of the major ancient philosophers, and a wide range of the modern speculative and experimental philosophers. No other woman in the seventeenth century, indeed, no woman until Laura Bassi and the marquise du Châtelet in the eighteenth century, would develop her own views in natural philosophy in a series of publications. Thus, *Observations* is an important document in the history of women's contributions to science and philosophy.

More broadly, Cavendish's system of nature, as articulated in *Observations*, fills a unique position in the logical space of early modern philosophy. In opposition to Hobbes and the materialists, she maintains that there can be no mechanical transfer of motion – nor need there be. Motion, perception, life, and reason are inherent within every part of nature. So for Cavendish, in contrast with the mechanical philosophers, matter is not inert, inanimate, and completely characterizable in terms of geometrical properties. She agrees with the mechanical atomists that nature is wholly material, but she opposes their particulate theory of matter in favor of the continuum theory of matter. Thus, her position is to be differentiated from any type of vitalistic atomism as well. In reply to those vitalists who hold that nature is a continuum insofar as all of its parts are links in the great chain of being, she responds that in her system none of the links are incorporeals. She is a thoroughgoing materialist, with respect to nature. For her, the ultimate explanations of natural phenomena make no reference to incorporeal substances or properties. In this way, her position is also distinct from that of the Platonists, Cartesians, vitalistic chemists and hermeticists, and Leibnizians.

nice (6)

In her first publication Cavendish wrote: "[I]f I am condemned, I shall be annihilated to nothing: but my ambition is such, as I would either be a world, or nothing" (*Poems*, "To Naturall Philosophers," unpaginated). The quotation demonstrates how closely she associated her desire for fame with the "world" or system of nature that she produced. Perhaps the most judicious appraisal was given by Cavendish's contemporary, Bathsua Makin: "The present Duchess of Newcastle, by her own genius, rather than any timely instruction, over-tops many grave gownmen."[31]

---

[31] [Bathsua Makin], *An Essay to Revive the Antient Education of Gentlewomen* . . . (London, 1673), p. 10.

1623- 1673

Chronology

c. 1623	Margaret Lucas, youngest of eight children of Thomas Lucas and Elizabeth Leighton Lucas, born on the site of St. John's Abbey, Colchester in Essex
1625	Margaret's father dies. Charles I accedes to the throne of England, and marries the Catholic Henrietta Maria, sister of Louis XIII and daughter of Marie de Medici
c. 1630	Thomas Hobbes writes the "little treatise," marking his initial departure from scholasticism towards mechanical philosophy; Hobbes begins teaching natural philosophy to William Cavendish, Earl (and later Marquis and Duke) of Newcastle, and to William's brother, Charles
1635–36	Hobbes joins the scholarly circle in Paris that includes Pierre Gassendi and Marin Mersenne, who also mediate his interactions with René Descartes; Hobbes visits Galileo in Florence
1638	Anna Maria van Schurman's Latin *The Learned Maid, or, Whether a Maid May Be a Scholar? A Logick Exercise* (English tr., 1659) published
1639	Schurman's Latin *On the Endpoint of Life* published; Schurman corresponds with Princess Elisabeth of Bohemia, and with Marie le Jars de Gournay, author of the French *The Equality of Men and Women* (1622)
1641	Descartes' Latin *Meditations on First Philosophy* published
1642	A mob plunders the Lucas' home in St. John's Abbey and desecrates the family vault in the cemetery. The English civil war begins

xxxvii

1643	Margaret becomes a maid of honor to Queen Henrietta Maria, who had fled from anti-Royalist insurgents in London to the safety of Merton College, Oxford. Princess Elisabeth of Bohemia begins a correspondence with Descartes on metaphysical and moral issues
1644	Descartes' Latin *Principles of Philosophy*, Mersenne's Latin *Synopsis of Universal Geometry and Mixed Mathematics* and *Physico-Mathematical Thoughts*, and Kenelm Digby's *Two Treatises* published. Prince Rupert of Bohemia, brother of Princess Elisabeth, fails to give fellow commander William Cavendish the needed tactical support; the Royalist forces are defeated at the Battle of Marston Moor. William flees England for Hamburg with John Bramhall, philosophical correspondent of Thomas Hobbes. Margaret follows Queen Henrietta Maria into exile in Paris
1645	William Cavendish travels throughout the Netherlands, visiting the exiled Queen Elizabeth of Bohemia in The Hague; he settles in Paris to wait on Queen Henrietta Maria, and there meets and corresponds with Margaret, whom he marries near the end of the year in Sir Richard Browne's chapel. Anna Maria van Schurman corresponds with Bathsua Makin
1647	Margaret's sister, Mary Killigrew; her mother, Elizabeth Leighton Lucas; and illegitimate brother, Sir Thomas, die
1648	Mersenne dies. At the request of Henrietta Maria, Margaret and her husband follow King Charles I to Holland; they rent the house formerly owned by the painter, Peter Paul Rubens, in Antwerp. Parliamentary troops execute Margaret's brother, Sir Charles, in Colchester
1649	King Charles I is executed in London
1650	Descartes dies in Stockholm, where he had been tutoring Queen Christina. Hobbes' *The Elements of Law, Natural and Politic* published in two parts; Walter Charleton publishes medical treatises of J. B. Van Helmont in *A Ternary of Paradoxes*. An unpublished English verse translation of Lucretius' Latin *On the Nature of Things* by Lucy Hutchinson (now in the British Library), and an unpublished prose translation (now in the Bodleian Library, Oxford) by an anonymous author are circulated

1651   Margaret and her brother-in-law, the mathematician
        Charles Cavendish, sail to London to petition for
        compensation for the loss of her husband's estate; her
        petition is unsuccessful. An English translation of Johann
        Amos Comenius' *Naturall Philosophie Reformed by Divine
        Light or a Synopsis of Physics*, Hobbes' *Leviathan* and
        William Harvey's Latin *Anatomical Exercises On the
        Generation of Animals* published
1652   Charleton's *The Darknes of Atheism Dispelled by the Light of
        Nature* published
1653   Henry More's *An Antidote Against Atheisme* and the first
        English edition of William Harvey's *On the Motion of the
        Heart and Blood in Animals* published. Charles Cavendish
        buys back Bolsover (house of his brother, William) from a
        purchaser about to destroy it for building materials. In March,
        Margaret returns to her husband in Antwerp before seeing her
        first volume, *Poems, and Fancies*, in print; additional material
        is completed too late to be included in this volume, and is
        published separately in May as *Philosophicall Fancies*.
1654   Charleton's *Physiologia-Epicuro-Gassendo-Charltoniana*
        published. Charles Cavendish dies
1655   Margaret's shorter literary pieces, including Shakespeare
        criticism and discussion of Harvey on the circulation of the
        blood, published as *The World's Olio*; her *Philosophical and
        Physical Opinions*, the first volume of Stanely's *The History
        of Philosophy*, and Hobbes' Latin *Elements of Philosophy, The
        First Section Concerning Body* (Eng. tr., 1656) also published.
        Gassendi dies
1656   Margaret's *Nature's Pictures*, which includes her
        biographical essay "A True Relation of My Birth, Breeding
        and Life," and John Evelyn's *An Essay on the First Book of
        T. Lucretius Carus De Rerum Natura* published
1657   Margaret corresponds with Constantijn Huygens on the
        topic of "exploding glasses"
1658   William Cavendish's French *The New Method and
        Extraordinary Invention to Dress Horses and Work Them
        According to Nature; As Also to Perfect Nature By the
        Subtlety of Art* published

1659	More's *The Immortality of the Soul* published
1660	Charles II is restored to the throne; Margaret and her husband return to England and retire to Welbeck, a country estate in Nottingham. She becomes honorary member of the literary salon of Katherine Philips. Robert Boyle's *New Experiments Physico-Mechanicall, touching the Spring of the Air and Its Effects . . .* published
1661	Joseph Glanvill's *The Vanity of Dogmatizing*, and Boyle's *The Sceptical Chymist* published
1662	Margaret's *Playes* and *Orations of Divers Sorts*, as well as Johannes Baptista Van Helmont's *Oriatrike, Or, Physick Refined* published
1663	A revised version of Margaret's *Philosophical and Physical Opinions*, Boyle's *Some Considerations touching the Usefulness of Experimental Natural Philosophy*, volume 1, and Henry Power's *Experimental Philosophy* published
1664	Margaret's *CCXI Sociable Letters* and *Philosophical Letters* published; Margaret discussed by More in his letter of March 1664/65 to philosopher Anne Conway; Boyle's *Experiments and Considerations touching Colours* published
1665	Robert Hooke's *Micrographia*, and Boyle's *New Experiments and Observations touching Cold* published; William is made Duke of Newcastle
1666	Margaret's *Observations upon Experimental Philosophy. To which is added, The Description of a New Blazing World*, Boyle's *Origine of Formes and Qualities according to the Corpuscular Philosophy* and Margaret Fell Fox's *Womens Speaking Justified* published. Margaret Cavendish's eldest brother, John, is expelled from the Royal Society of London
1667	Margaret's *The Life of the Thrice Noble . . . William Cavendishe* published (Latin translation by Charleton, 1668); she corresponds with Glanvill on metaphysical issues, and visits the Royal Society of London
1668	Margaret's *Grounds of Natural Philosophy* and *Plays, never before Printed* published
1670	Princess Elisabeth of Bohemia, now Abbess at Hereford, gives sanctuary to Anna Maria van Schurman and the persecuted Labadist community

1673	Bathsua Makin's *An Essay to Revive the Antient Education of Gentlewomen* and François Poulain de la Barre's French *The Equality of the Two Sexes* published; Margaret dies on December 15; she is buried in Westminster Abbey on January 7, 1674
1676	William Cavendish edits and publishes *Letters and Poems in Honour of the Incomparable Princess, Margaret, Dutchess of Newcastle*; he dies, and is buried next to Margaret in Westminster Abbey

Further reading

There is no standard edition of Cavendish's works. Only a few of her books exist in modern editions; see the List of Abbreviations for information about these editions.

Documents important for reconstructing Cavendish's intellectual circle, including letters to her by More, Hobbes, Glanvill, Charleton, and Digby, can be found in *Letters and Poems in Honour of the Incomparable Princess, Margaret, Dutchess of Newcastle* (London: Printed in the Savoy, 1676; repr. as *A Collection of Letters and Poems . . . to the Late Duke and Dutchess of Newcastle*, London: Langly Curtis, 1678). Her correspondence with Constantijn Huygens about "exploding glasses" can be found in *De Briefwisseling van Constantijn Huygens*, ed. J. A. Worp (The Hague: Martinus Nijhoff, 1916–17), vols. 5 and 6.

One of the only published critical responses to Cavendish's works by one of her contemporaries is S. Du Verger, *Humble Reflections Upon some Passages of the Right Honorable the Lady Marchioness of Newcastle's Olio Or An Appeal from her mesinformed to her own better judgement* (London, 1657).

Cavendish, the literary figure, was introduced to twentieth-century readers by Henry Ten Eyck Perry, *The First Duchess of Newcastle and Her Husband As Figures in Literary History* (Boston/London: Ginn and Company, 1918), which critically examines her corpus, and outlines its critical reception; and by Virginia Woolf, "The Duchess of Newcastle," in *The Common Reader* (London: Published by Leonard and Virginia Woolf at the Hogarth Press, 1925).

For a treatment of Cavendish's natural philosophy from a feminist perspective on literary history and criticism, see Sylvia Bowerbank,

"The Spider's Delight: Margaret Cavendish and the 'Female' Imagination," *English Literary Renaissance* 14 (1984): 392–408; repr. in K. Farrell, E. H. Hageman, A. F. Kinney (eds.), *Women in the Renaissance: Selections from English Literary Renaissance* (Amherst: University of Massachusetts Press, 1991).

Biographies of Cavendish include: [Thomas Longueville], *The First Duke and Duchess of Newcastle-Upon-Tyne* (New York/Bombay/Calcutta: Longmans, Green and Co., 1919); Douglas Grant, *Margaret the First: A Biography of Margaret Cavendish, Duchess of Newcastle, 1623– 1673* (London: Rupert Hart-Davis, 1957); and Kathleen Jones, *A Glorious Fame: The Life of Margaret Cavendish, Duchess of Newcastle, 1623– 1673* (London: Bloomsbury, 1988), which places Cavendish within the context of other women intellectuals of the period. Useful historical information can also be found in A. S. Turberville, *A History of Welbeck Abbey and Its Owners, Volume One: 1539–1755* (London: Faber and Faber Limited, 1938).

There is a long tradition in Hobbes scholarship of exploring the connection between his natural philosophy and his political views; John Rogers, in *The Matter of Revolution: Science, Poetry, and Politics in the Age of Milton* (Ithaca/London: Cornell University Press, 1996), does the same for Cavendish.

Work in the history of science that helps to illuminate the context in which Cavendish is constructing her system of nature include: Robert Hugh Kargon, *Atomism in England from Hariot to Newton* (Oxford: Clarendon Press, 1966); Peter Barker and Bernard Goldstein, "Is Seventeenth Century Physics Indebted to the Stoics?," *Centaurus* 27, 2 (1984): 148–64; and Christoph Meinel, "Early Seventeenth-Century Atomism: Theory, Epistemology, and the Insufficiency of Experiment," *Isis* 79, 296 (1988): 68–103. Samuel Mintz, in "The Duchess of Newcastle's Visit to the Royal Society," *The Journal of English and Germanic Philology* 51 (1952): 168–76, provides details about that meeting, the events leading up to it, and the critical reaction to Cavendish's presence. Gerald Meyer, in *The Scientific Lady in England 1650–1760* (Berkeley: University of California Press, 1955), focuses on *Observations* and places it in the context of other early modern scientific works by Englishwomen. In the past twenty years, important contributions to our understanding of Cavendish's natural philosophy have been made by historians of science interested in reevaluating women's contributions to early modern science, for example: Carolyn Merchant, *The Death of Nature* (San Francisco: Harper & Row, 1980); Lisa Sarasohn, "A Science Turned Upside Down: Feminism and the Natural Philosophy of Margaret Cavendish," *Huntington Library Quarterly* 47 (1984): 299–307; and Londa Schiebinger,"Margaret Cavendish, Duchess of Newcastle," in Mary Ellen Waithe (ed.), *A History of Women Philosophers* (Dordrecht: Kluwer Academic Publishers, 1991), vol. 3.

Recent contributions by historians of philosophy and the philosophy of science that examine aspects of Cavendish's organicist materialism and contrast her system of nature with the views of her contemporaries include: Elisabeth Strauss, "Organismus versus Maschine: Margaret Cavendish' Kritik am mechanistischen Naturmodell," in J. F. Maas (ed.), *Das Sichtbare Denken, Modelle und Modellhaftigkeit in der Philosophie und den Wissenschaften* (Amsterdam: Rodopi, 1993); Stephen Clucas, "The Atomism of the Cavendish Circle: A Reappraisal," *The Seventeenth Century* 9, 2 (1994): 247–73; Sarah Hutton, "In Dialogue with Thomas Hobbes: Margaret Cavendish's Natural Philosophy," *Women's Writing* 4, 3 (1997): 421–32; Eileen O'Neill, "Margaret Lucas Cavendish," in *Routledge Encyclopedia of Philosophy* (London/New York: Routledge, 1998); and Susan James, "The Innovations of Margaret Cavendish," *British Journal for the History of Philosophy* 7, 2 (1999): 219–44.

Finally, recent work in the history of philosophy which places Cavendish's contributions within the framework of philosophy written by other early modern women philosophers includes: Sarah Hutton, "Anne Conway, Margaret Cavendish and Seventeenth-Century Scientific Thought," in Lynette Hunter and Sarah Hutton (eds.), *Women, Science and Medicine 1500–1700* (Phoenix Mill/Stroud/ Gloucestershire: Sutton Publishing, 1997); and Eileen O'Neill, "Disappearing Ink: Early Modern Women Philosophers and Their Fate in History," in Janet Kourany (ed.), *Philosophy in a Feminist Voice* (Princeton: Princeton University Press, 1998); and "Women Cartesians, 'Feminine Philosophy,' and Historical Exclusion," in Susan Bordo (ed.), *Feminist Interpretations of René Descartes* (University Park, Pa.: Pennsylvania State University Press, 1999).

Note on the text

Observations has not appeared in print since Margaret Cavendish's life-time. There are only two editions of the work: the first was published in 1666, the second in 1668. I have taken the 1668 publication as the copy text for the present edition, and I have checked it against the 1666 publication. I refer to these editions in the notes for the text by their date.

There are extensive differences in spelling and punctuation between the two seventeenth-century editions. It is not clear which changes are due to the editorial hand of Cavendish, and which are due to the printer. I have remained silent about these alterations, and have simply followed the second edition. In a number of places, Cavendish added sentences and whole paragraphs of further explication to the text in the second edition; in only a few cases did she delete any material from the first edition and replace it with new material in the second. I have marked the significant additions in the text by placing them within square brackets, and I have indicated in the notes that this material was lacking in the first edition. In the exceptional cases where Cavendish actually revised the text, I have marked the revised material in the text by placing it within square brackets, and I have given the alternative material in the notes, indicating that it is from the 1666 edition. Finally, the 1666 edition included two items which Cavendish chose not to reproduce in the second edition; I follow the second edition in not including this material, which is extraneous to the project of *Observations*. The first was "A Catalogue of All the Works Hitherto Published by the Authoresse"; the second was a final section of the text "An Explanation of Some Obscure and Doubtful Passages Occurring in the Philosophical Works Hitherto Published by the Authoresse." This final section of the first edition may have been deleted from the second because Cavendish now felt that *Observations* surpassed her earlier publications in clarity.

In keeping with the aim of Cambridge Texts in the History of Philosophy to make works more accessible to the modern reader, I have modernized the text in accordance with these conventions:

Capitalization and spelling have been consistently modernized, including the removal of archaic contractions such as "dress'd" and "'tis." The symbol "&c" has been replaced by "etc." But archaic words and expressions have been retained; many of these, together with particularly obscure modern usages and references, are given in the Glossary. Certain changes that fall between spelling change and grammatical correction have also been made, e.g., uniformly and correctly distinguishing "then" from "than."

Italics were used by Cavendish and her contemporaries for a variety of functions. I have eliminated the conventional use of italics for names, for distinguishing key words or phrases from items in a series, and for extensive use, in place of normal type, in prefatory material, as in To the Reader. Where they were used to indicate technical terms or recurrent key-words; to mention a word or expression; or to use a word or phrase in a special way, for which we would use scare-quotes, italics have been eliminated and replaced with quotation marks. On several occasions I have silently added quotation marks for these purposes for the sake of consistency. Italics have also been eliminated and replaced with quotation marks where they were used for actual or purported quotation, or for close paraphrase. Italics have been retained for foreign words and expressions, book titles, and to mark stress.

An exception to the policy of modernizing the text has been made in the case of Cavendish's earmark punctuation, which has been retained, as has the location of her paragraph breaks. When the punctuation of the 1668 edition has been unreadable or missing, I have followed the first edition's punctuation.

Editorial footnotes are assigned Arabic numerals; Cavendish's own notes are assigned letters. Editorial references to *Observations* give the pagination from the present edition; editorial references to Cavendish's other publications give the pagination from the first editions of these texts, unless otherwise noted.

Cavendish is responding to quite a number of authors in *Observations*.

In those cases where she implicitly refers to authors via her characterization of an opinion which they jointly hold, I have attempted to identify the relevant authors and texts in the editorial notes. In these citations, I refer to the books' parts, chapters, sections and items, rather than to page numbers. When Cavendish explicitly quotes or semi-quotes an author, even if she gives neither the author's name nor the title of the text from which she is quoting, and when she refers to well-known arguments and positions, I have identified the text in the editorial notes and given exact page numbers. I refer to the editions and translations given above in the List of Abbreviations, or to first editions, unless otherwise noted. In the case of quotations from Aristotle, I also specify the exact locations via Bekker numbers. I have provided a translation for each foreign title that I cite; they are given within square brackets following the title.

Observations upon Experimental Philosophy

To
Her Grace
The
Duchess of Newcastle,
On her *Observations upon*
Experimental Philosophy

This book is book of books, and only fits
Great searching brains, and quintessence of wits;
For this will give you an eternal fame,
And last to all posterity your name:
You conquer death, in a perpetual life;
And make me famous too in such a wife.
So I will prophesy in spite of fools,
When dead, then honoured, and be read in schools.
And *ipse dixit* lost, not he, but she
Still cited in your strong philosophy.

William Newcastle

To His
Grace
The
Duke of Newcastle

My Noble Lord,

In this present treatise, I have ventured to make some observations upon experimental philosophy, and to examine the opinions of some of our modern microscopical or dioptrical writers: and, though your Grace is not only a lover of virtuosos, but a virtuoso yourself, and have as good, and as many sorts of optic glasses as anyone else; yet you do not busy yourself much with this brittle art, but employ most part of your time in the more noble and heroic art of horsemanship and weapons, as also in the sweet and delightful art of poetry, and in the useful art of architecture, etc. which shows that you do not believe much in the informations of those optic glasses, at least think them not so useful as others do, that spend most of their time in dioptrical inspections. The truth is, My Lord, that most men in these latter times, busy themselves more with other worlds, than with this they live in, which to me seems strange, unless they could find out some art that would carry them into those celestial worlds, which I doubt will never be; nay, if they did, it would be no better than Lucian's,[1] or the Frenchman's[2] art, with bottles, bladders, etc. or like the man's that would screw himself up into the moon:[3] And therefore, I confess, I have but little faith in such arts, and as little in telescopical, microscopical, and the like inspections; and prefer rational and judicious observations, before deluding glasses and experiments; which, as I have more at large declared in this following work, so I leave it to your Grace's perusal and judgment, which I know is so just, so exact,

---

[1] Lucian of Samosata (c. 120–200 AD) wrote two satirical dialogues about travel to other worlds: *Ikaromenippos, or the Sky Man* and *A True Story*.

[2] Probably a reference to Savinien de Cyrano de Bergerac, *Histoire comique contenant les états et empires de la lune* [Comic Story Containing the States and Empires of the Moon] (Paris, 1657); but cf. Pierre Borel, *Discours nouveau prouvant la pluralité des mondes* [New Discourse Proving the Plurality of Worlds] (Geneva, 1657).

[3] Probably a reference to John Wilkins, *The Discovery of a New World; or, A Discourse Tending to Prove, That (It Is Probable) There May Be Another Habitable World in the Moon* . . . (London, 1638); but cf. Domingo Gonsales, The speedy Messenger [Francis Godwin], *The Man in the Moone: or A Discourse of a Voyage Thither* (London, 1638).

and so wise, that I may more safely rely upon it, than all others besides; and if your Grace do but approve of it, I care not if all the world condemn it; for, your Grace's approbation is all that can be desired from,

    My Lord,

        Your Grace's honest wife, and humble servant,

        M.N.

formality!

To the
Most Famous
University
of Cambridge

Most Noble, and Eminently-Learned,

Do not judge it an impertinency, that now again I presume to offer unto you, another piece of my philosophical works; for, when I reflect upon the honour you have done me, I am so much sensible of it, that I am troubled I cannot make you an acknowledgment answerable to your great civilities.

You might, if not with scorn, with silence have passed by, when one of my sex, and, what is more, one that never was versed in the sublime arts and sciences of literature, took upon her to write, not only of philosophy, the highest of all human learning, but to offer it to so famous and celebrated an university as yours; but your goodness and civility being as great as your learning, would rather conceal, than discover or laugh at those weaknesses, and imperfections which you know my sex is liable to; nay, so far you were from this, that by your civil respects, and undeserved commendations, you were pleased to cherish rather, than quite to suppress or extinguish my weak endeavours.

For which favour, as I found myself doubly indebted to you, so I thought it my duty to pay you my double acknowledgments; thanks, you know, can never be unseasonable, when petitions may; neither can they be unpleasing, when petitions often are troublesome: And since there is no sacrifice, which God is more delighted with, than that of thanksgiving, I live in hopes you will not refuse this repeated offer of gratitude, but favourably, as a due to your merits, receive it from her, who both of your ingenuity, learning and civility is the greatest admirer, and shall always profess herself,

Your most obliged and devoted servant,
M.N.

The Preface to the Ensuing Treatise

It is probable, some will say, that my much writing is a disease; but what disease they will judge it to be, I cannot tell; I do verily believe they will take it to be a disease of the brain; but surely they cannot call it an apoplectical or lethargical disease: Perhaps they will say, it is an extravagant, or at least a fantastical disease; but I hope they will rather call it a disease of wit. Let them give it what name they please; yet of this I am sure, that if much writing be a disease, then the best philosophers, both moral and natural, as also the best divines, lawyers, physicians, poets, historians, orators, mathematicians, chemists, and many more have been grievously sick: and Seneca, Pliny, Aristotle, Cicero, Tacitus, Plutarch, Euclid, Homer, Virgil, Ovid, St. Augustine, St. Ambrose, Scotus, Hippocrates, Galen, Paracelsus, and hundreds more, have been at death's door with the disease of writing.[4] Now, to be infected with the same disease, which the devoutest, wisest, wittiest, subtlest, most learned and eloquent men have been troubled withal, is no disgrace; but the greatest honour that can happen to the most ambitious person in the world: and next to the honour of being thus infected, it is also a great delight and pleasure to me, as being the only pastime which employs my idle hours; insomuch, that, were I sure nobody did read my works, yet I would not

---

[4] The "divines" include Christian neoplatonist St. Augustine (354–430 AD) and Franciscan logician and metaphysician John Duns Scotus (1265/6–1308); St. Ambrose, Bishop of Milan (*c.* 339/40–397 AD) was originally a lawyer; Hippocrates of Cos (*c.* 460–*c.* 380 BC) and Galen of Pergamum (129–? 199 AD) are famous physicians of the ancient world; Homer (? prior to 700 BC), Virgil (70–19 BC) and Ovid (43 BC–17 AD) are ancient epic poets; the "historians" are Cornelius Tacitus (*c.* 56 – *c.* 115 AD) and Plutarch (before 50 AD – after 120 AD); philosopher Marcus Tullius Cicero (106 BC–43 BC) is admired as a master of the oration; Euclid (fl. *c.* 300 BC) is the famed mathematician of Alexandria; and the "chemist" is physican/alchemist Theophrastus Bombast von Hohenheim, known as "Paracelsus" (?1493–1541).

quit my pastime for all that: for although they should not delight others, yet they delight me; and if all women that have no employment in worldly affairs, should but spend their time as harmlessly as I do, they would not commit such faults as many are accused of.

I confess, there are many useless and superfluous books, and perchance mine will add to the number of them; especially it is to be observed, that there have been in this latter age, as many writers of natural philosophy, as in former ages there have been of moral philosophy; which multitude, I fear, will produce such a confusion of truth and falsehood, as the number of moral writers formerly did, with their over-nice divisions of virtues and vices, whereby they did puzzle their readers so, that they knew not how to distinguish between them. The like, I doubt, will prove amongst our natural philosophers, who by their extracted, or rather distracted arguments, confound both divinity and natural philosophy, sense and reason, nature and art, so much as in time we shall have, rather a chaos, than a well-ordered universe, by their doctrine: Besides, many of their writings are but parcels taken from the ancient; but such writers are like those unconscionable men in civil wars, which endeavour to pull down the hereditary mansions of noblemen and gentlemen, to build a cottage of their own;[5] for, so do they pull down the learning of ancient authors, to render themselves famous in composing books of their own. But though this age does ruin palaces, to make cottages; churches, to make conventicles; and universities to make private colleges; and endeavour not only to wound, but to kill and bury the fame of such meritorious persons as the ancient were; yet, I hope God of his mercy will preserve state, church, and schools, from ruin and destruction: Nor do I think their weak works will be able to overcome the strong wits of the ancient; for, setting aside some few of our moderns, all the rest are but like dead and withered leaves, in comparison to lovely and lively plants; and as for arts, I am confident, that where there is one good art found in these latter ages, there are two better old arts lost, both of the Egyptians, Greeks, Romans, and many other ancient nations; (when I say lost, I mean in relation to our knowledge, not in nature; for nothing can be lost in nature.) Truly, the art of augury was far more beneficial than the lately invented art of micrography; for I cannot

---

[5] Cavendish chronicles such acts and her family's losses during the English Civil War in *Life*.

perceive any great advantage this art doth bring us. The eclipse of the sun and moon was not found out by telescopes; nor the motions of the loadstone, or the art of navigation, or the art of guns and gunpowder, or the art of printing, and the like, by microscopes; nay, if it be true, that telescopes make appear the spots in the sun and moon, or discover some new stars, what benefit is that to us? Or if microscopes do truly represent the exterior parts and superficies of some minute creatures, what advantageth it our knowledge? For unless they could discover their interior, corporeal, figurative motions, and the obscure actions of nature, or the causes which make such or such creatures; I see no great benefit or advantage they yield to man: Or if they discover how reflected light makes loose and superficial colours, such as no sooner perceived but are again dissolved; what benefit is that to man? For neither painters nor dyers can enclose and mix that atomical dust, and those reflexions of light to serve them for any use. Wherefore, in my opinion, it is both time and labour lost: for, the inspection of the exterior parts of vegetables, doth not give us any knowledge how to sow, set, plant, and graft; so that a gardener or husbandman will gain no advantage at all by this art: The inspection of a bee, through a microscope, will bring him no more honey; nor the inspection of a grain, more corn; neither will the inspection of dusty atoms, and reflexions of light, teach painters how to make and mix colours, although it may perhaps be an advantage to a decayed lady's face, by placing herself in such or such a reflexion of light, where the dusty atoms may hide her wrinkles. The truth is, most of these arts are fallacies, rather than discoveries of truth; for sense deludes more than it gives a true information, and an exterior inspection through an optic glass, is so deceiving, that it cannot be relied upon: Wherefore, regular reason is the best guide to all arts, as I shall make it appear in this following treatise.

It may be, the world will judge it a fault in me, that I oppose so many eminent and ingenious writers: but I do it not out of a contradicting or wrangling nature, but out of an endeavour to find out truth, or at least the probability of truth, according to that proportion of sense and reason nature has bestowed upon me: for as I have heard my noble lord[6] say, that in the art of riding and fencing, there is but one truth, but many

---

[6] I.e., her husband William Cavendish.

falsehoods and fallacies: So it may be said of natural philosophy and divinity; for there is but one fundamental truth in each,[7] and I am as ambitious of finding out the truth of nature, as an honourable dueler is of gaining fame and repute; for, as he will fight with none but an honourable and valiant opposite, so am I resolved to argue with none but those which have the renown of being famous and subtle philosophers; and therefore as I have had the courage to argue heretofore with some famous and eminent writers in speculative philosophy;[8] so have I taken upon me in this present work, to make some reflexions also upon some of our modern experimental and dioptrical writers.[9] They will perhaps think me an inconsiderable opposite, because I am not of their sex, and therefore strive to hit my opinions with a side-stroke, rather covertly, than openly and directly; but if this should chance, the impartial world, I hope, will grant me so much justice as to consider my honesty, and their fallacy, and pass such a judgment as will declare them to be patrons, not only to truth, but also to justice and equity; for which heaven will grant them their reward, and time will record their noble and worthy actions in the register of fame, to be kept in everlasting memory.

[7] Cf. Cavendish's publication of her husband's view that since natural philosophers are "all guessers, not knowing, it gives every man room to think what he lists . . ." (*Opinions*, 1663, p. 459).

[8] In *Phil. Letters* Cavendish had critically examined the views in the following texts: Thomas Hobbes, *Leviathan* (London, 1651) and *Elements of Philosophy, The First Section concerning Body* (London, 1656); René Descartes, *Discours de la methode . . . Plus la dioptrique. Les meteores. Et la geometrie . . .* [Discourse on the Method . . . And in addition the Dioptrics. The Meteorology. And the Geometry] (Leiden, 1637) and *Principia philosophiae* [Principles of Philosophy] (Amsterdam, 1644); Henry More, *An Antidote Against Atheisme* (London, 1653) and *The Immortality of the Soul* (London/Cambridge, 1659); Johannes Baptista Van Helmont, *Oriatrike, or, Physick Refined . . .*, tr. J.[ohn] C.[handler] (London, 1662); Walter Charleton, *Physiologia Epicuro-Gassendo-Charltoniana, or a Fabrick of Science Upon the Hypothesis of Atoms* (London, 1654) and William Harvey, *Exercitationes de generatione animalium* [Anatomical Exercises On the Generation of Animals] (London, 1651).

[9] The principal "experimental and dioptrical writers" to whom Cavendish will now critically respond are: Thomas Hobbes, René Descartes, Henry Power, Robert Hooke and Robert Boyle.

To the Reader

Courteous Reader,

I do ingenuously confess, that both for want of learning and reading philosophical authors, I have not expressed myself in my philosophical works, especially in my *Philosophical and Physical Opinions*, so clearly and plainly as I might have done, had I had the assistance of art, and the practice of reading other authors: But though my conceptions seem not so perspicuous in the mentioned book of philosophical opinions; yet my *Philosophical Letters*, and these present *Observations*, will, I hope, render it more intelligible: which I have writ, not out of an ambitious humour, to fill the world with useless books, but to explain and illustrate my own opinions. For, what benefit would it be to me, if I should put forth a work, which by reason of its obscure and hard notions, could not be understood? especially it being well known, that natural philosophy is the hardest of all human learning, by reason it consists only in contemplation; and to make the philosophical conceptions of one's mind known to others, is more difficult than to make them believe, that if A. B. be equal to C. D. then E. F. is equal to A. B. because it is equal to C. D. But that I am not versed in learning, nobody, I hope, will blame me for it, since it is sufficiently known, that our sex being not suffered to be instructed in schools and universities, cannot be bred up to it. I will not say, but many of our sex may have as much wit, and be capable of learning as well as men; but since they want instructions, it is not possible they should attain to it: for learning is artificial, but wit is natural. Wherefore, when I began to read the philosophical works of other authors, I was so troubled with their hard words and expressions at first, that had they not been explained to me, and had I not found out some of them by the context and connexion of the sense, I should have been far enough to seek; for their hard words did more obstruct, than instruct me. The truth is, if anyone intends to write philosophy, either in English, or any other language, he ought to consider the propriety of the language, as much as the subject he writes of; or else to what purpose would it be to write? If you do write philosophy in English, and use all the hardest words and expressions which none but scholars are able to understand, you had better to write it in Latin; but if you will write for those that do not understand Latin, your reason will tell you, that you must explain those hard words, and English them in the easiest manner you can; What are words but marks of things? and what are philosophical terms, but to express the conceptions of one's mind in that science? And truly I do not think that there is any language so poor, which cannot do that; wherefore those that fill their writings with hard words, put the horses behind the coach, and instead of making hard things easy, make easy things hard, which especially in our English writers is a great fault; neither do I see any reason for it, but that they think to make themselves more famous by those that admire all what they do not understand, though it be non-sense; but I am not of their mind, and therefore although I do understand some of their hard expressions now, yet I shun them as much in my writings as is possible for me to do, and all this, that they may be the better understood by all, learned as well as unlearned; by those that are professed philosophers as well as by those that are none: And though I could employ some time in studying all the hardest phrases and words in other authors, and write as learnedly perhaps as they; yet will I not deceive the world, nor trouble my conscience by being a mountebank in learning, but will rather prove naturally wise than artificially foolish; for at best I should but obscure my opinions, and render them more intricate instead of clearing and explaining them; but if my readers should spy any errors slipt into my writings for want of art and learning, I hope they'll be so just as not to censure me too severely for them, but express their wisdom in preferring the kernel before the shells.

It is not possible that a young student, when first he comes to the university, should hope to be master of arts in one month, or one year; and so do I likewise not persuade myself, that my philosophy being new, and but lately brought forth, will at first sight prove master of under-standing, nay, it may be, not in this age; but if God favour her, she may attain to it in after-times: And if she be slighted now and buried in silence, she may perhaps rise more gloriously hereafter; for her ground being sense and reason, she may meet with an age where she will be more regarded, than she is in this.

But, Courteous Reader, all what I request of you at present, is, that if you have a mind to understand my philosophical conceptions truly, you would be pleased to read them not by parcels, here a little, and there a little, (for I have found it by myself, that when I read not a book thoroughly from beginning to end, I cannot well understand the author's design, but may easily mistake his meaning; I mean, such books as treat of philosophy, history, etc. where all parts depend upon each other.) But if you'll give an impartial judgment of my philosophy, read it all, or else spare your censures; especially do I recommend to you my *Philosophical Opinions*, which contain the grounds and principles of my philosophy, but since they were published before I was versed in the reading of other authors, I desire you to join my *Philosophical Letters*, and these *Observations* to them, which will serve as commentaries to explain what may seem obscure in the mentioned *Opinions*; but before all, read this following "Argumental Discourse," wherein are contained the principles and grounds of natural philosophy, especially concerning the constitutive parts of nature, and their properties and actions; as also be pleased to peruse the later discourse of the first part of this book, which treats of perception;[10] for perception being the chief and general action of nature, has occasioned me to be more prolix in explaining it, than any other subject; you'll find that I go much by the way of argumentation, and framing objections and answers; for I would fain hinder and obstruct as many objections as could be made against the grounds of my opinions; but it being impossible to resolve all (for, as nature and her parts and actions are infinite, so may also endless objections be raised) I have endeavoured only to set down such as I thought might be most material; but this I find, that there is no objection but one may find an answer to it; and as soon as I have made an answer to one objection, another offers itself again, which shows not only that nature's actions are infinite, but that they are poised and balanced, so that they cannot run into extremes.

However I do not applaud myself so much, as to think that my works can be without errors, for nature is not a deity, but her parts are often irregular: and how is it possible that one particular creature can know all

---

[10] Probably a reference to chs. 35–37; but see ch. 1 as well.

the obscure and hidden infinite varieties of nature? if the truth of nature were so easily known, we had no need to take so much pains in searching after it; but nature being material, and consequently divisible, her parts have but divided knowledges, and none can claim an universal infinite knowledge. Nevertheless, although I may err in my arguments, or for want of artificial terms; yet I believe the ground of my opinion is true, because it is sense and reason.

I found after the perusal of this present book, that several places therein might have been more perspicuously delivered, and better cleared; but since it is impossible that all things can be so exact, that they should not be subject to faults and imperfections; (for as the greatest beauties are not without moles, so the best books are seldom without errors;) I entreat the ingenuous reader to interpret them to the best sense; for they are not so material, but that either by the context or connexion of the whole discourse, or by comparing one place with another, the true meaning thereof may easily be understood; and to this end I have set down this following explanation of such places, as in the perusal I have observed, whereby the rest may also easily be mended.

When I say, that "discourse shall sooner find out nature's corporeal figurative motions, than art shall inform the senses";[a] by discourse, I do not mean speech, but an arguing of the mind, or a rational enquiry into the causes of natural effects; for discourse is as much as reasoning with ourselves; which may very well be done without speech or language, as being only an effect or action of reason.

When I say, that "art may make pewter, brass, etc."[b] I do not mean as if these figures were artificial, and not natural; but my meaning is, that if art imitates nature in producing of artificial figures, they are most commonly such as are of mixt natures, which I call hermaphroditical.

When I say, that "respiration is a reception and emission of parts through the pores or passages proper to each particular figure, so that when some parts issue, others enter";[c] I do not mean at one and the same time, or always through the same passages; for, as there is variety of natural creatures and figures, and of their perceptions; so of the manner of their perceptions, and of their passages and pores; all which no particular creature is able exactly to know, or determine: And therefore when I add in the following chapter, that "nature has more ways of

[a] Part I, c. 2, pag. 6. [I, ch. 2, p. 49.]   [b] C. 3, pag. 8. [I, ch. 3, p. 50.]
[c] C. 4, pag. 15. [I, ch. 4, p. 54.]

composing and dividing of parts, than by the way of drawing in, and sending forth by pores"; I mean, that not all parts of nature have the like respirations: The truth is, it is enough to know in general, that there is respiration in all parts of nature, as a general or universal action; and that this respiration is nothing else but a composition and division of parts; but how particular respirations are performed, none but infinite nature is capable to know.

When I say that "there is a difference between respiration and perception; and that perception is an action of figuring or patterning; but respiration an action of reception and emission of parts":[d] first, I do not mean, that all perception is made by patterning or imitation; but I speak only of the perception of the exterior senses in animals, at least in man, which I observe to be made by patterning or imitation; for, as no creature can know the infinite perceptions in nature, so he cannot describe what they are, or how they are made. Next, I do not mean, that respiration is not a perceptive action; for if perception be a general and universal action in nature, as well as respiration, both depending upon the composition and division of parts; it is impossible but that all actions of nature must be perceptive, by reason perception is an exterior knowledge of foreign parts and actions; and there can be no commerce or intercourse, nor no variety of figures and actions; no productions, dissolutions, changes, and the like, without perception; for how shall parts work and act, without having some knowledge or perception of each other? Besides, whereso-ever is self-motion, there must of necessity be also perception; for self-motion is the cause of all exterior perception. But my meaning is, that the animal, at least human respiration, which is a receiving of foreign parts, and discharging or venting of its own, in an animal or human figure or creature, is not the action of animal perception, properly so called; that is, the perception of its exterior senses, as seeing, hearing, tasting, touching, smelling; which action of perception is properly made by way of patterning and imitation, by the innate, figurative motions of those animal creatures, and not by receiving either the figures of the exterior objects into the sensitive organs, or by sending forth some invisible rays from the organ to the object; nor by pressure and reaction. Nevertheless, as I said, every action of nature is a knowing and perceptive action; and so is respiration, which of necessity presupposes a knowledge of exterior

[d] C. 5, pag. 16. [I, ch. 5, p. 55.]

15

parts; especially those that are concerned in the same action, and can no ways be performed without perception of each other.

When I say, that "if all men's opinions and fancies were rational, there would not be such variety in nature as we perceive there is";[e] by rational I mean regular, according to the vulgar way of expression by which a rational opinion is called, that which is grounded upon regular sense and reason; and thus, rational is opposed to irregular: Nevertheless, irregular fancies and opinions are made by the rational parts of matter, as well as those that are regular; and therefore in a philosophical and strict sense, one may call irregular opinions as well rational, as those that are regular; but according to the vulgar way of expression, as I said, it is sooner understood of *regular*, than of *irregular* opinions, fancies or conceptions.

When I say, that "none of nature's parts can be called inanimate, or soulless";[f] I do not mean the constitutive parts of nature, which are, as it were, the ingredients whereof nature consists, and is made up; whereof there is an inanimate part or degree of matter, as well as animate; but I mean the parts or effects of this composed body of nature, of which I say, that none can be called inanimate; for, though some philosophers think that nothing is animate, or has life in nature, but animals and vegetables; yet it is probable, that since nature consists of a commixture of animate and inanimate matter, and is self-moving, there can be no part or particle of this composed body of nature, were it an atom, that may be called inanimate, by reason there is none that has not its share of animate, as well as inanimate matter, and the commixture of these degrees being so close, it is impossible one should be without the other.

When enumerating the requisites of the perception of sight in animals, I say, that "if one of them be wanting, there is either no perception at all, or it is an imperfect perception";[g] I mean, there is either no animal perception of seeing, or else it is an irregular perception.

When I say, that "as the sensitive perception knows some of the other parts of nature by their effects; so the rational perceives some effects of the omnipotent power of God":[h] my meaning is not, as if the sensitive part of matter has no knowledge at all of God; for since all parts of Nature, even the inanimate, have an innate and fixt self-knowledge, it is probable that they may also have an interior self-knowledge of the existency of the eternal and omnipotent God, as the author of nature: But

e chap. 15, pag. 44. [I, ch. 15, p. 71.]   f C. 18, pa. 47. [I, ch. 16, p. 72.]
g Cap. 20, pag. 63. [I, ch. 20, p. 82.]   h Cap. 21, pag. 77. [I, ch. 21, p. 90.]

because the rational part is the subtlest, purest, finest, and highest degree of matter; it is most conformable to truth, that it has also the highest and greatest knowledge of God, as far as a natural part can have; for God being immaterial, it cannot properly be said, that sense can have a perception of him, by reason he is not subject to the sensitive perception of any creature, or part of nature; and therefore all the knowledge which natural creatures can have of God, must be inherent in every part of nature; and the perceptions which we have of the effects of nature, may lead us to some conceptions of that supernatural, infinite, and incomprehensible deity, not what it is in its essence or nature, but that it is existent, and that nature has a dependence upon it, as an eternal servant has upon an eternal master.

But some might say, How is it possible that a corporeal finite part, can have a conception of an incorporeal infinite being; by reason that which comprehends, must needs be bigger than that which is comprehended? Besides, no part of nature can conceive beyond itself, that is, beyond what is natural or material; and this proves, that at least the rational part, or the mind, must be immaterial to conceive a deity? To which I answer, that no part of nature can or does conceive the essence of God, or what God is in himself; but it conceives only, that there is such a divine being which is supernatural: And therefore it cannot be said, that a natural figure can comprehend God; for it is not the comprehending of the substance of God, or its patterning out, (since God having no body, is without all figure) that makes the knowledge of God ; but I do believe, that the knowledge of the existency of God, as I mentioned before, is innate, and inherent in nature and all her parts, as much as self-knowledge is.

Speaking of the difference between oil and other liquors;[i] for the better understanding of that place, I thought fit to insert this note: *Flame* is fluid, but not liquid, nor wet: *Oil* is fluid and liquid, but not wet; but *water* is both fluid, liquid and wet. *Oil* will turn into flame, and increase it; but *water* is so quite opposite to flame, that if a sufficient quantity be poured upon it, it will totally extinguish it.

When I say, that "sense and reason shall be the ground of my philosophy, and not particular natural effects";[j] my meaning is, that I do not intend to make particular creatures or figures, the principle of all the

---

[i] Cap. 24, pag. 84. [I, ch. 24, p. 95.]   [j] Cap. 25, pag. 94. [I, ch. 25, p. 100.]

infinite effects of nature, as some other philosophers do; for there is no such thing as a prime or principal figure of nature, all being but effects of one cause. But my ground is sense and reason, that is, I make self-moving matter, which is sensitive and rational, the only cause and principle of all natural effects.

When it is said, that "ice, snow, hail, etc. return into their former figure of water, whensoever they dissolve";[k] I mean, when they dissolve their exterior figures, that is, change their actions.

When I say that the "exterior object is the agent; and the sentient body, the patient":[l] I do not mean, that the object does chiefly work upon the sentient, or is the immediate cause of the perception in the sentient body, and that the sentient suffers the agent to act upon it; but I retain only those words, because they are used in schools: But as for their actions, I am quite of a contrary opinion, to wit, that the sentient body is the principal agent, and the external body the patient; for the motions of the sentient in the act of perception, do figure out or imitate the motions of the object, so that the object is but as a copy that is figured out, or imitated by the sentient, which is the chief agent in all transforming and perceptive actions that are made by way of patterning or imitation.

When I say, that "one finite part can undergo infinite changes and alterations";[m] I do not mean one single part, whereof there is no such thing in nature; but I mean, one part may be infinitely divided and composed with other parts; for as there are infinite changes, compositions, and divisions in nature, so there must be of parts; there being no variety but of parts; and though parts be finite, yet the changes may be infinite; for the finiteness of parts is but concerning the bulk or quantity of their figures; and they are called finite, by reason they have limited and circumscribed figures; nevertheless, as for duration, their parts being the same with the body of nature, are as eternal, and infinite as nature herself, and thus are subject to infinite and eternal changes.

When I say "a world of gold is as active interiorly, as a world of air is exteriorly";[n] I mean, it is as much subject to changes and alterations, as air; for, gold though its motions are not perceptible by our exterior senses, yet it has no less motion than the activest body of nature; only its motions are of another kind than the motions of air, or of some other bodies; for, retentive motions are as much motions, as dispersing, or

---

[k] Cap. 27, pag. 110. [I, ch. 27, p. 110.]   [l] Cap. 29, pag. 129. [I, ch. 29, p. 121.]
[m] Cap. 31, pag. 139. [I, ch. 31, p. 126.]   [n] Ibid., p. 140. [I, ch. 31, p. 128.]

some other sorts of motions, although not so visible to our perception as these; and therefore we cannot say, that gold is more at rest than other creatures of nature; for there is no such thing as rest in nature; although there be degrees of motion.

When I say, that "the parts of nature do not drive or press upon each other, but that all natural actions are free and easy, and not constrained";[o] my meaning is not, as if there was no pressing or driving of parts at all in nature, but only that they are not the universal or principal actions of nature's body, as it is the opinion of some philosophers, who think there is no other motion in nature, but by pressure of parts upon parts:[11] Nevertheless, there is pressure and reaction in nature, because there are infinite sorts of motions.

Also, when I say in the same place, that "nature's actions are voluntary"; I do not mean, that all actions are made by rote, and none by imitation; but, by voluntary actions I understand self actions; that is, such actions whose principle of motion is within themselves, and doth not proceed from such an exterior agent, as doth the motion of the inanimate part of matter; which, having no motion of itself, is moved by the animate parts, yet so, that it receives no motion from them, but moves by the motion of the animate parts, and not by an infused motion into them; for the animate parts in carrying the inanimate along with them, lose nothing of their own motion, nor impart no motion to the inanimate; no more than a man who carries a stick in his hand, imparts motion to the stick, and loses so much as he imparts; but they bear the inanimate parts along with them, by virtue of their own self-motion, and remain self-moving parts, as well as the inanimate remain without motion.

Again, when I make a distinguishment between voluntary actions, and exterior perceptions;[p] my meaning is not, as if voluntary actions were not made by perceptive parts; for whatsoever is self-moving and active, is perceptive; and therefore since the voluntary actions of sense and reason are made by self-moving parts, they must of necessity be perceptive actions: but I speak of perceptions properly so called, which are occasioned by foreign parts; and to those I oppose voluntary actions, which

---

[o] Cap. 31, pag. 138. [I, ch. 31, p. 127.]   [p] Cap. 37, pag. 212. [I, ch. 37, p. 170.]
[11] A reference to the view of the mechanical philosophers, who held that all natural change is explainable in terms of the impact of corporeal particles upon one another; see the Introduction for a discussion of Cavendish's criticisms of mechanism.

are not occasioned, but made by rote;[12] as for example, the perception of sight in animals, when outward objects present themselves to the optic sense to be perceived, the perception of the sentient is an occasioned perception; but whensoever, either in dreams, or in distempers, the sensitive motions of the same organ, make such or such figures, without any presentation of exterior objects, then that action cannot properly be called an exterior perception; but it is a voluntary action of the sensitive motions in the organ of sight, not made after an outward pattern, but by rote, and of their own accord.

When I say that "ignorance is caused by division, and knowledge by composition of parts";[q] I do not mean an interior, innate self-knowledge, which is and remains in every part and particle of nature, both in composition and division; for wheresoever is matter, there is life and self-knowledge; nor can a part lose self-knowledge, any more than it can lose life, although it may change from having such or such a particular life and knowledge; for to change and lose, are different things; but I mean an exterior, perceptive knowledge of foreign parts, caused by self-motion; of which I say that, as a union or combination of parts, makes knowledge, so a division or separation of parts, makes ignorance.

When I say "there's difference of sense and reason in the parts of one composed figure"[13];[r] I mean not, as if there were different degrees of sense, and different degrees of reason in their own substance or matter; for sense is but sense, and reason is but reason; but my meaning is, that there are different, sensitive and rational motions, which move differently in the different parts of one composed creature.

These are (Courteous Reader) the scruples which I thought might puzzle your understanding in this present work, which I have cleared in the best manner I could: and if you should meet with any other of the like nature, my request is, you would be pleased to consider well the grounds of my philosophy; and, as I desired of you before, read all before you pass your judgments and censures; for then, I hope, you'll find but few obstructions, since one place will give you an explanation of the other. In doing thus, you'll neither wrong yourself, nor injure the authoress, who should be much satisfied, if she could benefit your knowledge in the least;

---

[q] Cap. 9, pag. 289. [II, ch. 9, p. 214.]   [r] Cap. 15, pag. 303. [II, ch. 15, p. 223.]

[12] The distinction is between mental representations "occasioned" or triggered by an external object, and those that arise from within the agent out of the storehouse of memory; see the Glossary entry on "by rote."

[13] Quotation marks have been added by the editor for consistency.

if not, she has done her endeavour, and takes as much pleasure and delight in writing and divulging the conceptions of her mind, as perhaps some malicious persons will do in censuring them to the worst.

[But, I have heard, some men are pleased to say, that "in my philosophy there is neither ground or foundation, nor method."

Whereto I answer, that if this philosophy of mine were both groundless, and immethodical, I could not with reason expect my readers should either consider the connexion and mutual dependence of my several opinions; or defer their making a judgment of their probability, until they had read them all. But, truly, neither my sensitive, nor my rational faculties could enable me to perceive a more substantial ground, or firmer foundation, than that of "material nature": nor to follow a better method, than that of "sense" and "reason." Again, many, who have been conversant with the writings of the old philosophers, pretend therefore to understand all the moderns. But these men may be deceived. For, although the ancient philosophers might indeed be as subtle, and quicksighted as the modern, and perchance more: yet the difference betwixt their several conceptions being so great, may easily cause trouble and difficulty in the reader's understanding, and consequently lead them into an erroneous censure, while they examine the truth of these, by the correspondency or agreeableness they hold with those. Like as young students are more troubled to read and understand an old author, than their seniors are, who have formerly, by long study and frequent reading, made themselves familiar with his style and notions: and old scholars, on the other side, may be but young students in new authors. My philosophy, therefore, being new; I do not wonder, if they, who made this objection, do not yet understand it: and, I hope, if they please, but to study seriously the sense and reason thereof; that cloud of obscurity will soon vanish, and the light of knowledge appear in the room of it.

There remains yet one obstruction more to be removed. Perhaps the wise among my readers cannot, and the superstitious will not, allow "nature" to be infinite or eternal. If so, I am not unwilling, that both sorts should waive that opinion, and enjoy their own: nor is it necessary for me to be rigorous in asserting it. For, it is no absurdity to conceive that God might endow nature with "self-motion"; though not only the world, but even the chaos itself be supposed to have been made six thousand or more years ago. And as for "mechanical motion"; that seems but a mechanic opinion: nor have those, who make God the "First Mechanical

Mover," any other but an irreverent concept of the "divine nature." As for others, who hold the "immaterial soul" to move the body; if their tenet be admitted, then it will follow, that the souls of beasts also are immaterial: because they appear to do such actions, and have such passions, as men. Furthermore, I observe this by the by, that such who are accounted wise and subtle philosophers, usually endeavour to prove intricate and confused opinions, by sophistical and irrational arguments, more becoming raw schoolboys, than men of ripe judgment. Besides, there are [those]¹⁴ who suppose a "general soul," or "universal spirit" in the world, that moves all bodies, or all material nature. If so, then I cannot conceive, but this "universal soul" must move the body of man also: and so man must have two distinct "immaterial souls" in one body, that general one diffused through the world, and his own particular soul; which in my judgment is very absurd. In fine, as for their various arguments concerning the "will," "understanding," "memory," etc. they are sufficient to obstruct the will, amuse the understanding, and confound the memory of those who read them. But, surely the decrees of God are wise, good, and just; and nature's actions are poised, equal, and fit, and also rational and sensible, and consequently methodical. And if men allow nature to have sensitive and rational self-motions (as I cannot see why even the most serious should not) it would be an occasion of allaying at least, if not composing all the eager and inveterate disputes between the Academians, Epicureans, and Sceptics, and other the like sects, which have rendered philosophy perplex and confused. But this is not easily brought to pass; for, nature being a perpetual motion, and as full of division as composition, will not perhaps admit of such a general conformity of men's judgments.]¹⁵

¹⁴ Added by the editor.   ¹⁵ Lacking in 1666.

An Argumental Discourse

Concerning some principal subjects in natural philosophy;
necessary for the better understanding, not only of this,
but all other philosophical works, hitherto written by the authoress.

When I was setting forth this book of *Observations upon Experimental Philosophy*, a dispute chanced to arise between the rational parts of my mind concerning some chief points and principles in natural philosophy; for, some new thoughts endeavouring to oppose and call in question the truth of my former conceptions, caused a war in my mind: which in time grew to that height, that they were hardly able to compose the differences between themselves, but were in a manner necessitated to refer them to the arbitration of the impartial reader, desiring the assistance of his judgment to reconcile their controversies, and, if possible, to reduce them to a settled peace and agreement.

The first difference did arise about the question, How it came, that matter was of several degrees, as animate and inanimate, sensitive and rational? For, my latter thoughts would not believe that there was any such difference of degrees of matter: To which my former conceptions answered, that nature, being eternal and infinite, it could not be known how she came to be such, no more than a reason could be given how God came to be: For nature, said they, is the infinite servant of God, and her origin cannot be described by any finite or particular creature; for, what is infinite, has neither beginning nor end; but that natural matter consisted of so many degrees as mentioned, was evidently perceived by her effects or actions; by which it appeared first, that nature was a self-moving body, and that all her parts and creatures were so too: Next, that there was not only an animate or self-moving and active, but also an inanimate, that is, a dull and passive degree of matter; for if there were no animate degree, there would be no motion, and so no action nor variety of figures; and if no inanimate, there would be no degrees of natural figures and actions, but all actions would be done in a moment, and the figures would all be so pure, fine and subtle, as not to be subject to any grosser perception, such as our human, or other the like perceptions are. This inanimate part of matter, said they, had no self-motion, but was carried along in all the actions of the animate degree, and so was not moving, but moved; which animate part of matter being again of two degrees, viz. sensitive and rational, the rational being so pure, fine and subtle, that it gave only directions to the sensitive, and made figures in its own degree, left the working with and upon the inanimate part, to the sensitive degree of matter, whose office was to execute both the rational part's design, and to work those various figures that are perceived in nature; and those three degrees were so inseparably commixt in the body of nature, that none could be without the other in any part or creature of nature, could it be divided to an atom; for as in the exstruction of a house there is first required an architect or surveyor, who orders and designs the building, and puts the labourers to work; next the labourers or workmen themselves; and lastly the materials of which the house is built: so the rational part, said they, in the framing of natural effects, is, as it were, the surveyor or architect; the sensitive, the labouring or working part; and the inanimate, the materials: and all these degrees are necessarily required in every composed action of nature.

To this, my latter thoughts excepted, that in probability of sense and reason, there was no necessity of introducing an inanimate degree of matter; for all those parts which we call gross, said they, are no more but a composition of self-moving parts, whereof some are denser, and some rarer than others; and we may observe, that the denser parts are as active, as the rarest: For example; earth is as active as air or light, and the parts of the body are as active as the parts of the soul or mind, being all self-moving, as it is perceivable by their several, various compositions, divisions, productions, and alterations; nay, we do see, that the earth is more active in the several productions and alterations of her particulars, than what we name celestial lights: which observation is a firm argument to prove, that all matter is animate or self-moving; only there are degrees of motion, that some parts move slower, and some quicker.

Hereupon my former thoughts answered, that the difference consisted not only in the grossness, but in the dullness of the inanimate parts; and that, since the sensitive animate parts were labouring on, and with, the inanimate; if these had self-motion, and that their motion was slower than that of the animate parts, they would obstruct, cross, and oppose each other in all their actions; for the one would be too slow, and the other too quick.

The latter thoughts replied, that this slowness and quickness of motion would cause no obstruction at all; For, said they, a man that rides on a horse is carried away by the horse's motion, and has nevertheless also his own motions himself; neither does the horse and man transfer or exchange motion into each other, nor do they hinder or obstruct one another.[16]

The former thoughts answered, It was true, that motion could not be transferred from one body into another without matter or substance; and that several self-moving parts might be joined, and each act a part without the least hindrance to one another; for, not all the parts of one composed creature (for example, man) were bound to one and the same action; and this was an evident proof that all creatures were composed of parts, by reason of their different actions; nay, not only of parts, but of self-moving parts: also they confessed, that there were degrees of motion, as quickness and slowness, and that the slowest motion was as much motion as the quickest. But yet, said they, this does not prove, that nature consists not of inanimate matter as well as of animate; for, it is one thing to speak of the parts of the composed and mixed body of nature, and another thing to speak of the constitutive parts of nature, which are, as it were, the ingredients of which nature is made up as one entire self-moving body; for sense and reason does plainly perceive, that some parts are more dull, and some more lively, subtle and active: the rational parts are more agile, active, pure and subtle than the sensitive; but the inanimate have no activity, subtlety and agility at all, by reason they want self-motion; nor no perception, for self-motion is the cause of all perception; and this triumvirate of the degrees of matter, said they, is so necessary to balance and poise nature's actions, that otherwise the

---

[16] Cf. Descartes, *Principles of Philosophy*, II, § 31.

creatures which nature produces, would all be produced alike, and in an instant; for example, a child in the womb would as suddenly be framed, as it is figured in the mind; and a man would be as suddenly dissolved as a thought: But sense and reason perceives that it is otherwise; to wit, that such figures as are made of the grosser parts of matter, are made by degrees, and not in an instant of time, which does manifestly evince, that there is and must of necessity be such a degree of matter in nature as we call inanimate; for surely, although the parts of nature are infinite, and have infinite actions, yet they cannot run into extremes, but are balanced by their opposites, so that all parts cannot be alike rare or dense, hard or soft, dilating or contracting, etc. but some are dense, some rare, some hard, some soft, some dilative, some contractive, etc. by which the actions of nature are kept in an equal balance from running into extremes. But put the case, said they, it were so, that nature's body consisted altogether of animate matter, or corporeal self-motion, without an intermixture of the inanimate parts, we are confident that there would be framed as many objections against that opinion as there are now against the inanimate degree of matter; for, disputes are endless, and the more answers you receive, the more objections you will find; and the more objections you make, the more answers you will receive; and even shows, that nature is balanced by opposites: for, put the case the inanimate parts of matter were self-moving, then first there would be no such difference between the rational and sensitive parts, as now there is, but every part, being self-moving, would act of, and in itself, that is, in its own substance, as now the rational part of matter does. Next, if the inanimate part was of a slower motion than the rational and sensitive, they would obstruct each other in their actions; for one would be too quick, and the other too slow: neither would the quicker motion alter the nature of the slower, or the slower retard the quicker; for the nature of each must remain as it is; or else if it could be thus, then the animate part might become inanimate, and the rational, the sensitive, etc. which is impossible, and against all sense and reason.

At this declaration of my former thoughts, the latter appeared somewhat better satisfied, and had almost yielded to them, but that they had yet some scruples left, which hindered them from giving a full assent to my former rational conceptions. First, they asked, How it was possible, that that part of matter which had no innate self-motion, could be moved? For, said they, if it be moved, it must either be moved by its own motion, or by the motion of the animate part of matter: By its own motion it cannot move, because it has none: but if it be moved by the motion of the animate, then the animate must of necessity transfer motion into it; that so, being not able to move by an innate motion, it might move by a communicated motion.

The former thoughts answered, that they had resolved this question heretofore, by the example of a horse and a man, where the man was moved and carried along by the horse, without any communication or translation of motion from the horse into the man: Also a stick, said they, carried in a man's hand, goes along with the man, without receiving any motion from his hand.

My latter thoughts replied, that a man and a stick were parts or creatures of nature, which consist of a commixture of animate or self-moving matter; and that they did move by their own motions, even at the time when they were carried along by other parts: but with the inanimate part of matter it was not so; for it having no self-motion, could no ways move.

You say well, answered my former thoughts, that all the parts of nature, whensoever they move, move by their own motions; which proves, that no particular creature or effect of composed nature, can act upon another, but that one can only occasion another to move thus or thus; as, in the mentioned example, the horse does not move the man, but occasions him only to move after such or such a manner: Also, the hand does not move the stick, but is only an occasion that the stick moves thus, for the stick moves by its own motion.[17]

But, as we told you before, this is to be understood of the parts of the composed body of nature, which, as they are nature's creatures and effects, so they consist also of a commixture of the aforementioned degrees of animate and inanimate matter; but our discourse is now of those parts which do compose the body of nature, and make it what it is: and, as of the former parts none can be said moved, but all are moving, as having self-motion within them; so the inanimate part of matter, considered as it is an ingredient of nature, is no ways moving, but always moved. The former parts being effects of the body of nature, for distinction's sake may be called effective parts; but these, that is, the animate and inanimate, may be called constitutive parts of nature: Those

---

[17] See Hobbes, *Elements of Philosophy*, II, ch. 8, § 21 (*EW*, I, 117).

follow the composition of nature, but these are the essential parts, which constitute the body of nature; whereof the animate, by reason of their self-motion, are always active and perceptive; but the inanimate are neither active nor perceptive, but dull and passive; and you may plainly perceive it, (added my former thoughts) by the alleged example: for, as the stick has no animal motion, but yet is carried along by and with the animal wheresoever it goes; so the inanimate matter, although it has no motion at all, yet it goes along with the animate parts wheresoever they'll have it; the only difference is this, as we told you before, that the stick being composed of animate as well as inanimate matter, cannot properly be said moved, but occasioned to such a motion, by the animal that carries it; whenas the inanimate part cannot be said occasioned, but moved.

My latter thoughts replied, that the alleged example of the carried stick, could give them no full satisfaction as yet; for, said they, put the case the stick had its own motion, yet it has not a visible, exterior, local, progressive motion, such as animals have, and therefore it must needs receive that motion from the animal that carries it; for nothing can be occasioned to that which it has not in itself.

To which the former answered, first, that although animals had a visible exterior progressive motion, yet not all progressive motion was an animal motion. Next, they said, that some creatures did often occasion others to alter their motions from an ordinary, to an extraordinary effect; and if it be no wonder, said they, that cheese, roots, fruits, etc. produce worms, why should it be a wonder for an animal to occasion a visible progressive motion in a vegetable or mineral, or any other sort of creature? For each natural action, said they, is local, were it no more than the stirring of a hairsbreadth, nay, of an atom; and all composition and division, contraction, dilatation, nay, even retention, are local motions; for there is nothing in so just a measure, but it will vary more or less; nay, if it did not to our perception, yet we cannot from thence infer that it does not at all; for our perception is too weak and gross to perceive all the subtle actions of nature; and if so, then certainly animals are not the only creatures that have local motion, but there is local motion in all parts of nature.

Then my latter thoughts asked, that if every part of nature moved by its own inherent self-motion, and that there was no part of the composed body of nature which was not self-moving, how it came that children could not go as soon as born? Also, if the self-moving part of matter was of two degrees, sensitive and rational, how it came that children could not speak before they are taught? And if it was perceptive, how it came that children did not understand so soon as born?

To which the former answered, that although there was no part of matter that was figureless, yet those figures that were composed by the several parts of matter, such as are named natural creatures, were composed by degrees, and some compositions were sooner perfected than others; and some sorts of such figures or creatures, were not so soon produced or strengthened as others: For example, most of four-legged creatures, said they, can go, run, and skip about, so soon as they are parted from the dam, that is, so soon as they are born; also they can suck, understand, and know their dams; whenas a bird can neither feed itself, nor fly, so soon as it is hatched, but requires some time before it can hop on its legs, and be able to fly; but a butterfly can fly so soon as it comes out of the shell; by which we may perceive, that all figures are not alike, either in their composing, perfecting, or dissolving; no more than they are alike in their shapes, forms, understanding, etc. for if they were, then little puppies and kitlings would see so soon as born, as many other creatures do, whenas now they require nine days after their birth, before they can see. And as for speech, although it be most proper to the shape of man, yet he must first know or learn a language, before he can speak it; and although when the parts of his mind, like the parts of his body, are brought to maturity, that is, to such a regular degree of perfection as belongs to his figure, he may make a language of his own; yet it requires time, and cannot be done in an instant. The truth is, although speech be natural to man, yet language must be learned; and as there are several self-active parts, so there are several languages; and by reason the actions of some parts can be imitated by other parts, it causes what we name learning not only in speech, but in many other things.

Concerning the question, why children do not understand so soon as born? They answered, that as the sensitive parts of nature did compose the bulk of creatures, that is, such as were usually named bodies; and as some creatures' bodies were not finished or perfected so soon as others, so the self-moving parts, which by conjunction and agreement, composed that which is named the mind of man, did not bring it to the perfection of an animal understanding so soon as some beasts are brought to their understanding, that is, to such an understanding as was proper to their figure. But this is to be noted, said they, that although nature is in perpetual motion, yet her actions have degrees, as well as her parts; which is the reason that all her productions are done in that which is vulgarly named time; that is, they are not executed at once, or by one act: In short, as a house is not finished until it be thoroughly built; nor can be thoroughly furnished, until it be thoroughly finished; so is the strength and understanding of man, and all other creatures: And as perception requires objects, so learning requires practice; for, though nature is self-knowing, self-moving, and so perceptive; yet her self-knowing, self-moving, and perceptive actions, are not all alike, but differ variously: neither doth she perform all actions at once; otherwise all her creatures would be alike in their shapes, forms, figures, knowledges, perceptions, productions, dissolutions, etc. which is contradicted by experience.

After this, my latter thoughts asked, How it came, that the inanimate part of matter had more degrees than the animate?

The former answered, that as the animate part had but two degrees, to wit, the sensitive and rational; so the inanimate was but grosser and purer; and as for density, rarity, softness, hardness, etc. they were nothing but various compositions and divisions of parts, or particular effects: Nor was it density or hardness that made grossness; and thinness or rarity of parts, that made fineness and purity: for, gold is more dense than dross, and yet is more pure and fine: But this is most probable, said they, that the rarest compositions are most suddenly altered: Nor can the grossness and fineness of the parts of nature, be without animate and inanimate matter; for the dullness of one degree, poises the activity of the other; and the grossness of one, the purity of the other: All which, keeps nature from extremes.

But, replied my latter thoughts, You say, that there are infinite degrees of hardness, thickness, thinness, density, rarity, etc.

Truly, answered the former, if you'll call them degrees, you may; for so there may be infinite degrees of magnitude, as bigger and bigger; but these degrees are nothing else but the effects of self-moving matter, made by a composition of parts, and cannot be attributed to one single part, there being no such thing in nature; but they belong to the infinite parts of nature joined in one body: And as for matter itself, there are no more degrees but animate and inanimate; that is, a self-moving, active, and perceptive, and a dull, passive and moved degree.

My latter thoughts asked, Since nature's parts were so closely joined in one body, how it was possible that there could be finite, and not single parts?

The former answered, that finite and single parts, were not all one and the same: for single parts, said they, are such as can subsist by themselves; neither can they properly be called parts, but are rather finite wholes: for it is a mere contradiction to say single parts, they having no reference to each other, and consequently, not to the body of nature: But, what we call finite parts, are nothing else but several corporeal figurative motions, which make all the difference that is between the figures or parts of nature, both in their kinds, sorts, and particulars. And thus finite and particular parts are all one, called thus, by reason they have limited and circumscribed figures, by which they are discerned from each other; but not single figures, for they are all joined in one body, and are parts of the one infinite whole, which is nature; and these figures being all one and the same with their parts of matter, change according as their parts change, that is, by composition and division: for, were nature an atom, and material, that atom would have the properties of a body, that is, be divisible and compoundable, and so be subject to infinite changes, although it were not infinite in bulk.

My latter thoughts replied, that if a finite body could have infinite compositions and divisions, then nature need not to be infinite in bulk or quantity: Besides, said they, it is against sense and reason, that a finite should have infinite effects.

The former answered: first, as for the infiniteness of nature, it was certain that nature consisted of infinite parts; which if so, she must needs also be of an infinite bulk or quantity; for wheresoever is an infinite number of parts or figures, there must also be an infinite whole, since a whole and its parts differ not really, but only in the manner of our conception: for, when we conceive the parts of nature, as composed in one body, and inseparable from it, the composition of them is called a whole; but, when we conceive their different figures, actions and changes, and that they are divisible from each other, or amongst themselves, we call them parts; for by this, one part is discerned from the other part; as (for example) a mineral from a vegetable, a vegetable from an element, an element from an animal, etc. and one part is not another part; but yet these parts are, and remain still, parts of infinite nature, and cannot be divided into single parts, separated from the body of nature, although they may be divided amongst themselves infinite ways, by the self-moving power of nature. In short, said they, a whole is nothing but a composition of parts, and parts are nothing but a division of the whole.

Next, as for the infinite compositions and divisions of a finite whole, said they, it is not probable that a finite can have infinite effects, or can be actually divided into infinite parts; but yet a body cannot but have the proprieties of a body, as long as it lasts; and therefore if a finite body should last eternally, it would eternally retain the effects, or rather proprieties of a body, that is, to be divisible and compoundable, and if it have self-motion, and was actually divided and composed, then those compositions and divisions of its parts, would be eternal too; but what is eternal, is infinite, and therefore in this sense one cannot say amiss, but that there might be eternal compositions and divisions of the parts of a finite whole; for wheresoever is self-motion, there is no rest: But, mistake us not, for we do not mean divisions or compositions into single or infinite parts, but a perpetual and eternal change and self-motion of the parts of that finite body, or whole, amongst themselves.

But because we speak now of the parts of infinite nature, which are infinite in number, though finite, or rather, distinguished by their figures; it is certain, said they, that there being a perpetual and eternal self-motion in all parts of nature, and their number being infinite, they must of necessity be subject to infinite changes, compositions, and divisions, not only as for their duration, or eternal self-motion, but as for the number of their parts: for, parts cannot remove, but from, and to parts; and as soon as they are removed from such parts, they join to other parts, which is nothing else but a composition and division of parts; and this composition and division of the infinite parts of nature, hinders that there are no actual divisions or compositions of a finite part, because the one counterbalances the other: for, if by finite you understand a single part, there can be no such thing in nature, since what we call the finiteness of parts, is nothing else but the difference and change of their figures, caused by self-motion: And therefore, when we say, infinite nature consists of an infinite number of finite parts, we mean of such parts as may be distinguished or discerned from each other by their several figures; which figures are not constant, but change perpetually in the body of nature. So that there can be no constant figure allowed to no part, although some do last longer than others.

Then my latter thoughts desired to know, Whether there were not degrees of motion, as well as there are of matter?

The former answered, that, without question, there were degrees of motion; for the rational parts were more agile, quick, and subtle in their corporeal actions, than the sensitive, by reason they were of a purer and finer degree of matter, and free from labouring on the inanimate parts: But, withal, they told them, that the several different and opposite actions of nature, hindered each other from running into extremes. And as for the degrees of matter, there could not possibly be more than animate and inanimate; neither could any degree go beyond matter, so as to become immaterial. The truth is, said they, to balance the actions of nature, it cannot be otherwise, but there must be a passive degree of matter, opposite to the active; which passive part is what we call inanimate: for, though they are so closely intermixt in the body of nature, that they cannot be separated from each other, but by the power of God; nevertheless, sense and reason may perceive that they are distinct degrees, by their distinct and different actions, and may distinguish them so far, that one part is not another part, and that the actions of one degree are not the actions of the other. Wherefore, as several self-moving parts may be joined in one composed body, and may either act differently without hindrance and obstruction to each other, or may act jointly and agreeably to one effect; so may the sensitive parts carry or bear along with them the inanimate parts, without either transferring and communicating motion to them, or without any co-operation or self-action of the inanimate parts: And as for matter, as there can be no fewer degrees than animate and inanimate, sensitive and rational; so neither can there be more: for, as we mentioned heretofore, were there nothing but animate or self-moving matter in nature, the parts of nature would be too active and quick in their several productions, alterations, and dissolutions; and all things would be as soon made, as thoughts. Again, were there no inanimate degree of matter, the sensitive corporeal motions would retain the figures or patterns of exterior objects, as the rational do; which yet we perceive otherwise: for, so soon as the object is removed, the sensitive perception is altered; and though the sensitive parts can work by rote, as in dreams, and some distempers; yet their voluntary actions are not so exact as their exterior perceptive actions, nor altogether and always so regular as the rational; and the reason is, that they are bound to bear the inanimate parts along with them in all their actions. Also, were there no degree of inanimate matter, nature's actions would run into extremes; but because all her actions are balanced by opposites, they hinder both extremes in nature, and produce all that harmonious variety that is found in nature's parts.

But, said my latter thoughts, wheresoever is such an opposition and crossing of actions, there can be no harmony, concord, or agreement, and consequently, no orderly productions, dissolutions, changes and alterations, as in nature we perceive there be.

The former answered, that though the actions of nature were different and opposite to each other, yet they did cause no disturbance in nature, but they were ruled and governed by nature's wisdom; for nature being peaceable in herself, would not suffer her actions to disturb her government: Wherefore, although particulars were crossing and opposing each other, yet she did govern them with such wisdom and moderation, that they were necessitated to obey her, and move according as she would have them; but sometimes they would prove extravagant and refractory, and hence came that we call irregularities. The truth is, said they, contrary and opposite actions are not always at war: For example, two men may meet each other contrary ways, and one may not only stop the other from going forward, but even draw him back again the same way he came; and this may be done with love and kindness, and with his good will, and not violently, by power and force. The like may be in some actions of nature. Nevertheless, we do not deny but there is many times force and power used between particular parts of nature, so that some do overpower others; but this causes no disturbance in nature: for, if we look upon a well-ordered government, we find that the particulars are often at strife and difference with each other, whenas yet the government is as orderly and peaceable as can be.

My latter thoughts replied, that although the several and contrary actions in nature, did not disturb her government, yet they moving severally in one composed figure, at one and the same time, proved, that "motion," "figure," and "body," could not be one and the same thing.

The former answered, that they had sufficiently declared heretofore, that matter was either moving, or moved, viz. that the animate part was self-moving, and the inanimate moved, or carried along with, and by the animate; and these degrees or parts of matter, were so closely intermixt in the body of nature, that they could not be separated from each other, but did constitute but one body, not only in general, but also in every particular; so that not the least part (if least could be) nay not that which some call an atom, was without this commixture; for, wheresoever was inanimate, there was also animate matter; which animate matter, was nothing else but corporeal self-motion; and if any difference could be apprehended, it was, said they, between these two degrees, to wit, the animate and inanimate part of matter, and not between the animate part, and self-motion, which was but one thing, and could not so much as be conceived differently: And since this animate matter, or corporeal self-motion, is thoroughly intermixt with the inanimate parts, they are but as one body, (like as soul and body make but one man) or else it were impossible that any creature could be composed, consist, or be dissolved; for if there were matter without motion, there could be no composition or dissolution of such figures as are named creatures; nor any, if there were motion without matter, or (which is the same) an immaterial motion: for, can any part of reason, that is regular, believe, that, that which naturally is nothing, should produce a natural something? Besides, said they, material and immaterial are so quite opposite to each other, as it is impossible they should commix and work together, or act one upon the other: nay, if they could, they would make but a confusion, being of contrary natures: Wherefore, it is most probable, and can, to the perception of regular sense and reason, be no otherwise, but that self-moving matter, or corporeal figurative self-motion, does act and govern wisely, orderly and easily, poising or balancing extremes with proper and fit oppositions, which could not be done by immaterials, they being not capable of natural compositions and divisions; neither of dividing matter, nor of being divided[.] In short, although there are numerous corporeal figurative motions in one composed figure, yet they are so far from disturbing each other, that no creature could be produced without them: And as the actions of retention are different from the actions of digestion or expulsion, and the actions of contraction from those of dilatation; so the actions of imitation or patterning, are different from the voluntary actions, vulgarly called conceptions, and all this to make an equal poise or balance between the actions of nature. Also, there is difference in the degrees of motions, in swiftness, slowness, rarity, density, appetites, passions, youth, age, growth, decay, etc. as also, between several sorts of perceptions; all which proves, that nature is composed of self-moving parts, which are the cause of all her varieties. But this is well to be observed, said they, that the rational parts are the purest, and consequently, the most active parts of nature, and have the quickest actions: wherefore, to balance them, there must be a dull part of matter, which is the inanimate, or else a world would be made in an instant, and every-thing would be produced, altered, and dissolved on a sudden, as they had mentioned before.

Well, replied my latter thoughts, if there be such oppositions between the parts of nature, then I pray inform us, whether they be all equally and exactly poised and balanced?

To which the former answered, that though it was most certain that there was a poise and balance of nature's corporeal actions; yet no particular creature was able to know the exactness of the proportion that is between them, because they are infinite.

Then my latter thoughts desired to know, whether motion could be annihilated?

The former said, No: because nature was infinite, and admitted of no addition nor diminution; and consequently, of no new creation nor annihilation of any part of hers.

But, said the latter, If motion be an accident, it may be annihilated.

The former answered, They did not know what they meant by the word "accident."

The later said, that an accident was something in a body, but nothing without a body.

If an accident be something, answered the former, then certainly it must be body; for, there is nothing but what is corporeal in nature: and if it be body, then it cannot be nothing at no time, but it must of necessity be something.

But it cannot subsist of, and by itself, replied my latter thoughts, as a substance: for, although it hath its own being, yet its being is to subsist in another body.

The former answered, that if an accident was nothing without a body, or substance, and yet something in a body; then they desired to know, how, being nothing, it could subsist in another body, and be separated from another body: for, composition and division, said they, are at-tributes of a body, since nothing can be composed or divided, but what has parts; and nothing has parts, but what is corporeal, or has a body: and therefore, if an accident can be in a body, and be separated from a body, it would be nonsense to call it nothing.

But then my latter thoughts asked, that when a particular motion ceased, what became of it?

The former answered, It was not annihilated, but changed.

The latter said, How can motion be corporeal, and yet one thing with body? Certainly, if body be material, and motion too, they must needs be two several substances.

The former answered, that motion and body were not two several substances; but motion and matter made one self-moving body; and so was place, colour, figure, etc. all one and the same with body.

The latter replied, that a man, and his action, were not one and the same, but two different things.

The former answered, that a man, and his actions, were no more different, than a man was different from himself; for, said they, although a man may have many different actions; yet, were not that man existent, the same actions would not be: for, though many men have the like actions, yet they are not the same.

But then, replied the latter, place cannot be the same with body, nor colour; because a man may change his place, and his colour, and yet retain his body.

Truly, said the former, if place be changed, then body must change also; for wheresoever is place, there is body: and though it be a vulgar phrase, that a man changes his place when he removes, yet it is not a proper philosophical expression; for he removes only from such parts, to such parts: so that it is a change, or a division and composition of parts, and not of place. And as for colour, though it changes, yet that proves not, that it is not a body, or can be annihilated. The truth is, though figure, motion, colour, etc. do change, yet they remain still in nature, and it is impossible that nature can give away, or lose the least of her corporeal attributes or proprieties: for, nature is infinite in power, as well as in act; we mean, for acting naturally; and therefore, whatsoever is not in present act, is in the power of infinite nature.

But, said my latter thoughts, if a body be divided into very minute parts, as little as dust, where is the colour then?

The colour, answered the former, is divided as well as the body; and though the parts thereof be not subject to our sensitive perception, yet they have, nevertheless, their being; for all things cannot be perceptible by our senses.

The latter said, that the colour of a man's face could change from pale to red, and from red to pale, and yet the substance of the face remain the same; which proved, that colour and substance was not the same.

The former answered, that although the colour of a man's face did change, without altering the substance thereof; yet this proved no more that colour was immaterial, than that motion was immaterial: for, a man may put his body into several postures, and have several actions, and yet without any change of the substance of his body; for, all actions do not necessarily import a change of the parts of a composed figure, there being infinite sorts of actions.

We will leave accidents, said my latter thoughts, and return to the inanimate part of matter; and since you declare, that all parts of nature do worship and adore God, you contradict yourself, in allowing an inanimate degree of matter; by reason, where there is no self-motion, there can be no perception of God, and consequently, no worship and adoration.

The former answered, that the knowledge of God did not consist in exterior perception: for God, said they, being an infinite, incomprehensible, supernatural, and immaterial essence, void of all parts, can no ways be subject to perception. Nevertheless, although no part can have an exterior perception of the substance of God, as it has of particular natural creatures, yet it has conceptions of the existence of God, to wit, that there is a God above nature, on which nature depends; and from whose immutable and eternal decree, it has its eternal being, as God's eternal servant: but, what God is in his essence, neither nature, nor any of her parts or creatures, is able to conceive. And therefore, although the inanimate part of matter is not perceptive; yet, having an innate knowledge and life of itself, it is not improbable but it may also have an interior, fixt and innate knowledge of the existency of God, as, that he is to be adored and worshipped. And thus the inanimate part may, after its own manner, worship and adore God, as much as the other parts in their ways: for, it is probable, that God having endued all parts of nature with self-knowledge, may have given them also an interior knowledge of himself, that is, of his existency, how he is the God of nature, and ought to be worshipped by her, as his eternal servant.

My latter thoughts excepted, that not any creature did truly know itself, much less could it be capable of knowing God.

The former answered, that this was caused through the variety of self-motion: for, all creatures (said they) are composed of many several parts, and every part has its own particular self-knowledge, as well as self-motion, which causes an ignorance between them; for, one part's knowledge is not another part's knowledge; nor does one part know what another knows; but all knowledge of exterior parts, comes by perception: Nevertheless, each part knows itself, and its own actions. And as there is an ignorance between parts, so there is also an acquaintance (especially in the parts of one composed creature) and the rational parts being most subtle, active and free, have a more general acquaintance than the sensitive: Besides, the sensitive many times informs the rational, and the rational the sensitive, which causes a general agreement of all the parts of a composed figure, in the execution of such actions as belong to it.

But, how is it possible, replied my latter thoughts, that the inanimate part of matter can be living and self-knowing, and yet not self-moving? for, life and knowledge cannot be without self-motion; and therefore, if the inanimate parts have life and knowledge, they must necessarily also have self-motion.

The former answered, that life and knowledge did no ways depend upon self-motion: for, had nature no motion at all, yet might she have life and knowledge; so that self-motion is not the cause of life and knowledge, but only of perception, and all the various actions of nature; and this is the reason, said they, that the inanimate part of matter is not perceptive, because it is not self-moving: for, though it hath life and self-knowledge as well as the animate part, yet it has not an active life, nor a perceptive knowledge. By which you may see, that a fixt and interior self-knowledge, may very well be without exterior perception: for, though perception presupposes an innate self-knowledge as its ground and principle, yet self-knowledge does not necessarily require perception, which is only caused by self-motion: for self-motion, as it is the cause of the variety of nature's parts and actions, so it is also of their various perceptions. If it were not too great a presumption, said they, we could give an instance of God, who has no local self-motion, and yet is infinitely knowing. But we'll forebear to go so high, as to draw the infinite, incomprehensible God, to the proofs of material nature.

My latter thoughts replied, first, that if it were thus, then one and the same parts of matter would have a double life, and a double knowledge.

Next, they said, that if perception were an effect of self-motion, then God Himself must necessarily be self-moving, or else he could not perceive nature, and her parts and actions.

Concerning the first objection, my former thoughts answered, that the parts of nature could have a double life and knowledge, no more than one man could be called double or treble: You might as well, said they, make millions of men of one particular man; nay, call every part or action of his, a peculiar man, as make one and the same part of matter have a double life and knowledge.

But mistake us not, added my former thoughts, when we say, that one and the same part cannot have a double life and knowledge: for, we mean not the composed creatures of nature, which, as they consist of several degrees of matter; so they have also, several degrees of lives and knowledges; but it is to be understood of the essential or constitutive parts of nature: for, as the rational part is not, nor can be the sensitive part, so it can neither have a sensitive knowledge; no more can a sensitive part have a rational knowledge, or either of these the knowledge of the inanimate part; but each part retains its own life and knowledge. Indeed, it is with these parts as it is with particular creatures; for, as one man is not another man, nor has another man's knowledge; so it is likewise with the mentioned parts of matter; and although the animate parts have an interior, innate self-knowledge, and an exterior, perceptive knowledge; yet these are not double knowledges; but perception is only an effect of interior self-knowledge, occasioned by self-motion.

And as for the second, they answered, that the divine perception and knowledge was not any ways like a natural perception, no more than God was like a creature: for, nature (said they) is material, and her perceptions are amongst her infinite parts, caused by their compositions and divisions: but God is a supernatural, indivisible, and incorporeal being, void of all parts and divisions; and therefore he cannot be ignorant of any the least thing; but, being infinite, he has an infinite knowledge, without any degrees, divisions, or the like actions belonging to material creatures. Nor is he naturally, that is, locally self-moving: but he is a fixt, unalterable, and, in short, an incomprehensible being; and therefore no comparison can be made between him and nature, he being the eternal God and nature his eternal servant.

Then my latter thoughts said, that as for the knowledge of God, they would not dispute of it; but if there was a fixt and interior innate knowledge in all nature's parts and creatures, it was impossible that there could be any error, or ignorance between them.

The former answered, that although errors belonged to particulars, as well as ignorance; yet they proceeded not from interior self-knowledge, but either from want of exterior particular knowledges, or from the irregularity of motions; and ignorance was likewise a want not of interior, but exterior knowledge, otherwise called perceptive knowledge: for, said they, parts can know no more of other parts, but by their own perceptions: and since no particular creature or part of nature, can have an infallible, universal, and thorough perception of all other parts; it can neither have an infallible and universal knowledge: but it must content itself with such knowledge as is within the reach of its own perceptions; and hence it follows, that it must be ignorant of what it does not know: for, perception has but only a respect to the exterior figures and actions of other parts; and though the rational part is more subtle and active than the sensitive, and may have also some perceptions of some interior parts and actions of other creatures; yet it cannot have an infallible and thorough perception of all their interior parts and motions, which is a knowledge impossible for any particular creature to attain to.

Again, my latter thoughts objected, that it was impossible that the parts of one and the same degree could be ignorant of each other's actions, how various soever; since they were capable to change their actions to the like figures.

The former answered, first, that although they might make the like figures, yet they could not make the same, because the parts were not the same. Next, they said, that particular parts could not have infinite perceptions, but that they could but perceive such objects as were subject to that sort of perception which they had; no, not all such: for, oftentimes objects were obscured and hidden from their perceptions, that although they could perceive them if presented, or coming within the compass and reach of their perceptive faculty or power; yet, when they were absent, they could not: Besides, said they, the sensitive parts are not so subtle as to make perceptions into the interior actions of other parts; no, not the rational are able to have exact perceptions thereof: for, perception extends but to adjoining parts, and their exterior figures and actions; and if they know anything of their interior parts, figures or motions, it is only by guess, or probable conclusions, taken from their exterior actions or figures, and made especially by the rational parts, which, as they are the most inspective, so they are the most knowing parts of nature.

After these, and several other objections, questions and answers, between the latter and former thoughts and conceptions of my mind, at last some rational thoughts, which were not concerned in this dispute, perceiving that they became much heated, and fearing they would, at last, cause a faction, or civil war, amongst all the rational parts, which would breed that which is called "a trouble of the mind"; endeavoured to make a peace between them; and to that end they propounded, that the sensitive parts should publicly declare their differences and controversies, and refer them to the arbitration of the judicious and impartial reader. This proposition was unanimously embraced by all the rational parts; and thus, by their mutual consent, this "Argumental Discourse" was set down, and published after this manner. In the meantime, all the rational parts of my mind inclined to the opinion of my former conceptions, which they thought much more probable than those of the latter. And now, since it is your part, Ingenious Reader, to give a final decision of the cause, consider well the subject of their quarrel, and be impartial in your judgment; let not self-love or envy corrupt you, but let regular sense and reason be your only rule, that you may be accounted just judges, and your equity and justice be remembered by all that honour and love it.

The Table of All the Principal Subjects Contained and Discoursed of in This Book

[18] 1666 and 1668 erroneously give: "Of Parts."

II) Further Observations upon *Experimental Philosophy*;
Reflecting Withal, upon Some Principal Subjects in
Contemplative Philosophy

III Observations upon the Opinions of Some Ancient Philosophers

---

[19] 1666 listed an additional section entitled, "An Explanation of Some Obscure and Doubtful Passages Occurring in the Philosophical Works Hitherto Published by the Authoress"; on the next page, this edition gives "A Catalogue of All the Works Hitherto Published by the Authoress."

Q. What is nature? 'One body'
or
MICRO-MACROCOSM! variety?

I Observations upon Experimental Philosophy[20]

wrong!

x5

I Of Human Sense and Perception

Before I deliver my observations upon that part of philosophy which is called experimental, I thought it necessary to premise some discourse concerning the perception of human sense. It is known that man has five exterior senses, and every sense is ignorant of each other; for the nose knows not what the eyes see, nor the eyes what the ears hear, neither do the ears know what the tongue tastes; and as for touch, although it is a general sense, yet every several part of the body has a several touch, and each part is ignorant of each other's touch: And thus there is a general ignorance of all the several parts, and yet a perfect knowledge in each part; for the eye is as knowing as the ear, and the ear as knowing as the nose, and the nose as knowing as the tongue, and one particular touch knows as much as another, at least is capable thereof: Nay, not only every several touch, taste, smell, sound or sight, is a several knowledge by itself, but each of them has as many particular knowledges or perceptions as there are objects presented to them: Besides, there are several degrees in each particular sense; As for example, some men (I will not speak of other animals) their perception of sight, taste, smell, touch, or hearing, is quicker to some sorts of objects, than to others, according either to the

[20] In this part of the book, Cavendish responds to the views of some contemporary scientists and some ancient philosophers, especially Aristotle – as understood by her contemporaries. Of particular importance are the arguments in ch. 31 against both the vacuum and a particulate theory of matter – key elements in her attack against atomism and corpuscularianism – and her extended treatment of the anti-mechanical theory of perception in chs. 35–37. See the Introduction for a discussion of these issues.

perfection or imperfection, or curiosity, or purity of the corporeal figurative motions of each sense, or according to the presentation of each object proper to each sense; for if the presentation of the objects be imperfect, either through variation or obscurity, or any other ways, the sense is deluded. Neither are all objects proper for one sense; but as there are several senses, so there are several sorts of objects proper for each several sense. Now if there be such variety of several knowledges, not only in one creature, but in one sort of sense; to wit, the exterior senses of one human creature; what may there be in all the parts of nature? It is true, there are some objects which are not at all perceptible by any of our exterior senses; as for example, rarefied air, and the like. But although they be not subject to our exterior sensitive perception, yet they are subject to our rational perception, which is much purer and subtler than the sensitive; nay, so pure and subtle a knowledge, that many believe it to be immaterial, as if it were some God, whenas it is only a pure, fine and subtle figurative motion or perception: It is so active and subtle, as it is the best informer and reformer of all sensitive perception; for the rational matter is the most prudent and wisest part of nature, as being the designer of all productions, and the most pious and devoutest part, having the perfectest notions of God; I mean, so much as nature can possibly know of God: so that whatsoever the sensitive perception is either defective in, or ignorant of, the rational perception supplies. But, mistake me not: by rational perception and knowledge, I mean regular reason, not irregular; where I do also exclude "art," which is apt to delude sense, and cannot inform so well as reason doth; for reason reforms and instructs sense in all its actions. But both the rational and sensitive knowledge and perception being dividable as well as composable, it causes ignorance as well as knowledge amongst nature's creatures: For though nature is but one body, and has no sharer or co-partner, but is entire and whole in itself, as not composed of several different parts or substances, and consequently has but one infinite natural knowledge and wisdom; yet by reason she is also dividable and composable, according to the nature of a body, we can justly and with all reason say, that, as nature is divided into infinite several parts, so each several part has a several and particular knowledge and perception, both sensitive and rational, and again that each part is ignorant of the other's knowledge and perception; whenas otherwise, considered altogether and in general, as they make up but one infinite body of nature, so they make also but one infinite general "body & place"...

knowledge. And thus nature may be called both "individual," as not having single parts subsisting without her, but all united in one body; and "dividable," by reason she is partible in her own several corporeal figurative motions, and not otherwise: for, there is no "vacuum" in nature, neither can her parts start or remove from the infinite body of nature, so as to separate themselves from it; for there's no place to flee to, but body and place are all one thing; so that the parts of nature can only join and disjoin to and from parts, but not to and from the body of nature. And since nature is but one body, it is entirely wise and knowing, ordering her self-moving parts with all facility and ease, without any disturbance, living in pleasure and delight, with infinite varieties and curiosities, such as no single part or creature of hers can ever attain to.

II Of Art, and Experimental Philosophy

Some are of opinion, that "By art there may be a reparation made of the mischiefs and imperfections mankind has drawn upon itself by negligence and intemperance, and a willful and superstitious deserting the prescripts and rules of nature; whereby every man, both from a derived corruption, innate and born with him, and from his breeding and converse with men, is very subject to slip into all sorts of errors."[21] But the all-powerful God, and his servant nature, know, that art, which is but a particular creature, cannot inform us of the truth of the infinite parts of nature, being but finite itself: for though every creature has a double perception, rational and sensitive, yet each creature or part has not an infinite perception; nay, although each particular creature or part of nature may have some conceptions of the infinite parts of nature, yet it cannot know the truth of those infinite parts, being but a finite part itself, which finiteness causes errors in perceptions: Wherefore it is well said, when they confess themselves, that "the uncertainty and mistakes of human actions proceed either from the narrowness and wandering of our

[21] R.[obert] Hooke, *Micrographia: or Some Physiological Descriptions of Minute Bodies Made by Magnifying Glasses, with Observations and Inquiries Thereupon* (London, 1665), "The Preface," unpaginated. Cavendish alters the beginning of the quotation, which reads: "And as this is the peculiar privilege of human nature in general, so is it capable of being so far advanced by the helps of art, and experience, as to make some men excel others in their observations, and deductions, almost as much as they do beasts. By the addition of such *artificial instruments* and *methods*, there may be, in some manner, a reparation made for the mischiefs and imperfection . . ."

senses, or from the slipperiness or delusion of our memory, or from the confinement or rashness of our understanding."[22] "But," say they, "it is no wonder that our power over natural causes and effects is so slowly improved, seeing we are not only to contend with the obscurity and difficulty of the things whereon we work and think, but even the forces of our minds conspire to betray us: And, these being the dangers in the process of human reason, the remedies can only proceed from the real, the mechanical, the experimental philosophy; which hath this advantage over the philosophy of discourse and disputation, that, whereas that chiefly aims at the subtlety of its deductions and conclusions, without much regard to the first groundwork, which ought to be well laid on the sense and memory; so this intends the right ordering of them all, and making them serviceable to each other."[23] In which discourse I do not understand, first, what they mean by our power over natural causes and effects: For we have no power at all over natural causes and effects; but only one particular effect may have some power over another, which are natural actions: but neither can natural causes nor effects be overpowered by man so, as if man was a degree above nature, but they must be as nature is pleased to order them; for man is but a small part, and his powers are but particular actions of nature, and therefore he cannot have a supreme and absolute power. Next, I say, that sense, which is more apt to be deluded than reason, cannot be the ground of reason, no more than art can be the ground of nature: Wherefore discourse shall sooner find or trace nature's corporeal figurative motions, than deluding arts can inform the senses; For how can a fool order his understanding by art, if nature has made it defective? or, how can a wise man trust his senses, if either the objects be not truly presented according to their natural figure and shape, or if the senses be defective, either through age, sickness, or other accidents, which do alter the natural motions proper to each sense? And hence I conclude, that experimental and mechanic philosophy cannot be above the speculative part, by reason most experiments have their rise from the speculative, so that the artist or mechanic is but a servant to the student.

[22] Ibid.; slightly altered.   [23] Ibid.; slightly altered.

III Of Micrography, and of Magnifying and Multiplying Glasses

Although I am not able to give a solid judgment of the art of "micrography," and the several dioptrical instruments belonging thereto, by reason I have neither studied nor practised that art; yet of this I am confident, that this same art, with all its instruments, is not able to discover the interior natural motions of any part or creature of nature; nay, the question is, whether it can represent yet the exterior shapes and motions so exactly, as naturally they are; for art doth more easily alter than inform: As for example; art makes cylinders, concave and convex glasses, and the like, which represent the figure of an object in no part exactly and truly, but very deformed and misshaped: also a glass that is flawed, cracked, or broke, or cut into the figure of lozenges, triangles, squares, or the like, will present numerous pictures of one object. Besides, there are so many alterations made by several lights, their shadows, refractions, reflexions, as also several lines, points, mediums, interposing and intermixing parts, forms and positions, as the truth of an object will hardly be known; for the perception of sight, and so of the rest of the senses, goes no further than the exterior parts of the object presented; and though the perception may be true, when the object is truly presented, yet when the presentation is false, the information must be false also. And it is to be observed, that art, for the most part, makes hermaphroditical, that is, mixt figures, partly artificial, and partly natural: for art may make some metal, as pewter, which is between tin and lead, as also brass, and numerous other things of mixt natures; In the like manner, may artificial glasses present objects, partly natural, and partly artificial; nay, put the case they can present the natural figure of an object, yet that natural figure may be presented in as monstrous a shape, as it may appear misshapen rather than natural: For example; a louse by the help of a magnifying glass appears like a lobster, where the microscope enlarging and magnifying each part of it, makes them bigger and rounder than naturally they are. The truth is, the more the figure by art is magnified, the more it appears misshapen from the natural, insomuch as each joint will appear as a diseased, swelled and tumid body, ready and ripe for incision. But, mistake me not; I do not say, that no glass presents the true picture of an object: but only that magnifying, multiplying, and the like optic glasses, may, and do oftentimes present falsely the picture of an exterior object; I say, the picture, because it is not the real body of the object which the glass presents, but the glass only figures or patterns out the picture presented in and by the glass, and there mistakes may easily be committed in taking copies from copies. Nay, artists do confess themselves, that flies, and the like, will appear of several figures or shapes, according to the several reflexions, refractions, mediums and positions of several lights; which if so, how can they tell or judge which is the truest light, position, or medium, that doth present the object naturally as it is?[24] And if not, then an edge may very well seem flat, and a point of a needle a globe:[25] but if the edge of a knife, or point of a needle were naturally and really so as the microscope presents them, they would never be so useful as they are; for, a flat or broad plain-edged knife would not cut, nor a blunt globe pierce so suddenly another body, neither would nor could they pierce without tearing and rending, if their bodies were so uneven: And if the picture of a young beautiful lady should be drawn according to the representation of the microscope, or according to the various refraction and reflexion of light through such like glasses; it would be so far from being like her, as it would not be like a human face, but rather a monster, than a picture of nature. Wherefore those that invented microscopes, and such like dioptrical glasses, at first, did, in my opinion, the world more injury than benefit; for this art has intoxicated so many men's brains, and wholly employed their thoughts and bodily actions about phenomena, or the exterior figures of objects, as all better arts and studies are laid aside; nay, those that are not as earnest and active in such employments as they, are; by many of them, accounted unprofitable subjects to the commonwealth of learning. But though there be numerous books written of the wonders of these glasses, yet I cannot perceive any such, and at best, they are but superficial wonders, as I may call them. But could experimental philosophers find out more beneficial arts than our forefathers have done, either for the better increase of vegetables and brute animals to nourish our bodies, or better and commodious contrivances in the art of architecture to build us houses, or for

[24] Cf. Hooke, *Micrographia*, "Preface," where he notes that of microscopic bodies "there is much more difficulty to discover the true shape, than of those visible to the naked eye, the same object seeming quite differing, in one position to the light, from what it really is, and may be discovered in another . . . The eyes of a fly in one kind of light appear almost like a lattice, drilled through with abundance of small holes . . . In the sunshine they look like a surface covered with golden nails . . ." (unpaginated).

[25] Cf. Hooke, *Micrographia*, "Observation I: Of the Point of a Sharp Small Needle" and "Observation II: Of the Edge of a Razor."

NB Hooke's preface!

the advancing of trade and traffic to provide necessaries for us to live, or
for the decrease of nice distinctions and sophistical disputes in churches,
schools and courts of judicature, to make men live in unity, peace and
neighbourly friendship; it would not only be worth their labour, but of as
much praise as could be given to them: But, as boys that play with watery
bubbles[s] or fling dust[t] into each other's eyes, or make a hobbyhorse[u] of
snow, are worthy of reproof rather than praise, for wasting their time
with useless sports; so those that addict themselves to unprofitable arts,
spend more time than they reap benefit thereby. Nay, could they benefit
men either in husbandry, architecture, or the like necessary and profitable employments; yet before the vulgar sort would learn to understand
them, the world would want bread to eat, and houses to dwell in, as also
clothes to keep them from the inconveniences of the inconstant weather.
But truly, although spinsters were most experienced in their art, yet they
will never be able to spin silk, thread, or wool, etc. from loose atoms;
neither will weavers weave a web of light from the sun's rays; nor an
architect build an house of the bubbles of water and air, (unless they be
poetical spinsters, weavers and architects:) and if a painter should draw a
louse as big as a crab, and of that shape as the microscope presents, can
anybody imagine that a beggar would believe it to be true? but if he did,
what advantage would it be to the beggar? for it does neither instruct him
how to avoid breeding them, or how to catch them, or to hinder them
from biting. Again, if a painter should paint birds according to those
colours the microscope presents, what advantage would it be for fowlers
to take them? truly, no fowler will be able to distinguish several birds
through a microscope, neither by their shapes nor colours; They will be
better discerned by those that eat their flesh, than by micrographers that
look upon their colours and exterior figures through a magnifying glass.
In short, magnifying glasses are like a high heel to a short leg, which if it
be made too high, it is apt to make the wearer fall, and at the best, can do
no more than represent exterior figures in a bigger, and so in a more
deformed shape and posture than naturally they are; but as for the
interior form and motions of a creature, as I said before, they can no more
represent them, than telescopes can the interior essence and nature of the
sun, and what matter it consists of; for if one that never had seen milk
before, should look upon it through a microscope, he would never be able

---

[s] Glass-tubes.   [t] Atoms.   [u] Exterior figures.

to discover the interior parts of milk by that instrument, were it the best that is in the world; neither the whey, nor the butter, nor the curds. Wherefore the best optic is a perfect natural eye, and a regular sensitive perception; and the best judge, is reason; and the best study, is rational contemplation joined with the observations of regular sense, but not deluding arts; for art is not only gross in comparison to nature, but, for the most part, deformed and defective, and at best produces mixt or hermaphroditical figures, that is, a third figure between nature and art: which proves, that natural reason is above artificial sense, as I may call it: wherefore, those arts are the best and surest informers, that alter nature least, and they the greatest deluders that alter nature most, I mean, the particular nature of each particular creature; (for art is so far from altering infinite nature, that it is no more in comparison to it, than a little fly to an elephant; no not so much, for there is no comparison between finite and infinite.) But wise nature taking delight in variety, her parts, which are her creatures, must of necessity do so too.

IV   Of the Production of Fire by a Flint and Steel[26]

Some learned writers of micrography, having observed the fiery sparks that are struck out by the violent motion of a flint against steel, suppose them to be little parcels either of the flint or steel, which by the violence of the stroke, are at the same time severed and made red hot; nay, sometimes to such a degree, as they are melted together into glass. But whatsoever their opinion be, to my sense and reason it appears very difficult to determine exactly how the production of fire is made, by reason there are so many different sorts of productions in nature, as it is impossible for any particular creature to know or describe them: Nevertheless, it is most probable, that those two bodies do operate not by incorporeal but corporeal motions, which either produce a third corporeal figure out of their own parts, or by striking against each other, do alter some of their natural corporeal figurative parts, so as to convert them into fire, which if it have no fuel to feed on, must of necessity die; or it may be, that by the occasion of striking against each other, some of

---

[26] Cf. Power, *Experimental Philosophy, In Three Books: Containing New Experiments Microscopial, Mercurial, Magnetical* . . . (London, 1664 [correct date 1663]), "Observation XLIX: The Sparks of Flint and Steel," and Hooke, *Micrographia*, "Observation VIII: Of the Fiery Sparks Struck from a Flint or Steel."

their looser parts are metamorphosed, and afterwards return to their former figures again; like as flesh, being bruised and hurt, becomes numb and black, and after returns again to its proper figure and colour; or like water, which by change of motion in the same parts, being turned into snow, ice, or hail, may return again into its former figure and shape; for nature is various in her corporeal figurative motions. But it is observable, that fire is like seeds of corn sown in earth, which increases or decreases according as it has nourishment; by which we may see, that fire is not produced from a bare immaterial motion, as I said before; (for a spiritual issue cannot be nourished by a corporeal substance:) but it is with fire as it is, with almost all other natural creatures, which require respiration as well as perception; for, fire requires air as well as animals do. By respiration, I do not mean only that animal respiration which in man, and other animal creatures, is performed by the lungs; but a dividing and uniting, or separating and joining of parts from and to parts, as of the exterior from and to the interior, and of the interior from and to the exterior; so that when some parts issue, other do enter: And thus by the name of respiration I understand a kind of reception of foreign matter, and emission of some of their own; as for example, in animals, I mean not only the respiration performed by the lungs, but also the reception of food, and of other matter entering through some proper organs and pores of their bodies, and the discharging of some other matter the same way; and if this be so, as surely it is, then all or most creatures in nature have some kind of respiration or reciprocal breathing, that is, attraction and expiration, receiving of nourishment and evacuation, or a reception of some foreign parts, and a discharging and venting of some of their own. But yet it is not necessary that all the matter of respiration in all creatures should be air; for every sort of creatures, nay every particular, has such a matter of respiration, as is proper both to the nature of its figure, and proper for each sort of respiration. Besides, although air may be a fit substance for respiration to fire, and to some other creatures; yet I cannot believe, that the sole agitation of air is the cause of fire, no more than it can be called the cause of man: for, if this were so, then houses that are made of wood, or covered with straw, would never fail to be set on fire by the agitation of the air. Neither is it requisite that all respirations in all creatures should be either hot or cold, moist or dry, by reason there are many different sorts of respiration, according to the nature and propriety of every creature: whereof some may be hot, some cold; some hot and dry, some cold and dry; some hot and moist, some cold and moist, etc. And in animals, at least in mankind, I observe, that the respiration performed by the help of their lungs, is an attraction of some refrigerating air and an emission of some warm vapour. What other creatures' respirations may be, I leave for others to enquire.

V Of Pores[27]

As I have mentioned in my former discourse, that I do verily believe all or most natural creatures have some certain kind of respiration; so do I also find it most probable, that all or most natural creatures have pores: not empty pores; for there can be no vacuum in nature, but such passages as serve for respiration, which respiration is some kind of receiving and discharging of such matter as is proper to the nature of every creature: And thus the several organs of animal creatures, are, for the most part, employed as great large pores; for nature being in a perpetual motion, is always dissolving and composing, changing and ordering her self-moving parts as she pleases. But it is to be well observed, that there is difference between perception and respiration; for, perception is only an action of figuring or patterning, whenas the rational and sensitive motions do figure or pattern out something: but respiration is an action of drawing, sucking, breathing in, or receiving any ways outward parts; and of venting, discharging, or sending forth inward parts. Next, although there may be pores in most natural creatures, by reason that all, or most, have some kind of respiration; yet nature hath more ways of dividing and uniting of parts, or of ingress and egress, than the way of drawing in, and sending forth by pores: for nature is so full of variety, that not any particular corporeal figurative motion can be said the prime or fundamental, unless it be self-motion, the architect and creator of all figures: Wherefore, as the globular figure is not the prime or fundamental of all other figures, so neither can respiration be called the prime or fundamental motion; for, as I said, nature has more ways than one, and there are also retentive motions in nature which are neither dividing nor composing, but keeping or holding together.

[27] Cf. Hooke, *Micrographia*, "Observation xv: Of Kettering Stone, and of the Pores of Inanimate Bodies."

VI   Of the "Effluviums" of the Loadstone

It is the opinion of some, that, "the magnetical effluviums do not proceed intrinsically from the stone, but are certain extrinsical particles, which approaching to the stone, and finding congruous pores and inlets therein, are channeled through it; and having acquired a motion thereby, do continue their current so far, till being repulsed by the ambient air, they recoil again, and return into a vortical motion, and so continue their revolution forever through the body of the magnet."[28] But if this were so, then all porous bodies would have the same magnetical effluviums, especially a charcoal, which, they say, is full of deep pores: besides, I can hardly believe, that any microscope is able to show how those flowing atoms enter and issue, and make such a vortical motion as they imagine. Concerning the argument drawn from the experiment, that "a magnet being made red hot in the fire, not only admits the magnetical vigour it had before, but acquires a new one";[29] doth not evince or prove that the magnetical effluviums are not innate or inherent in the stone: for fire may overpower them so as we cannot perceive their vigour or force, the motions of the fire being too strong for the motions of the loadstone; but yet it doth not follow hence, that those motions of the loadstone are lost, because they are not perceived, or that afterwards, when by cooling the loadstone they may be perceived again, they are not the same motions; but new ones, no more than when a man does not move his hand, the motion of it can be lost or annihilated. But, say they, "If the polary direction of the stone should be thought to proceed intrinsically from the stone, it were as much as to put a soul or intelligence into the stone, which must turn it about, as angels are [feigned][30] to do celestial orbs."[31] To which I answer; that although the turning of the celestial orbs by angels may be a figment; yet that there is a soul and intelligence in the loadstone, is as true, as that there is a soul in man. I will not say, that the loadstone has a spiritual or immaterial soul, but a corporeal or material one, to wit, such a soul as is a particle of the soul of nature, that is, of rational matter, which moves in the loadstone according to the propriety and nature of its figure. Lastly, as for their argument concluding from

---

[28] Power, *Experimental Philosophy*, p. 157; slightly altered.
[29] Ibid.; slightly altered.
[30] Power's own word gives this phrase a quite different meaning: ". . . as angels are fained [i.e., obliged] to do the celestial orbs."
[31] Power, *Experimental Philosophy*, p. 158; slightly altered and condensed.

the different effluviums of other, as for example, electrical and odoriferous bodies, etc. as camphor, and the like, whose expirations, they say, fly away into the open air, and never make any return again to the body from whence they proceeded; I cannot believe this to be so: for if odoriferous bodies should effluviate and waste after that manner, then all strong odoriferous bodies would be of no continuance; for where there are great expenses, there must of necessity follow a sudden waste: but the contrary is sufficiently known by experience. Wherefore, it is more probable, that the effluviums of the loadstone, as they call them, or the disponent and directive faculty of turning itself towards the north, is intrinsically inherent in the stone itself, (and is nothing else but the interior, natural, sensitive, and rational corporeal motions proper to its figure, as I have more at large declared in my *Philosophical Letters*, and *Philosophical Opinions*;) than that a stream of exterior atoms, by beating upon the stone, should turn it to and fro, until they have laid it in such a position.

VII   Of the Stings of Nettles and Bees[32]

I cannot approve the opinion of those, who believe that the swelling, burning, and smarting pain caused by the stinging of nettles and bees, doth proceed from a poisonous juice, that is contained within the points of nettles, or stings of bees; for it is commonly known, that nettles, when young, are oftentimes eaten in salads, and minced into broths; nay, when they are at their full growth, good housewives used to lay their cream cheeses in great nettles; whereas, if there were any poison in them, the interior parts of animal bodies, after eating them, would swell and burn more than the exterior only by touching them. And as for stings of bees, whether they be poisonous or not, I will not certainly determine anything, nor whether their stings be of no other use (as some say) than only for defence or revenge; but this I know, that if a bee once loseth its sting, it becomes a drone: which if so, then surely the sting is useful to the bee, either in making wax and honey, or in drawing, mixing and tempering the several sorts of juices, or in penetrating and piercing into vegetables, or other bodies, after the manner of broaching or tapping, to cause the liquor to issue out; or in framing the structure of their comb, and the like;

[32] Cf. Power, *Experimental Philosophy*, "Observation II: The Bee" and "Observation XLV: Of Nettles," and Hooke, *Micrographia*, "Observation XXV: Of the Stinging Points and Juice of Nettles, and Some Other Venomous Plants."

for surely nature doth not commonly make useless and unprofitable things, parts, or creatures. Neither doth her design tend to an evil effect; although I do not deny but that good and useful instruments may be and are often employed in evil actions. The truth is, I find that stings are of such kind of figures as fire is, and fire of such a kind of figure as stings are; but although they be all of one general kind, nevertheless they are different in their particular kinds; for, as animal kind contains many several and different particular kinds or sorts of animals; so the like do vegetables, and other kinds of creatures.

VIII   Of the Beard of a Wild Oat[33]

Those who have observed through a microscope, the beard of a wild oat, do relate that it is only a small black or brown bristle, growing out of the side of the inner husk; which covers the grain of a wild oat, and appears like a small wreathed sprig with two clefts: if it be wetted in water, it will appear to unwreathe itself, and by degrees to straighten its knee, and the two clefts will become straight; but if it be suffered to dry again, it will by degrees wreathe itself again, and so return into its former posture: The cause of which they suppose to be the differing texture of its parts, which seeming to have two substances, one very porous, loose and spongy, into which the watery streams of air may very easily be forced, which thereby will grow swelled and extended; and a second, more hard and close, into which the water cannot at all or very little penetrate; and this retaining always the same dimensions, but the other stretching and shrinking, according as there is more or less water or moisture in its pores, it is thought to produce this unwreathing and wreathing. But that this kind of motion (whether it be caused by heat and cold, or by dryness and moisture, or by any greater or less force, proceeding either from gravity and weight, or from wind, which is the motion of the air, or from some springing body, or the like) should be the very first footstep of sensation and animate motion, and the most plain, simple and obvious contrivance that nature has made use of to produce a motion next to that of rarefaction and condensation by heat and cold, as their opinion is; I shall not easily be persuaded to believe. For if animate motion was produced

---

[33] Cf. Hooke, *Micrographia*, "Observation xxvii: Of the Beard of a Wild Oat, and the Use that May Be Made of It for Exhibiting Always to the Eye the Temperature of the Air, As to Dryness and Moisture."

this way, it would, in my opinion, be but a weak and irregular motion. Neither can I conceive how these, or any other parts, could be set amoving, if nature herself were not self-moving, but only moved: Nor can I believe, that the exterior parts of objects are able to inform us of all their interior motions; for our human optic sense looks no further than the exterior and superficial parts of solid or dense bodies, and all creatures have several corporeal figurative motions one within another, which cannot be perceived neither by our exterior senses, nor by their exterior motions: as for example, our optic sense can perceive and see through a transparent body; but yet it cannot perceive what that transparent body's figurative motions are, or what is the true cause of its transparentness; neither is any art able to assist our sight with such optic instruments as may give us a true information thereof: for what a perfect natural eye cannot perceive, surely no glass will be able to present.

IX   Of the Eyes of Flies[34]

I cannot wonder enough at the strange discovery made by the help of the microscope concerning the great number of eyes observed in flies; as that, for example, in a gray drone-fly should be found clusters which contain about 14,000 eyes: which if it be really so, then those creatures must needs have more of the optic sense than those that have but two, or one eye; for my reason cannot believe, that so many numerous eyes should be made for no more use than one or two eyes are: for though art, the emulating ape of nature, makes often vain and useless things; yet I cannot perceive that nature herself doth so.[35] But a greater wonder it is to me, that man with the twinkling of one eye, can observe so many in so small a creature, if it be not a deceit of the optic instrument: for, as I have mentioned above, art produces most commonly hermaphroditical figures, and it may be, perhaps, that those little pearls or globes, which were taken for eyes in the mentioned fly, are only transparent knobs, or glossy shining spherical parts of its body, making refractions of the rays of light, and reflecting the pictures of exterior objects; there being many creatures, that have such shining protuberances and globular parts, and those

[34] Cf. Power, *Experimental Philosophy*, "Observation III: The Common Fly," and Hooke, *Micrographia*, "Observation XXXIX: Of the Eyes and Head of a Grey Drone-Fly, and of Several Other Creatures."

[35] Cavendish may have in mind the scholastic dictum: *frustra fit per plura quod potest fieri per pauciora* [in vain is something produced by many things which can be produced by fewer].

full of quick motion, which yet are not eyes. Truly, my reason can hardly be persuaded to believe, that this artificial informer (I mean the microscope) should be so true as it is generally thought; for, in my opinion it, more deludes, than informs. It is well known, that if a figure be longer, broader, and bigger than its nature requires, it is not its natural figure; and therefore, those creatures, or parts of creatures, which by art appear bigger than naturally they are, cannot be judged according to their natural figure, since they do not appear in their natural shape; but in an artificial one, that is, in a shape or figure magnified by art, and extended beyond their natural figure; and since man cannot judge otherwise of a figure than it appears: besides, if the reflexions and positions of light be so various and different as experimental philosophers confess themselves, and the instrument not very exact (for who knows but hereafter there may be many faults discovered of our modern microscopes which we are not able to perceive at the present) how shall the object be truly known? Wherefore I can hardly believe the truth of this experiment concerning the numerous eyes of flies; they may have, as I said before, glossy and shining globular protuberances, but not so many eyes; as for example, bubbles of water, ice, as also blisters and watery pimples, and hundreds the like, are shining and transparent hemispheres, reflecting light, but yet not eyes; nay, if flies should have so many numerous eyes, why can they not see the approach of a spider until it be just at them; also, how comes it that sometimes (as for example, in cold weather) they seem blind, so as one may take or kill them, and they cannot so much as perceive their enemy's approach? surely if they had 14,000 eyes, all this number would seem useless to them; since other creatures which have but two, can make more advantage of those two eyes, than they of their vast number. But perchance some will say, that, flies having so many eyes, are more apt to be blind than others that have but few, by reason the number is the cause that each particular is the weaker. To which I answer, that if two eyes be stronger than a thousand, then nature is to be blamed that she gives such numbers of eyes to so little a creature. But nature is wiser than we or any creature is able to conceive: and surely she works not to no purpose, or in vain; but there appears as much wisdom in the fabric and structure of her works, as there is variety in them. Lastly, I cannot well conceive the truth of the opinion of those, that think all eyes must have a transparent liquor, or humour within them, for in crabs' and lobsters' eyes, I can perceive none such; and there may also be many other animal creatures which have none: for nature is not tied to one way, but as she makes various creatures, so she may and doth also make their parts and organs variously, and not the same in all, or after one and the same manner or way.

X Of a Butterfly[36]

Concerning the generation of butterflies, whether they be produced by the way of eggs, as some experimental philosophers do relate, or any other ways; or whether they be all produced after one and the same manner, shall not be my task now to determine; but I will only give my readers a short account of what I myself have observed: When I lived beyond the seas in banishment with my noble lord, one of my maids brought upon an old piece of wood, or stone (which it was I cannot perfectly remember) something to me which seemed to grow out of that same piece; it was about the length of half an inch or less, the tail was short and square, and seemed to be a vegetable, for it was as green as a green small stalk, growing out of the aforesaid piece of stone or wood; the part next the tail was like a thin skin, wherein one might perceive a perfect pulsation, and was big in proportion to the rest of the parts; The part next to that, was less in compass, and harder, but of such a substance as it was like pewter or tin: The last and extreme part opposite to the first mentioned green tail or stalk, seemed like a head, round, only it had two little points or horns before, which head seemed to the eye and touch like a stone; so that this creature appeared partly a vegetable, animal and mineral; But what is more, it was in a continual motion, for the whole body of it seemed to struggle as if it would get loose from that piece of wood or stone the tail was joined to, or out of which it grew; But, I cutting and dividing its tail from the said piece, it ceased to move, and I did not regard it any further. After some while I found just such another insect, which I laid by upon the window; and one morning I spied two butterflies playing about it; which, knowing the window had been close shut all the while, and finding the insect all empty, and only like a bare shell or skin, I supposed had been bred out of it; for the shell was not only hollow and thin, but so brittle as it straight fell into pieces, and did somewhat resemble the skin of a snake when it is cast; And it is

---

[36] Cf. Power, *Experimental Philosophy*, "Observation v: The Butterfly."

observable, that two butterflies were produced out of one shell, which I supposed to be male and female. But yet this latter I will not certainly affirm, for I could not discern them with my eyes, except I had had some microscope, but a thousand to one I might have been also deceived by it: and had I opened this insect, or shell, at first; it might perhaps have given those butterflies an untimely death, or rather hindered their production. This is all I have observed of butterflies: but I have heard also that caterpillars are transformed into butterflies; whether it be true or not, I will not dispute: only this I dare say, that I have seen caterpillars spin, as silkworms do, an oval ball about their seed, or rather about themselves.

XI Of the Walking Motions of Flies, and Other Creatures[37]

What experimental writers mention concerning the feet of flies, and their structure, to wit, that they have two claws or talons, and two palms or soles, by the help of which they can walk on the sides of glass, or other smooth bodies perpendicularly upwards; If this be the only reason they can give, then certainly a dormouse must have the same structure of feet; for she will, as well as a fly, run straight upwards on the sharp edge of a glazed or well polished sword, which is more difficult than to run up the side of glass: And as for flies, that they can suspend themselves against the undersurface of many bodies; I say, not only flies, but many other creatures will do the same: for not only great caterpillars, or such worms as have many legs, as also spiders; but a newt, which is but a little creature, will run up a wall in a perpendicular line; nay, walk as flies do with its back down, and its legs upwards. Wherefore it is not, in my opinion, the pores of the surface of the body, on which those creatures walk; as for example, that a fly should run the tenters or points of her feet, which some have observed through a microscope, into the pores of such bodies she walks on, or make pores where she finds none; (for I cannot believe, that in such close and dense bodies, where no pores at all can be perceived, the small and weak leg of a fly should pierce a hole so suddenly, and with one step;) Nor an imaginary glue, nor a dirty or smokey substance adhering to the surface of glass, as some do conceive; Nor so much the lightness of their bodies that makes those creatures walk in such a posture; for many can do the same that are a thousand times

[37] Cf. Hooke, *Micrographia*, "Observation xxxvii: Of the Feet of Flies, and Several Other Insects."

heavier than a little fly; but the chief cause is the shape of their bodies; which being longer than they are deep, one counterpoises the other; for the depth of their bodies has not so much weight as their length, neither are their heads and legs just opposite: Besides, many have a great number of feet, which may easily bear up the weight of their bodies; and although some creatures, as horses, sheep, oxen, etc. have their legs set on in the same manner as mice, squirrels, cats, etc. yet they cannot run or climb upwards and downwards in a perpendicular line, as well as these creatures do, by reason of the depth of their bodies from the soles of their feet to the surface of their back, the weight of their depth overpowering the strength of their legs. Wherefore the weight of a creature lies for the most part in the shape of its body, which shape gives it such sorts of actions as are proper for it; as for example, a bird flies by its shape, a worm crawls by its shape, a fish swims by its shape, and a heavy ship will bear itself upon the surface of water merely by its exterior shape; it being not so much the interior figure or nature of wood that gives it this faculty of bearing up, by reason we see that many pieces of timber will sink down to the bottom in water. Thus "heaviness and lightness" is for the most part caused by the shape or figure of the body of a creature, and all its exterior actions depend upon the exterior shape of its body.

[XII][38]   Whether It Be Possible to Make Man and Other Animal Creatures that Naturally Have No Wings, Fly as Birds Do

Some are of opinion, that it is not impossible to make man, and such other creatures that naturally have no wings, fly as birds do; but I have heard my noble lord and husband give good reasons against it; For when he was in Paris, he discoursing one time with Mr. H.[39] concerning this subject, told him that he thought it altogether impossible to be done: A man, said he, or the like animal that has no wings, has his arms set on his body in a quite opposite manner than birds' wings are; for the concave part of a bird's wings, which joins close to his body, is in man outward; and the inward part of a man's arm where it joins to his body, is in birds placed outward: so that which is inward in a bird, is outward in man; and what is inward in man, is outward in birds; which is the reason that a man

---

[38] Lacking in 1666 and 1668.
[39] I.e., Hobbes. Cavendish notes that Hobbes liked William Cavendish's views on this issue and on witchcraft so much that he incorporated them into his *Leviathan* (*Life*, III, ch. 9, p. 143).

has not the same motion of his arm which a bird has of his wing. For flying is but swimming in the air; and birds, by the shape and posture of their wings, do thrust away the air, and so keep themselves up; which shape, if it were found the same in man's arms, and other animals' legs, they might perhaps fly as birds do, nay, without the help of feathers; for we see that bats have but flesh wings: neither would the bulk of their bodies be any hindrance to them; for there be many birds of great and heavy bodies, which do nevertheless fly, although more slowly, and not so nimbly as flies, or little birds: Wherefore it is only the different posture and shape of men's arms, and other animals' legs, contrary to the wings of birds, that makes them unapt to fly, and not so much the bulk of their bodies. But I believe, that a four-legged creature, or animal, may more easily and safely go upright like man, although it hath its legs set on in a contrary manner to man's arms and legs; for a four-legged animal's hind legs resemble man's arms, and its forelegs are just as man's legs. Nevertheless there is no art that can make a four-legged creature imitate the actions of man, no more than art can make them have or imitate the natural actions of a bird: For, art cannot give new motions to natural parts, which are not proper or natural for them, but each part must have such proper and natural motions and actions as nature has designed for it. I will not say, but art may help to mend some defects, errors, or irregularities in nature, but not make better that which nature has made perfect already. Neither can we say, man is defective, because he cannot fly as birds: for flying is not his natural and proper motion; We should rather account that man monstrous that could fly, as having some motion not natural and proper to his figure and shape; for that creature is perfect in its kind, that has all the motions which are naturally requisite to the figure of such a kind: But, man is apt to run into extremes, and spoils nature with doting too much upon art.

XIII   Of Snails and Leeches: And, Whether All Animals Have Blood[40]

Whether snails have a row of small teeth, orderly placed in the gums, and divided into several smaller and greater; or, whether they have but one small bended hard bone, which serves them instead of teeth, to bite out

---

[40] Cf. Power, *Experimental Philosophy*, "Observation xxxi: Of the Great Black Snail."

pretty large and half-round bits of the leaves of trees to feed on; experimental philosophers may enquire by the help of their microscopes: My opinion is, that snails are like leeches, which will not only bite, but suck; but this I do verily believe, that snails only bite vegetables, not animals as leeches do; and though leeches bite into the skin, yet they do not take any part away, but suck out only the juicy part, that is, the blood, and leave the grosser substance of flesh behind; and so do snails bite into herbs, to suck out the juicy substance, or else there would be found flesh in leeches, and herbs in snails, which is not; so that snails and leeches bite for no end but only to make a passage to suck out the juicy parts; and therefore I cannot perceive that they have bones, but I conceive their teeth or parts they pierce withal, to be somewhat of the nature of stings, which are no more bones than the points of fire are. I do not certainly affirm they are stings, but my meaning is, that they are pointed or piercing figures, that is, as I said, of the nature of stings, there being many several sorts of pointed and piercing figures, which yet are not stings, as there are several sorts of grinding and biting figures which are not teeth; for there are so many several sorts of figures in vegetables, minerals, animals, and elements, as no particular creature is able to conceive. Again, it is questioned, whether those creatures that suck blood from others, have blood themselves, as naturally belonging to their own substance; and my opinion is, that it is no necessary consequence, that that should be a part of their substance on which they feed: food may be converted into the substance of their bodies by the figurative transforming motions, but it is not part of their substance before it is converted; and so many creatures may feed on blood, but yet have none of themselves as a natural constitutive part of their being: Besides, there are maggots, worms, and several sorts of flies, and other creatures, that feed upon fruits and herbs, as also lobsters, crabs, etc. which neither suck blood, nor have blood; and therefore blood is not requisite to the life of every animal, although it is to the life of man, and several other animal creatures: Neither do I believe, that all the juice in the veins, is blood (as some do conceive;) for some of the juice may be in the way of being blood, and some may have altered its nature from being blood, to corruption, which later will never be blood again, and some may only be metamorphosed from blood, and reassume its own colour again; for it is as natural for blood to be red, as for the sun to be light: Wherefore when some learned are of opinion, that those white, or yellow, or black juices which are found in the veins of small insects, are their blood, they might as well say, that brains are blood, or that the marrow in the bones, is blood; or, if the brain should all be turned to water, say, that this water is brains; which would be as much as if one should call a man's body, turned to dust and ashes, an animal creature, or a man: for there are natural properties which belong to every creature, and to each particular part of a creature; and so is blood in some animals a natural vital part proper to the conservation of its life, without which it cannot subsist: For example, a young maid in the greensickness, when her veins are fuller of water, than blood, appears pale and is always sickly, weak and faint, not able to stir, by reason her veins are fuller of water than blood; but, were it all water, she would presently die. Wherefore all juices are not blood; nay, I cannot believe as yet, that those they call veins in some insects, are veins, much less that they contain blood, and have a circulation of blood, nor that their motions proceed from muscles, nerves and tendons; but this I may say, that the veins are the proper and convenient vehicles or receptacles of blood, as the head is of brains, and the bones of marrow; also it is as proper for blood to be red, as for veins to contain blood, for bones to contain marrow, and for the head to contain brains; and when they alter or change from their particular natures, they are no more blood, brains, nor marrow: Wherefore those creatures that have a juice which is not red, have no blood; and if no blood, they have no veins. I will not say, that all those that have veins must of necessity have them full of blood; for in dropsies, as also in the greensickness, as I mentioned above, they are fuller of water than blood; but they must of necessity have some blood in their veins, by reason the veins are the most proper receptacles for blood, and no man can live without blood; but when all blood is turned to water, he must of necessity die.

XIV   Of Natural Productions

I cannot wonder with those, who admire that a creature which inhabits the air, doth yet produce a creature, that for some time lives in the water as a fish, and afterward becomes an inhabitant of the air; for this is but a production of one animal from another: but, what is more, I observe that there are productions of and from creatures of quite different kinds; as for example, that vegetables can and do breed animals, and animals, minerals and vegetables, and so forth: Neither do I so much wonder at this, because

I observe that all creatures of nature are produced but out of one matter, which is common to all, and that there are continual and perpetual generations and productions in nature, as well as there are perpetual dissolutions. But yet I cannot believe, that some sorts of creatures should be produced on a sudden by the way of transmigration or translation of parts, which is the most usual way of natural productions; for both natural and artificial productions are performed by degrees, which requires time, and is not done in an instant. Neither can I believe, that all natural things are produced by the way of seeds or eggs; for when I consider the variety of nature, it will not give me leave to think that all things are produced after one and the same manner or way; by reason the figurative motions are too different, and too diversely various, to be tied to one way of acting in all productions. Wherefore as some productions are done by the way of transmigration or translation of parts; as for example, the generation of man, and other animals, and others by a bare metamorphosis or trans-formation of their own parts into some other figure, as in the generation of maggots out of cheese, or in the production of ice out of water, and many the like; so each way has its own particular motions, which no particular creature can perfectly know. I have mentioned in my *Philosophical Letters*,[v] that no animal creature can be produced by the way of metamor-phosing, which is a change of motions in the same parts of matter; but (as I do also express in the same place) I mean such animals which are produced one from another, and where the production of one is not caused by the destruction of the other; such creatures, I say, it is impossible should be produced by a bare metamorphosis, without transmigration or translation of parts from the generator: but such insects, as maggots, and several sorts of worms and flies, and the like, which have no generator of their own kind, but are bred out of cheese, earth and dung, etc. their production is only by the way of metamorphosing, and not translation of parts. Neither can I believe, as some do, that the sun is the common generator of all those insects that are bred within the earth; for, there are not only productions of minerals and vegetables, but also of animals in the earth deeper than the sun can reach; and the heat of the sun can pierce no further than cold can, which is not above two yards from the surface of the earth, at least in our climate. But, why may not the earth, without the help of the sun, produce animal creatures, as well as a piece of cheese in a deep cellar where neither

---

[v] Sect. 4, Let. 2. [*Phil. Letters*, IV, § 2; p. 426.]

the sun nor his beams enter? Truly, I wonder men will confine all productions to one principal agent, and make the sun the common generator of all or most living insects, and yet confess that nature is so full of variety, and that the generations and productions of insects are so various, as not only the same kind of creature may be produced from several kinds of ways, but the very same creature may produce several kinds. Nevertheless, I believe that natural creatures are more numerously and variously produced by dissolution of particulars by the way of metamorphosing, than by a continued propagation of their own species by the way of translation of parts; and that nature hath many more ways of productions, than by seeds or seminal principles, even in vegetables: witness the generation or production of moss, and the like vegetables that grow on stones, walls, dead animals' skulls, tops of houses, etc. So that he who doth confine nature but to one way of acting or moving, had better to deprive her of all motion; for nature being infinite, has also infinite ways of acting in her particulars. Some are of opinion, that the seed of moss being exceeding small and light, is taken up, and carried to and fro in the air into every place, and by the falling drops of rain, is washed down out of it, and so dispersed into all places, and there takes only root and propagates where it finds a convenient soil for it to thrive in: But this is only a wild fancy, and has no ground; and no experimental writer shall ever persuade me, that by his dioptrical glasses he has made any such experiment: wherefore I insist upon sense and reason, which inform me of the various productions of nature, which cannot be reduced to one principal kind, but are more numerous than man's particular and finite reason can conceive. Neither is it a wonder to see plants grow out of the earth without any waste of the earth, by reason there are perpetual compositions and divisions in nature, which are nothing else but an uniting and disjoining of parts, to and from parts, and prove that there is an interchangeable ingress and egress, or a reciprocal breathing in all nature's parts; not perceptible by man: so that no man can tell the association of parts, and growing motions of anyone, much less of all creatures.

XV   Of the Seeds of Vegetables

Some do call the seeds of vegetables, "the cabinet of nature, wherein are laid up her jewels":[41] But this, in my opinion, is a very hard and

---

[41] Hooke, *Micrographia*, p. 152; slightly altered.

improper expression; for I cannot conceive, what jewels nature has, nor in what cabinet she preserves them. Neither are the seeds of vegetables more than other parts or creatures of nature. But I suppose some conceive nature to be like a granary or storehouse of pine-barley, or the like; which if so, I would fain know in what grounds those seeds should be sown to produce and increase: for no seeds can produce of themselves if they be not assisted by some other matter; which proves, that seeds are not the prime or principal creatures in nature, by reason they depend upon some other matter which helps them in their productions: for if seeds of vegetables did lie never so long in a storehouse, or any other place, they would never produce, until they were put into some proper and convenient ground: It is also an argument, that no creature or part of nature can subsist singly and divided from all the rest, but that all parts must live together; and since no part can subsist and live without the other, no part can also be called prime or principal. Nevertheless all seeds have life as well as other creatures; neither is it a paradox to say, seeds are buried in life, and yet do live; for what is not in present act, we may call buried, entombed or inurned in the power of life; as for example, a man, when his figure is dissolved, his parts dispersed, and joined with others, we may say his former form or figure of being such a particular man is buried in its dissolution, and yet liveth in the composition of other parts, or, which is all one, he doth no more live the life of a man, but the life of some other creature he is transformed into by the transforming and figuring motions of nature; nay, although every particle of his former figure were joined with several other parts and particles of nature, and every particle of the dissolved figure were altered from its former figure into several other figures; nevertheless, each of these particles would not only have life, by reason it has motion, but also the former figure would still remain in all those particles, though dispersed, and living several sorts of lives, there being nothing in nature that can be lost or annihilated; but nature is and continues still the same as she was, without the least addition or diminution of any the least thing or part, and all the varieties and changes of natural productions proceed only from the various changes of motion. But to return to seeds; some experimental writers have observed, that the seed of corn violets, which looks almost like a very small flea, through the microscope appears a large body covered with a tough, thick, and bright reflecting skin, very irregularly shrunk and pitted, insomuch that it is almost an impossibility to find two of them wrinkled

69

alike, and wonder that there is such variety even in this little seed:[42] But to me it is no wonder, when I consider the variety of nature in all her works, not only in the exterior, but also in the interior parts of every creature; but rather a wonder to see two creatures just alike each other in their exterior figures. And since the exterior figures of creatures are not the same with the interior, but in many or most creatures quite different; it is impossible that the exterior shape and structure of bodies can afford us sure and excellent instructions to the knowledge of their natures and interior motions, as some do conceive; for how shall a feather inform us of the interior nature of a bird? we may see the exterior flying motions of a bird by the help of its wings, but they cannot give us an information of the productive and figurative motions of all the interior parts of a bird, and what makes it to be such a creature; no more than the exterior view of a man's head, arms, legs, etc. can give an information of his interior parts, viz. the spleen, liver, lungs, etc. Also in vegetables; although those sorts of vegetables which are outwardly burning may be outwardly pointed, and they that are hot and burning within may be inwardly pointed, yet no microscope is able to present to our view those inward points by the inspection of the exterior figure and shape of those vegetables: Neither doth it follow, that all those which are outwardly pointed, must needs be of a hot and burning nature, except they be also pointed inwardly. Nay although some particular creatures should seem to resemble each other in their exterior shapes and figures so much as not to be distinguished at the first view, yet upon better acquaintance we shall find a great difference betwixt them; which shows that there is more variety and difference amongst nature's works, than our weak senses are able to perceive; nay, more variety in one particular creature, as for example, in man, than all the kind or sort of that creature, viz. mankind, is able to know. And if there be such difference betwixt the exterior figures of creatures of one sort, what may there be betwixt their exterior shapes and interior natures? Nevertheless, although there be such variety, not only in the general kinds of creatures, but in every particular, yet there is but one ground or principle of all this variety, which is self-motion, or self–moving matter. And I cannot enough admire the strange conceits of some men, who perceiving and believing such a curious variety and

---

[42] Hooke, *Micrographia*, "Observation xxviii: Of the Seeds of Venus Looking-glass, or Corn Violet."

various curiosity of nature in the parts of her body, and that she is in a perpetual motion, and knows best her own laws, and the several proprieties of bodies, and how to adapt and fit them to her designed ends, nay, that God hath implanted a faculty of knowing in every creature; do yet deny, nay, rail against nature's self-moving power, condemning her as a dull, inanimate, senseless and irrational body: as if a rational man could conceive, that such a curious variety and contrivance of natural works should be produced by a senseless and irrational motion; or, that nature was full of immaterial spirits, which did work natural matter into such various figures; or that all this variety should be caused by an immaterial motion, which is generated out of nothing, and annihilated in a moment: for no man can conceive or think of motion without body; and if it be above thought, then surely it is above act. But I rather cease to wonder at those strange and irregular opinions of mankind, since even they themselves do justify and prove the variety of nature; for what we call irregularities in nature, are really nothing but a variety of nature's motions; and therefore if all men's conceits, fancies and opinions were rational, there would not be so much variety as there is. Concerning those that say, there is no variety in the elemental kingdom, as air, water, and earth; air and water having no form at all, unless a potentiality to be formed into globules, and that the clods and parcels of earth are all irregular. I answer, This is more than man is able to know: But, by reason their microscopes cannot make such hermaphroditical figures of the elements, as they can of minerals, vegetables, and animals, they conclude there is no such variety in them; whenas yet we do plainly perceive that there are several sorts of air, fire, water, earth; and no doubt but these several sorts, and their particulars, are as variously figured as other creatures: Truly it is no consequence to deny the being of that which we do not see or perceive; for this were to attribute an universal and infinite knowledge to our weak and imperfect senses. And therefore I cannot believe, that the Omnipotent Creator has written and engraven his most mysterious designs and counsels only in one sort of creatures; since all parts of nature, their various productions and curious contrivances, do make known the omnipotency of God, not only those of little, but also those of great sizes; for in all figures, sizes and actions, is apparent the curious variety of nature, and the omnipotency of the creator, who has given nature a self-moving power to produce all these varieties in herself; which varieties do evidently prove, that nature doth not work in all creatures alike: nor that she has but one primary or principal sort of motions, by which she produces all creatures, as some do conceive the manner of wreathing and unwreathing, which they have observed in the beard of a wild oat, mentioned before, to be the first footstep of sensation and animate motion, and the most plain, simple and obvious contrivance nature has made use of to produce a motion next to that of rarefaction and condensation by heat and cold; for this is a very wild and extravagant conceit, to measure the infinite actions of nature according to the rule of one particular sort of motions; which any one that has the perfect use of his sense and reason may easily see, and therefore I need not to bring many arguments to contradict it.

XVI Of the Providence of Nature, and of Some Opinions Concerning Motion

Concerning those that speak of the providence of nature, and the preserving of vegetables, to wit, that nature is very curious and careful in preserving their seminal principles,[43] and lays them in most convenient, strong and delicate cabinets for their safer protection from outward danger: I confess, nature may make such protections, that one creature may have some defence from the injuries and assaults of its fellow creatures; but these assaults are nothing but dissolving motions, as friendly and amiable associations are nothing else but composing motions: neither can anything be lost in nature; for even the least particle of nature remains as long as nature herself. And if there be any providence in nature, then certainly nature has knowledge and wisdom; and if she hath knowledge and wisdom, then she has sense and reason; and if sense and reason, then she has self-motion; and if nature has self-motion, then none of her parts can be called inanimate or soulless: for motion is the life and soul of nature, and of all her parts; and if the body be animate, the parts must be so too, there being no part of the animate body of nature that can be dead, or without motion; whereof an instance might be given of animal bodies, whose parts have all animal life, as well as the body itself: Wherefore those that allow a soul, or an informing, actuating and animating form or faculty in nature and her parts, and yet call some

[43] Ibid.: "The providence of nature about vegetables, is in no part manifested more, than in the various contrivances about the seed . . ." (p. 152).

parts inanimate or soulless, do absolutely contradict themselves. And those that say, all the varieties of nature are produced, not by self-motion, but that one part moves another, must at last come to something that moves itself: besides, it is not probable, that one part moving another, should produce all things so orderly and wisely as they are in nature.[44] But those that say, motion is no substance, and consequently not material, and yet allow a generation and annihilation of motion, speak, in my opinion, nonsense: for first, how can self-motion, the author and producer of all things, work all the varieties that are in nature, and be nothing itself? Next, how can that which is nothing (for all that is not material is nothing in nature, or no part of nature[45]) be generated and annihilated? Nay, if motion be material, as surely it is, yet there can neither be a new generation, nor an annihilation of any particular motion in nature; for all that is material in nature has its being in and from infinite matter, which is from eternity; it being impossible that any other new matter should be created besides this infinite matter out of which all natural things consist, or that any of this matter should be lost or annihilated. But perhaps those that believe new generations and annihilations of particular motions, may say, that their opinion is not as if those particular motions were generated out of some new matter, but that the matter of such motions is the same with the matter of all other natural creatures, and that their perishing or annihilation is not an utter destruction or loss of their being out of nature, but only of being such or such a motion, as some vegetables and elements are generated and perish in one night: Truly if their meaning be thus, then it were better to name it an alteration or change of motion, rather than a new generation, and a perishing or annihilation. But my intention is not to plead for other men's opinions, but rather to clear my own, which is, that motion is material; for figure, motion and matter are but one thing; and that no particular motion is or can be lost in nature, nor created anew; as I have declared more at large elsewhere.[46]

---

[44] Cavendish is criticizing the mechanical philosophers with an argument against atomism that derives from the ancient Stoics; see the Introduction.

[45] Cf. Hobbes' claim in the Third Objections to Descartes' *Meditationes de prima philosophiae* . . . [Meditations on First Philosophy] (Paris, 1641) (AT, vii, 173; CSM, ii, 122).

[46] Cavendish especially has in mind her *Opinions* (1663).

XVII   Descartes' Opinion of Motion, Examined

I cannot well apprehend what Descartes means, by matter being at first
set amoving by a strong and lively action, and by his extraordinary swift
rotation or whirling motion about the center; as also by the shavings of
his ethereal subtle matter which filled up all vacuities and pores, and his
ethereal globules; I would ask, Whether this kind of motion did still
continue?[47] if so, then not only the rugged and uneven parts, but also the
ethereal globules would become less by this continual rotation, and
would make this world a very weak, dizzy, and tottering world; and if
there be any such shaving and lessening, then, according to his principles, there must also be some reaction, or a reacting and resisting
motion, and then there would be two opposite motions which would
hinder each other. But I suppose he conceived, that nature, or the God of
nature, did produce the world after a mechanical way, and according as
we see turners, and such kind of artificers work; which if so, then the art
of turning is the prime and fundamental of all other mechanical arts, and
ought to have place before the rest, and a turner ought to be the prime
and chief of all mechanics, and highly esteemed: But alas! that sort of
people is least regarded; and [though][48] by their turning art they make
many dusty shavings, yet they get but little profit by them; for all they get
is by their several wooden figures they make, as spoons, ladles, cups,
bowls, trenchers, and the like; and not by their shavings. Wherefore, as
all other mechanics do not derive their arts from turners; so neither is it
probable, that this world and all natural creatures are produced by a
whirling motion, or a spherical rotation, as if some spirits were playing at
bowls or football; for, as I have often mentioned, nature has infinite ways
of motions, whereof none is prime or principal, but self-motion; which is
the producer of all the varieties nature has within herself. Next, as for his
opinion of transferring and imparting motion to other bodies, and that
that body which imparts motion to another body, loses as much as it
gives, I have answered in my *Philosophical Letters*; to wit, that it is most
improbable: because, motion being material and inseparable from mat-

---

[47] See Descartes' *Principles of Philosophy*, III, § 46ff. Descartes assumes three types of particles whose
motions explain all the phenomena in the visible world: the swiftly moving, globular particles of
the second element comprising the heavens, the extremely fine particles of the first element
comprising the sun and the fixed stars, and the bulkier particles composing the planets and
comets. Physical bodies on the surface of the earth contain all three types of particles.
[48] As in 1666; 1668: hought.

ter, cannot be imparted without matter; and if not, then the body that receives motion would increase in bulk, and the other that loses motion would decrease, by reason of the addition and diminution of the parts of matter, which must of necessity increase and lessen the bulk of the body: the contrary whereof is sufficiently known.

XVIII   Of the Blackness of a Charcoal; and of Light

I cannot in reason give my consent to those dioptrical writers,[49] who conceive that the blackness of a charcoal proceeds from the porousness of its parts, and the absence of light, viz. that light, not being reflected in the pores of a charcoal, doth make it obscure, and consequently appear black: For the opinion which holds that all colours are caused by the various reflexion of light, has but a weak and uncertain ground, by reason the refraction or reflexion of light is so inconstant, as it varies and alters continually; and there being so many reflexions and positions of light, if they were the true cause of colours, no colour would appear constantly the same, but change variously, according to the various reflexion of light; whereas, on the contrary, we see that natural and inherent colours continue always the same, let the position and reflexion of light be as it will. Besides, there being different coloured creatures, if all had the same position and reflexion of light, they would not appear of divers, but all of one colour: the contrary whereof is proved by experience. I will not say, but the refraction and various position of light may vary and alter a natural and inherent colour exteriorly so, as to cause, for example, a natural blue to appear green, or a natural green to appear red, etc. but those figures which light makes, being but superficially and loosely spread upon other natural and substantial figures, are so uncertain, inconstant and momentary, that they do change according as the reflexion and position of light alters; and therefore they cannot cause or produce any natural or inherent colours; for these are not superficial, but fixt, and remain constantly the same. And as for blackness, that it should be caused by the absence of light, I think it to be no more probable, than, that light is the cause of our sight; for if the blackness of a charcoal did

---

[49] For variations on this position, see, e.g., Hobbes, *Elements of Philosophy*, IV, ch. 27, § 16 (*EW*, I, 464–65); Descartes, *Dioptrics*, Discourse I; Hooke, *Micrographia*, "Observation XVI: Of Charcoal, or Burnt Vegetables," and Boyle, *Experiments and Considerations touching Colours . . .* (1664) (*WRB*, I, esp. 696ff.).

proceed from the absence of light in its pores, then a black horse would have more or deeper pores than a white one, or a sorrel, or any other coloured horse; also a black Moor would have larger pores than a man of a white complexion; and black satin, or any black stuff, would have deeper pores than white stuff: But if a fair white lady should bruise her arm, so as it did appear black, can anyone believe that light would be more absent from that bruised part than from any other part of her arm that is white? or that light should reflect otherwise upon that bruised part, than on any other? Also, can anybody believe, that the reflexion of light on a decayed lady's face should be the cause that her complexion is altered from what it was when she was young, and appeared beautiful and fair? Certainly, light is no more the cause of her complexion than of her wrinkles, or else she would never complain of age, but of light. But to prove further, that the entering of light into the pores of exterior bodies, can neither make perception nor colours; if this were so, then the entering of light into the pores of the eye, would make it perceive all things of as many colours as a rainbow hath: besides, if several eyes should have several shaped pores, none would agree in the perception of the colour of an exterior object; or else it would so dazzle the sight, as no object would be truly perceived in its natural colour: for it would breed a confusion between those reflexions of light that are made in the pores of the eye, and those that are made in the pores of the object, as being not probable they would agree, since all pores are not just alike, or of the same bigness; so as what with air, light, particles, and pores jumbled together, and thrust or crowded into so small a compass, it would make such a confusion and chaos of colours, as I may call it, that no sight would be able to discern them; wherefore it is no more probable that the perception of sight is caused by the entering of light into the pores of the eye, than that the perception of smoke is caused by its entrance into the eye: And I wonder rational men do believe, or at least conceive nature's actions to be so confused and disordered, whenas yet sense and reason may perceive that nature works both easily and orderly: and therefore I rather believe, that as all other creatures, so also light is patterned out by the corporeal figurative and perceptive motions of the optic sense, and not that its perception is made by its entrance into the eye, or by pressure and reaction, or by confused mixtures; by reason the way of patterning is an easy alteration of parts, whenas all others are forced and constrained, nay, unsettled, inconstant and uncertain: for how should the fluid particles of air and light be able to produce a constant and settled effect, being so changeable themselves, what instances soever of geometrical figures be drawn hither to evince it? If man knew nature's geometry, he might perhaps do something; but his artificial figures will never find out the architecture of nature, which is beyond his perception or capacity. But some may object, that neither colour, nor any other object can be seen or perceived without light, and therefore light must needs be the cause of colours, as well as of our optic perception. To which I answer, Although we cannot regularly see any other bodies without light, by reason darkness doth involve them, yet we perceive darkness and night without the help of light. They will say, We perceive darkness only by the absence of light: I answer, If all the perception of the optic sense did come from light, then the perception of night or darkness would be no perception at all; which is a paradox, and contrary to common experience, nay, to sense and reason; for black requires as much perception as white, and so doth darkness and night. Neither could we say, It is dark, or it is night, if we did not perceive it to be so, or had no perception at all of it: The truth is, we perceive as much darkness as we do light, and as much black as we do white: for although darkness doth not present to our view other objects, so as light doth, but conceals them, yet this doth not infer that darkness is not perceived; for darkness must needs do so, by reason it is opposite to light, and its corporeal figurative motions are quite contrary to the motions of light, and therefore must also of necessity have contrary effects; Wherefore the error of those that will not allow darkness to be a corporeal figurative motion, as well as light, but only a privation or absence of light, cannot make it nothing; but it is on the contrary well known, that darkness has a being as well as light has, and that it is something, and not nothing, by reason we do perceive it; but he that perceives, must needs perceive something, for no perception can be of nothing: besides, I have declared elsewhere, that we do see in dreams; and that madmen see objects in the dark, without the help of light: which proves, it is not the presence or entering of light into the eye, that causes our seeing, nor the absence of light, which takes away our optic perception; but light only doth present exterior objects to our view, so as we may the better perceive them. Neither is a colour lost or lessened in the dark, but it is only concealed from the ordinary perception of human sight; for truly, if colours should not be colours in the dark, then it might as rationally be said, that a man's flesh and blood is not flesh and blood in the dark, when it is not seen by a human eye: I will not say, that the smallness and fineness of parts may not make colours appear more glorious; for colours are like artificial paintings, the gentler and finer their draughts and lines are, the smoother and glossier appear their works; but smallness and fineness is not the true cause of colours, that is, it doth not make colours to be colours, although it makes colours fine. And thus black is not black through the absence of light, no more than white can be white by the presence of light; but blackness is one sort of colour, whiteness another, redness another, and so of the rest: Whereof some are superficial and changeable, to wit, such as are made by the reflexion of light, others fixt and inherent, viz. such as are in several sorts of minerals, vegetables, and animals; and others again are produced by art, as by dyeing and painting; which artists know best how to order by their several mixtures.

XIX   Of the Pores of a Charcoal; and of Emptiness

Although I cannot believe, that the absence of light in the pores of a charcoal is the cause of its blackness; yet I do not question the truth of its pores: for that all, or most creatures have pores, I have declared before; which pores are nothing else but passages to receive and discharge some parts of matter; and therefore the opinion of those that believe an entering of some particles of exterior bodies through the pores of animal creatures, and an intermixing with their interior parts; as, that for example, in the bathing in mineral waters, the liquid and warm vehicles of the mineral particles, do by degrees insinuate themselves into the pores of the skin, and intermix with the inner parts of the body, is very rational; for, this is a convenient way of conveying exterior parts into the body, and may be effectual either to good or bad: and although the pores be very small, yet they are numerous, so that the number of the pores supplies the want of their largeness. But yet although pores are passages for other bodies to issue or enter, nevertheless they are not empty, there being no such thing as an emptiness in nature; for surely God, the fullness and perfection of all things, would not suffer any vacuum in nature, which is a pure nothing; "vacuum" implies a want and imperfection of something, but all that God made by his all-powerful command, was good and perfect; Wherefore, although charcoals and other bodies have pores, yet they are filled with some subtle matter not subject to our sensitive perception; and are not empty, but only called so, by reason they are not filled up with some solid and gross substance perceptible by our senses. But, some may say, If there be no emptiness in nature, but all fullness of body, or bodily parts, then the spiritual or divine soul in man, which inhabits his body, would not have room to reside in it: I answer, The spiritual or divine soul in man is not natural, but supernatural, and has also a supernatural way of residing in man's body; for place belongs only to bodies, and a spirit being bodiless, has no need of a bodily place. But then they will say, that I make spirit and vacuum all one thing, by reason I describe a spirit to be a natural nothing, and the same I say of vacuum; and hence it will follow, that particular spirits are particular emptinesses, and an infinite spirit an infinite vacuum. My answer is, that although a spirit is a natural nothing, yet it is a supernatural something; but a vacuum is a pure nothing, both naturally and supernaturally; and God forbid I should be so irreligious, as to compare spirits, and consequently *God*, who is an infinite spirit, to a vacuum; for God is all-fulfilling, and an infinite fullness and perfection, though not a corporeal or material, yet a supernatural, spiritual, and incomprehensible fullness; whenas vacuum, although it is a corporeal word, yet in effect or reality is nothing, and expresses a want or imperfection, which cannot be said of any supernatural creature, much less of *God*.

XX   Of Colours[50]

Although the sensitive perception doth pattern out the exterior figure of colours, as easily as of any other object; yet all perceptions of colours are not made by patterning; for as there are many perceptions which take no patterns from outward objects; so there are also perceptions, of colours which never were presented to our sensitive organs: Neither is any perception made by exterior objects, but by interior, corporeal, figurative motions; for the object doth not print or act any way upon the eye, but it is the sensitive motions in the eye which pattern out the figure of the object: and it is to be observed, that as the parts of some bodies do consist

---

[50] Cf. Hobbes, *Elements of Philosophy*, IV, chs. 25 and 27; Descartes, *Dioptrics*, Discourses I and VI; *Meteorology*, Discourse VIII; and *Principles of Philosophy*, IV §§ 195ff.; Hooke, *Micrographia*, "Observation IX: Of the Colours Observable in Muscovy Glass, and Other Thin Bodies" and "Observation X: Of Metalline, and Other Real Colours"; Power, *Experimental Philosophy*, "A Digression of the Animal Spirits," Fourth Deduction; Boyle, *Experiments and Considerations touching Colours* (*WRB*, I, 662ff.).

of several different figures, which the learned call "heterogeneous," one figure being included within another; and of some again, the parts are but of one kind of figure, which they call "homogeneous" bodies; as for example, water:[51] So it may be with colours; for in some, their parts may be quite thorough of one colour, and others again, may be of several colours; and indeed, most creatures, as they have different parts, so those different parts have also different colours; and as those parts do alter, so do their colours: For example, a man that is in good health, looks of a sanguine complexion; but being troubled with the yellow or black jaundices, his complexion is of the colour of the humour, either black or yellow; yet it doth not proceed always from the overflowing of the humour towards the exterior parts; for many times, when the humour is obstructed, it will cause the same effect; but then the corporeal motions in the extreme parts alter by way of imitation or metamorphosing, as from a sanguine colour, into the colour of the predominant humour: Wherefore it [is][52] no more wonder to see colours change in the tempering of steel (as some are pleased to allege this experiment)[53] than to see steel change and rechange its temper from being hard, to soft; from tough to brittle, etc. which changes prove, that colours are material, as well as steel; so that the alteration of the corporeal parts, is the alteration of the corporeal figures of colours. They also prove, that light is not essential to colours; for although some colours are made by several reflexions, refractions and positions of light; yet light is not the true and natural cause of all colours; but those colours that are made by light, are most inconstant, momentary and alterable, by reason light and its effects are very changeable: Neither are colours made by a bare motion, for there is no such thing as a bare or immaterial motion in nature; but both light and colours are made by the corporeal figurative motions of nature; and according to the various changes of those motions, there are also various and different lights and colours; and the perception of light and colours is made and dissolved by the sensitive figurative motions in the optic "sensorium," without the exchange of exterior objects; but as the slackest, loosest or rarest parts, are of least solid or composed corporeal figures, so are they most apt to change and rechange upon the least

---

[51] On "homogeneous" and "heterogeneous" bodies, see Aristotle, *Meteorology*, IV, especially chs. 8–12.

[52] As in 1666; lacking in 1668.

[53] The reference is to Boyle; see *Experiments and Considerations touching Colours* (*WRB*, I, 669ff.).

disorder; as may well be observed in colours raised by passions, as, fear, anger, or the like, which will change not only the complexion and countenance, but the very features will have some alteration for a short time; and many times the whole body will be so altered, as not to be rightly composed again for a good while; nay, often there follows a total dissolution of the whole figure, which we call death. And at all this we need not wonder, if we do but consider, that nature is full of sense and reason, that is, of sensitive and rational perception: which is the cause that oftentimes the disturbance of one part, causes all other parts of a composed figure to take an alarm; for, as we may observe, it is so in all other composed bodies, even in those composed by art: As for example, in the politic body of a commonwealth, one traitor is apt to cause all the kingdom to take arms; and although every member knows not particularly of the traitor, and of the circumstances of his crime; yet every member, if regular, knows its particular duty, which causes a general agreement to assist each other. And as it is with a commonwealth, so it is also with an animal body; for if there be factions amongst the parts of an animal body, then straight there arises a civil war. Wherefore to return to colours: A sudden change of colours may cause no wonder, by reason there is oftentimes in nature a sudden change of parts, that is, an alteration of figures in the same parts: Neither is it more to be admired, that one colour should be within another, than one figurative part is within another; for colours are figurative parts: And as there are several creatures, so there are also several colours; for the colour of a creature is as well corporeal, as the creature itself; and (to express myself as clearly as I can) colour is as much a body, as place and magnitude, which are but one thing with body. Wherefore when the body, or any corporeal part varies, whether solid or rare: place, magnitude, colour, and the like, must of necessity change or vary also; which change is no annihilation or perishing; for as no particle of matter can be lost in nature, nor no particular motion; so neither can colour: and therefore the opinion of those who say, that when flax or silk is divided into very small threads, or fine parts, those parts lose their colours, and being twisted, regain their colours, seems not conformable to truth: For the division of their parts doth not destroy their colours, nor the composing of those parts regain them; but they being divided into such small and fine parts, it makes their colours, which are the finest of their exterior parts, not to be subject to our optic perception; for what is very small or rare, is not subject to the human optic sense; wherefore there are these following conditions required to the optic perception of an exterior object: First, the object must not be too subtle, rare, or little, but of a certain degree of magnitude; Next, it must not be too far distant, or without the reach of our sight; then, the medium must not be obstructed, so as to hinder our perception; And lastly, our optic "sensorium" must be perfect, and the sensitive motions regular; of which conditions, if any be wanting, there is either no perception at all, or it is an imperfect perception: for, the perception of seeing an exterior object, is nothing else but a patterning out of the figure of that same object by the sensitive figurative and perceptive motions; but there are infinite parts that are beyond our human perception, and it would be but a folly for us to deny that which we cannot see or perceive: And if the perceptive motions be not regular in our optic sense, we may see different colours in one object; nay, the corporeal figurative motions in the eye may make several figurative colours, even without the patterns of outward objects. And as there are several colours, so there are also several corporeal figurative motions that make several colours in several parts; and the more solid the parts are, the more fixt are their inherent natural colours: But superficial colours are more various, though not so various as they would be, if made by dusty atoms, flying about as flies in sunshine; for, if this opinion were true, all colours, and other creatures would be composed or made by chance, rather than by reason; and, chance being so ignorantly inconstant, not any two parts would be of the like colour, nor any kind of species would be preserved; but wise nature, although she be full of variety, yet she is also full of reason, which is knowledge; for there is no part of nature that has not sense and reason, which is life and knowledge; and if all the infinite parts have life and knowledge, infinite nature cannot be a fool or insensible: But mistake me not; for I do not mean, that her parts in particular are infinitely knowing; but I say, infinite nature hath an infinite knowledge; and by reason nature is material, she is dividable as well as composable, which is the cause that there is an obscurity in her parts, in particular, but not in general, that is, in nature herself: nay, if there were not an obscurity in the particulars, men would not endeavour to prove inherent and natural figures by superficial phenomena. But as for colour, some do mention the example of a blind man, who could discover colours by touch;[54] and truly I cannot

---

[54] Boyle, in *Experiments and Considerations touching Colours*, discusses John Vermaasen, the "blind Dutchman," who allegedly distinguished black objects from red, yellow or green ones by means

account it a wonder, because colours are corporeal figurative motions, and touch being a general sense, may well perceive by experience (which is gained by practice) some notions of other sensitive perceptions; as for example, a blind man may know by relation the several touches of water, milk, broth, jelly, vinegar, vitriol, etc. as well as what is hot, cold, rare, dense, hard, soft, or the like; and if he have but his touch, hearing, speaking and smelling, perfectly, he may express the several knowledges of his several senses, by one particular sense; or he may express one sense's knowledge by another; but if the senses be imperfect, he cannot have a true knowledge of any object. The same may be said of colours; for several colours being made by several corporeal figurative motions, may well be perceived by a general sense, which is touch: I will not say, that touch is the principle of all sensitive knowledge; for then I should be of the opinion of those experimental philosophers, which will have one principal motion or figure to be the cause of all natural things; but I only say, animal touch may have some notion of the other animal senses, by the help of rational perception. All which proves, that every part is sensible, and every sense knowing, not only in particular, but that one sense may have some general notion or knowledge of the rest; for there are particular and general perceptions in sensitive and rational matter, which is the cause both of the variety and order of nature's works; and therefore it is not necessary that a black figure must be rough, and a white figure smooth: Neither are white and black, the ground-figures of colours, as some do conceive, or as others do imagine, blue and yellow; for no particular figure can be a principle, but they are all but effects; and I think it is as great an error to believe effects for principles, as to judge of the interior natures and motions of creatures by their exterior phenomena or appearances, which I observe in most of our modern authors, whereof some are for incorporeal motions; others for prime and principal figures; others for first matter; others for the figures of dusty and insensible atoms, that move by chance: whenas neither atoms, corpuscles or particles; nor pores, light or the like, can be the cause of fixt and natural colours; for if it were so, then there would be no stayed or solid colour; insomuch, as a horse, or any other creature, would be of more various colours than a rainbow: But that several colours, are of several

of the roughness of the surface of the former in comparison with the others; Boyle also considers the case of the "blind Earl of Mansfield" who could distinguish black objects from white ones solely by touch (*WRB*, I, 68off.; 707–08).

figures, was always, and is still my opinion, and that the change of colours proceeds from the alteration of their figures, as I have more at large declared in my other philosophical words: Indeed art can no more force certain atoms or particles to meet and join to the making of such a figure as art would have, than it can make by a bare command, insensible atoms to join into a uniform world. I do not say this, as if there could not be artificial colours, or any artificial effects in nature; but my meaning only is, that although art can put several parts together, or divide and disjoin them; yet it cannot make those parts move or work, so as to alter their proper figures, or interior natures, or to be the cause of changing and altering their own, or other parts, any otherwise than they are by their natures. Neither do I say, that no colours are made by light; but I say only, that fixt colours are not made by light: and as for the opinion, that white bodies reflect the light outward, and black bodies inward, as some authors do imagine:[55] I answer, It is probable some bodies may do so; but all white and black colours are not made by such reflexions: The truth is, some conceive all colours to be made by one sort of motion, as some do believe that all sensation is made by pressure and reaction, and all heat by parts tending outward, and all cold by parts tending inward;[56] whenas there are not only several kinds of heat and cold, as animal, vegetable, mineral and elemental heat and cold; but several sorts in each kind; and different particulars in each sort; for there is a moist heat, a dry heat, a burning, a dissolving, a composing, a dilating, a contracting heat, and many more. The like for colds; all which several kinds, sorts and particulars, are made by the several changes of the corporeal figurative motions of nature, and not by pressure and reaction, or by tending inward and outward. And as there is so great a variety and difference amongst natural creatures, both in their perceptions and interior natures; so there are also varieties of their colours, the natural colours of men being different from the natural colours of beasts, birds, fish, worms, flies, etc. Concerning their interior natures, I'll allege but few examples: although a peacock, parrot, pie, or the like, are gay birds; yet there is difference in their gaiety. Again, although all men have flesh and blood, and are of one particular kind; yet their interior natures and dispositions are so different, that seldom any two men are of the same complexion;

---

[55] Eg., Robert Boyle, *Experiments and Considerations touching Colours* (*WRB*, I, 696ff.).
[56] The reference is to Hobbes; see *Elements of Philosophy*, IV, ch. 27, § 3, and ch. 28, § 1 (*EW*, I, 448ff.; 466ff.).

and as there is difference in their complexions, so in the exterior shapes and features of their exterior parts; insomuch that it is a wonder to see two men just alike; nay, as there is difference in the corporeal parts of their bodies, so in the corporeal parts of their minds, according to the old proverb, "So many men, so many minds": For there are different understandings, fancies, conceptions, imaginations, judgments, wits, memories, affections, passions, and the like. Again, as in some creatures there is difference both in their exterior features, and interior natures; so in others there is found a resemblance only in their exterior, and a difference in their interior parts; and in others again, a resemblance in their interior, and a difference in their exterior parts: As for example, black *ebony*, and black *marble*, are both of different natures, one being wood, and the other stone; and yet they resemble each other in their exterior colour and parts; also, white, black and gray *marble*, are all of one interior nature, and yet do differ in their exterior colour and parts. The same may be said of chalk and milk, which are both white, and yet of several natures; as also of a turquoise, and the sky, which both appear of one colour, and yet their natures are different; besides, there are so many stones of different colours, nay, stones of one sort; as for example, diamonds, which appear of divers colours, and yet are all of the same nature; also man's flesh, and the flesh of some other animals, doth so much resemble, as it can hardly be distinguished, and yet there is great difference betwixt man and beast: Nay, not only particular creatures, but parts of one and the same creature are different; for example, every part of man's body has a several touch, and every bit of meat we eat, has a several taste; witness the several parts, as legs, wings, breast, head, etc. of some fowl; as also the several parts of fish, and other creatures. All which proves the infinite variety in nature, and that nature is a perpetually self-moving body, dividing, composing, changing, forming and transforming her parts by self-corporeal figurative motions; and as she has infinite corporeal figurative motions, which are her parts, so she has an infinite wisdom to order and govern her infinite parts; for she has infinite sense and reason, which is the cause that no part of hers, is ignorant, but has some knowledge or other; and this infinite variety of knowledge makes a general infinite wisdom in nature. And thus I have declared how colours are made by the figurative corporeal motions, and that they are as various and different as all other creatures; and when they appear either more or less, it is by the variation of their parts. But as for the experiment of snow, which some do allege, that in a darkened room, it is not perceived to have any other light than what it receives,[57] doth not prove that the whiteness of snow is not an inherent and natural colour, because it doth not reflect light, or because our eye doth not see it; no more than we can justly say, that blood is not blood, or flesh is not flesh in the dark, if our eye do[th] not perceive it, or that the interior parts of nature are colourless, because the exterior light makes no reflexion upon them. Truly, in my judgment, those opinions, that no parts have colour, but those which the light reflects on, are neither probable to sense nor reason; for how can we conceive any corporeal part, without a colour? In my opinion, it is as impossible to imagine a body without colour,[58] as it is impossible for the mind to conceive a natural immaterial substance; and if so pure a body as the mind, cannot be colourless, much less are grosser bodies. But put the case all bodies that are not subject to exterior light, were black as night, yet they would be of a colour; for black is as much a colour; as green, or blue, or yellow, or the like; but if all the interior parts of nature be black, then, in my opinion, nature is a very sad and melancholy lady; and those which are of such an opinion, surely their minds are more dark than the interior parts of nature; I will not hope that clouds of dusty atoms have obscured them; But if no creature can have imagination without figure and colour, much less can the optic sensitive parts; for the exterior sensitive parts are more gross than the rational; and therefore they cannot be without colour, no more than without figure: and although the exterior parts of animals are subject to our touch; yet the countenances of those several exterior parts are no more perceptible by our touch, than several colours are: By countenances, I mean the several exterior postures, motions, or appearances of each part; for as there is difference betwixt a face, and a countenance; (for a face remains constantly the same, whenas the countenance of a face may, and doth change every moment; as for example, there are smiling, frowning, joyful, sad, angry countenances, etc.) so there is also a difference between the exterior figure or shape of a creature, and the several and various motions, appearances or postures of the exterior parts of that creature's exterior figure; whereof the former may be compared to a face, and the

---

[57] Boyle's experiment is described in *Experiments and Considerations touching Colours* (*WRB*, I, 699).
[58] Descartes held that we can conceive of colorless bodies; color is not essential to the nature of body. See his "wax argument" in the *Meditations* (AT, VII, 30ff.; CSM, II, 20ff.), and *Principles of Philosophy*, II, §§ 4 and 11.

latter to a countenance. But leaving this nice distinction; If anyone should ask me, Whether a Barbary horse, or a jennet, or a Turkish, or an English horse, can be known and distinguished in the dark? I answer: They may be distinguished as much as the blind man (whereof mention hath been made before) may discern colours, nay, more; for the figure of a gross exterior shape of a body may sooner be perceived, than the more fine and pure countenance of colours. To shut up this my discourse of colours, I will briefly repeat what I have said before, viz. that there are natural and inherent colours which are fixt and constant, and superficial colours, which are changeable and inconstant; as also artificial colours made by painters and dyers, and that it is impossible that any constant colour should be made by inconstant atoms, and various lights. It is true, there are streams of dust or dusty atoms, which seem to move variously, upon which the sun or light makes several reflexions and refractions; but yet I do not see, nor can I believe, that those dusty particles, and light, are the cause of fixt and inherent colours; and therefore if experimental philosophers have no firmer grounds and principles than their colours have; and if their opinions be as changeable as inconstant atoms, and variable lights, then their experiments will be of no great benefit and use to the world. Neither will artificial characters and geometrical figures be able to make their opinions and experiments more probable; for they appear to me like Dr. Dee's numbers, who was directed by I know not what spirits, which Kelly saw in his holy stone, which neither of them did understand;[59] much less will dioptrical glasses give any true information of them, but they rather delude the sight; for art is not only intricate and obscure, but a false informer, and rather blinds than informs any particular creature of the truth of nature: but my reason perceives that nature loves sometimes to act or work blindfolded in the actions of art; for although they be natural, yet they are but nature's blind, at least her winking or juggling actions, causing some parts or creatures to deceive others; or else they are her politic actions by which she deceives her creatures' expectations, and by that means keeps them from knowing and understanding her subtle and wise government.

---

[59] John Dee (1527–1608), scientist, mathematician and hermetic philosopher, chronicles, in *A True and Faithful Relation* (London, 1659), his use of numerical and alphabetical tables to summon angels, which appeared in a crystal ball, and spoke to Dee through his assistant Edward Kelley.

XXI Whether an Idea have a Colour, and of the Idea of a Spirit

I have declared in my former discourse, that there is no colour without body, nor a body without colour; for we cannot think of a body without we think of colour too. To which some may object, that if colour be as proper to a body as matter, and if the mind be corporeal, then the mind is also coloured. I answer, The mind, in my opinion, has as much colour as other parts of nature. But then perhaps they will ask me, What colour the mind is of? My answer is, that the mind, which is the rational part of nature, is no more subject to one colour, than the infinite parts of nature are subject to one corporeal figurative motion; for you can no more confine the corporeal mind to a particular complexion, than you can confine infinite matter to one particular colour, or all colours to one particular figure. Again, they may ask, Whether an idea have a colour? and if so, whether the idea of God be coloured? To which I answer, If the ideas be of corporeal finite figures, they have colours according to the nature, or property, or figure of the original; but as for the idea of God, it is impossible to have a corporeal idea of an infinite incorporeal being; for though the finite parts of nature may have a perception or knowledge of the existence of God, yet they cannot possibly pattern or figure him; he being a supernatural, immaterial, and infinite being: But put the case (although it is very improbable, nay, against sense and reason) there were natural immaterial ideas, if those ideas were finite, and not infinite, yet they could not possibly express an infinite, which is without limitation, by a finite figure which hath a circumference. Some may say, An immaterial idea hath no circumference. But then I answer, It is not a finite idea, and it is impossible for an idea to be infinite: for I take an idea to be the picture of some object, and there can be no picture without a perfect form; neither can I conceive how an immaterial can have a form, not having a body; wherefore it is more impossible for nature to make a picture of the infinite God, than for man, which is but a part of nature, to make a picture of infinite nature; for nature being material, has also figure and matter, they being all one, so that none can be without the other, no more than nature can be divided from herself. Thus it is impossible for man to make a figure, or picture of that which is not a part of nature; for pictures are as much parts of nature, as any other parts; nay, were they monstrous, as we call them: for nature being material, is also figurative;

and being a self-moving matter or substance, is dividable, and composable: and as she hath infinite, corporeal, figurative motions, and infinite parts; so she hath infinite figures, of which, some are pictures, others originals: And if any one particular creature could picture out those infinite figures, he would picture out nature; but nature being infinite, cannot be pictured or patterned by any finite and particular creature, although she is material; nevertheless she may be patterned in parts: And as for God, he being individable, and immaterial, can neither be patterned in part, nor in whole, by any part of nature which is material, nay, not by infinite nature herself: Wherefore the notions of God can be no otherwise but of His existence; to wit, that we know there is something above nature, who is the author, and God of nature; for though nature hath an infinite natural knowledge of the infinite God; yet, being dividable as well as composable, her parts cannot have such an infinite knowledge or perception; and being composable as much as dividable, no part can be so ignorant of God, as not to know there is a God. Thus nature hath both an infinite and finite perception; infinite in the whole, (as I may say for better expression's sake) and finite in parts. But mistake me not, I do not mean, that either the infinite perception of nature, or the finite perceptions of natural parts and creatures, are any otherwise of that supernatural and divine being, than natural; but yet they are the most purest parts, being of the rational part of nature, moving in a most elevating and subtle manner, as making no exact figure or form, because God hath neither form nor figure; but that subtle matter, or corporeal perceptive motion patterns out only an over-ruling power: which power all the parts of nature are sensible of, and yet know not what it is; like as the perception of sight seeth the ebbing and flowing of the sea, or the motion of the sun, yet knows not their cause; and, the perception of hearing, hears thunder, yet knows not how it is made; and if there be such ignorance of the corporeal parts of nature, what of God? [For whatsoever is corporeal, hath a being; but what being an immaterial hath, no corporeal can perceive: Wherefore no part of nature (her parts being corporeal) can perceive an immaterial; because it is impossible to have a perception of that which is not perceptible, as not being an object fit or proper for corporeal perception. Indeed, an immaterial is no object, because it is not a body. But some may say, that a corporeal may have a conception, although not a perception of an immaterial. I answer, that a corporeal cannot have a conception of that which in nature is not a body.

Thus far the corporeal motions can conceive somewhat above nature, but can conceive no more than what that is which is above, or is more powerful than nature: And for proof; How many several opinions [are][60] there concerning God, as of his being, existence, attributes, and the like? insomuch, that there are few of one and the same opinion: But such a conception, as, that there is something more powerful than nature, all the parts of nature (which are infinite) certainly have: And so God, being an infinite and eternal God, hath an infinite and eternal worship; for every part conceiving something about itself, and above its nature, worships that supreme, either through fear, or love, or both; yet knows not what the supreme being is.][61] But to conclude, my opinion is, that, as the sensitive perception knows some of the other parts of nature by their effects; so the rational perceives some effects of the omnipotent power of God; which effects are perceptible by finite creatures, but not his infinite nature, nor essence, nor the cause of his infiniteness and omnipotency. Thus, although God's power may be perceived by nature's parts; yet what God is, cannot be known by any part: And nature being composable, there is a general acknowledgment of God in all her parts, but being also dividable, it is the cause there are particular religions and opinions of God, and of his divine worship and adoration.

XXII   Of Wood Petrified[62]

I cannot admire, as some do, that wood doth turn into stone, by reason I observe, that slime, clay, dirt, nay, water, may and doth often the same, which is further off from the nature of stone, than wood is, as being less dense, and its interior figurative motions, being dilating; but yet this does not prove that all other creatures may as easily be metamorphosed into stone, as they; for the parts of water are composed but of one sort of figure, and are all of the same nature; and so is wood, clay, shells, etc. whose parts are but of one figure, at least, not of so many different figures as the parts of animals, or other creatures; for as animals have different parts, so these parts are of different figures, not only exteriorly, but interiorly; as for example, in some or most animals there are bones,

[60] 1668: "is."   [61] Lacking in 1666.
[62] Cf. Hooke, *Micrographia*, "Observation xvii: Of Petrifyed Wood, and Other Petrifyed Bodies"; Robert Boyle, *New Experiments and Observations touching Cold, or an Experimental History of Cold begun . . .* (1665), "Of a Place in England Where, without Petrifying Water, Wood is Turned into Stone. A Further Account of an Observation about White Blood." (*WRB*, ii, 736ff.).

gristles, nerves, sinews, muscles, flesh, blood, brains, marrow, choler, phlegm, and the like: Besides, there are several sorts of flesh, witness their interior and exterior parts, as the heart, lungs, liver, spleen, guts, and the like; as also the head, brain, arms, body, legs, and the like; all which would puzzle and withstand the power of Ovid's metamorphosing of gods and goddesses. Wherefore it is but a weak argument to conclude, because some creatures or parts can change out of one figure into another, without a dissolution of their composed parts, therefore all creatures can do the like: For, if all creatures could or should be metamorphosed into one sort of figure, then this whole world would perhaps come to be one stone, which would be a hard world. But this opinion, I suppose, proceeds from chemistry; for, since the last act of chemistry (as I have heard) is the production of glass,[63] it makes, perhaps, chemists believe, that at the last day, when this world shall be dissolved with fire, the fire will calcine, or turn it into glass. A brittle world indeed! But whether it will be transparent, or no, I know not; for it will be very thick.

XXIII   Of the Nature of Water[64]

The ascending of water in pipes, pumps, and the like engines, is commonly alleged as an argument to prove there is no vacuum:[65] But, in my opinion, water, or the like things that are moist, liquid and wet, their interior, corporeal, and natural motion is flowing, as being of a dilating figure; and when other parts or creatures suppress those liquors, so that they cannot rise, they will dilate; but when solid and heavy bodies are put into them, as stones, metals, etc. which do sink, then they will rise above them, as being their nature to overflow any other body, if they can have the better of it, or get passage. For, concerning the floating of some

---

[63] Johannes Baptista Van Helmont claimed that his "alkahest" (a universal solvent or, alternatively, superior process of chemical analysis) could convert bodies into salt; see *Oriatrike*, p. 48. "Vitriol," with the glassy appearance of its sulfates, was the salt commonly held by chemists to be the first principle of things. Perhaps this can explain Cavendish's obscure remark. (All future references to Van Helmont will be to Johannes, Van Helmont the Elder.)

[64] Cf. Descartes, *Meteorology*, Discourse v; *Principles of Philosophy*, IV, § 48; Van Helmont, *Oriatrike*, pp. 53ff.

[65] Cavendish rejects the seventeenth-century scholastic view that phenomena such as suction and the rise of water in a pump result from nature's "abhorrence of a vacuum"; but she accepts Stoic reasons for denying the existence of vacua. For an alternative view, see Robert Boyle, *New Experiments Physico-Mechanical, touching the Spring of the Air and its Effects . . .* (1660) (*WRB*, I, 1ff.).

bodies, the reason is not so much their levity or porousness, but both their exterior shape, and the water's restlessness or activity; the several parts of water endeavouring to drive those floating bodies from them; as when several men playing at ball, or shuttlecock, or the like, endeavour to beat those things from, and to each other; or as one should blow up a feather into the air, which makes it not only keep up in the air, but to wave about. The like doth water with floating bodies: and the lighter the floating parts are, the more power have the liquid parts to force and thrust them about. And this is also the reason why two floating bodies of one nature, endeavour to meet and join; because by joining, they receive more strength to resist the force of the watery parts: The same may be said, whenas floating bodies stick or join to the sides of vessels; but many times the watery parts will not suffer them to be at rest or quiet, but drive them from their strongholds or defences. Concerning the suppression of water, and of some floating bodies in water, by air or light, as that air and light should suppress water, and bodies floating upon it, (as some do conceive)[66] I see no reason to believe it; but the contrary rather appears by the levity of air, which is so much lighter, and therefore of less force than either the floating bodies, or the water on which they float. Some again are of the opinion, that water is a more dense body than ice,[67] and prove it by the refractions of light; because water doth more refract the rays of light, than ice doth: But whatsoever their experiments be, yet my reason can hardly believe it; for, although ice may be more transparent than water, yet it may be more dense than water; for glass is more transparent than water, and yet more dense than water: and some bodies will not be transparent, if they be thick, that is, if they have a great number of parts upon parts; whenas they will be transparent, if they be thin, that is, if they have few thin parts upon each other: so that transparent bodies may be darkened; and those that are not transparent of themselves, may be made so, by the thickness or thinness of parts, that one may see, or not see through them: and thus a thin body of water may

---

[66] Cf. Kenelm Digby, *Two Treatises. In One of Which, the Nature of Bodies; in the Other, the Nature of Mans Soule; Is Looked Into* . . . (Paris, 1644), First Treatise, ch. 11, esp. § 6ff.; Charleton, *Physiologia*, III, ch. 11, § II, 7; Descartes, *Principles of Philosophy*, IV, § 23ff.

[67] See Hobbes, *Elements of Philosophy*, IV, ch. 28, § 7: ". . . ice is lighter than water. The cause whereof is . . . that air is received in and mingled with the particles of the water whilst it is congealing" (*EW*, I, 474). Cf. Boyle, *New Experiments and Observations touching Cold*, Title IX: "Experiments in Consort, Touching the Bubbles, from which the Levity of Ice is Supposed to Proceed" (*WRB*, II, 542–50).

be more transparent than a thick body of ice; and a thin body of ice may be more transparent than a thick body of water. As for the expansion of water, it doth not prove that water is more dense than ice; but on the contrary, it rather proves, that it is more rare: for, that body whose parts are close and united, is more dense than that whose parts are fluid and dilating. Neither doth expansion alter the interior nature of a body, any more than contraction; but it alters only the exterior posture: As for example, when a man puts his body into several postures, it doth not alter him from being a man, to some other creature; for the stretching of his legs, spreading out of his arms, puffing up his cheeks, etc. changes his nature, or natural figure, no more than when he contracts his limbs close together, crumpling up his body, or folding his arms, etc. but his posture is only changed; the like for the expansions and contractions of other sorts of creatures. Nor can I readily give my assent to their opinion, that some liquors are more dense than others; I mean such as are perfectly moist, liquid and wet, as water is: for there be numerous sorts of liquors, which are not thoroughly wet as water; and although their circular-lines may be different, as, some edged, some pointed, some twisted, and the like; yet they do not differ so much, but that their inherent figures are all of circular-lines; for the interior nature or figure of water, and so of all other moist and wet liquors, is circular: and it is observable, that as art may be an occasion of diminishing those points or edges of the circular-lines of some liquors, or of untwisting them, so it may also be an occasion that some liquid and wet bodies may become so pointed, edged, twisted, etc. as may occasion those circles to move or turn into such or such exterior figures, not only into triangular, square, round, and several other forms or figures, as appears in ice, hail, frost, and flakes of snow; but into such figures as they name spirits: which several sorts of figures belonging all to one sort of creatures, may cause several refractions, reflexions, and inflexions of the rays of light. Wherefore mechanics may be very much mistaken concerning the truth of the interior nature of bodies, or natural creatures, by judging them only according to their exterior figures.[68]

---

[68] Cf. Descartes, *Meteorology*, Discourse I. See Cavendish's related discussion in *Phil. Letters*, pp. 117ff.

XXIV Of Salt; and of Sea or Salt Water[69]

The reason why salt is made, or extracted out of salt water, is, that the circular-lines of sea or salt water, are pointed exteriorly, but not interiorly; which is the cause that the saltish parts may be easily divided from those watery lines: and it is to be observed, that those points when joined to the watery circles, are rare; but being once separated, either by art, or a more natural way, by some sorts of dividing motions, they become more dense; yet not so dense, but they may melt, or return again into the first figure, (which is a rare figure) and so become liquid salt; and afterwards they may be densed or contracted again; for there is no other difference between dry and liquid salt, but what is made by the rarity or density of those sort of points. As for that sort of salt which is named "volatile," it is when some of those rare points become more dilated or rarefied, than when they are joined to the watery circle-lines; I say, some, not all: For, as some points do condense, or contract into fixt salt; so others do dilate or arise into "volatile" salt.[70] But perchance some will say, "How can there be several sorts of points, since a point is but a point?" I answer, There may very well be several sorts, considering the nature of their substance; for some sorts are rare, some dense, some contracting, some dilating, some retenting, etc. Besides, all points are not alike, but there is great difference amongst several pointed figures; for all are not like the point of a pin or needle; but (to allege some gross examples) there be points of pyramids, points of knives, points of pins, points of the flame of a candle, and numerous other sorts, which are all several points, and not one like another; for I do not mean a "mathematical," or imaginary point, such as is only made by the rational matter in the mind, (although even amongst those imaginary points there is difference; for you cannot imagine, or think of the several pointed figures of several sorts or kinds of creatures, or parts; but you will have a difference in your mind) but I mean pointed figures, and not single points. It is also to be observed, that as some watery circles will, and may have points outwardly; so some have also points inwardly; for some watery circles, as I have mentioned in my *Philosophical Opinions*, are edged, to wit, such as are in "vitriol" water;

[69] Cf. Aristotle, *Meteorology*, II, ch. 2; Descartes, *Meteorology*, Discourse III; *Principles of Philosophy*, IV, § 66ff.; Robert Boyle, *The Sceptical Chymist* (London, 1661).

[70] Chemists, such as Boyle and Van Helmont, distinguished "fixed" from "volatile" salts. The latter are salts disposed to evaporate, or to turn into fumes or vapor; the former are salts that are not easily volatilized.

others pointed, as those in salt water; and others are of other sorts of points, as those in cordial or hot waters; but those last are more artificial: And all these are different in their sorts or kinds, although a little difference in their own natures, may appear great in our human perception. Concerning oil, there is also difference between oil and other wet bodies; for oil, although it be rare, liquid and moist, yet we cannot say it is absolutely that which we name wet, as other liquors are, viz. water and wine, or natural juices: and since the interior natural figure of oil is burning and hot, it is impossible to divide those interior fiery points from the circle figure of oil, without dissolving those liquid circle- lines. But as the penetrations of other acid and salt liquors, are caused by their exterior points; so oil, whose points are interiorly in the circle-lines, cannot have such quick effects of penetration, as those that are exteriorly pointed. But mistake me not, I do not mean such exterior parts as are only subject to our human perception; but such as cause those creatures or parts to be of such a figure or nature.

XXV   Of the Motions of Heat and Cold[71]

Those which affirm that heat and cold are the two primary and only causes of the productions of all natural things;[72] do not consider sufficiently the variety of nature, but think that nature produces all by art; and since art is found out and practised by man, man conceits himself to be above nature: But as neither art, nor any particular creature can be the cause or principle of all the rest; so neither can heat and cold be the prime cause of all natural productions, no more than paint can produce all the parts of man's face, and the eyes, nose, forehead, chin, cheeks, lips, and the like; or a periwig can produce a natural head, or a suit of clothes can make the body of man; for then whensoever the fashioned

[71] Cf. Francis Bacon, *Novum organum* [The New Organon], II, §§ 20ff. in *Instauratio magna . . .* [The reat Instauration] (London, 1620); Hobbes, *Elements of Philosophy*, IV, ch. 27, §§ 3ff. and ch. 28 §§1ff (*EW*, I, 448ff.; 466ff.); Descartes, *Principles of Philosophy*, IV, §§ 29ff.; Charleton, *Physiologia*, III, ch. 12; Boyle, *New Experiments and Observations touching Cold* (*WRB*, II, 462ff.) and *Experiments, Notes, &c. about the Mechanical Origin or Production of Divers Particular Qualities . . .* (1675) (*WRB*, IV, 230ff.).

[72] Anaximenes (fl. *c.* 546 BC) held that all phenomena can be explained in terms of two types of change that air undergoes: the "warming" process of rarefaction, and the "cooling" of condensation. But cf. Aristotle, *Meteorology*, IV, ch. 8: "bodies are formed by heat and cold and . . . these agents operate by thickening and solidifying" (384b24–25; *CWA*, I, 617). Bernadino Telesio (1509–88), in *De rerum natura iuxta propria principia* [On the Nature of Things According to their Proper Principles] (Naples, 1565) argues for heat and cold as the incorporeal, active principle of nature.

garments of mode dresses do change, men would of necessity change also; but art causes gross mistakes and errors, not only in sensitive, but also in rational perceptions; for sense being deluded, is apt to delude reason also, especially if reason be too much indulgent to sense; and therefore those judgments that rely much upon the perception of sense, are rather sensitive than rational judgments; for sense can have but a perception of the exterior figures of objects, and art can but alter the outward form or figure, but not make or change the interior nature of anything; which is the reason that artificial alterations cause false, at least, uncertain and various judgments; so that nature is as various in men's judgments, as in her other works. But concerning heat and cold, my opinion is, that they are like several colours, some natural, and some artificial; of which the artificial are very inconstant, at least not so lasting as those that are not made by art; and they which say, that both heat and cold are not made by the sensories, or sensitive organs, are in the right, if their meaning be, that both heat and cold, in their natures, and with all their properties, as they are particular creatures, are not made or pro-duced by human or animal senses; nevertheless, the sensitive animal perception of heat and cold, is made by the sensitive motions, in their sensitive organs: for what heat and cold soever an animal creature feels, the perception of it is made in the sense of touch, or by those sensitive motions in the parts of its body; for, as the perception of any other outward object is not made by a real entrance of its parts into our sensories; so neither is all perception of heat and cold made by the intermixture of their particles with our flesh, but they are patterned and figured out by the sensitive motions in the exterior parts of the body, as well as other objects: I will not say, that cold or heat may not enter and intermix with the parts of some bodies, as fire doth intermix with fuel, or enters into its parts; but my meaning is, that the animal perception of heat and cold, is not made this way, that is, by an intermixture of the parts of the agent, with the parts of the patient, as the learned call them; that is, of the exterior object, and the sentient; or else the perception of all exterior objects, would be made by such an intermixture, which is against sense and reason: and therefore even in such a commixture, where the parts of the object enter into the body of the sentient, as fire doth into fuel, the perception of the motions of the fire in the fuel, and the fuel's consumption or burning, is not made by the fire, but by the fuel's own perceptive motions, imitating the motions of the fire; so that fire doth not turn the fuel into ashes, but the fuel doth change by its own corporeal figurative motions, and the fire is only an occasion of it. The same may be said of cold. Neither is every creature's perception alike, no more than it can be said, that one particular creature, as (for example) man, hath but one perception: for, the perceptions of sight and smelling, and so of every sense, are different; nay, one and the same sense may have as many several perceptions, as it hath objects; and some sorts of perceptions in some creatures, are either stronger or weaker than in others: For, we may observe, that in one and the same degree of heat or cold, some will have quicker, and some slower perceptions than others: For example, in the perception of touch, if several men stand about a fire, some will sooner be heated than others. The like for cold; some will apprehend cold weather sooner than others; the reason is, that in their perception of touch, the sensitive motions work quicker or slower in figuring or patterning out heat or cold, than in the perception of others. The same may be said of other objects; where some sentient bodies will be more sensible of some, than of others, even in one and the same kind of perception. But if in all perceptions of cold, cold should intermix with the bodies of animals, or other creatures, like several ingredients; then all bodies, upon the perception of cold, would dissolve their figures, which we see they do not: for, although all dissolving motions are knowing and perceptive, because every particular motion is a particular knowledge and perception; yet, not every perception requires a dissolution or change of its figure. It is true some sorts or degrees of exterior heat and cold, may occasion some bodies to dissolve their interior figures, and change their particular natures; but they have not power to dissolve or change all natural bodies. Neither doth heat or cold change those bodies by an intermixture of their own particles with the parts of the bodies: but the parts of the bodies change themselves by way of imitation, as men put themselves into a mode fashion; although oftentimes the senses will have fashions of their own, without imitating any other objects. For, not all sorts of perceptions are made by imitation or patterning, but some are made voluntarily, or by rote: As for example, when some do hear and see such or such things, without any outward objects. Wherefore, it is not certain streams, or agitated particles in the air,[73] nor the vapours and effluviums of exterior objects, insinuating

---

[73] See, e.g., Descartes, *Principles of Philosophy*, IV, § 29.

themselves into the pores of the sentient,[74] that are the cause of the perception of heat and cold, as some do imagine; for there cannot probably be such differences in the pores of animal creatures of one sort, (as for example, of men) which should cause such a different perception as is found in them: For, although exterior heat or cold be the same, yet several animals of the same sort, will have several and different perceptions of one and the same degree of exterior heat and cold, as above mentioned; which difference would not be, if their perception was caused by a real entrance of hot and cold particles, into the pores of their bodies: Besides, burning fevers, and shaking agues, prove that such effects can be without such exterior causes. Neither can all sorts of heat and cold be expressed by wind, air and water, in weather glasses; for, they being made by art, cannot give a true information of the generation of all natural heat and cold; but as there is great difference between natural and artificial ice, snow, colours, light, and the like; so between artificial and natural heat and cold; and there are so many several sorts of heat and cold, that it is impossible to reduce them all to one certain cause or principle, or confine them to one sort of motions; as some do believe that all sorts of heat and cold are made by motions tending inward and outward; and others, that by ascending and descending, or rising and depressing motions: which is no more probable, than that all colours are made by the reflexion of light, and that all white is made by reflecting the beams of light outward; and all black by reflecting them inward: or that a man when he is on horseback, or upon the top of an house or steeple, or in a deep pit or mine, should be of another figure, than of the figure and nature of man, unless he were dissolved by death, which is a total alteration of his figure. For neither gravity nor levity of air, nor atmospherical pillars, nor any weather glasses, can give us a true information of all natural heat and cold; but the several figurative corporeal motions, which make all things in nature, do also make several sorts of heat and cold, in several sorts of creatures. But I observe, experimental philosophers do first cry up several of their artificial instruments, then make doubts of them, and at last disprove them; so that there is no trust nor truth in them, to be relied on: For, it [is][75] not an age since weather glasses were held the only divulgers of heat and cold, or change of

---

[74] Boyle atributes to Pierre Gassendi the view that cold is due to "nitrous exhalations" in *New Experiments and Observations touching Cold* (*WRB*, II, 594ff.).

[75] As in 1666; lacking in 1668.

weather; and now some do doubt, they are not such infallible informers of those truths. By which it is evident, that experimental philosophy has but a brittle, inconstant, and uncertain ground. And these artificial instruments, as microscopes, telescopes, and the like, which are now so highly applauded, who knows but they may within a short time have the same fate; and upon a better and more rational enquiry, be found deluders, rather than true informers. The truth is, there's not anything that has, and doth still delude most men's understandings more, than that they do not enough consider the variety of nature's actions, and do not employ their reason so much in the search of nature's actions, as they do their senses; preferring art and experiments, before reason; which makes them stick so close to some particular opinions, and particular sorts of motions or parts; as if there were no more motions, parts, or creatures in nature, than what they see and find out by their artificial experiments.

Thus the variety of nature, is a stumbling block to most men, at which they break their heads of understanding, like blind men, that run against several posts or walls: and how should it be otherwise, since nature's actions are infinite, and man's understanding finite? For, they consider not so much the interior natures of several creatures, as their exterior figures and phenomena; which makes them write many paradoxes, but few truths; supposing that sense and art can only lead them to the knowledge of truth; whenas they rather delude their judgments, instead of informing them. But, nature has placed sense and reason together, so that there is no part or particle of nature, which has not its share of reason, as well as of sense: for, every part having self-motion, has also knowledge, which is sense and reason; and therefore it is fit we should not only employ our senses, but chiefly our reason, in the search of the causes of natural effects: for, sense is only a workman, and reason is the designer and surveyor; and as reason guides and directs, so ought sense to work. But seeing that in this age, sense is more in fashion than reason, it is no wonder there are so many irregular opinions and judgments amongst men. However, although it be the mode, yet I, for my part, shall not follow it; but leaving to our moderns, their experimental, or mode philosophy, built upon deluding art, I shall addict myself to the study of contemplative philosophy, and reason shall be my guide. Not that I despise sense, or sensitive knowledge: but, when I speak of sense, I mean the perception of our five exterior senses, helped (or rather deluded) by art, and artificial instruments: for I see, that in this present age, learned men are full of art, and artificial trials; and when they have found out something by them, they presently judge that all natural actions are made the same way: As for example, when they find by art that salt will make snow congeal into ice,[76] they instantly conclude from thence, that all natural congelations, are made by saline particles; and that the *primum frigidum*, or the principal cause of all natural cold, must needs be salt;[77] by reason they have found by art, that salt will do the same effect, in the aforesaid commixture with snow. But how grossly they are deceived, rational men may judge. If I were a chemist, and acknowledged their common principles, I might, perchance, have some belief in it, but not whilst I follow reason. Nay, I perceive, that oftentimes our senses are deluded by their own irregularities, in not perceiving always truly and rightly, the actions of art, but mistaking them, which is a double error: and therefore that particular sensitive knowledge in man, which is built merely upon artificial experiments, will never make him a good philosopher, but regular sense and reason must do it; that is, a regular, sensitive, and rational inquisition, into the various actions of nature: For, put the case a microscope be true, concerning the magnifying of an exterior object; but yet the magnitude of the object, cannot give a true information of its interior parts, and their motions; or else great and large bodies would be interiorly known, even without microscopes. The truth is, our exterior senses can go no further than the exterior figures of creatures, and their exterior actions: but our reason may pierce deeper, and consider their inherent natures, and interior actions. And although it do sometimes err, (for there can be no perfect or universal knowledge in a finite part, concerning the infinite actions of nature) yet it may also probably guess at them, and may chance to hit the truth. Thus sense and reason shall be the ground of my philosophy, and no particular natural effects, nor artificial instruments; and if anyone can show me a better and surer ground or principle, than this, I shall most willingly and joyfully embrace it.

---

[76] Consider William Cavendish's view: "Ice is made of salt, for who knows not, that put snow and salt in a pot and stir it by the fire, and it becomes ice? This is salt. The world is nothing but salt, and that salt is the ground of everything, life and motion" (*Opinions*, 1663, p. 461).

[77] A view commonly held by the chemists, and by Gassendi; cf. Charleton, *Physiologia*, III, ch. 12, § II, 7.

XXVI   Of the Measures, Degrees, and Different Sorts of Heat and Cold

Some experimental philosophers, are much inquisitive into the measures of heat and cold; and as we have settled standards for weight, magnitude, and time; so they endeavour to measure the varying temperature, and gradual differences of heat and cold.[78] But do what they can, their artificial measures or weights, neither will, nor can be so exact as the natural are, to wit, so as not to make them err in more or less: Neither is it possible, that all the degrees of heat and cold in nature can be measured; for no man can measure what he doth not know; and who knows all the different sorts of heats and colds? Nay, if man did endeavour to measure only one sort of heat or cold: As for example, the degrees of the heat or coldness of the air, how is it possible that he should do it, by reason of the continual change of the motions of heat or cold of the air, which are so inconstant, that it were surer to measure the fluidity of the air, than to measure the degrees of heat or cold of the air: for, the temper of the air, and of its heat and cold, may vary so, as many times we shall never find the same measure again. Wherefore, if we desire to have some knowledge of the degrees of some sorts of heat or cold, my opinion is, that we may more easily attain to it by the help of rational perception, than by a sensitive inspection of artificial weather glasses, or the like; for reason goes beyond sense: and although the sensitive perception is best next the rational; yet the rational is above the sensitive. But some of the learned conceive the degrees of heat and cold, are made by bare divisions; whenas, in my opinion, they are made by the several degrees of their corporeal figurative motions. They do also imagine, that there's no degree but must ascend from one to two; from two, to three; and so forth, through all numbers; and that from one to twenty, there be so many degrees as there be numbers; whenas, in my opinion, there's no more but one degree required from one, to a million, or more: for though both in nature and art, there are degrees from one single figure to another; yet there may also be but one degree from one to a million, without reckoning any intermediate degrees or figures: so that a body, when it

[78] E.g., Bacon, *Novum organum*, II, § 13; Athanasius Kircher, *Magnes, sive de arte magnetica* [Magnets, or the Magnetic Art] (Rome, 1641); Hooke, *Micrographia*, "Observation VII: Of Some Phenomena of Glass Drops"; Robert Boyle, *New Experiments and Observations touching Cold*, "New Thermometrical Experiments and Thoughts," (*WRB*, II, 481ff.) and "The Experimental History of Cold begun," Title IV (*WRB*, II, 518–24).

moves quick or slow, needs not to go through all the intermediate degrees of quickness or slowness, as to move quicker and quicker, slower and slower; but may immediately move from a very slow, to a very quick degree: The truth is, no man is able to measure the infinite degrees of natural motions; for though nature consists of particular finites, yet it doth also consist of infinite particulars; finite in figure, infinite in number; and who can number from finite to infinite? But having discoursed hereof elsewhere, I return to heat and cold: and let others dispute whether the degrees of heat and cold in the air, be the same with the degrees of animal perceptions, or with the degrees of animal cold and heat: My opinion is, that there being several sorts, and several particular heats and colds, they cannot be just alike each other, but there's some difference betwixt them: As for example, there are shaking, freezing, chilly, windy, numb, stiff, rare, dense, moist, dry, contracting, dilating, ascending, descending, and other numerous sorts of colds; nay, there are some sorts of candied figures made by heat, which appear as if they were frozen: Also, there are fluid colds which are not wet, as well as fluid heats that are not dry; for phlegm is fluid, and yet not wet; and some sorts of air are fluid, and not wet; I say, some, not all: For, some are hot and moist, others hot and dry. The same may be said of some sorts of heat and cold; for some are moist, and some dry: and there may be at one and the same time, a moist cold in the air, and a dry cold in water; which, in my opinion, is the reason, that in sealed weather glasses, (according to some experimenters' relations) sometimes the air doth not shrink, but rather seems to be expanded when the weather grows colder, and that the water contracts: not that the cold contraction of water, causes an expansion of the air, to prevent a vacuum; for there cannot be any such thing as a vacuum in nature: But, that there is a moist cold in the air, and a dry cold in the water, whereof the dry cold causes a contraction, and the moist cold an expansion; nay, there is often a moist and dry cold in the air at one and the same time; so that some parts of the air may have a moist cold, and the next adjoining parts a dry cold, and that but in a very little compass; for there maybe such contractions and dilatations in nature, which make not a hairsbreadth difference; nature being so subtle and curious, as no particular can trace her ways; and therefore when I speak of contractions and dilatations, I do not mean they are all such gross actions perceptible by our exterior senses, as the works of art; but such as the curiosity of nature works. Concerning the several sorts of animal heat and cold, they are quite different from the elemental, and other sorts of heat and cold; for some men may have cold fits of an ague, under the line, or in the hottest climates; and others burning fevers, under the poles, or in the coldest climates. It is true, that animals, by their perceptions may pattern out the heat or cold of the air, but these perceptions are not always regular or perfect; neither are the objects at all times exactly presented as they should, which may cause an obscurity both in art, and in particular sensitive perceptions; and through this variety, the same sort of creatures may have different perceptions of the same sorts of heat and cold. Besides, it is to be observed, that some parts or creatures, as for example, water, and the like liquors, if kept close from the perception either of heat or cold, will neither freeze, nor grow hot; and if ice or snow be kept in a deep pit, from the exterior object of heat, it will never thaw, but continue ice or snow; whenas being placed near the perception of the sun, fire, or warm air, its exterior figure will alter from being ice, to water; and from being cold, to hot; or to an intermediate temper betwixt both; nay, it may alter from an extreme degree of cold, to an extreme degree of heat, according as the exterior object of heat doth occasion the sensitive perceptive motions of water or ice to work; for, extremes are apt to alter the natural temper of a particular creature, and many times so as to cause a total dissolution of its interior natural figure; (when I name extremes, I do not mean any uttermost extremes in nature; for nature being infinite, and her particular actions being poised and balanced by opposites, can never run into extremes; but I call them so, in reference only to our perception; as we used to say, "It is *extreme* hot, or *extreme* cold.") And the reason of it is, that water by its natural perceptive motions, imitates the motions of heat or cold; but being kept from the perception of them, it cannot imitate them. The same reason may be given upon the experiment, that some bodies being put into water, will be preserved from being frozen or congealed; for they being in water, are not only kept from the perception of cold, but the water doth, as a guard, preserve them; which guard, if it be overcome, that is, if the water begin to freeze, then they will do so too. But yet all colds are not airy, nor all heats sunny or fiery: for, a man, as I mentioned before, may have shaking fits of an ague, in the hottest climate, or season; and burning fits of a fever in the coldest climate or season: and as there is difference between elemental and animal cold and heat, so betwixt other sorts; so that it is but in vain to prove all sorts of heat and cold by artificial weather glasses, suppressions and elevations of water, atmospherical parts, and the like: for, it is not the air that makes all cold; no, not that cold which is called elementary, no more than it makes heat; but the corporeal, figurative, self-moving, perceptive, rational and sensitive parts of nature, which make all other creatures, make also heat and cold. Some learned make much ado about "antiperistasis," and the flight of those two contrary qualities, heat and cold, from each other; where, according to their opinion, one of them being surrounded and besieged by the other, retires to the innermost parts of the body, which it possesses; and there by recollecting its forces, and animating itself to a defence, is extended or increased in its degree, and so becomes able to resist its adversary; which they prove by the cold expelled from the earth, and water by the sunbeams, which, they say, retires to the middle region of the air, and there defends itself against the heat that is in the two other, viz. the upper and lower regions; and so it doth in the earth; for, say they, we find in summer, when the air is sultry hot, the cold retreats into cellars and vaults; and in winter, when the air is cold, they are the sanctuary and receptacle of heat; so that the water in wells and springs, and the like places under ground, is found warm and smoking; whenas the water which is exposed to the open air, by cold is congealed into ice. But whatsoever their opinion be, I cannot believe that heat and cold run from each other, as children at bo-peep: for, concerning the earth's being warm in winter, and cold in summer, it is not, in my opinion, caused by hot or cold atoms, flying, like birds, out of their nests, and returning to the same; nor is the earth, like a storehouse, that hoards up cold and heat at several seasons in the year; but there is a natural temper of cold and heat, as well in the earth, as in other creatures; and that vaults, wells, and springs under ground, are warm in winter, when the exterior air is cold: the reason is not, that the heat of the air, or the "calorific atoms,"[79] as they call them, are retired thither, to defend themselves from the coldness of the air; but, they being so deep in the earth, where the cold cannot enter, are kept from the perception of cold, so as they cannot imitate, so well, the motions of cold, as other creatures that are exposed to the open air. The like may be said of the heat of the sun in summer, which cannot penetrate deeper into the bowels of the earth, than cold can. The truth is, the earth is to them like an umbrella, which defends or

---

[79] See Charleton, *Physiologia*, III, ch. 12, § 1, 5.

keeps men from the sun, rain, wind, dust, etc. but although it defends them from the heat of the sun, or coldness of wind; yet they have those qualities naturally within themselves, sometimes more, and sometimes less: and so has the earth its natural temper of heat and cold. But what umbrella the middle region has, whether it be some planet, or anything else, I am not able to determine, unless I had been there, and observed it: Nay, ten to one but I might even then have been mistaken. Wherefore all the contentions and disputes about the doctrine of "antiperistasis," are, in my judgment, to little purpose, since we are not able to know all the differences of heat and cold; for if men conceive there is but one heat and cold in nature, they are mistaken: and much more, if they think they can measure all the several sorts of heat and cold in all creatures, by artificial experiments; for as much as a natural man differs from an artificial statue or picture of a man, so much differs a natural effect from an artificial, which can neither be so good, nor so lasting as a natural one. If Charles' Wain, the axes of the earth, and the motions of the planets, were like the pole, or axes, or wheels of a coach, they would soon be out of order. Indeed, artificial things are pretty toys to employ idle time: Nay, some are very useful for our conveniency; but yet they are but nature's bastards or changelings, if I may so call them: and though nature takes so much delight in variety, that she is pleased with them, yet they are not to be compared to her wise and fundamental actions: for, Nature being a wise and provident lady, governs her parts very wisely, methodically, and orderly: Also, she is very industrious, and hates to be idle, which makes her employ her time as a good housewife does, in brewing, baking, churning, spinning, sowing, etc. as also in preserving, for those that love sweetmeats; and in distilling, for those that take delight in cordials; for she has numerous employments; and being infinitely self–moving, never wants work; but her artificial works, are her works of delight, pleasure and pastime: Wherefore those that employ their time in artificial experiments, consider only nature's sporting or playing actions; but those that view her wise government, in ordering all her parts, and consider her changes, alterations, and tempers in particulars, and their causes, spend their time more usefully and profitable: and truly, to what purpose should a man beat his brains, and weary his body with labours about that wherein he shall lose more time, than gain knowledge? But if anyone would take delight in such things, my opinion is, that our female sex would be the fittest for it; for they most commonly take pleasure in making of sweetmeats, possets, several sorts of pies, puddings, and the like; not so much for their own eating, as to employ their idle time; and it may be, they would prove good experimental philosophers, and inform the world how to make artificial snow, by their creams, or possets beaten into froth: and ice, by their clear, candied, or crusted quiddities, or conserves of fruits: and frost, by their candied herbs and flowers: and hail, by their small comfits made of water and sugar, with whites of eggs: And many other the like figures, which resemble beasts, birds, vegetables, minerals, etc. But the men should study the causes of those experiments: and by this society, the commonwealth would find a great benefit. For the woman was given to man, not only to delight, but to help and assist him; and I am confident, women would labour as much with fire and furnace, as men; for they'll make good cordials and spirits; but whether they would find out the philosophers' stone, I doubt; for our sex is more apt to waste, than to make gold: However, I would have them try, especially those that have means to spend; for, who knows but women might be more happy in finding it out, than men; and then would men have reason to employ their time in more profitable studies, than in useless experiments.

XXVII   Of Congelation and Freezing[80]

The congelation of water into ice, snow, hail, and the like, is made by its own corporeal figurative motions, which upon the perception of the exterior object of cold, by the way of imitation, do contract and condense water into such or such a figure. Some are of opinion, that water, or the like liquors, are not contracted, but expanded, or rarefied by freezing;[81] which they prove both by the levity of congealed water, and the breaking of glasses, earthen bottles, or other the like vessels, in which water is contained when it freezes. But although I mentioned in my former discourse, that there are several sorts of colds; as for example, moist and dry colds; whereof these contract and condense, those dilate and rarefy; so that there are cold dilatations, as well as cold contractions; yet freezing

---

[80] Cf. Aristotle, *Meteorology*, I, chs. 10–12; and IV; Hobbes, *Elements of Philosophy*, IV, ch. 28; Descartes, *Meteorology*, Discourses I and VI; Hooke, *Micrographia*, "Observation XIV: Of Several Kindes of Frozen Figures"; Boyle, *New Experiments and Observations touching Cold* (*WRB*, II, 462ff.).

[81] E.g., in *Meteorology*, Discourse VI and *Principles of Philosophy*, IV, § 31, Descartes offers a mechanical explanation of why water, unlike other bodies, expands when it freezes.

or congelation being none of the sorts of moist, but of dry colds; it is not made by expanding or dilating, but by contracting and condensing motions; for, that liquid bodies when frozen, are more extended, it is not the freezing motions that cause those extensions; but water being of a dilative nature, its interior parts strive against the exterior; which figurative motions do imitate the motions of cold, or frost; and in that strife, the water becomes extended or dilated, when congealed into ice. But the question is, Whether solid bodies do dilate or extend, when they freeze? And my opinion is, they do not; for, that solid bodies, as metal, and like, are apt to break in a hard frost, does not prove an expansion, but the division of their parts is rather made by contraction: for, though the motions of cold in metal, are not so much exteriorly contracting, as to be perceived by our optic sense, in its bulk or exterior magnitude, as they are in the body of water, whose interior nature is dilative: yet, by the division which cold causes, it may well be believed, that freezing hath an interior contractive effect, otherwise it could not divide so, as many times it doth. Wherefore I believe, that solid bodies break by an extreme, and extraordinary contraction of their interior parts, and not by an extraordinary expansion. Besides, this breaking shows a strong self-motion in the action of congealing or freezing; for, the motions of cold are as strong and quick, as the motions of heat: nay, even those experimental philosophers which are so much for expansion, confess themselves, that water is thicker and heavier in winter, than in summer; and that ships draw less water, and that the water can bear greater burdens in winter, than in summer; which doth not prove a rarefaction and expansion, but rather a contraction and condensation of water by cold. They likewise affirm, that some spirituous liquors of a mixt nature, will not expand, but on the contrary, do visibly contract in the act of freezing. Concerning the levity of ice, I cannot believe it to be caused by expansion; for expansion will not make it lighter, but it is only a change of the exterior shape or figure of the body: Neither doth ice prove light, because it will float above water: for, a great ship of wood, which is very heavy, will swim; whenas other sorts of bodies that are light, and little, will sink. Nor are minute bubbles, the cause of the ice's levity, which some do conceive to stick within the ice, and make it light: for, this is but a light and airy opinion, which has no firm ground; and it might as well be said, that airy bubbles are the cause that a ship keeps above water: but though wind and sails make a ship swim faster, yet they will not hinder it from sinking. The truth is, the chief cause of the levity or gravity of bodies, is quantity of bulk, shape, purity and rarity, or grossness and density, and not minute bubbles, or insensible atoms, or pores, unless porous bodies be of less quantity in water, than some dense bodies of the same magnitude. And thus it is the triangular figure of snow that makes it light, and the squareness that makes ice heavier than snow: for, if snow were porous, and its pores were filled with atoms, it would be much heavier than its principle, water. Besides, it is to be observed, that not all kind of water is of the same weight, by reason there are several sorts of circle-lines which make water; and therefore those that measure all water alike, may be mistaken: For, some circle-lines may be gross, some fine, some sharp, some broad, some pointed, etc. all which may cause a different weight of water. Wherefore freezing, in my opinion, is not caused by rarefying and dilating, but by contracting, condensing and retenting motions. And truly, if ice were expanded by congelation, I would fain know, whether its expansions be equal with the degrees of its hardness; which if so, a drop of water might be expanded to a great bigness: Nay, if all frozen liquors should be enlarged or extended in magnitude, according to the strength of the freezing motions, a drop of water at the poles would become (I will not say a mountain, but) a very large body. Neither can rarefaction, in my opinion, be the cause of the ice's expansion; for, not all rarefied bodies do extend: and therefore I do rather believe a clarifaction in ice, than a rarefaction, which are different things. But some may object, that hot and swelling bodies do dilate, and diffuse heat and scent without an expansion of their substance. I answer, That is more than anyone is able to prove: the truth is, when a fiery coal, and an odoriferous body cast heat and scent, (as we used to say) it is not, that they do really and actually expand or dilate heat or scent without body; for there can be no such thing as an immaterial heat or scent; neither can "nothing" be dilated or expanded, but both heat and scent being one thing with the hot and smelling body, are as exterior objects patterned out by the sensitive motions of the sentient body; and so are felt and smelt, not by an actual emission of their own parts, or some heating and smelling atoms, or an immaterial heat and smell, but by an imitation of the perceptive motions in the sentient subject. The like for cold: for, great shelves, or mountains of ice, do not expand cold beyond their icy bodies; but the air patterns out the cold: and so doth the perception of those seamen that sail into cold countries. For, it is well to be observed, that there is a stint or proportion in all nature's corporeal figurative motions, to wit, in her particulars, as we may plainly see in every particular sort or species of creatures, and their constant and orderly productions; for though particular creatures may change into an infinite variety of figures, by the infinite variety of nature's corporeal figurative motions; yet each kind or sort is stinted so much, as it cannot run into extremes, nor make a confusion, although it make a distinguishment between every particular creature, even in one and the same sort. And hence we may conclude, that nature is neither absolutely necessitated, nor has an absolute free will: for, she is so much necessitated, that she depends upon the all-powerful God, and cannot work beyond herself, or beyond her own nature; and yet hath so much liberty, that in her particulars she works as she pleaseth, and as God has given her power; but she being wise, acts according to her infinite natural wisdom, which is the cause of her orderly government in all particular productions, changes and dissolutions; so that all creatures in their particular kinds, do move and work as nature pleases, orders and directs: And therefore, as it is impossible for nature to go beyond herself; so it is likewise impossible, that any particular body should extend beyond itself, or its natural figure. I will not say, that heat or cold, or other parts and figures of nature, may not occasion other bodies to dilate or extend: but, my meaning is, that no heat or cold can extend without body, or beyond body; and that they are figured and patterned out by the motions of the sentient; which imitating or patterning motions of the sentient body, cannot be so perfect or strong, as the original motions in the object itself. Neither do I say, that all parts or bodies do imitate, but some; and at some times there will be more imitators, than at others; and sometimes none at all: and the imitations are according as the imitating or patterning parts are disposed, or as the object is presented. Concerning the degrees of a visible expansion, they cannot be declared otherwise than by the visibly extended body; nor be perceived by us, but by the optic sense. But mistake me not, I do not mean, that the degrees of heat and cold can only be perceived by our optic sense; but I speak of bodies visibly expanded by heat and cold: for, some degrees and sorts of heat and cold, are subject to the human perception of sight, some to the perception of touch, some to both, and some to none of them; there being so many various sorts and degrees both of heat and cold, as they cannot be altogether subject to our grosser exterior senses; but those which are, are perceived, as I said, by our perception of sight and touch; for although our sensitive perceptions do often commit errors and mistakes, either through their own irregularity, or some other ways; yet, next to the rational, they are the best informers we have: for, no man can naturally go beyond his rational and sensitive perception. And thus, in my opinion, the nature of congelation is not effected by expanding or dilating, but contracting and condensing motions in the parts of the sentient body; which motions in the congelation of water, do not alter the interior nature of water, but only contract its exterior figure into the figure either of ice, snow, hail, hoarfrost, or the like, which may be proved by their return into the former figure of water, whensoever they dissolve; for, wheresoever is a total change, or alteration of the interior natural motions of a creature, when once dissolved, it will never regain its former figure; and therefore, although the exterior figures of congealed water are various and different, yet they have all but one interior figure, which is water, into which they return, as into their principle, whensoever they change their exterior figures by dissolving and dilating motions; for as a laughing and frowning countenance doth not change the nature of a man, so neither do they the nature of water. I do not speak of artificial, but of natural congealed figures, whose congelation is made by their own natural figurative motions. But although all congelations are some certain kind of motions, yet there may be as many particular sorts of congelations, as there are several sorts of frozen or congealed bodies; for though I name but one figure of snow, another of ice, another of hail, etc. yet I do not deny but there may be numerous particular sorts and figures of ice, snow, hail, etc. all which may have their several freezing or congealing motions: nay, freezing in this respect may very well be compared to burning, as being opposite actions: And as there are various sorts of burning, much differing from each other, so there are of freezing: for, although all burning is of the nature of fire, yet not all burning is an elemental fire: for example, lime, and some vegetables, and other creatures, have burning effects, and yet are not an elemental fire: neither doth the sun, and ordinary fire, burn just alike. The same may be said of freezing. And I observe, that fluid and rare parts are more apt to freeze, than solid and dense bodies; for, I do not believe all sorts of metal can freeze, so as water, or watery liquors, unless they were made liquid. I will not say, that minerals are altogether insensible of cold or frost; but they do not freeze like liquid bodies; nay, not all liquid bodies will freeze: As for example, some sorts of spirituous liquors, oil, vinous spirits, chemical extracts, etc. which proves, that not all the infinite parts of nature, are subject to one particular kind of action, to wit, the action of freezing: for, if congelation did extend to the infinite parts of nature, it would not be a finite and particular, but an infinite action: but, as I said, liquid bodies are more apt to freeze, (especially water, and watery liquors) than dense and hard bodies, or some sorts of oil, and spirits; for, as we see that fire cannot have the same operation on all bodies alike, but some it causes to consume and turn to ashes; some it hardens, some it softens, and on some it hath no power at all. So its opposite frost or cold cannot congeal every natural body, but only those which are apt to freeze or imitate the motions of cold. Neither do all these bodies freeze alike, but some slower, some quicker; some into such, and some into another figure: As for example, even in one kind of creatures, as animals, some beasts, as foxes, bears, and the like, are not so much sensible of cold, as man, and some other animal creatures; and dead animals or parts of dead animals, will freeze much sooner than those which are living; not that living animals have more natural life than those we call dead: for animals, when dissolved from their animal figure, although they have not animal life, yet they have life according to the nature of the figure into which they did change; but, because of their different perceptions: for, a dead or dissolved animal, as it is of another kind of figure than a living animal, so it has also another kind of perception, which causes it to freeze sooner than a living animal doth. But I cannot apprehend what some learned mean by the powerful effects of cold upon inanimate bodies; whether they mean, that cold is only animate, and all another bodies inanimate; or, whether both cold and other bodies on which it works, be inanimate: If the latter, I cannot conceive how inanimate bodies can work upon each other, I mean such bodies as have neither life nor motion; for without life or motion, there can be no action: but if the former, I would fain know whether cold be self-moving? If not, I ask, What is that which moves it? Is it an imma-terial spirit, or some corporeal being? If an immaterial spirit, we must allow, that the spirit is either self-moving, or must be moved by another; if it be moved by another being, and that same being, again by another, we shall after this manner run into infinite, and conclude nothing: But if that immaterial spirit have self-motion, why may not a natural corporeal being, have the like? they being both creatures of God, who can as well grant self-motion to a corporeal, as to an incorporeal being: nay, I am not able to comprehend how motion can be attributed to a spirit; I mean, natural motion, which is only a propriety of a body, or of a corporeal being: but if cold is self-moving, then nature is self moving; for the cause can be no less than the effect: and if nature be self-moving, no part of nature can be inanimate; for, as the body is, so are its parts; and as the cause, so its effects. Thus some learned do puzzle themselves and the world with useless distinctions, into animate and inanimate creatures; and are so much afraid of self-motion, as they will rather maintain absurdities and errors, than allow any other self-motion in nature, but what is in themselves: for, they would fain be above nature, and petty gods, if they could but make themselves infinite; not considering that they are but parts of nature, as all other creatures: Wherefore I, for my part, will rather believe as sense and reason guides me, and not according to interest, so as to extol my own kind above all the rest, or above nature herself. And thus, to return to cold: As congelation is not an universal or infinite action, which extends to the infinite parts of nature, and causes not the like effects in those creatures that are perceptible of it; so I do also observe, that not any other sorts of bodies but water, will congeal into the figure of snow, whenas there are many that will turn into the figure of ice: besides, I observe, that air doth not freeze beyond its degree of consistency; for if it did, no animal creature would be able to breathe, since all, or most of them are subject to such a sort of respiration, as requires a certain intermediate degree of air, neither too thick, nor too thin: What respirations other creatures require, I am not able to determine; for as there are several infinite parts and actions of nature, so also several sorts of respirations; and I believe, that what is called the ebbing and flowing of the sea, may be the sea's respiration; for nature has ordered for every part or creature, that which is most fitting and proper for it.

Concerning artificial congelations, as to turn water or snow into the figure of ice, by the commixture of salt, nitre, alum, or the like, it may, very probably, be effected: for water, and watery liquors, their interior figure being circular, may easily change, by contracting that circular figure into a triangle or square; that is, into ice or snow (for water, in my opinion, has a round or circular interior figure, snow a triangular, and ice a square; I do not mean an exact mathematical triangle or square, but such an one as is proper for their figure) and that the mixture of those, or the like ingredients, being shaken together in a vial, doth produce films of ice on the outside of the glass, as experimenters relate; proves, not only that the motions of cold are very strong, but also that there is perception in all parts of nature, and that all congelations, both natural and artificial, are made by the corporeal perceptive motions, which the sentient has of exterior cold; which is also the reason that salt being mixt with snow, makes the liquor always freeze first on that side of the vessel where the mixture is: for, those parts which are nearest, will imitate first the motions of frost, and after them, the neighbouring parts, until they be all turned into ice. The truth is, that all or most artificial experiments, are the best arguments to evince, there is perception in all corporeal parts of nature: for, as parts are joined, or commix with parts, so they move or work accordingly into such or such figures, either by the way of imitation, or otherwise; for their motions are so various, as it is impossible for one particular to describe them all; but no motion can be without perception, because every part or particle of nature, as it is self-moving, so it is also self-knowing and perceptive; for matter, self-motion, knowledge, and perception, are all but one thing, and no more differing nor separable from each other, than body, place, magnitude, colour and figure. Wherefore experimental philosophers cannot justly blame me for maintaining the opinion of self-motion, and a general perception in nature.

But to return to artificial congelations: There is as much difference between natural and artificial ice and snow, as there is between chalk and cheese, or between a natural child, and a baby made of paste or wax, and gummed silk; or between artificial glass, and natural diamonds: The like may be said of hail, frost, wind, etc. for though their exterior figures do resemble, yet their interior natures are quite different; and therefore, although by the help of art, some may make ice of water or snow, yet we cannot conclude from hence, that all natural ice is made the same way, by saline particles, or acid spirits, and the like; for if nature should work like art, she would produce a man like as a carver makes a statue, or a painter draws a picture: beside, it would require a world of such saline or acid particles, to make all the ice that is in nature. Indeed, it is as much absurdity, as impossibility, to constitute some particular action the common principle of all natural heat and cold, and to make an universal cause, of a particular effect: for, no particular part or action, can be prime in nature, or a fundamental principle of other creatures or actions, although it may occasion some creatures to move after such or such a way. Wherefore, those that will needs have a *primum frigidum*, or some body which they suppose must of necessity be supremely cold, and by participation of which, all other cold bodies obtain that quality, whereof some do contend for earth, some for water, others for air; some for nitre, and others for salt, do all break their heads to no purpose:[82] for first, there are no extremes in nature, and therefore no body can be supremely cold, nor supremely hot. Next, as I said, it is impossible to make one particular sort of creatures, the principle of all the various sorts of heat or cold that are in nature: for, there is an elemental heat and cold, a vegetable, mineral, animal heat and cold; and there may be many other sorts which we do not know: And how can either earth, or water, or nitre, or salt, be the principle of all these different colds? Concerning the earth, we see that some parts of the earth are hot, and some cold; the like of water and air: and the same parts which are now hot, will often in a moment grow cold; which shows they are as much subject to the perception of heat and cold, as some other creatures, and doth plainly deny to them the possibility of being a *primum frigidum*. I have mentioned in my poetical works, that there is a sun in the center of the earth; and in another place, I have described a chemical heat; but these being but poetical fancies, I will not draw them to any serious proofs; only this I will say, that there may be degrees of heat and cold in the earth, and in water, as well as there are in the air; for certainly the earth is not without motion, a dull, dead, moveless and inanimate body; but it is as much internally active, as air and water are externally; which is evident enough by the various productions of vegetables, minerals, and other bodies that derive their offspring out of the earth: And as for nitre and salt, although they may occasion some sorts of colds, in some sorts of bodies, like some sorts of food, or tempers of air, or the like, may work such or such effects in some sorts of creatures; yet this doth not prove that they are the only cause of all kinds of heat and cold that are in nature. The truth is, if air, water, earth, nitre, or salt, or insensible, roving, and wandering atoms, should be the only cause of cold, then there would be no difference of hot and cold climates, but it would freeze as well under the line, as it doth at the poles. But there's such a stir kept about atoms, as that they are so full of action, and produce all

[82] Boyle, in *New Experiments and Observations touching Cold*, summarizes the major positions on the question of whether there is "some body or other, that is of its own nature supremely cold, and by participation of which, all other cold bodies obtain that quality"; he notes that Plutarch took the *primum frigidum* to be earth; Aristotle took it to be water; the Stoics and modern non-Aristotelians held that it was air; Gassendi and others said that it was nitrous exhalations, or steams of salt-peter, sea salt or spirit of nitre (*WRB*, II, 585ff.). Cf. Charleton, *Physiologia*, III, ch. 12, § II, 6ff.

things in the world, and yet none describes by what means they move, or from where they have this active power.

[Here some perhaps may say, that my position implies an absurdity; it being unreasonable to constitute some particular action, the common principle of all natural heat and cold.

I answer, therefore, that it is not more absurd, than that all men should be produced from one man, or at least, from one kind or sort of action: But, all animals are not produced from man, nor from one sort of action: For, fowls are not produced as fishes are; nor fishes as beasts; nor beasts as worms; nor all worms as silkworms; nor any of the forementioned living creatures, as maggots, out of cheese, or fruits; or as lice out of men; and a million of other insects, which I can neither enumerate, nor declare how they are produced.

But this one question I ask, Were all *black Moors*, who seem a kind or race of men different from the white, produced from *Adam?* Doubtless they were. For *Negroes* are still produced by the same action, or way of generation, as white men are. So are *beasts*, yet *Adam* had no hand in their production. And though all beasts have one common way of production, yet must every several kind or sort of them have a several original or principle; that is, they must arise from some corporeal thing of a different species. Now the like may be said of all sorts of heat or cold; so that one prime action or motion cannot produce all sorts of heat or cold. For, though all sorts of heat or cold, are still heat and cold (as all sorts of animals, are still animals) yet all the several sorts or kinds of them, are not one and the same kind, but different. Nor does one particular action, produce all those several sorts or kinds. For, if there were no differences in their productions, then would not only all men be exactly like, but all beasts also; that is, there would be no difference between a horse and a cow, a cow and a lion, a snake and an oyster. The same holds good, likewise, of all *vegetables*; though all of them be either sowed, or planted, or engrafted, yet the actions of their productions are different, otherwise there could be no difference between a pear and a plum. But man is apt to judge according to what he, by his senses, perceives of the exterior parts of corporeal actions of objects, and not by their interior difference; and nature's variety is beyond man's sensitive perception. I conclude therefore, with what I formerly said, namely, that, "nor all animals, nor all vegetables are produced after one and the same manner or way, much less by one and the same kind or sort of motion or action."[83] For, a maggot is not produced as an ass is; and for vegetables, there is no less difference in the manner of their production; sowing being different from setting, and engrafting different from both.][84]

Lastly, some are of opinion, that the chief cause of all cold, and its effects, is wind;[85] which they describe to be air moved in a considerable quantity, and that either forwards only, or in an undulating motion: which opinion, in my judgment, is as erroneous as any of the former, and infers another absurdity, which is, that all winds are of the same nature; whenas there are as many several sorts, and differences of winds, as of other creatures; for there are several winds in several creatures: Winds in the earth are of another kind than those in the air; and the wind of an animal breath, is different from both; nay, those that are in the air, are of different sorts; some cold and dry, some hot and moist, and some temperate, etc. which, how they can all produce the effect of cold or freezing, by the compression of the air, I am not able to judge: Only this I dare say, that if wind causes cold or frost, then in the midst of the summer, or in hot climates, a vehement wind would always produce a great frost; besides, it would prove, that there must of necessity be far greater winds at the poles, than under the equinoctial, there being the greatest cold. Neither will this principle be able to resolve the question, why a man that has an ague, feels a shaking cold, even under the line, and in the coldest weather, when there is no stirring of the least wind. All which proves, that it is very improbable that wind should be the principle of all natural cold; and therefore it remains firm, that self-moving matter, or corporeal, figurative self-motion, as it is the prime and only cause of all natural effects, so it is also of cold, and heat, and wind, and of all the changes and alterations in nature; which is, and hath always been my

---

[83] Cf. "when I consider the variety of nature, it will not give me leave to think that all things are produced after one and the same manner or way; by reason the figurative motions are too different, and too diversely various, to be tied to one way of acting in all productions" (*Observations*, p. 67) and "in animal kind, creations or productions are not after one and the same manner o[r] way . . . so for vegetables, as some by the way of sowing seeds, some by the way of planting slips, and some by the way of grafting or inoculating . . ." (*Opinions*, 1663, pp. 24–25).

[84] Lacking in 1666.

[85] See, e.g., Hobbes, *Elements of Philosophy*, IV, ch. 28. Her own view may be influenced by Van Helmont's doctrine of *blas*, the vital force that accounts for all motion and change: *blas humanum* controls pulse, motion of the blood and heart, and vital heat; *blas metereon* directs the motions of heavenly bodies and meteorological change; *blas alterativum* governs heat and cold, and so condensation and rarefaction. On the nature of wind, see also Aristotle, *Meteorology*, II. chs. 4–6; Descartes, *Meteorology*, Discourse IV.

constant, and, in my simple judgment, the most probable and rational opinion in natural philosophy.

XXVIII   Of Thawing or Dissolving of Frozen Bodies

As freezing or congelation is caused by contracting, condensing, and retentive motions; so thawing is nothing else but dissolving, dilating, and extending motions: for, freezing and thawing are two contrary actions; and as freezing is caused several ways, according to the various disposition of congealable bodies, and the temper of exterior cold; so thawing, or a dissolution of frozen bodies, may be occasioned either by a sympathetic agreement, (as for example, the thawing of ice in water, or other liquors) or by some exterior imitation, as by hot dilating motions. And it is to be observed, that, as the time of freezing, so the time of dissolving, is according to the several natures and tempers both of the frozen bodies themselves, and the exterior objects applied to frozen bodies, which occasion their thawing or dissolution: for, it is not only heat that doth cause ice, or snow, or other frozen bodies to melt quicker or slower; but, according as the nature of the heat is, either more or less dilative, or more or less rarefying: for surely, an exterior actual heat, is more rarefying than an interior virtual heat; as we see in strong spirituous liquors which are interiorly contracting, but being made actually hot, become exteriorly dilating: The like of many other bodies; so that actual heat is more dissolving than virtual heat. And this is the reason why ice and snow will melt sooner in some countries or places, than in others; and is much harder in some, than in others: for we see, that neither air, water, earth, minerals, nor any other sorts of creatures are just alike in all countries or climates: The same may be said of heat and cold. Besides, it is to be observed, that oftentimes a different application of one and the same object, will occasion different effects; as for example, if salt be mixed with ice, it may cause the contracted body of ice to change its present motions into its former state or figure, viz. into water; but being applied outwardly, or on the outside of the vessel wherein snow or ice is contained, it may make it freeze harder instead of dissolving it. Also, ice will oftentimes break into pieces of its own accord, and without the application of any exterior object: And the reason, in my opinion, is, that some of the interior parts of the ice endeavouring to return to their proper and natural figure by virtue of their interior dilative motions, do break and divide some of the exterior parts that are contracted by the motions of frost, especially those which have not so great a force or power as to resist them.

But concerning thawing, some by their trials have found, that if frozen eggs, apples, and the like bodies, be thawed near the fire, they will be thereby spoiled: but if they be immersed in cold water, or wrapt into ice or snow, the internal cold will be drawn out, as they suppose, by the external; and the frozen bodies will be harmlessly, though not so quickly, thawed. And truly, this experiment stands much to reason; for, in my opinion, when frozen bodies perceive heat or fire, the motions of their frozen parts, upon the perception, endeavour to imitate the motions of heat or fire; which being opposite to the motions of cold, in this sudden and hasty change, they become irregular, insomuch as to cause in most frozen parts a dissolution of their interior natural figure: Wherefore it is very probable, that frozen bodies will thaw more regularly in water, or being wrapt into ice or snow, than by heat or fire: for, thawing is a dilating action; and water, as also ice and snow, (which are nothing but congealed water) being of a dilative nature, may easily occasion a thawing of the mentioned frozen parts, by sympathy; provided the motions of the exterior cold do not overpower the motions of the interior frozen parts: for, if a frozen body should be wrapt thus into ice or snow, and continue in an open, cold, frosty air, I question whether it would cause a thaw in the same body; it would preserve the body in its frozen state, from dissolving or disuniting, rather than occasion its thawing. But that such frozen bodies, as apples, and eggs, etc. immersed in water, will produce ice on their outsides, is no wonder, by reason the motions of water imitate the motions of the frozen bodies; and those parts of water that are nearest, are the first imitators, and become of the same mode. By which we may see, that some parts will clothe themselves, others only veil themselves with artificial dresses; most of which dresses are but copies of other motions, and not original actions: It makes also evident, that those effects are not caused by an ingress of frigorific atoms in water, or other congealable bodies, but by the perceptive motions of their own parts. And what I have said of cold, the same may be spoken of heat; for it is known, that a part of a man's body being burned with fire, the burning may be cured by the heat of the fire; which, in my opinion, proceeds from a sympathetical agreement betwixt the motions of the fire, and the motions of the burned part: for every part of a man's body hath its natural heat, which is of an intermediate temper; which heat being heightened by the burning motions of fire, beyond its natural degree, causes a burning and smarting pain in the same part: And therefore, as the fire did occasion an immoderate heat, by an intermixture of its own parts with the parts of the flesh; so a moderate heat of the fire may reduce again the natural heat of the same parts, and that by a sympathetical agreement betwixt the motions of the elemental and animal heat. But it is to be observed, first, that the burning must be done by an intermixture of the fire with the parts of the body: Next, that the burning must be but skin-deep, (as we used to call it) that is, the burned part must not be totally overcome by fire, or else it will never be restored again. Neither are all burned bodies restored after this manner, but some; for one and the same thing will not in all bodies occasion the like effects; as we may see by fire, which being one and the same, will not cause all fuels to burn alike; and this makes true the old saying, "One man's meat, is another man's poison." The truth is, it cannot be otherwise: for, though nature, and natural self-moving matter is but one body, and the only cause of all natural effects; yet, nature being divided into infinite, corporeal, figurative self-moving parts; these parts, as the effects of that only cause, must needs be various, and again, proceeding from one infinite cause, as one matter, they are all but one thing, because they are infinite parts of one infinite body. But some may say, If nature be but one body, and the infinite parts are all united into that same body; how comes it that there is such an opposition, strife and war, betwixt the parts of nature? I answer: Nature being material, is composable and dividable; and as composition is made by a mutual agreement of parts, so division is made by an opposition or strife betwixt parts; which opposition or division, doth not obstruct the union of nature, but, on the contrary, rather proves, that without an opposition of parts, there could not be a union or composition of so many several parts and creatures, nor no change or variety in nature; for if all the parts did unanimously conspire and agree in their motions, and move all but one way, there would be but one act or kind of motion in nature; whenas an opposition of some parts, and a mutual agreement of others, is not only the cause of the miraculous variety in nature, but it poises and balances, as it were, the corporeal figurative motions, which is the cause that nature is steady and fixt in herself, although her parts be in a perpetual motion.

XXIX   Several Questions Resolved Concerning Cold, and Frozen Bodies

First, I will give you my answer to the question, which is much agitated among the learned, concerning cold, to wit, Whether it be a positive quality, or a bare privation of heat?[86] And my opinion is, that cold is both a positive quality, and a privation of heat: For, whatsoever is a true quality of cold, must needs be a privation of heat; since two opposites cannot subsist together in one and the same part, at one point of time. By privation, I mean nothing else, but an alteration of nature's actions in her several parts; or, which is all one, a change of natural, corporeal motions: and so the death of animals may be called a privation of animal life; that is, a change of the animal motions in that particular creature, which made animal life, to some other kind of action which is not animal life.[87] And in this sense, both cold and heat, although they be positive qualities, or natural beings; yet they are also privations; that is, changes of corporeal, figurative motions, in several particular creatures, or parts of nature. But what some learned mean by "bare privation," I cannot apprehend: for, there's no such thing as a bare privation, or bare motion in nature; but all motion is corporeal, or material; for matter, motion and figure, are but one thing: Which is the reason, that to explain myself the better, when I speak of motion, I do always add the word "corporeal," or "figurative"; by which, I exclude all bare or immaterial motion, which expression is altogether against sense and reason.

The second question is, Whether winds have the power to change the exterior temper of the air? To which I answer: that winds will not only occasion the air to be either hot or cold, according to their own temper, but also animals and vegetables, and other sorts of creatures: for, the

---

[86] Descartes held that heat is caused by the rapid motion of corpuscles; see, e.g., *Le monde . . ., ou Traité de la lumière . . .* [The World or Treatise on Light] (Paris, 1664), ch. 2. There was a debate between those who held that cold is simply a privation or lack of that motion, and those, e.g., Gassendi, who held that cold is a positive quality caused by the slowing and deadening activity of "frigorifick atoms"; see Charleton, *Physiologia*, III, ch. 12, § II. Cf. Boyle, *Of the Mechanical Origins of Heat and Cold* (1675) (*WRB*, IV, 244ff.).

[87] Cf. Cavendish's gloss with that of the schoolmen: "The term privation is used . . . when a thing does not have in any way some attribute which it is capable of having, for example, when an animal does not have sight. And this occurs in two ways: first, if it does not have it in any way at all; and second, if it does not have it in some definite respect, for example at some definite time or in some definite manner . . ." (St. Thomas Aquinas, *Commentary on Aristotle's Metaphysics*, tr. John Rowan (Notre Dame: Dumb Ox Books, 1995), bk X, lesson 6, no. 2043. See also Aristotle, *Categories*, 10 and *Metaphysics*, V, 22.

sensitive, corporeal motions in several kinds of creatures, do often imitate and figure out the motions of exterior objects, some more, some less; some regularly, and some irregularly; and some not at all, according to the nature of their own perceptions. By which we may observe, that the agent, which is the external object, has only an occasional power; and the patient, which is the sentient, works chiefly the effect by virtue of the perceptive, figurative motions in its own sensitive organs or parts.

Question 3. Why those winds that come from cold regions, are most commonly cold; and those that come from hot regions, are for the most part hot? I answer: The reason is, that those winds have more constantly patterned out the motions of cold or heat in those parts from which they either separated themselves, or which they have met withal. But it may be questioned, Whether all cold and hot winds do bring their heat and cold along with them, out of such hot and cold countries? And I am of opinion they do not; but that they proceed from an imitation of the nearest parts, which take patterns from other parts; and these again from the remoter parts; so that they are but patterns of other patterns, and copies of other copies.

Question 4. Why fire in some cold regions, will hardly kindle, or at least, not burn freely? I answer: This is no more to be wondered at, than that some men do die with cold: For, cold being contrary to fire, if it have a predominant power, it will, without doubt, put out the fire: Not that the cold corporeal motions do destroy fire by their actual power over it; but, that fire destroys itself by an imitation of the motions of cold: So that cold is only an occasional cause of the fire's destruction, or at least, of the alteration of its motions, and the diminution of its strength. But some might ask, What makes, or causes this imitation in several sorts of creatures? I answer, The wisdom of nature, which orders her corporeal actions to be always in a mean, so that one extreme (as one may call it) does countervail another. But then, you'll say, There would always be a right and mean temper to all things. I answer: So there is in the whole; that is, in infinite nature, although not in every particular: for, nature's wisdom orders her particulars to the best of the whole; and although particulars do oppose each other, yet all opposition tends to the conservation of a general peace and unity in the whole. But to return to fire: Since air is the proper matter of respiration for fire, extreme colds and frosts, either of air or vapour, are as unfit for the respiration of fire, as water is; which if it do not kill it quite, yet it will at least make it sick, pale and faint; but if water be rarefied to such a degree, that it becomes thin vapour, then it is as proper for its respiration, as air. Thus we see, although fire hath fuel, which is its food; yet no food can keep it alive, without breath or respiration. The like may be said of some other creatures.

Question 5. Whether wood be apt to freeze? My answer is, that I believe that the moist part of wood, which is sap, may freeze as hard as water; but the solid parts cannot do so: for, the cracking noise of wood is no proof of its being frozen, because wainscot will make such a noise in summer, as well as in winter. And it is to be observed, that some bodies will be apter to freeze in a weak, than in a hard frost, according to their own dispositions; which is as much to be considered, as the object of cold or frost itself: for, some bodies do more, and some less imitate the motions of some objects, and some not at all. And thus we see, that solid bodies do only imitate the contractive motions of cold, but not the dilative motions of moisture, which is the cause they break in a hard frost, as a string, which being tied too hard, will fly asunder; and as they imitate cold, so they do also imitate thaw.

Question 6. Whether water be fluid in its nature, or but occasionally, by the agitation of the air? I answer: that water is fluid in its own nature, needs no proof, but is known enough by the force of its dilating motions: for water, when it gets but liberty, it overflows all, and dilates every-where: Which proves, it is not air that makes it fluid; but it is so in its own nature.

Question 7. What produces those great precipices and mountains of ice which are found in the sea, and other great waters? I answer: that snow, as also thick fogs and mists, which are nothing but rarefied water, falling upon the ice, make its outside thicker; and many great shelves, and broken pieces of ice, joining together, produce such precipices and mountains as mentioned.

Question 8. Whether fishes can live in frozen water? I answer: If there be as much water left unfrozen, as will serve them for respiration, they may live: for it is well known, that water is the chief matter of respiration for fish, and not air: for, fish being out of water, cannot live long; but whilst they live, they gasp and gape for water. I mean, such kinds of fish which do live altogether in water, and not such creatures as are of a mixt kind, and live in water as well as land, which the learned call amphibious creatures, as otters, and the like, which may live in the air, as well as in water: Those fish, I say, if the water be thoroughly frozen, or if but the surface of water be quite frozen over to a pretty depth, will often die; by reason the water that remains unfrozen, by the contraction of ice, has altered for that time, its dilative motions, to retentive motions: and, like as men are smothered in a close air, so fish in close water; that is, in water which is quite covered and enclosed with ice: But, as some men have not so nice and tender natures as others; and some have larger organs for respiration, than others; and some are more accustomed to some sorts of air, than others; which may cause them to endure longer, or respire more freely than others: so some fishes do live longer in such close waters, than others: And some may be like men that are frostbitten, which may chance to live even in those waters that are quite thoroughly frozen, as experimenters relate; but yet I cannot believe, that the water, in which fishes have been observed to live, can be so thoroughly frozen to solid ice, that it should not leave some liquidity or wetness in it, although not perceptible by our sight, by which those fishes were preserved alive: However, it is more probable for fish to live in ice, than other creatures; because the principle of ice, is water, which is the matter of the fishes' respiration, which keeps them alive.

Question 9. Whether in decoctions of herbs, when congealed or frozen into ice, the figures of the herbs do appear in the ice? This is affirmed for truth by many learned; and though I do not deny, but that such liquors, in freezing, may have some resemblance of their solid parts; yet I do not believe it to be universal: for, if the blood of an animal should be congealed into ice, I doubt it would hardly represent the figure of an animal. Indeed there's much difference between the exterior figures of creatures, and their interior natures; which is evident even in frozen water, whose exterior icy figures are numerous, whenas their interior nature is but water: And there may also several changes and alterations of exterior figures be made by art, when their interior nature is but one and the same.

Question 10. Whether cold doth preserve bodies from corruption? I answer: that, in my opinion, it may be very probable: For, corruption or putrefaction, is nothing but irregular dissolving motions; whenas freezing or congelation is made by regular, contracting and condensing motions; and so long as these motions of freezing are in force, it is impossible the motions that make corruption, should work their effect. But that such bodies as have been thoroughly frozen, after being thawed, are most commonly spoiled; the reason is, that the freezing or congealing motions, being not natural to those bodies, have caused such a thorough alteration of the natural motions of their parts, as a hundred to one; but they will never move regularly and orderly again afterward; but on the contrary, their interior motions do quite and absolutely change; by which the figure is totally altered from its former nature. But if a solid body be not thoroughly frozen, it may be reduced to a perfect regularity again; for those natural motions that are not altered, may occasion the rest to act as formerly, to the preservation of that figure.

XXX   Of Contraction and Dilatation

There have been, and are still great disputes amongst the learned, concerning contraction and extension of bodies: but, if I were to decide their controversy, I would ask, first, Whether they did all agree in one principle? that is, whether their principle was purely natural, and not mixt with divine or supernatural things: for, if they did not well apprehend one another's meaning, or argued upon different principles, it would be but a folly to dispute, because it would be impossible for them to agree. But concerning contraction and dilatation, my opinion is, that there can be no contraction nor extension of a single part, by reason there is no such thing as a single or indivisible part in nature: for, even that which the learned call an atom, although they make it a single body, yet being material or corporeal, it must needs be divisible: Wherefore all contraction and dilatation consists of parts, as much as body doth; and there is no body that is not contractive and dilative, as well as it is dividable and composable: for, parts are, as it were, the effects of a body, by reason there is no body without parts; and contraction and extension, are the effects of parts; and magnitude and place are the effects of contraction and extension: And all these are the effects of corporeal, figurative self-motion, which I have more fully declared in several places of my philosophical works.

But some may say, It is impossible that a body can make itself bigger or less, than by nature it is. My answer is: I do not conceive what is meant by being little or great by nature: for, nature is in a perpetual motion, and so are her parts, which do work, intermix, join, divide, and move according as nature pleases, without any rest or intermission. Now if there be such changes of parts and motions, it is impossible that there can be any constant figure in Nature; I mean, so as not to have its changes of motions, as well as the rest, although they be not all after the same manner: and, if there can be no constant figure in nature, there can neither be a constant littleness or greatness, nor a constant rarity or density; but all parts of nature must change according to their motions: for, as parts divide and compose, so are their figures: and since there are contracting and dilating motions, as well as there are of other sorts; there are also contracting and dilating parts; and if there be contracting and dilating parts, then their magnitude changes accordingly: for, magnitude doth not barely consist in quantity, but in the extension of the parts of the body; and as the magnitude of a body is, so is place; so that place is larger, or less, according as the body contracts or dilates; for it is well to be observed, that it is not the interior figure of any part or creature of nature, that alerts by contraction or dilatation: For example; gold or quicksilver is not changed from being gold or quicksilver, when it is rarefied; but only that figure puts itself into several postures. Which proves, that the extension of a body, is not made by an addition or intermixture of foreign parts, as composition; nor contraction, by a diminution of its own parts, as division; for dilatation and composition, as also division and contraction, are different actions: The dilatation of a body, is an extension of its own parts, but composition is an addition of foreign parts; and contraction, although it makes the body less in magnitude, yet it loses nothing of its own parts. The truth is, as division and composition, are natural corporeal motions, so are contraction and dilatation: and as both composition and division belong to parts, so do contraction and dilatation; for there can be no contraction or dilatation of a single part.

XXXI   Of the Parts of Nature, and of Atoms

Although I am of opinion, that nature is a self-moving, and consequently a self-living and self-knowing infinite body, divisible into infinite parts; yet I do not mean, that these parts are atoms; for there can be no atom, that is, an indivisible body in nature; because whatsoever has body, or is material, has quantity; and what has quantity, is divisible. But some may say, If a part be finite, it cannot be divisible into infinite. To which I answer, that there is no such thing as one finite single part in nature: for when I speak of the parts of nature, I do not understand, that those parts are like grains of corn or sand in one heap, all of one figure or magnitude, and separable from each other: but, I conceive nature to be an infinite body, bulk or magnitude, which by its own self-motion, is divided into infinite parts; not single or indivisible parts, but parts of one continued body, only discernible from each other by their proper figures, caused by the changes of particular motions: for, it is well to be observed, first, that nature is corporeal, and therefore divisible. Next, that nature is self-moving, and therefore never at rest: I do not mean exteriorly moving; for nature being infinite, is all within itself, and has nothing without, or beyond it, because it is without limits or bounds: but interiorly, so that all the motions that are in nature, are within herself; and being various and infinite in their changes, they divide the substance or body of nature into infinite parts; for the parts of nature, and changes of motion, are but one thing: for, were there no motion, there would be no change of figures. It is true, matter in its own nature would be divisible, because wheresoever is body, there are parts: but, if it had no motion, it would not have such various changes of figures as it hath: Wherefore it is well to be considered, that self-motion is throughout all the body of nature; and that no part or figure, how small soever, can be without self-motion; and according as the motions are, so are the parts; for infinite changes of motions, make infinite parts: nay, what we call one finite part, may have infinite changes, because it may be divided and composed infinite ways. By which it is evident, first, that no certain quantity or figure can be assigned to the parts of nature, as I said before of the grains of corn or sand; for infinite changes of motions, produce infinite varieties of figures; and all the degrees of density, rarity, levity, gravity, slowness, quickness; nay, all the effects that are in nature. Next, that it is impossible to have single parts in nature, that is, parts which are indivisible in themselves, as atoms; and may subsist single, or by themselves, precised or separated from all other parts: for, although there are perfect and whole figures in nature, yet are they nothing else but parts of nature, which consist of a composition of other parts, and their figures make them discernible from other parts or figures of nature. For example: an eye, although it be composed of parts, and has a whole and perfect figure, yet it is but part of the head, and could not subsist without it. Also the head, although it has a whole and perfect figure, yet it is a part of the body, and could not subsist without it. The same may be said of all other particular and perfect figures: As for example, an animal, though it be a whole and perfect figure, yet it is but a part of earth, and some other elements, and parts of nature, and could not subsist without them; nay, for anything we know to the contrary, the elements cannot subsist without other creatures. All which proves, that there are no single parts, nor vacuum, nor no[88] composition of loose atoms in nature; for if such a whole and perfect figure would be divided into millions of other parts and figures, yet it is impossible to divide it into single parts, by reason there is as much composition, as there is division in nature; and as soon as parts are divided from such or such parts, at that instant of time, and by the same act of division, they are joined to other parts, and all this, because nature is a body of a continued infiniteness, without any holes or vacuities. Nay, were it possible that there could be a single part, that is, a part separated from all the rest; yet being a part of nature, it must consist of the same substance as nature herself; but nature is an infinite composition of rational, sensitive and inanimate matter: which although they do constitute but one body, because of their close and inseparable conjunction and commixture; nevertheless, they are several parts, (for one part is not another part) and therefore every part or particle of nature, consisting of the same commixture, cannot be single or indivisible. Thus it remains firm, that self-motion is the only cause of the various parts and changes of figures; and that when parts move or separate themselves from parts, they move and join to other parts, at the same point of time: I do not mean, that parts do drive or press upon each other; for those are forced and constraint actions; whenas natural self-motions are free and voluntary. And although there are pressures and reactions in nature, yet they are not universal actions. Neither is there any such thing as a stoppage in the actions of nature, nor do parts move though empty spaces; but as some parts join, so others divide by the same act: for, although some parts can quit such or such parts, yet they cannot quit all parts: For example, a man goes a hundred miles, he leaves or quits those parts from whence he removed first; but as soon as he removes from such parts, he joins to other parts, were his motion no more than a hairsbreadth; so that all his journey is nothing else but a division and composition of parts, wheresoever he goes, by water, or by land; for it is impossible for him to quit parts in general, although it be in his choice to quit such or such particular parts, and to join to what parts he will.

[88] The reader needs to be aware that a double negative is typically used by Cavendish to express a negative sense; this is one of those instances.

When I speak of motion, I desire to be understood, that I do not mean any other but corporeal motion; for there is no other motion in nature: So that generation, dissolution, alteration, augmentation, diminution, transformation; nay, all the actions of sense and reason, both interior, and exterior, and what motions soever in nature, are corporeal; although they are not all perceptible by our exterior senses: for, our senses are too gross to perceive all the curious and various actions of nature; and it would be but a folly to deny, what our senses cannot perceive: for, although sense and reason are the same in all creatures and parts of nature, not having any degrees in themselves, no more than self-knowledge hath; (for self-knowledge can but be self-knowledge, and sense and reason can but be sense and reason;) yet they do not work in all parts of nature alike, but according as they are composed: and therefore it is impossible for any human eye to see the exterior motions of all creatures, except they be of some grosser bodies: for, who can see the motion of the air, and the like? Nay, I believe not, that all exterior motions of grosser bodies can be perceived by our sight, much less their interior actions: And by this, I exclude rest; for, if matter, or corporeal nature, be in a perpetual motion, there can be no rest in nature; but what others call rest, is nothing else but retentive motions; which retentive motions, are as active, as dispersing motions; for Mr. Descartes says well, that it requires as much action or force to stay a ship, as to set it afloat; and there is as much action required in keeping parts together, as in dispersing them.[89] Besides, interior motions are as active as some exterior, nay, some more: and I believe, if there were a world of gold, whose parts are close and dense, it would be as active interiorly, as a world of air, which is fluid and rare, would be active exteriorly. But some may say, How is it possible that there can be a motion of bodies, without an empty space; for one body cannot move in another body? I answer: Space is change of division, as place is change of magnitude; but division and magnitude belong to body; therefore space and place cannot be without body, but wheresoever is body, there is place also: neither can a body leave a place behind it. So that the distinction of interior and exterior place, is needless; because no body can have two places, but place and body are but one thing; and whensoever the body changes, its place changes also. But some do not consider, that there are degrees of matter; for, nature's body doth not consist of one degree, as to be all hard or dense like a stone; but as there are infinite changes of motion, so there are in nature infinite degrees of density, rarity, grossness, purity, hardness, softness, etc. all caused by self-motion; which hard, gross, rare fluid, dense, subtle, and many other sorts of bodies, in their several degrees, may more easily move, divide and join, from, and with each other, being in a continued body, than if they had a vacuum to move in: for, were there a vacuum, there would be no successive motions, nor no degrees of swiftness and slowness, but all motion would be done in an instant. The truth is, there would be such distances of several gaps and holes, that parts would never join, if once divided; insomuch, as a piece of the world would become a single particular world, not joining to any part besides itself; which would make a horrid confusion in nature, contrary to all sense and reason. Wherefore the opinion of vacuum is, in my judgment, as absurd, as the opinion of senseless and irrational atoms, moving by chance: for, it is more probable that atoms should have life and knowledge to move regularly, than that they should move regularly and wisely by chance, and without life and knowledge; for, there can be no regular motion, without knowledge, sense and reason: and therefore those who are for atoms, had best to believe them to be self-moving, living and knowing bodies, for else their opinion is very irrational. But the opinion of atoms, is fitter for a poetical fancy, than for serious philosophy; and this is the reason that I have waived it in my philosophical works: For, if there can be no single parts, there cannot be atoms in nature, or else nature would be like a beggar's coat full of lice: Neither would she be able to rule those wandering and straggling atoms, because they are not parts of her body, but each is a single body by itself, having no dependence upon each other. Wherefore, if there should be a composition of atoms, it would not be a body made of parts, but of so many whole and entire single bodies, meeting together as a swarm of bees. The truth is, every atom being single, must be an absolute body by itself, and have an absolute power and knowledge, by which it would become a kind of a deity; and the concourse of them would rather cause a confusion, than a conformity in nature; because, all atoms being absolute, they would all be governors, but none would be governed.

Thus I have declared my opinion concerning the parts of nature, as also vacuum, and atoms; to wit, that it is impossible there can be any such things in nature. I will conclude, after I have given my answer to these two following questions.

First, it may be asked, Whether the parts of a composed figure do continue in such a composition until the whole figure be dissolved? I answer, My opinion is, that in some compositions they do continue, at least some longer than others; but, although some parts of a figure do disjoin from each other, and join with others; yet the structure of the creature may nevertheless continue. Neither is it necessary, that those which begin a building, must needs stay to the end or perfection of it; for some may begin, others may work on, and others may finish it; also, some may repair, and some may ruin: and it is well to be observed, that the compositions of all creatures are not alike, nor do they continue or dissolve all alike, and at the same time.

Secondly, it may be questioned, Whether there can be an infinite distance between two or more parts? And my answer is, that distance properly doth not belong to infinite, but only to finite parts; for distance is a certain measure between parts and parts; and wheresoever is a measure, there must be two extremes; but there are no extremes nor ends in infinite, and therefore there can be no infinite distance between parts. Indeed, it is a mere contradiction, and nonsense to say, "infinite between parts," by reason the word "between," implies a finiteness as between such a part, and such a part. But you will say, Because nature is an infinite body, it must have an infinite measure; for wheresoever is body, there is magnitude and figure; and wheresoever is magnitude and figure, there is measure. I answer: It is true, body, magnitude and figure, are all but one thing; and according as the body is, so is its magnitude and figure; but the body of nature being infinite, its magnitude and figure must also be infinite. But mistake me not, I do not mean a circumscribed and perfect exterior magnitude, by reason there's nothing exterior in respect to infinite, but in relation to its infinite parts. The truth is, men do often mistake, in ascribing to infinite, that which properly belongs to particulars; or at least, they consider the attributes of an infinite and a finite body, after one and the same manner; and no wonder, because a finite capacity cannot comprehend what infinite is: But although we cannot positively know what infinite is, yet we may guess at it by its opposite, that is, by finite: for, infinite is that which has no terms, bounds or limits, and therefore it cannot be circumscribed; and if it cannot be circumscribed as a finite body, it cannot have an exterior magnitude and figure, as a finite body; and consequently, no measure. Nevertheless, it is no contradiction to say, it has an infinite magnitude and figure: for, although infinite nature cannot have anything without, or beyond itself, yet it may have magnitude and figure within itself, because it is a body: and by this the magnitude and figure of infinite nature is distinguished from the magnitude and figure of its finite parts; for these have each their exterior and circumscribed figure, which nature has not. And as for measure, it is only an effect of a finite magnitude, and belongs to finite parts: that have certain distances from each other. It is true, one might in a certain manner say, "an infinite distance"; as for example, if there be an infinite line which has no ends, one might call the infinite extension of that line "an infinite distance"; but this is an improper expression; and it is better to keep the term of "an infinite extension," than call it "an infinite distance"; for, as I said before, distance is measure, and properly belongs to parts: Nay, if it were possible that there could be an infinite distance of parts in nature, yet the perpetual changes of motions, by which parts remove, and join from and to parts, would not allow any such thing in nature: for the parts of nature are always in action, working, intermixing, composing, dividing perpetually; so as it would be impossible for them to keep certain distances.

But to conclude this discourse, I desire it may be observed,

1. That whatsoever is body, were it an atom, must have parts; so that body cannot be without parts.

2. That there is no such thing as rest or stoppage in infinite matter; but there is self-motion in all parts of nature, although they are not all exteriorly, locally moving to our perception; for reason must not deny what our senses cannot comprehend. Although a piece of wood or metal has no exterior progressive motion, such as is found in animals; nevertheless, it is not without motion, for it is subject to generation and dissolution, which certainly are natural corporeal motions, besides many others: The truth is, the harder, denser, and firmer bodies are, the stronger are their motions; for it requires more strength to keep and hold parts together, than to dissolve and separate them.

3. That, without motion, parts could not alter their figures; neither would there be any variety in infinite nature.

4. If there were any such thing as atoms, and vacuum, there would be no conformity, nor uniformity in nature.

Lastly, as there is a perpetual self-motion in nature, and all her parts, so it is impossible that there can be perfect measures, constant figures, or single parts in nature.

XXXII   Of the Celestial Parts of This World; and Whether They Be Alterable

It may be questioned, Whether the celestial parts of the world never alter or change by their corporeal figurative motions, but remain constantly the same, without any change or alteration?[90] I answer: Concerning the general and particular kinds or sorts of creatures of this world, human sense and reason doth observe, that they do not change, but are continued by a perpetual supply and succession of particulars, without any general alteration or dissolution; but as for the singulars or particulars of those kinds and sorts of creatures, it is most certain, that they are subject to perpetual alterations, generations, and dissolutions: for example, human sense and reason perceives, that the parts of the earth do undergo continual alterations; some do change into minerals, some into vegetables, some into animals, etc. and these change again into several other figures, and also some into earth again, and the elements are changed one into another; when as yet the globe of the earth itself, remains the same, without any general alteration or dissolution; neither is there any want or decay of general kinds of creatures, but only a change of their particulars: and though our perception is but finite, and must contain itself within its own compass or bounds, so that it cannot judge of all particulars that are in nature; nevertheless, I see no reason why the celestial parts of the world should not be subject to alteration, as well as those of the terrestrial globe: for, if nature be full of self-motion, no particular can be at rest, or without action; but the chief actions of nature are composition and division, and changes of parts. Wherefore, although to our human perception, the stars and planets do not change from their general nature, as from being such or such composed figures, but appear the same to us, without any general or remarkable change of their exterior figures; yet we cannot certainly affirm, that the parts thereof be either moveless or unalterable, they being too remote from our perception, to discern all their particular motions: For, put the case the moon, or any other of the planets, were inhabited by animal creatures, which could see as much of this terrestrial globe, as we see of the

---

[90] Aristotle, *On the Heavens*, I, ch. 3 argues that the celestial bodies are "ungenerated and indestructible and exempt from increase and alteration" (270a13–14; *CWA*, I, 450). Cavendish was familiar with the evidence against Aristotle in Galileo's *Dialogue Concerning the Two Chief World Systems – Ptolemaic and Copernican*; a translation is included in *Mathematical Collections and Translations*, tr. Thomas Salisbury (London, 1661).

[moon];[91] although they could perceive, perhaps, the progressive motion of the whole figure of this terrestrial globe, in the same manner as we do perceive the motion of the moon, yet they would never be able to discern the particular parts thereof, viz. trees, animals, stones, water, earth, etc. much less their particular changes and alterations, generations and dissolutions. In the like manner do the celestial orbs appear to us; for, none that inhabit this globe, will ever be able to discern the particular parts of which the globe of the moon consists, much less their changes and motions. Indeed, it is with the celestial orbs, as it is with other composed parts or figures of nature, which have their interior, as well as exterior; general, as well as particular motions: for, it is impossible that nature, consisting of infinite different parts, should have but one kind of motion; and therefore, as a man, or any other animal, has first his exterior motions or actions, which belong to his whole composed figure, next his internal figurative motions by which he grows, decays, and dissolves, etc. Thirdly, as every several part and particle of his body has its interior and exterior actions; so it may be said of the stars and planets, which are no more than other parts of nature, as being composed of the same matter which all the rest consists of, and partaking of the same self-motion; for although our sight cannot discern more than their progressive, and shining or twinkling motion; nevertheless, they being parts of nature, must of necessity have their interior and exterior, particular and general motions; so that the parts of their bodies may change as much as the parts of this globe, the figure of the whole remaining still the same: for, as I said before, they being too far from our perception, their particular motions cannot be observed; nay, were we able to perceive the exterior actions of their parts, yet their interior motions are no ways perceptible by human sight. We may observe the effects of some interior motions of natural creatures; for example, of man, how he changes from infancy to youth, from youth to old age, etc. but how these actions are performed inwardly, no microscope is able to give us a true information thereof. Nevertheless, mankind is as lasting, as the sun, moon and stars: Nay, not only mankind, but also several other kinds and species of creatures, as minerals, vegetables, elements, and the like: for, though particulars change, yet the species do not; neither can the species be impaired by the changes of their particulars:

[91] As in 1666; 1668 erroneously gives: month.

for example, the sea is no less salt, for all there is so much salt extracted out of salt water; besides, that so many fresh rivers and springs do mingle and intermix with it. Neither doth the earth seem less, for all the productions of vegetables, minerals and animals, which derive their birth and origin from thence. Nor doth the race of mankind seem either more or less now, than it was in former ages: for, every species of creatures, is preserved by a continued succession or supply of particulars; so that when some die, or dissolve from being such natural figures, others are generated, and supply the want of them. And thus it is with all parts of nature, both what we call celestial, and terrestrial; nor can it be otherwise, since nature is self-moving, and all her parts are perpetually active.

XXXIII   Of the Substance of the Sun, and of Fire

There are diverse opinions concerning the matter or substance of the sun: Some imagine the sun to be a solid body set on fire: Others, that it is a fluid body of fire: and others again, that it is only a body of light and not of fire: so that I know not which opinion to adhere to:[92] but yet, I do rather believe the sun be a solid, than a fluid body, by reason fluid bodies are more inconstant in their motions, than solid bodies; witness lightning, which is a fluid fire, and flashes out through the divided clouds, with such a force as water that is pumped; and being extended beyond the degree of flame, alters to something else that is beyond our human perception. Indeed, it is of the nature of air, or else air inflamed; and as some sorts of air are more rare, subtle and searching than others; so are some sorts of lightning, as it is known by experience: or it is like several sorts of flame, that have several sorts of fuel to feed on; as for example, the flame of oil, the flame of wood, the flame of "aqua-vitae," the flame of gums, and the like; all which are very different, not only in their several tempers and degrees of heat, but also in their several manners of burning or flaming; for, the flame of aqua-vitae is far thinner and bluer, than the flame of wax, wood, tallow, or the like; insomuch, that there is as much difference between them, as there is between the azure sky, and a white cloud; which shows, that the flame of spirituous bodies is more airy and rare, than the flame of others: for, flame is only the rare and airy parts of

---

[92] See, e.g., Hobbes, *Elements of Philosophy*, IV, ch. 27, §§ 1–4 (*EW*, I, 445–53); Descartes, *Principles of Philosophy*, III, §§ 21–24; Digby, *Two Treatises*, First Treatise, ch. 10, §§ 2ff.

fire; and there is a natural body of fire, as well as of air, earth and water: and as there are several sorts of earth, water and air, so there are also several sorts of fire: and as there are springs of water, and springs of air; so there may also be springs of fire and flame. But to return to the sun; though I am not able certainly to determine of what substance it is, yet to our perception it appears not to be a fluid, but a solid body, by reason it keeps constantly the same exterior figure, and never appears either ebbing or flowing, or flashing, as lightning is; nor does the whole figure of its body dissolve and change into another figure: nevertheless, it being a natural creature, and consisting of self-moving parts, there is no question but its parts are subject to continual changes and alterations, although not perceptible by our sight, by reason of its distance, and the weakness of our organs; for although this terrestrial globe which we inhabit, in its outward figure, nay, in its interior nature, remains still the same; yet its parts do continually change by perpetual compositions and dissolutions, as is evident, and needs no proof. The same may be said of the sun, moon, stars and planets; which are like a certain kind of species of creatures; as for example, animal, or mankind; which species do always last, although their particulars are subject to perpetual productions and dissolutions. And thus it is with all composed figures or parts of nature, whose chief action is respiration, (if I may so call it) that is, composition and division of parts, caused by the self-moving power of nature.

XXXIV   Of Telescopes[93]

Many ingenious and industrious artists take much labour and pains in studying the natures and figures of celestial objects, and endeavour to discover the causes of their appearances, by telescopes, and such like optic instruments; but if art be not able to inform us truly of the natures of those creatures that are near us; how may it delude us in the search and enquiry we make of those things that are so far from us? We see how multiplying glasses do present numerous pictures of one object, which he that has not the experience of the deceitfulness of such glasses, would really think to be so many objects. The like deceits may be in other optic instruments, for ought man knows. It is true, we may, perhaps, through a

---

[93] Cf. Descartes, *Dioptrics*, Discourse IX; Hooke, *Micrographia*, "Observation LVIII: Of a New Property in the Air, and Several Other Transparent Mediums Named 'Inflection', Whereby Very Many Considerable Phenomena are Attempted to be Solved, and Divers Other Uses are Hinted."

telescope, see a steeple a matter of twenty or thirty miles off; but the same can a natural eye do, if it be not defective, nor the medium obstructed, without the help of any such instrument, especially if one stand upon a high place. But, put the case a man should be upon the Alps, he would hardly see the city of Paris from thence, although he looked through a telescope never so perfect, and had no obstruction to hinder his sight. And truly, the stars and planets are far more distant from us, than Paris from the Alps. It is well known, that the sense of sight requires a certain proportion of distance betwixt the eye and the object; which being exceeded, it cannot perform its office: for, if the object be either too near, or too far off, the sight cannot discern it; and, as I have made mention in my *Philosophical Letters* of the nature of those guns, that according to the proportion of the length of the barrel, shoot either further or shorter; for the barrel must have its proportioned length, which being exceeded, the gun will shoot so much shorter as the barrel is made longer: so may [perspective][94] glasses, perhaps, direct the sense of seeing within a certain compass of distance; which distance, surely, the stars and planets do far exceed; I mean so, as to discern their figures, as we do of other objects that are near us: for, concerning their exterior progressive motions, we may observe them with our natural eyes, as well as through artificial tubes: We can see the sun's rising and setting, and the progressive motion of the moon, and other planets; but yet we cannot see their natural figures, what they are, nor what makes them move; for, we cannot perceive progressive local motion otherwise, than by change of distance, that is, by composition and division of parts, which is commonly (though improperly) called change of place; and no glasses or tubes can do more. Some affirm, they have discovered many new stars, never seen before, by the help of telescopes; but whether this be true, or not, or whether it be only a delusion of the glasses, I will not dispute; for I having no skill, neither in the art of optics, nor in astronomy, may chance to err; and therefore I will not eagerly affirm what I do not certainly know; I only endeavour to deliver my judgment as reason directs me, and not as sense informs, or rather deludes me; and I chose rather to follow the guidance of regular reason, than of deluding art.

[94] 1666 and 1668: prospective.

XXXV   Of Knowledge and Perception in General

Since natural knowledge and perception, is the ground and principle, not only of philosophy both speculative and experimental, but of all other arts and sciences, nay, of all the infinite particular actions of nature; I thought it not amiss to join to the end of this part, a full declaration of my opinion concerning that subject.

First, it is to be observed, that matter, self-motion, and self-knowledge, are inseparable from each other, and make nature one material, self-moving, and self-knowing body. [To say "inseparable from each other," in my opinion, seems as if they were different parts, and not different properties of the same part.][95]

2. Nature being material, is dividable into parts; and being infinite in quantity or bulk, her parts are infinite in number.

3. No part can subsist singly, or by itself, precised from the rest; but they are all parts of one infinite body; for though such parts may be separated from such parts, and joined to other parts, and by this means may undergo infinite changes, by infinite compositions and divisions; yet no part can be separated from the body of nature.

4. And hence it follows, that the parts of nature are nothing else but the particular changes of particular figures, made by self-motion.

5. As there can be no annihilation, so there can neither be a new creation of the least part or particle of nature, or else nature would not be infinite.

6. Nature is purely corporeal or material, and there is nothing that belongs to, or is a part of nature, which is not corporeal; so that natural and material, or corporeal, are one and the same; and therefore spiritual-beings, non-beings, mixt-beings, and whatsoever distinctions the learned do make, are no ways belonging to nature. Neither is there any such thing as an incorporeal motion; for all actions of nature are corporeal, being natural; and there can no abstraction be made of motion or figure, from matter or body, but they are inseparably one thing. [Wherefore no spiritual being, can have local motion.][96]

7. As infinite matter is divided into infinite parts; so infinite knowledge is divided into infinite particular knowledges; and infinite self-motion, into infinite particular self-actions.

---

[95] Lacking in 1666.   [96] Lacking in 1666.

re, time or space?

8. There is no other difference between self-knowledge, and particular knowledges, than betwixt self-motion, and particular self-actions; or betwixt a whole, and its parts; a cause, and its effects: for, self-knowledge is the ground and principle of all particular knowledges, as self-motion is the ground and principle of all particular actions, changes and varieties of natural figures.

9. As infinite nature has an infinite self-motion and self-knowledge; so every part and particle has a particular and finite self-motion and self-knowledge, by which it knows itself, and its own actions, and perceives also other parts and actions; which latter is properly called perception; not as if there were two different principles of knowledge in every particular creature or part of nature; but they are two different acts of one and the same interior and inherent self-knowledge, which is a part of nature's infinite self-knowledge.

10. Thus perception, or a perceptive knowledge, belongs properly to parts, and may also be called an exterior knowledge, by reason it extends to exterior objects.

11. Though self-knowledge is the ground and principle of all particular knowledges and perceptions; yet, self-motion, since it is the cause of all the variety of natural figures, and of the various compositions and divisions of parts; it is also the cause of all perceptions.

12. As there is a double degree of corporeal self-motion, viz. rational and sensitive; so there is also a double degree of perception, rational and sensitive.

13. A whole may know its parts; and an infinite a finite; but no particular part can know its whole, nor one finite part, that which is infinite: I say, no particular part; for, when parts are regularly composed, they may by a general conjunction or union of their particular knowledges and perceptions, know more, and so judge more probably of the whole, or of infinite; and although by the division of parts, those composed knowledges and perceptions, may be broke asunder like a ruined house or castle, kingdom or government; yet some of the same materials may chance to be put to the same uses, and some may be joined to those that formerly employed themselves other ways. And hence I conclude, that no particular parts are bound to certain particular actions, no more than nature herself, which is self-moving matter; for, as nature is full of variety of motions or actions, so are her parts; or else she could not be said self-moving, if she were bound to certain actions, and had not

liberty to move as she pleases: for, though God, the author of nature, has ordered her, so that she cannot work beyond her own nature, that is, beyond matter; yet has she freedom to move as she will; neither can it be certainly affirmed, that the successive propagation of the several species of creatures, is decreed and ordained by God, so that nature must of necessity work to their continuation, and can do no otherwise; but human sense and reason may observe, that the same parts keep not always to the same particular actions, so as to move to the same species or figures; for, those parts that join in the composition of an animal, alter their actions in its dissolution, and in the framing of other figures; so that the same parts which were joined in one particular animal, may, when they dissolve from that composed figure, join severally to the composition of other figures; as for example, of minerals, vegetables, elements, etc. and some may join with some sorts of creatures, and some with others, and so produce creatures of different sorts, whenas before they were all united in one particular creature: for, particular parts are not bound to work or move to a certain particular action, but they work according to the wisdom and liberty of nature, which is only bound by the omnipotent God's decree, not to work beyond herself, that is, beyond matter; and since matter is dividable, nature is necessitated to move in parts; for matter can be without parts, no more than parts can be without a whole; neither can nature, being material, make herself void of figure; nor can she rest, being self-moving; but she is bound to divide and compose her several parts into several particular figures, and dissolve and change those figures again infinite ways: All which proves the variety of nature, which is so great, that even in one and the same species, none of the particulars resemble one another so much, as not to be discerned from each other.

But to return to knowledge and perception: I say, they are general and fundamental actions of nature; it being not probable that the infinite parts of nature should move so variously, nay, so orderly and methodically as they do, without knowing what they do, or why, and whether they move; and therefore all particular actions whatsoever in nature, as respiration, digestion, sympathy, antipathy, division, composition, pressure, reaction, etc. are all particular perceptive and knowing actions: for, if a part be divided from other parts, both are sensible of their division: The like may be said of the composition of parts: and as for pressure and reaction, they are as knowing and perceptive as any other particular actions; but yet this does not prove, that they are the principle of perception, and that there's no perception but what is made by pressure and reaction; or that at least they are the ground of animal perception;[97] for as they are no more but particular actions, so they have but particular perceptions: and although all motion is sensible, yet no part is sensible but by [its own][98] motions in its own parts; that is, no corporeal motion is sensible but of or by itself. Therefore when a man moves a string, or tosses a ball, the string or ball is no more sensible of the motion of the hand, than the hand is of the motion of the string or ball; but the hand is only an occasion that the string or ball moves thus or thus. I will not say, but that it may have some perception of the hand, according to the nature of its own figure; but it does not move by the hand's motion, but by its own: for, there can be no motion imparted, without matter or substance.

Neither can I certainly affirm, that all perception consists in patterning out exterior objects; for, although the perception of our human senses is made that way, yet nature's actions being so various, I dare not conclude from thence, that all the perceptions of the infinitely various parts and figures of nature are all made after the same manner. Nevertheless, it is probable to sense and reason, that the infinite parts of nature have not only interior self-knowledge, but also exterior perceptions of other figures or parts, and their actions; by reason there is a perpetual commerce and intercourse between parts and parts; and the chief actions of nature, are composition and division, which produce all the variety of nature; which proves, there must of necessity be perception between parts and parts; but, how all these particular perceptions are made, no particular creature is able to know, by reason of their variety; for, as the actions of nature vary, so do the perceptions. Therefore it is absurd to confine all perception of nature, either to pressure and reaction, or to the animal kind of perception; since even in one and the same animal sense, (as for example, of seeing) there are numerous perceptions: for, every motion of the eye, were it no more than a hairsbreadth, causes a several perception: besides, it is not only the five organs in an animal, but every part and particle of his body, that has a peculiar knowledge and perception, because it consists of self-moving

---

[97] The target here is a mechanical account of sense perception, such as the theories of the ancient atomists Epicurus and Lucretius, and of Hobbes.

[98] As in 1666; 1668: own.

matter; which if so, then a looking glass, that patterns out the face of a man; and a man's eye, that patterns again the copy from the glass, cannot be said to have the same perception; by reason a glass, and an animal, are different sorts of creatures: for, though a piece of wood, stone, or metal, may have a perceptive knowledge of man, yet it hath not a man's perception;[99] because it is a vegetable, or mineral, and cannot have an animal knowledge or perception, no more than the eye patterning out a tree or stone, can be said to have a vegetable or mineral perception; nay, when one animal (as for example, one man) perceives another, he doth not perceive his knowledge; for, it is one thing to perceive the exterior figure of a creature, and another thing to perceive its interior, proper, and innate actions: also, it is one thing to perceive exterior objects, and another to receive knowledge: for, no part can give away to another its inherent and proper particular nature; neither can one part make itself another part; it may imitate some actions of another part, but not make itself the same part: which proves, that each part must have its own knowledge and perception, according to its own particular nature: for, though several parts may have the like perceptions, yet they are not the same; and although the exterior figures of some objects may be alike, yet the perceptions may be quite different. It is true, sensitive and rational knowledge, is general and infinite in nature; but every part being finite, can have but a finite and particular knowledge, and that according to the nature of its particular figure: for, as not all creatures, although they be composed of one matter, are alike in their figures; so not all can have the like knowledges and perceptions, though they have all self-motion: for, particular creatures and actions, are but effects of the only infinite self-moving matter, and so are particular perceptions; and although they are different, yet the difference of effects does not argue different causes, but one and the same cause may produce several and different effects; so that although there be infinite different motions in nature, yet they are all but motions, and cannot differ from each other in being motions, or self-moving parts; and although there be infinite, several, and different perceptions, yet they are all perceptions; for the effects cannot alter the cause, but the cause

---

[99] Hobbes, *Elements of Philosophy*, IV, ch. 25, § 5, agrees that if we consider perception made solely through pressure and reaction, it is unclear how the view – that all bodies are endowed with sense – can be refuted; but since animal sensation requires memory, and thus organs fit for retaining motions, not all bodies have animal sense (*EW*, I, 393–94).

may alter the effects. Wherefore rational and sensitive corporeal motions, cannot change from being motions, though they may change from moving thus, to move thus; nor perceptions from being perceptions, though they may change from being such or such particular perceptions; for the change is only in particulars, not in the ground or principle, which continues always the same. The truth is, as it is impossible that one figure should be another figure, or one part another part; so likewise it is impossible, that the perception of one part should be the perception of another; but being in parts, they must be several; and those parts being different, they must be different also; but some are more different than others: for, the perceptions of creatures of different sorts, as, for example, of a vegetable and an animal, are more different than the perception of particulars of one sort, or of one composed figure: for, as there is difference in their interior natures, so in their perceptions; so that a mineral or vegetable that perceives the figure of an animal, has no more the perception of an animal, than an animal which perceives or patterns out the figure of a mineral or vegetable, has the perceptions of those creatures; for example, when a man lies upon a stone, or leans on a tree, or handles and touches water, etc. although these parts be so closely joined to each other, yet their perceptions are quite different; for the man only knows what he feels, or sees, or hears, or smells, or tasteth, but knows not what sense or perception those parts have; nay, he is so far from that, that even one part of his body doth not know the sense and perception of another part of his body: as for example, one of his hands knows not the sense and perception of his other hand; nay, one part of his hand knows not the perception of another part of the same hand: for, as the corporeal figurative motions differ, so do particular knowledges and perceptions: and although sensitive and rational knowledge is general and infinite in infinite nature, yet every part being finite, has but finite and particular perceptions: besides, perception being but an effect, and not a cause, is more various in particulars: for, although creatures are composed of rational and sensitive matter, yet their perceptions are not alike; neither can the effect alter the cause; for, though the several actions of sensitive and rational matter be various, and make several perceptions, yet they cannot make several kinds of sensitive and rational matter; but when as perceptions change, the parts of the sensitive and rational matter remain the same in themselves; that is, they do not change from being sensitive or rational parts, although they may make numerous perceptions in their particular parts, according to the various changes of self-motion.

But some may say, If the particular parts of one composed figure, be so ignorant of each other's knowledge, as I have expressed, how can they agree in some action of the whole figure, where they must all be employed, and work agreeably to one effect? As for example, when the mind designs to go to such a place, or do such a work, how can all the parts agree in the performing of this act, if they be ignorant of each other's actions? I answer: Although every part's knowledge and perception, is its own, and not another's, so that every part knows by its own knowledge, and perceives by its own perception; yet it doth not follow from thence, that no part has any more knowledge than of itself, or of its own actions: for, as I said before, it is well to be observed, that there being an intercourse and commerce, as also an acquaintance and agreement between parts and parts, there must also of necessity be some knowledge or perception betwixt them, that is, one part must be able to perceive another part, and the action of that same part: for, wheresoever is life and knowledge, that is, sense and reason, there is also perception; and though no part of nature can have an absolute knowledge, yet it is neither absolutely ignorant; but it has a particular knowledge, and particular perceptions, according to the nature of its own innate and interior figure. In short; As there are several kinds, sorts and particular perceptions, and particular ignorances between parts, so there are more general perceptions between some parts, than between others; the like of ignorance: all which is according to the various actions of corporeal self-motion: But yet no part can have a thorough perception of all other parts and their actions, or be sure that that part which it perceives, has the like perception of it again: for, one part may perceive another part, and yet this part may be ignorant of that part, and its perception: For example, my eye perceives an object, but that object is not necessitated to perceive my eye again: also my eye may perceive the pattern of itself made in a looking glass, and yet be ignorant whether the glass do the like. Again, when two parts touch each other, one part may perceive the other, and yet be ignorant whether the other does the like: For example, a man joins both his hands together; they may have perception of each other, and yet be ignorant of each other's perception; and, most commonly, one part judges of another's perception by its own; for, when one man perceives the actions of another man, he judges by those actions, what perceptions he has; so that judgment is but a comparing of actions: for, as likeness of interior motions makes sympathy, so comparing of actions makes judgment, to know and distinguish what is alike, and what is not. Therefore perception of exterior objects, though it proceeds from an interior principle of self-knowledge, yet it is nothing else but an observation of exterior parts or actions; so that parts in their several compositions and divisions, may have several perceptions of each other, according to the nature of their figurative corporeal motions: and although each part's knowledge is its own, yet parts may have as much knowledge of each other, as they can perceive, or observe of each other; for, the perceptive motions of one part, may inform themselves of the actions of other parts. The truth is, every particular part has its own motion's figures, sense and reason, which by a conjunction or composition of parts, makes a general knowledge: for, as the division of parts causes a general obscurity; so composition of parts makes a general knowledge and understanding: and as every part has self-motion, so it has self-knowledge and perception.

But it is to be observed, that since there is a double perception in the infinite parts of nature, sensitive and rational; the perception and information of the rational parts is more general, than of the sensitive, they being the most prudent, designing and governing parts of nature, not so much encumbered with labouring on the inanimate parts of matter, as the sensitive: Therefore the rational parts in a composed figure, or united action, may sooner have a general knowledge and information of the whole, than the sensitive, whose knowledge is more particular: As for example, a man may have a pain in one of the parts of his body, although the perception thereof is made by the sensitive corporeal motions in that same part, yet the next adjoining sensitive parts may be ignorant thereof, whenas all the rational parts of the whole body may take notice of it. Thus the rational parts having a more general acquaintance than the sensitive, and being also the designing and architectonical parts, they employ the sensitive parts to work to the same effect; but these are not always ready to obey, but force sometimes the rational to obey them, which we call irregularity; which is nothing but an opposition or strife between parts: As for example, a man designs to employ the exterior strength and action of his exterior parts; but if through irregularity, the legs and arms be weak, the stomach sick, the head full of pain; they will not agree to the executing of the commands of the rational parts.

Likewise, the mind endeavours often to keep the sensitive motions of the body from dissolution; but they many times follow the mode, and imitate other objects, or cause a dissolution or division of that composed figure by voluntary actions.

Thus the sensitive and rational motions do oftentimes cross and oppose each other: for, although several parts are united in one body, yet are they not always bound to agree to one action; nor can it be otherwise; for, were there no disagreement between them, there would be no irregularities, and consequently no pain or sickness, nor no dissolution of any natural figure.

And such an agreement and disagreement, is not only betwixt the rational and sensitive parts, but also betwixt the rational and rational, the sensitive and sensitive. For some rational parts, may in one composed figure, have opposite actions; As for example, the mind of man may be divided, so as to hate one person, and love another: nay, hate and love one and the same person, for several things, at the same time: as also, rejoice and grieve at the same time. For example; a man has two sons, one is killed in the wars, and the other comes home with victory and honour; the father grieves for the slain son, and rejoices for the victorious son: for, the mind being material, is dividable as well as composable; and therefore its parts may as well oppose each other, as agree; for, agreement and friendship is made by composition, and disagreement by division; and sense and reason is either stronger or weaker, by composition or division, regularity or irregularity; for a greater number of parts may overpower a less: also, there are advantages and disadvantages amongst parts, according to the several sorts of corporeal figurative motions; so that some sorts of corporeal motions, although fewer or weaker, may overpower others that are more numerous and strong; but the rational being the most subtle, active, observing and inspective parts, have, for the most part, more power over the sensitive, than the sensitive have over them; which makes that they, for the most part, work regularly, and cause all the orderly and regular compositions, dissolutions, changes and varieties in the infinite parts of nature: Besides, their perception and observation being more general, it lasts longer; for, the rational continue the perception of the past actions of the sensitive, whenas the sensitive keep no such records.

Some say, that perception is made by the ideas of exterior objects entering into the organs of the sentient; but this opinion cannot be probable to sense and reason:[100] For, first, if ideas subsist of themselves, then they must have their own figures; and so the figures of the objects would not be perceived, but only the figures of the ideas. But if those ideas be the figures of the objects themselves, then by entering into our sensories, the objects would lose them; for one single object, can have no more but one exterior figure at one time, which surely it cannot lose and keep, at one and the same time. But if it be a print of the object on the air, it is impossible there could be such several sorts of prints as there are perceptions, without a notable confusion.[101] Besides, when I consider the little passages, (as in the sense of touch) the pores of the flesh, through which they must enter, I cannot readily believe it: nay, the motions and prints would grow so weak, and faint in their journey, especially if the object be a great way off, as they would become of no effect. But if their opinion be, that ideas can change and alter, then all immaterial substances may do the same, and spirits may change and alter into several immaterial figures; which, in my opinion cannot be: for, what is supernatural, is unalterable; and therefore the opinion of ideas in perception, is as irregular, as the opinion of senseless atoms in the framing of a regular world.

Again, some of our modern philosophers are of opinion, that the subject wherein colour and image are inherent, is not the object or thing seen; for image and colour, say they, may be there where the thing seen, is not: As for example, the sun, and other visible objects, by reflexion in water or glass; so that there is nothing without us, really, which we call image or colour: for the image or colour, is but an apparition unto us, of the motion and agitation which the object works in the brain or spirits;[102] and divers times men see directly the same object double, as two candles

---

[100] Seventeenth-century scholastics held that perception involves an object's production of an incorporeal "species," or form, in our sense organs via the "multiplication" (i.e., replication) of species in the air from that object to our organs. Critics worried about how these forms could subsist detached from any substance; see Leibniz, *Monadologie* [Monadology], § 7; and *Phil. Letters*, pp. 97ff. They also argued that if there were such forms, they would have to be corporeal, in which case a variety of problems arise; see Nicolas Malebranche, *De la recherche de la verité . . .* [The Search After Truth] (Paris, 1674–75), bk III, pt II, ch. 2; and John Norris, *Essay on the Ideal or Intelligible World* (London, 1701–04), vol. II, pp. 344ff.
[101] See Malebranche, ibid.; cf. Kenelm Digby, *Two Treatises*, First Treatise, ch. 32, § 9; and Joseph Glanvill, *Scepsis Scientifica: or, Confest Ignorance, the Way to Science; In an Essay of the Vanity of Dogmatizing . . .* (London, 1665), ch. VI, § 5.
[102] The reference is to the mechanical philosophers, e.g., Descartes and Hobbes, for whom sensible images and colors are just ideas (Descartes) or phantasms (Hobbes) in perceivers; external objects are properly characterized solely in terms of mechanical properties, e.g., extension and motion.

for one, and the like. To which I answer, that all this doth not prove that the object is not perceived, or that an object can be without image or colour, or that figure and colour are not the same with the object; but it proves, that the object enters not the eye, but is only patterned out by the perceptive motions in the optic sense; for the reflexion of the sun in water or glass, is but a copy of the original, made by the figurative perceptive motions in the glass or water, which may pattern out an object as well as we do; which copy is patterned out again by our optic perception, and so one copy is made by another. The truth is, our optic sense could not perceive either the original, or copy of an exterior object, if it did not make those figures in its own parts: and therefore figure and colour are both in the object, and the eye; and not, as they say, neither in the object, nor in the eye: for, though I grant that one thing cannot be in two places at once, yet there may be several copies made of one original, in several parts, which are several places, at one and the same time; which is more probable, than that figure and colour should neither be in the object, nor in the eye; or, according to their own words, that figure and colour should be there, where the thing seen is not; which is to separate it from the object, a thing against all possibility, sense and reason; or else, that a substanceless and senseless motion, should make a progressive journey from the object to the sentient, and there print, figure and colour upon the optic sense, by a bare agitation or concussion, so that the perception or apparition (as they call it) of an object, should only be according to the stroke the agitation makes: As for example, the perception of light, after such a manner, figure after such, and colour after another: for, if motion be no substance or body, and besides, void of sense, not knowing what it acts, I cannot conceive how it should make such different strokes upon both the sensitive organ, and the brain, and all so orderly, that everything is perceived differently and distinctly. Truly, this opinion is like Epicurus' of atoms; but how absurd it is to make senseless corpuscles, the cause of sense and reason, and consequently of perception, is obvious to everyone's apprehension, and needs no demonstration.

Next, as colour, according to their opinion, is not inherent any otherwise in the object, but by an effect thereof upon us, caused by such a motion in the object; so, neither (say they) is sound in the thing we hear, but in ourselves: for, as a man may see, so he may hear double, or treble, by multiplication of echoes, which are sounds as well as the original; and not being in one and the same place, cannot be inherent in the body; for the clapper has no sound in it, but motion, and maketh motion in the inward parts of the bell: neither has the bell motion, but sound, and imparts motion to the air, the air again imparts motion to the ear and nerves, until it comes to the brain, which has motion, not sound: from the brain it rebounds back into the nerves outward, and then it becomes an apparition without, which we call sound. But, good Lord! what a confusion would all this produce, if it were thus! What need is there of imparting motion, when nature can do it a much easier way. I wonder how rational men can believe that motion can be imparted without matter: Next, that all this can be done in an instant: Again, that it is the organ of the sentient that make colour, sound, and the like, and that they are not really inherent in the object itself. For were there no men to perceive such or such a colour, figure or sound; can we rationally think that object would have no colour, figure, nor sound at all? I will not say, that there is no pressure or reaction; but they do not make sense or reason: several parts may produce several effects by their several compositions; but yet this does not prove that there can be no perception but by pressure upon the organ, and consequently the brain; and that the thing perceived, is not really existent in the object, but a bare apparition to the sentient: the clapper gives no motion to the bell, but both the clapper, and the bell, have each their own motion, by which they act in striking each other; and the conjunction of such or such parts, makes a real sound, were there no ear to hear it.

Again, concerning the sense of touch, the heat, say they, we feel from the fire, is in us; for it is quite different from that in the fire: our heat is pleasure, or pain, according as it is, great or moderate; but in the coal there is no such thing. I answer: They are so far in the right, that the heat we feel, is made by the perceptive motions of, and in our own parts, and not by the fire's parts acting upon us: but yet, if the fire were not really such a thing as it is, that is, a hot and burning body, our sense would not so readily figure it out, as it does: which proves it is a real copy of a real object, and not a mere phantasm, or bare imparted motion from the object to the sentient, made by pressure and reaction: for if so, the fire would waste in a moment of time, by imparting so much motion to so many sentients; besides, the several strokes which the several imparted motions make upon the sentient, and the reaction from the sentient to the exterior parts, would cause such a strong and confused agitation in the sentient, that it would rather occasion the body to dissolve through the irregularities of such forced motions. But having discoursed enough of this subject heretofore, I will add no more, but refer both their, and my own opinions, to the judicious and impartial reader: Only concerning fire, because they believe it is the only shining body upon earth, I will say this: If it were true, then a glow-worm's tail, and cat's eyes, must be fire also; which yet experience makes us believe otherwise.

As for sleep, they call it a privation of the act of sense:[103] To which I can no ways give my consent, because I believe sense to be a perpetual corporeal self-motion, without any rest. Neither do I think the senses can be lockt up in sleep: for, if they be self-moving, they cannot be shut up; it being as impossible to deprive self-motion of acting, as to destroy its nature; but if they have no self-motion, they need no locking up at all, because it would be their nature to rest, as being moveless. In short, sense being self-motion, can neither rest nor cease; for what they call cessation, is nothing else but an alteration of corporeal self-motion: and thus cessation will require as much a self-moving agent, as all other actions of nature.

Lastly, say they, it is impossible for sense to imagine a thing past; for sense is only of things present.[104] I answer, It is true, by reason the sensitive corporeal motions work on, and with the parts of inanimate matter; nevertheless, when a repetition is made of the same actions, and the same parts, it is a sensitive remembrance; and thus is also experience made; which proves, there is a sensitive perception and self-knowledge, because the senses are well acquainted with those objects they have often figured or patterned out: And to give a further demonstration thereof, we see that the senses are amazed, and sometimes frighted at such objects as are unusual, or have never been presented to them before. In short, conception, imagination, remembrance, experience, observation, and the like, are all made by corporeal, self-knowing, perceptive self-motion, and not by insensible, irrational, dull, and moveless matter.

XXXVI   Of the Different Perceptions of Sense and Reason

Having declared in the former discourse, that there is a double perception in all parts of nature, to wit, rational and sensitive; some might ask,

---

[103] See Descartes, *Principles of Philosophy*, IV, § 196; but cf. Aristotle, *On Sleep*.
[104] Hobbes, *Elements of Philosophy*, IV, ch. 25, § 7 (*EW*, I, 396).

how these two degrees of motions work; whether differently or unitedly in every part, to one and the same perception.

I answer: that regularly, the animal perception of exterior objects, is made by its own sensitive, rational, corporeal and figurative motions; the sensitive patterning out the figure or action of an outward object in the sensitive organ; and the rational making a figure of the same object in their own substance; so that both the rational and sensitive motions, work to one and the same perception, and that at the same point of time, and, as it were, by one act; but yet it is to be observed, that many times they do not move together to one and the same perception; for, the sensitive and rational motions do many times move differently even in one and the same part: As for the rational, they being not encumbered with any other parts of matter, but moving in their own degree, are not at all bound to work always with the sensitive, as is evident in the production of fancies, thoughts, imaginations, conceptions, etc. which are figures made only by the rational motions in their own matter or substance, without the help of the sensitive; and the sensitive, although they do not commonly work without the rational, yet many times they do, and sometimes both the rational and sensitive work without patterns, that is, voluntarily, and by rote; and sometimes the sensitive take patterns from the rational, as in the invention of arts, or the like; so that there is no necessity that they should always work together to the same perception. Concerning the perception of exterior objects, I will give an instance, where both the rational and sensitive motions do work differently, and not to the same perception: Suppose a man be in a deep contemplative study, and somebody touch or pinch him, it happens oft that he takes no notice at all of it, nor doth feel it; whenas yet his touched or pinched parts are sensible, or have a sensitive perception thereof; also a man doth often see or hear something, without minding or taking notice thereof, especially when his thoughts are busily employed about some other things; which proves, that his mind, or rational motions, work quite to another perception than his sensitive do. But some perhaps will say, because there is a thorough mixture of animate (rational and sensitive) and inanimate matter, and so close and inseparable a union and conjunction betwixt them, that it is impossible they should work differently, or not together: Besides, the alleged example does not prove, that the rational and sensitive motions in one and the same part that is touched or pinched, or in the organ which hears or seeth, do not work together, but proves only, that the sensitive motions of the touched part or organ, and the rational motions in the head or brain, do not work together; whenas, nevertheless, although a man takes no notice of another man's touching or pinching, the rational motions of that same part may perceive it. To which I answer: First, I do not deny that there is a close conjunction and commixture of both the rational and sensitive parts in every body or creature, and that they are always moving and acting; but I deny that they are always moving to the same perception: for to be, and move together, and to move together to the same perception, are two different things. Next, although I allow that there are particular, both rational and sensitive figurative motions in every part and particle of the body; yet the rational being more observing and inspective than the sensitive, as being the designing and ordering parts, may sooner have a general information and knowledge of all other rational parts of the composed figure, and may all unitedly work to the conceptions or thoughts of the musing and contemplating man; so that his rational motions in the pinched part of his body, may work to his interior conceptions; and the sensitive motions of the same part, to the exterior perception: for, although I say in my *Philosophical Opinions*, that all thoughts, fancies, imaginations, conceptions, etc. are made in the head, and all passions in the heart; yet I do not mean, that all rational figurative actions, are only confined to the head, and to the heart, and are in no other parts of the body of an animal, or man; for surely, I believe there is sense and reason, or sensitive and rational knowledge, not only in all creatures, but in every part of every particular creature. But since the sensitive organs in man are joined in that part which is named the head; we believe that all knowledge lies in the head, by reason the other parts of the body do not see as the eyes, nor hear as the ears, nor smell as the nose, nor taste as the tongue, etc. All which makes us prefer the rational and sensitive motions that work to those perceptions in the mentioned organs, before the motions in the other parts of the body; whenas yet these are no less rational and sensible than they, although the actions of their sensitive and rational perceptions, are after another manner: for, the motions of digestion, growth, decay, etc. are as sensible, and as rational, as those five sensitive organs, or the head; and the heart, liver, lungs, spleen, stomach, bowels, and the rest, know as well their office and functions, and are as sensible of their pains, diseases, constitutions, tempers, nourishments, etc. as the eyes, ears, nostrils, tongue, etc. know their particular actions and perceptions: for, although no particular part can know the infinite parts of nature, yet every part may know itself, and its own actions, as being self-moving. And therefore, the head or brains cannot engross all knowledge to themselves; but the other parts of the body have as much in the designing and production of a creature, as the brain has in the production of a thought; for children are not produced by thoughts, no more than digestion or nourishment is produced by the eyes, or the making of blood by the ears, or the several appetites of the body, by the five exterior sensitive organs: But, although all, (interior, as well as exterior) parts of the body have their particular knowledges and perceptions, different from those of the head, and the five sensitive organs; and the head's and organ's knowledge and perception are differing from them; nevertheless, they have acquaintance or correspondence with each other: for, when the stomach has an appetite to food, the mouth and hands endeavour to serve it, and the legs are willing to run for it: The same may be said of other appetites. Also, in case of oppression, when one part of the body is oppressed, or in distress; all the other parts endeavour to relieve that distressed or afflicted part. Thus, although there is difference between the particular actions, knowledges, and perceptions of every part, which causes an ignorance betwixt them; yet, by reason there is knowledge and perception in every part, by which each part doth not only know itself, and its own actions; but has also a perception of some actions of its neighbouring parts: it causes a general intelligence and information betwixt the particular parts of a composed figure: which information and intelligence, as I have mentioned heretofore, is more general betwixt the rational, than the sensitive parts: for, though both the sensitive and rational parts are so closely intermixt, that they may have knowledge of each other; yet the sensitive parts are not so generally knowing of the concerns of a composed figure, as the rational; by reason the rational are more free and at liberty than the sensitive, which are more encumbered with working on, and with the inanimate parts of matter; and therefore it may very well be, that a man in a deep contemplative study, doth not always feel when he is pinched or touched; because all the rational motions of his body concur or join to the conception of his musing thoughts; so that only the sensitive motions in that part, do work to the perception of touch; whenas the rational, even of the same part, may work to the conception of his thoughts. Besides, it happeneth oft, that there is not always an agreement betwixt the rational and sensitive motions, even in the same parts; for the rational may move regularly, and the sensitive irregularly; or, the sensitive may move regularly, and the rational irregularly: nay, often there are irregularities and disagreements in the same degree of motions, as betwixt rational and rational, sensitive and sensitive: and although it be proper for the rational to inform the sensitive, yet the sensitive do often inform the rational; only they cannot give such a general information as the rational: for one rational part can inform all other rational parts in a moment of time, and by one act: And therefore rational knowledge is not only in the head or brains, but in every part or particle of the body.

Some learned conceive, that all knowledge is in the mind, and none in the senses: For the senses, say they, present only exterior objects to the mind; which sits as a judge in the kernel, or fourth ventricle of the brain,[105] or in the orifice of the stomach,[106] and judges of them; which, in my apprehension, is a very odd opinion: For first, they allow, that all knowledge and perception comes by the senses, and the sensitive spirits; who, like faithful servants, run to and fro, as from the sensitive organs, to the brain and back, to carry news to the mind; and yet they do not grant, that they have any knowledge at all: which shows, they are very dull servants; and I wonder how they can inform the mind of what they do not know themselves. Perchance, they'll say, it is after the manner or way of intelligence by letters, and not by word of mouth: for, those that carry letters to and fro, know nothing of the business that intercedes betwixt the correspondents; and so it may be between the mind, and the external object. I answer: First, I cannot believe there's such a correspondence between the object and the mind of the sentient or perceiver: for, if the mind and the object should be compared to such two intelligencers, they would always have the like perception of each other, which we see is not so: for, oftentimes I have a perception of such or such an object, but that object may have no perception of me. Besides, there's nothing carried from the object, to the mind of the sentient, by its officers, the sensitive spirits, as there is betwixt two correspondents: for, there's no perception made by an actual emission of parts, from the object to the mind: for, if perception were made that way, not only some

---

[105] Descartes held that the soul/mind has its principal seat in "gland H," the pineal gland; but this gland is at the root of the third ventricle: *L'Homme* . . . [Treatise on Man] (Paris, 1664) (AT, XI, 129, 176ff.; CSM, I, 100, 106ff.); *Passions de l'âme* [Passions of the Soul] (Paris, 1649), I, §§ 31ff. Cf. *Phil. Letters*, pp. 111ff.

[106] The view of Van Helmont in *Oriatrike*, pp. 283ff.; cf. *Phil. Letters*, pp. 327ff.

parts of the object, but the figure of the whole object would enter through the sensitive organ, and present itself before the mind, by reason all objects are not perceived in parts, but many in whole: And since the exterior figure of the object is only perceived by the senses, then the bare figure would enter into the brain, without the body or substance of the object; which how it could be, I am not able to conceive: nay, if it were possible, truly, it would not be hidden from the mind's officers, the sensitive spirits, except they did carry it veiled or covered; but then they would know, at least, from whence they had it, and to whom, and how they were to carry it. Wherefore it is absurd, in my opinion, to say, that the senses bring all knowledge of exterior objects to the mind, and yet have none themselves; and that the mind chiefly resides but in one part of the body; so that when the heel is touched, the sensitive spirits, who watch in that place, do run up to the head, and bring news to the mind. Truly, if the senses have no knowledge of themselves, how comes it that a man born blind, cannot tell what the light of sun is, or the light of a candle, or the light of a glow-worm's tail? For, though some objects of one sense may be guessed by the perception of another sense, as we may guess by touch, the perception of an object that belongs to sight, etc. yet we cannot perfectly know it, except we saw it, by reason the perception of sight belongs only to the optic sense. But some may ask, If a man be so blind, that he cannot make use of his optic sense; what is become of the sensitive motions in that same part of his body, to wit, the optic sensorium? I answer, The motions of that part are not lost, because the man is blind, and cannot see; for a privation or absence of a thing, doth not prove that it is quite lost; but, the same motions which formerly did work to the perception of sight, are only changed, and work now to some other action than the perception of sight; so that it is only a change or alteration of motions in the same parts, and not an annihilation: for, there's no such thing as an annihilation in nature, but all the variety in nature, is made by change of motions. Wherefore, to conclude, the opinion of sense and reason, or a sensitive and rational knowledge in all parts of nature, is, in my judgment, more probable and rational, than the opinion which confines all knowledge of nature to a man's brains or head, and allows none neither to the senses, nor to any part of nature.

XXXVII   Several Questions and Answers Concerning Knowledge and Perception

I am not ignorant, that endless questions and objections may be raised upon one subject; and, to answer them, would be an infinite labour. But, since I desire to be perspicuous in delivering my opinions, and to remove all those scruples which seem to obstruct the sense thereof, I have chosen rather to be guilty of prolixity and repetitions, than to be obscure by too much brevity. And therefore I will add to my former discourse of knowledge and perception, the resolution of these following questions, which, I hope, will render it more intelligible.

Q. 1.   What difference is there between self-knowledge and perception?

I answer: There is as much difference betwixt them, as betwixt a whole, and its parts; or a cause, and its effects: For, though self-motion be the occasional cause of particular perceptions, by reason it is the cause of all particular actions of nature, and of the variety of figures; yet self-knowledge is the ground, or fundamental cause of perception: for, were there not self-knowledge, there could not be perception; by reason perceptions are nothing else but particular exterior knowledges, or knowledges of exterior parts and actions, occasioned by the various compositions and divisions of parts: so that self-moving matter has a perceptive self-knowledge, and consisting of infinite parts; those parts have particular self-knowledges and perceptions, according to the variety of the corporeal figurative motions, which, as they are particular, cannot be infinite in themselves: for, although a whole may know its parts, yet the parts cannot possibly know the whole; because an infinite may know a finite, but a finite cannot know an infinite. Nevertheless, when many parts are regularly composed, those parts by a conjunction or union of their particular self-knowledges and perceptions of each other, may know more, and so judge more probably of infinite, as I have declared above: but, as for single parts, there is no such thing in nature, no more than there can be an infinite part.

*Q. 2.   Whether the inanimate part of matter, may not have
self-knowledge, as well as the animate?*

I answer: that, in my opinion, and according to the conceptions of my
sense and reason, the inanimate part of matter has self-knowledge, as
well as the animate, but not perception; for it is only the animate part of
matter that is perceptive, and this animate matter being of a two-fold
degree, sensitive and rational; the rational not being encumbered with
the inanimate parts, has a more clear and freer perception than the
sensitive, which is well to be observed: for, though the rational, sensitive,
and inanimate parts of matter, make but one infinite self-moving body of
nature, yet there are infinite particular self-knowledges; for, nature, is
divided into infinite parts, and all parts of nature are self-knowing. But,
as all are not animate, so all are not perceptive; for perception, though it
proceeds from self-knowledge, as its ground or principle, yet it is also an
effect of self-motion; for, were there no self-motion, there would be no
perception: and because nature is self-moving, all her parts are so too;
and, as all her parts are moving, so they have all compositions and
divisions; and as all are subject to compositions and divisions, so all have
variety of self-knowledge, so that no part can be ignorant. And by reason
self-knowledge is the ground and principle of perception, it knows all the
effects, by the variety of their changes: therefore the inanimate part of
matter may, for anything I know or perceive, be as knowing as the other
parts of nature: for, although it be the grossest part, and so the dullest,
wanting self-motion; yet, by the various divisions and compositions
which the animate parts do make, the inanimate may be as knowing as
the animate.

But some may say, If inanimate matter were knowing of itself, then it
would also be sensible of itself. I answer: Self-knowledge is so far
sensible of itself, that it knows itself; and therefore the inanimate part of
matter being self-knowing, may be sensible of its own self-knowledge;
but yet it is not such a sense as self-moving matter has, that is, a
perceptive sense: for the difference of animate and inanimate matter,
consists herein, that one is self-moving, and consequently perceptive,
but the other not. And as animate matter is self-moving as well as
self-knowing; so it is the chief and architectonical part of nature, which
causes all the variety that is in nature; for, without animate matter, there
could be no composition and division, and so no variety; and without

inanimate matter, there could not be such solid compositions of parts as there are; for, the animate part of matter cannot be so gross as the inanimate: and therefore without these degrees, there would be no variety of figures, nor no composition of solid figures, as animals, vegetables, minerals, etc. So that those effects which our sense and reason perceives, could not be without the degrees of animate and inanimate matter; neither could there be perception without animate matter, by which all the various effects of nature are perceived: for, though one creature cannot perceive all the effects; yet the infinite parts of nature, by their infinite actions, perceive infinitely.

Again: Some may object, that if the inanimate part of matter have self-knowledge and sense, it must of necessity have life also. To which I answer: that the inanimate part of matter may have life, according as it hath sense and knowledge; but not such a life as the animate part of matter has, that is, an active life, as to compose and divide the infinite body of nature, into infinite parts and figures, and to produce infinite varieties of them, for all this cannot be without motion; nevertheless, it has so much life, as to know itself; and so much sense, as to be sensible of its own self-knowledge. In short, the difference between animate and inanimate matter's life, sense and self-knowledge, is, that the animate matter has an active life, and a perceptive sense and self-knowledge, which the inanimate part of matter has not, because it wants self-motion, which is the cause of all actions and perceptions in nature.

Q. 3. Whether the inanimate matter could have parts, without self-motion?

I answer, Yes: for, wheresoever is body or matter, there are also parts, because parts belong to body, and there can be no body without parts; but yet, were there no self-motion, there could be no various changes of parts or figures. The truth is, nature considered as she is, and as much as our sense and reason can perceive by her various effects, must of necessity be composed, or consist of a commixture of animate, both rational and sensitive, and inanimate matter: for, were there no inanimate matter, there would be no ground, or grosser substance to work on, and so no solid figures: and, were there no animate sensitive matter, there would be no "labourer," or "workman," as I may call it, to form the inanimate part of matter into various figures; nor would there be such infinite changes, compositions, divisions, productions, dissolutions, etc. as we see there are. Again, were there no animate rational matter, there would be no "designer" or "surveyor," to order and direct all things methodically; nor no fancies, imaginations, conceptions, memory, etc. so that this "triumvirate" of the degrees of matter, is so necessary a constitutive principle of all natural effects, that nature could not be without it: I mean; nature considered, not what she might have been, but as she is, and as much as we are able to perceive by her actions; for, natural philosophy is no more but a rational inquisition into the causes of natural effects: and therefore, as we observe the effects and actions of nature, so we may probably guess at their causes and principles.

Q. 4.   How so fine, subtle and pure a part as the animate matter is, can work upon so gross a part as the inanimate?

I answer, More easily than vitriol, or aqua fortis, or any other high extracts, can work upon metal, or the like; nay, more easily than fire can work upon wood, or stone, or the like. But you will say, that, according to my opinion, these bodies are not wrought upon, or divided by the exterior agent, as by fire, vitriol, etc. but that they divide themselves by their own inherent self-motion, and that the agent is no more but an occasion that the patient moves or acts thus, or thus. I answer, It is very true: for, there is such a commixture of animate and inanimate matter, that no particle in nature can be conceived or imagined, which is not composed of animate matter, as well as of inanimate; and therefore the patient, as well as the agent, having both a commixture of these parts of matter, none can act upon the other, but the patient changes its own parts by its own self-motion, either of its own accord, or by way of imitation; but the inanimate part of matter, considered in itself, or in its own nature, hath no self-motion, nor can it receive any from the animate; but they being both so closely intermixt, that they make but one self-moving body of nature, the animate parts of matter, bear the inanimate with them in all their actions; so that it is impossible for the animate parts to divide, compose, contract, etc. but the inanimate must serve them, or go along with them in all such corporeal figurative actions.

Q. 5.   *How is it possible that parts, being ignorant of each other, should*
agree in the production of a figure?

I answer: When I speak of ignorance and knowledge, my meaning is, not
that there is as much ignorance in the parts of nature, as there is
knowledge; for all parts have self-knowledge: but, I understand a perceptive knowledge, by which parts do perceive parts: and as for the agreeing
actions of parts, they cannot readily err, unless it be out of willfulness to
oppose or cross each other: for, put the case the sensitive parts were as
ignorant of perceptions as the inanimate; yet the rational being thoroughly intermixt with them, would cause agreeable combinations and connexions of parts in all productions; because they, being not encumbered with
the burdens of other parts, make more general perceptions than the
sensitive; and moving freely in their own degree, there is a more perfect
acquaintance between them, than the sensitive parts; which is the cause
that the rational do design and order, whenas the sensitive labour and
work: I mean, when they move regularly, or to one and the same effect;
for then they must needs move agreeably and unitedly: But, because the
sensitive parts are perceptive as well as the rational, and perceive not only
the rational adjoining parts, but also those of their own degree, they
cannot so grossly err, as some believe; especially since the sensitive parts
do not only know their own work, but are also directed by the rational;
but, as I have often said, the several sorts, both of the sensitive and
rational perceptions are well to be considered, which are as various as the
actions of nature, and cannot be numbered, by reason every figurative
action is a several perception, both sensitive and rational; and infinite
matter being in a perpetual motion, there must of necessity be infinite
figures, and so infinite perceptions amongst the infinite parts of nature.
    [But this is farther to be observed, that although every part hath its
own knowledge and perception; yet, when many parts are conjoined into
one figure, then, by reason of that twofold relation of their actions and
near neighbourhood, they become better acquainted. And, as many men
assembled in a church, make but one congregation, and all agree to
worship one God, in one and the same manner or way; so, many parts
conjoined in one figure, are, as it were, so many communicants, all
agreeing, and being united in one body. For example, all parts concur-
ring to compose the figure of the *eye*, agree together, not only in the
composition, but in the act of seeing or perception, and in all other

things, if regular, that are proper to that figure. The same may be understood of the parts composing the *ear*, and requisite to its perception; and in like manner to the rest of the *senses*. So that, though the parts of the eye be ignorant of the parts of the ear, as being wholly and only employed about their own composition, and the properties thereof, yet are they not ignorant of what their own adjoining parts do. I say, they are ignorant, not of all distant parts, but only of some: for, both the eye and the ear perceive at a distance, though not at all distances; otherwise, neither of them could represent the several sorts of objects proper to its composition: the eye could not pattern or represent objects proper to the sight; nor the ear pattern objects proper to the hearing. Thus you may perceive that an eye, or any other sensitive figure, is composed of parts, not only self-knowing and perceptive, but also *agreeing*, as being connected, and acting in one common union.][107]

Q. 6.   Whether there be single self-knowledges, and single perceptions in nature?

I answer: If there can be no such thing as a single part in nature, there can neither be a single self-knowledge or perception: for, body and parts can never be separated from each other, but wheresoever is body, were it an atom, there are parts also; and when parts divide from parts, at the same time, and by the same act, they are joined to other parts; so that composition and division is done by one act. The like for knowledge: for knowledge, being material, consists of parts; and as it is impossible that there can be single parts, or parts subsisting by themselves, without reference to each other, or the body of nature; so it is impossible that there can be single knowledges. Neither can there be a single magnitude, figure, colour, place, etc. but all that is corporeal, has parts; and by reason nature is a self-moving, and self-knowing body, all her parts must of necessity be so too. But, particular composed figures, and particular degrees of matter, are not single parts; nor are particular actions, single actions, no more than a particular creature is a single part: for, it would be nonsense to say, single compositions, and single divisions; and therefore particular and single are not one and the same: and as there can be no such thing as single in nature, so there can neither be single knowledges

---

[107] Lacking in 1666.

and perceptions: which is well to be observed, lest we introduce a vacuum in nature, and so make a confusion between her parts and actions: [but, were it possible there could be a single part, there would be a single knowledge.][108]

Q. 7.   How is it possible, since there is but one self-knowledge in nature, as there is but one self-motion, that there can be a double degree of this self-knowledge, as also a double perception, viz. rational and sensitive?

I answer: As the several degrees of matter are not several kinds of matter; so neither are rational and sensitive knowledge, several kinds of self-knowledges, but only different degrees of one self-knowledge: for, as there is but one matter, and one self-motion; so there is also but one self-knowledge in nature, which consists of two degrees, rational and sensitive, whereof the rational is the highest degree of self-knowledge: for it is a more pure, subtle, active and piercing knowledge than the sensitive, by reason it is not bound to work on, and with the inanimate parts of matter, but moves freely in its own degree; whenas the sensitive is encumbered with labouring on the inanimate parts of matter: Indeed, there is as much difference between those two degrees of self-knowledge, as betwixt a chief architect, designer or surveyor, and betwixt a labourer or workman: for, as the labourer and surveyor, though they be different particulars, are yet both of one kind, viz. mankind: so it is likewise with self-knowledge; for, were matter divided into infinite degrees, it would still remain matter; and though self-motion be divided into infinite degrees of motions, yet it is still but self-motion. The like for self-knowledge: for, self-moving matter can but know itself; and as matter is the ground or constitutive principle of all the parts and figures in nature, (for, without matter, there could be no parts, and so no division) and self-motion is the ground or principle of all particular actions, so is self-knowledge the ground of all particular knowledges and perceptions. Again, as one part cannot be another part, so neither can one part's knowledge be another part's knowledge, although they may have perceptions of each other. When I speak of parts, I mean not single parts; for there can be no such thing as a single part in nature: but, by parts I understand particular self-moving figures, whether they be such

---

[108] Lacking in 1666.

composed figures as (for distinction sake) we call finite wholes; as for example, an animal, a tree, a stone, etc. or, whether they be parts of those finite figures: for it is impossible to describe or determine exactly what the parts of nature are, by reason nature, although it is but one body, yet being self-moving, it is divided into infinite figures, which, by self-motion, are infinitely changed, composed, dissolved, etc. which compositions and divisions, hinder that there can be no single parts; because no part, though it should be infinitely changed, composed and divided, can be separated from the body of nature, but as soon as it is divided from such parts, it is composed with other parts; nay, were it possible that it might be separated from the body of nature, it would not be a part then, but a whole; for it would have no reference to the body of nature: besides, if it continued body, or matter, it would still have parts; for wheresoever is body, there is a composition of parts.

But if anyone desires to know, or guess at the parts of nature, he cannot do it better, than by considering the corporeal figurative motions or actions of nature: for, what we name parts, are nothing but the effects of those figurative motions; so that motions, figures and parts, are but one thing. And it is to be observed, that in composed figures, there are interior and exterior parts; the exterior are those which may be perceived by our exterior senses, with all their proprieties, as, colour, magnitude, softness, hardness, thickness, thinness, gravity, levity, etc. But the interior parts are the interior, natural, figurative motions, which cause it to be such or such a part or creature: As for example, man has both his interior and exterior parts, as is evident; and each of them has not only their outward figure or shape, but also their interior, natural, figurative motions, which did not only cause them to be such or such parts; (as for example, a leg, a head, a heart, a spleen, a liver, blood, etc.) but do also continue their being: the only difference is, that those figurative motions which did first form or produce them; afterwards, when they were finished, became retentive motions: By retentive motions, I do not only mean such as keep barely the parts of the composed figures together; but, all those that belong to the preservation and continuance of them; under which are comprehended digestive motions, which place and displace parts; attractive motions, which draw nourishment into those parts; expulsive motions, which expel superfluous and hurtful parts: and many the like: for, there are numerous sorts of retentive motions, or such as belong to the preservation and continuance of a composed figure, as well as there are of creating or producing motions. By which we may plainly see, that one figure lies within another; that is, one corporeal figurative motion, is within another; and, that the interior and exterior parts or figures of creatures, are different in their actions: for example, the ebbing and flowing, or the ascending and descending motions of water, are quite different from those interior figurative motions that make it water: The like may be said of vegetables, minerals, animals, and all other sorts of creatures; nay, though both the interior and exterior parts, figures or motions, do make but one composed figure or creature, as for example, man; and are all but parts of that same figure; yet, each being a particular motion, has also its peculiar self-knowledge and perception: for, the difference of particular knowledges and perceptions, depends upon the difference of nature's actions; which, as by the division of parts, they cause an ignorance between them; so, by composition, they cause also perceptions. I do not mean, an interior or self-ignorance, which cannot be in nature, by reason every part and particle has self knowledge; but, an exterior, that is, an ignorance of foreign parts, figures or actions, although they be parts of one composed figure; for, the parts of the hand do not know the parts of the stomach, and their actions. Neither do I mean an interior self-perception, which can neither be in nature, because perception presupposes ignorance; and if there cannot be a self-ignorance, there can neither be a self-perception, although there may be an interior self-knowledge. Nor is it proper to say, a part may perceive itself, or have a perception of itself: But by perception, I mean an exterior or foreign knowledge; that is, a knowledge of other parts, figures or actions. These perceptions, I say, are different, according to the difference of the corporeal figurative motions; for, it is impossible that such or such parts, should have such or such perceptions, if they have not such or such corporeal motions. Therefore, though all parts have self-knowledge, as well as self-motion; yet, by reason all parts do not move alike, they cannot make the like perceptions: and though self-knowledge, as it is the ground and fountain, not only of all particular knowledges, but also of all exterior perceptions, is but one in itself, as a fixt being, and cannot be divided from its own nature; (for, as matter cannot be divided from being matter, or self-motion from being self-motion; so, neither can self-knowledge be divided from being self-knowledge; nor can they be separated from each other, but every part and particle of natural matter, has self-knowledge and perception, as well as it hath self-motion:) Yet, all this hinders not, but there may be degrees of self-knowledge, according to the degrees of matter: for, as there is rational and sensitive matter, so there is also rational and sensitive self-knowledge: nay, there are infinite particular self-knowledges and perceptions, according to the infiniteness of parts and motions; and yet all is but one self-moving and self-knowing nature: for, parts are nothing else but a division of the whole, and the whole is nothing else but a composition of parts. All which I desire may be taken notice of, lest my sense be misinterpreted; for, when I speak of rational and sensitive self-knowledge, I do not mean as if there were more self-knowledges than one, in the only infinite matter, to wit, a double kind of self-knowledge; but I speak in reference to the parts of matter: for, the rational part is more pure, and so more agile, quick and free, than the sensitive; and the animate part is self-moving, but the inanimate not: And thus in respect to parts; as they are divided, so they have several self-knowledges and perceptions, as also numerous lives and souls in one composed figure or creature: and as infinite parts belong to one infinite whole; so infinite self-knowledges, and infinite perceptions, belong to the infinite actions of those infinite parts. But some may ask, Why there are no more degrees of matter, but two, viz. animate and inanimate; and no more degrees of animate, but rational and sensitive? I answer, Human sense and reason cannot conceive it possible there should be more or fewer; for the rational and sensitive are the purest degrees matter can be capable of: and, were there any purer than these, they would be beyond the nature of matter; which is impossible, because nature cannot go beyond itself. Again, some may perhaps desire to know, Why there are more degrees of inanimate matter, than of animate; to wit, of thickness and thinness, rarity and density, lightness and heaviness, etc.? I answer, These are nothing else but the actions of the material parts, and do not belong to the nature of matter; so that they cannot make parts less or more material, for all is but matter; neither can they alter the nature of matter; for matter is still matter, however it moves. Lastly, some may ask, How it is possible that such an infinite variety can proceed from but two degrees of matter, to wit, animate, and inanimate? I answer, As well as infinite effects can proceed from one infinite cause: for, nature being an infinite body, must also have infinite parts; and having an infinite self-motion, must of necessity have an infinite variety of parts; and being infinitely self-knowing, must also have infinite self-knowing parts; which proves, that nature's body must of necessity consist of those two degrees, viz. animate, and inanimate matter: for, were there no animate matter, which is corporeal self-motion, there would never be such variety of figures, parts and actions in nature, as there is, nor no perceptions: for, self-knowledge, or matter, without self-motion, could never make any variety in nature; and therefore, although self-motion causes an obscurity by the division of parts, yet it causes also particular perceptions between parts; and as the motions vary, so do perceptions of parts. In short, there is but one infinite body, and infinite parts; one infinite self-knowledge, and infinite particular self-knowledges; one infinite self-motion, and infinite particular actions; as also, infinite particular perceptions: for, self-motion is the cause of all the variety of nature: and, as one figure or part of nature, lies within another, so one perception is within another.

Q. 8. How can there be self-knowledge and perception, in one and the same part?

I answer: As well as the being or substance of a thing, and its actions, can consist together; or as a cause and its effects: for, though they are so far different from each other, that the cause is not the effect, nor the effect the cause; as also, that the effect must of necessity depend upon the cause, but the cause may choose whether it will produce such or such effects: As for example, though action or motion depends upon matter, yet matter does not depend upon motion, as being able to subsist without it: and though perception depends upon self-knowledge, yet self-knowledge does not depend upon perception: Nevertheless, wheresoever is perception, there is also self-knowledge; by reason, that wheresoever there is an effect in act or being, there is also its cause. And although perception depends also upon outward objects, yet outward objects do not depend upon perceptions; but perception, as it depends upon self-knowledge, so it depends also upon self-motion; for, without self-knowledge and self-motion, there would be no perception: So that both exterior perceptions, and all interior voluntary actions, proceed from self-knowing, and self-moving matter; but the difference between particular interior self-knowledges and perceptions, is caused by the changes of corporeal, figurative self-motion.

Q. 9.   Whether particular parts or figures, be bound to particular perceptions?

I answer: Particular parts make perceptions, according to the nature of their corporeal, figurative motions, and their perceptions are as numerous as their actions: For example, those parts that are composed into the figure of an animal, make perceptions proper to that which figures corporeal, interior, natural motions: but, if they be dissolved from the animal figure, and composed into vegetables, they make such perceptions as are proper for vegetables; and being again dissolved and composed into minerals, they make perceptions proper to minerals, etc. so that no part is tied or bound to one particular kind of perception, no more than it is bound to one particular kind of figure; but when the interior motions of that figure change, the perceptions proper to that same figure, change also: for, though self-knowledge, the ground of all perceptions, is a fixt, and inherent, or innate knowledge; yet, the perceptions vary according to their objects, and according to the changes and compositions of their own parts: for, as parts are composed with parts, so are their perceptions: nay, not only perceptions, but also particular self-knowledges alter, according to the alteration of their own parts or figures, not from being self-knowledge; for, self-knowledge can be but self-knowledge, but from being such or such a particular self knowledge. And since there is no part or particle of nature, but is self-knowing, or has its particular self-knowledge, it is certain, that as the interior nature of the figure alters by the changes of motion, the interior self-knowledge of that figure, alters too: for, if a vegetable should turn into a mineral, it cannot retain the self-knowledge of a vegetable, but it must of necessity change into the self-knowledge of a mineral; for, nothing can have a knowledge of itself, otherwise than what it is: And because self-knowledge is the ground of perception, as self-knowledge alters, so doth perception: I mean, that kind of perception that belonged to such a figure, alters to another kind of perception proper to another figure; so that it is with perception, as it is with other creatures. For example; as there are several kinds of creatures, as elements, animals, minerals, vegetables, etc. so there are also several kinds of perceptions, as animal, vegetative, mineral, elemental perception: And as there are different particular sorts of these mentioned kinds of creatures, so there are also of perceptions; nay, as one particular creature of these sorts, consists of different parts; so every part has also different perceptions: for self-motion, as it is the cause of all the various changes of figures and parts of nature, so it is also of the variety of perceptions: for, put the case matter were of one infinite figure, it would have but self-knowledge, or at least no variety of perceptions, because it would have no variety of corporeal figurative motions; and it is well to be observed, that, although numerous different parts may agree in perception, that is, their sensitive and rational figurative motions, may all well perceive one and the same object; yet, the manner of their perceptions are different, according to the difference of their figures, or rather, of their interior, corporeal, figurative motions: For example, a man, a tree, and a stone, may all have perceptions of one object, but yet their perceptions are not alike: for, the tree has not an animal or mineral, but a vegetative perception; and so has the man, not a vegetative or mineral, but an animal perception; and the stone, not an animal or a vegetative, but a mineral perception; each according to the interior nature of its own figure.

Q. 10.   Whether there could be self-knowledge without perception?

I answer: Self-knowledge being the ground of all perceptions, which are nothing else but exterior knowledges, might as well subsist without them, as matter would subsist without motion: but, since self-motion is the cause of all the various changes of figures and parts, and of all the orderly productions, generations, transformations, dissolutions, and all other actions of nature; these cannot be performed without perception: for, all actions are knowing and perceptive; and, were there no perception, there could not possibly be any such actions: for, how should parts agree, either in the generation, composition or dissolution of composed figures, if they had no knowledge or perception of each other? Therefore, although self-knowledge is a fixt interior being, and the ground of all perceptions; yet, were there no self-motion, there could be no action, and consequently, no perception, at least no variety of perceptions in nature: but, since nature is one self-moving, and self-knowing body, self-knowledge can no more be separated from perception, than motion can be divided from matter; but every part and particle of nature, were it an atom, as it is self-moving, so it is also self-knowing and perceptive. But yet, it is not necessary that perception must only be betwixt neighbouring or adjoining parts: for some parts may very well perceive each other at a distance, and when other parts are between; nay, some perceptions do require a distance of the object: As for example, the optic perception in animals, as I have declared before,[w] where I do mention the requisites of the animal perception of sight; whereof if one be wanting, there is either no perception at all, (I mean, no perception of seeing in that animal) or, the perception is imperfect. But some may ask, Whether, in such a case, that is, in the perception of an object which is distant from the sentient, the intermediate parts are as well perceived, as the object itself, to which the perception directly tends? I answer, that, if the intermediate parts be subject to that kind of perception, they may as well be perceived, as the object that is distant; nay, sometimes better: but most commonly, the intermediate parts are but slightly or superficially perceived: For example, in the aforementioned sense of seeing, if the organ of sight be directed to some certain object that is distant, and there be some parts between the organ and the object, perceptible by the same sense, but such as do not hinder or obstruct the perception of the said object: not only the object, but also those intermediate parts will be perceived by the optic sense. Also, if I cast my eye upon an object that is before me, in a direct line, the eye will not only perceive the object to which it is chiefly directed, but also those parts that are joined to it, either beneath, or above, or on each side of that object, at the same point of time, and by the same act; the sole difference is, that the said object is chiefly, and of purpose patterned out by the sensitive and rational figurative motions of the eye; whenas the other intermediate or adjoining parts, are but superficially and slightly looked over.

And this proves, first, that nature is composed of sensitive, rational and inanimate matter, without any separation or division from each other; for, could matter be divided into an atom, that very atom would have a composition of these three degrees of matter. And therefore, although the parts of nature do undergo infinite divisions and compositions, so that parts may be composed and divided infinite ways; yet, these three degrees can never be separated or divided from one another, because of their close union and commixture through infinite nature.

Next, it proves, that there can be no single parts in nature; for, what commonly are called parts of nature, are nothing else but changes of motion in the infinite body of nature; so that parts, figures, actions and

---

[w] Part I, c. 20, Of Colours, p. 63. [I, ch. 20, p. 82.]

changes of motion, are one and the same, no more differing from each other, than body, place, magnitude, figure, colour, etc. For self-motion is the cause of the variety of figures and parts of nature, without which, although there would, nevertheless, be parts, (for, wheresoever is matter or body, there are parts also) yet nature would be but a confused heap, or chaos, without the distinction of any perfect figures; which figures make perfect perceptions of perfect objects; I say, of perfect objects: for, if the objects be not perfect, neither can the sensitive perceptions be perfect; but then the rational being joined with the sensitive, and being more subtle, active and piercing, may find out the error either of the object, or sense: for, both the rational and sensitive parts being united in one figure or action, can more easily perceive the irregularities of each other's actions, than of exterior objects; all which could not be, were there single parts in nature; neither could such acts be performed by chance, or senseless atoms: nay, could there be any single parts in nature, there would consequently be a vacuum, to discern and separate them from each other; which vacuum would breed such a confusion amongst them, as there would be no conformity or symmetry in any of their figures. Therefore I am absolutely against the opinion of senseless and irrational atoms, moving by chance: for, if nature did consist of such atoms, there would be no certain kinds and species of creatures, nor no uniformity or order: neither am I able to conceive how there could be a motion by chance, or an irrational and senseless motion; no more than I can conceive how motion can be without matter or body: for self-motion, as it is corporeal, so it is also sensitive and rational.

Q. 11.   Whether perception be made by patterning?

I answer: My sense and reason does observe, that the animal, at least, human perception, performed by the sensitive and rational motions in the organs appropriated for it, is made by patterning or framing of figures, according to the patterns of exterior objects; but whether all other kinds and sorts of perceptions in the infinite parts of nature, be made the same manner or way, neither myself, nor no particular creature is able to determine, by reason there are as many various sorts of perceptions, as there are of other actions of nature; and according as the corporeal figurative motions do alter and change, so do particular perceptions; for, perception is a corporeal, figurative action, and is generally in all parts and actions of nature: and, as no part can be without self-motion and self-knowledge, so none can be without perception. And therefore, I dare truly say, that all perceptions are made by figuring, though I cannot certainly affirm, that all are made by imitation or patterning. But it is well to be observed, that, besides those exterior perceptions of objects, there are some other interior actions both of sense and reason, which are made without the presentation of exterior objects, voluntarily, or by rote; and therefore are not actions of patterning, but voluntary actions of figuring: As for example, imaginations, fancies, conceptions, passions, and the like; are made by the rational, corporeal, figurative motions, without taking any copies of foreign objects; also, many generations, dissolutions, alterations, transformations, etc. are made by the sensitive motions, without any exterior patterns; for, the generation of maggot in a cheese, of a worm in the root of a tree, of a stone in the bladder, etc. are not made by patterning or imitation, because they are not like their producers, but merely by a voluntary figuring: And therefore it is well to be observed, that figuring and patterning are not one and the same; figuring is a general action of nature: for, all corporeal actions are figurative, whenas patterning is but a particular sort of figuring: and although I observe, that some perceptions are made by patterning, yet I cannot say the same of all; neither are the interior voluntary actions, made by patterning; but, both the sensitive and rational motions, frame such or such figures of their own accord: for, though each part in the composition of a creature, knows its own work, and all do agree in the framing and producing of it; yet they are not necessitated always to imitate each other: which is evident, because the composition of one and the same creature, is various and different, by reason of the variety of its parts.

And this is the difference between exterior perceptions, and interior voluntary actions: for, though both are effects of self-knowledge and self-motion, yet perceptions are properly concerning foreign parts, figures and actions, and are occasioned by them: but, the voluntary actions are not occasioned by any outward objects, but make figures of their own accord, without any imitation, patterns, or copies of foreign parts, or actions: And as the figures and parts alter by their compositions and divisions, so do both interior and exterior particular knowledges: for a tree, although it has sensitive and rational knowledge and perception, yet it has not an animal knowledge and perception; and if it should be divided into numerous parts, and these again be composed with other parts, each would have such knowledge and perception, as the nature of their figure required: for, self-knowledge alters as their own parts also; perception alters as the objects alter; figures alter as the actions alter; and the actions alter as nature pleases, or is decreed by God to work.

But I desire it may be observed, first, that, although there are both voluntary actions of figuring, and occasioned actions of perceiving exterior objects, both in sense and reason, whereof those I call interior, these exterior; yet both of them are innate and inherent actions of their own parts, as proceeding from the ground and fountain of self-knowledge: and the reason why I call the voluntary actions, interior, is, because they have no such respect to outward objects, at least, are not occasioned by them, as perceptions are, but are the figurative actions of sense and reason, made by rote; whenas perceptions do tend to exterior objects, and are made according to the presentation of their figures, parts or actions.

Next, it is to be observed, that many times the rational motions take patterns from the sensitive voluntary figures: As for example, in dreams, when the sensitive motions make voluntary figures on the inside of the sensitive organs, the rational take patterns of them; and again, the sensitive do many times take patterns of the rational, when they make figures by rote, as in the invention and delivery of arts and sciences; so that there is oftentimes an imitation between the rational and sensitive motions: for, the rational voluntary figures, are like exterior objects, to be patterned out by the sensitive perceptive motions; and the sensitive voluntary figures, are like exterior objects, to be patterned out by the rational perceptive motions; and yet all their perceptive actions are their own, and performed inwardly, that is, by their own motions: Which proves, that by calling perception an exterior action, I do not mean that it is an action externally perceptible or visible: for, if it were thus, then one part would presently know another part's perception, when and how it perceives; which we find it does not: for, although a man perceives a tree or stone, yet he does not know whether the tree or stone perceives him, much less, what perceptions they make: But, as I said before, perception I call an exterior action, because it is occasioned by an object that is without the perceiving parts: for, although both sensitive and rational perception are so closely intermixt, that none can be without the other in every part or particle of nature, were it no bigger than what is called an atom; yet, considered in themselves, they are without each other so far, that the rational perceptive part, is not the sensitive, nor the sensitive the rational; or else they would not be several parts or actions, neither would there by any imitation betwixt them.

Lastly, I desire that notice may be taken, when I say, that every action of nature is perceptive: for, since there are no single parts in nature; but, whatsoever is body, consists of parts: there can neither be any such thing as a single action, that is, an action of a single part; but, in all natural actions, there is a commerce, intercourse, or agreement of parts; which intercourse or agreement, cannot be without perception or knowledge of each other: Wherefore it must of necessity follow, that every action is perceptive, or that perception between parts, is required in every action of nature; nay, even in those which are called voluntary actions: for, though the rational and sensitive parts of a composed figure, can make voluntary figures within themselves, without taking any patterns of foreign objects; yet those parts must needs know and perceive each other, even in the composition or framing of their voluntary figures: so that exterior knowledge or perception, is as universal as self-motion; for, wheresoever is self-motion, there is perception also. But it is well to be observed, first, that perception, or perceptive knowledge, is only between parts. Next, that although every action in nature is perceptive; yet, not every action is the action of perception, properly so called; which perception, in composed figures, at least in animals, is an action of patterning out exterior parts or objects, performed by the rational and sensitive corporeal figurative motions, in their proper organs: But, there are infinite other actions, which, although they require perceptive parts, yet they are not such actions of perceptions as are made by patterning out, or imitating outward objects; as for example, respiration, digestion, contraction, dilatation, expulsion, generation, retention, dissolution, growth, decay, etc. Nevertheless, all those actions are perceptive; that is, the parts which perform those actions, have perception of each other, or else they would never agree to produce such effects. The truth is, that even the action of perception, properly so called, presupposes many particular perceptions between those parts that concur to the performance of that act: for it is impossible that both the rational and sensitive parts in a composed figure, should make the act of perception, without they know and agree what they are to do, and how they are to perform it, as I mentioned before. And this is the reason that I have made[x] a difference between perception and respiration, and called them different actions; not as if respiration was not a perceptive action, or presupposes not knowledge and perception between those parts that make respiration; but it is not the action of perception properly so called; as for example, the perception of seeing, hearing, smelling, tasting, etc. in animals: but it is properly an action of drawing, sucking, breathing in, or receiving any ways, outward parts; and of venting, discharging or sending forth inward parts: Nevertheless, all this cannot be done without perception or knowledge, no more than without motion; for, wheresoever is motion, there is perception also: and therefore respiration is a perceptive action. In short, I desire it may be observed, 1. That there is perception in every action, but not that every perception is made by patterning. 2. That all self-moving parts are perceptive. 3. That perception, perceptive knowledge, and exterior knowledge, are all one thing, and that I take them indifferently. 4. That all voluntary actions, both of sense and reason, are made by perceptive parts; and therefore, when I make a distinguishment between voluntary actions, and perceptions, I mean the perceptions of a composed figure, and not the particular perceptive knowledges between those parts that join in the act of such perceptions, or in the making of voluntary figures.

But it may be objected, that if all motions be perceptive, they would be wholly employed in nothing else, but in making copies of exterior parts or objects.

My answer is, Although I say, that all motions are perceptive; yet, I do not positively affirm, that all perceptions in nature are made by patterning or imitation: for, we are to consider, that there are as many different sorts of perceptions, as there are of motions; because every particular motion, has a particular perception: and though, in a composed figure or creature, some motions may work to the patterning out of exterior objects, yet all the rest may not do so, and be nevertheless, perceptive: For, as a man, or any other animal creature, is not altogether composed of eyes, ears, noses, or the like sensitive organs: so, not all perceptive motions are imitating or patterning; but some are retentive, some expulsive, some attractive, some contractive, some dilative, some creating or producing, some dissolving, some imitating or patterning, and so forth. And as there are degrees of parts and motions, so some perceptions may

---

[x] N. 5, Of Pores. [I, ch. 5, p. 55.]

be so much purer, finer, and subtler than others, as much as pure air is beyond gross earth. The truth is, we cannot judge of nature's actions any other ways than we observe them by our own sensitive and rational perceptions: and, since we find that the sensitive and rational motions in our sensitive organs, do work by the way of patterning or imitation, we may surely conclude, that some perceptions are made that way; but, that all other perceptions in all natural parts or creatures, should be after the same manner, would be too presumptuous for any particular creature to affirm, since there are infinite several sorts of perceptions: and although we may justly, and with all reason believe, that all parts of nature are perceptive, because they are self-moving, and self-knowing; yet no particular creature is able to judge how, and in what manner they perceive, no more than it can know how they move. And by this it is evident, how in one and the same organ of the eye, some motions or parts may work to the act of perception, properly so called, which is made by patterning out the figure of an exterior object; and other motions or parts may work to the retention of the eye, and preserving it in its being: others again may work to its shutting and opening; and others to its respiration, that is, venting of superfluous, and receiving of nourishing parts; which motions are properly subservient to the retentive motions, and hundreds the like; and yet all these motions are as knowing and perceptive, after their way, as those that work to the act of perception, properly so called; that is, to the act of seeing, made by patterning or imitation. But it is well to be observed, that although the eye has the quickest action in the perception of seeing; yet is this action most visible, not only by its motions, but by the figures of the objects that are represented in the eye: for, if you look into another's eye, you will plainly perceive therein, the picture of your own figure; and, had other objects but such an optic perception as animals, they would, without question, observe the same. Some will say, Those figures in the eye are made by reflexion; but reflexions cannot make such constant and exact patterns or imitations. Others believe it proceeds from pressure and reaction; but pressure and reaction, being but particular actions, cannot make such variety of figures. Others again say, that the species of the objects, pass from the objects to the optic organ, and make figures in the air; but then the multitude of those figures in the air, would make such a confusion, as would hinder the species passing through: besides, the species being corporeal, and proceeding from the object, would lessen its quantity or bulk.[109] Wherefore my opinion is, that the most rare and subtlest parts in the animal sensitive organs, do pattern out the figures of exterior objects, and that the perception of the exterior animal senses, to wit, sight, hearing, tasting, touching, smelling, is certainly made by no other way, than by figuring and imitation.

Q. 12. How the bare patterning out of the exterior figure of an object, can give us an information of its interior nature?

My answer is, that although our sensitive perception can go no further than the exterior shape, figure and actions of an object; yet, the rational being a more subtle, active, and piercing perception, by reason it is more free than the sensitive, does not rest in the knowledge of the exterior figure of an object, but, by its exterior actions, as by several effects, penetrates into its interior nature, and doth probably guess and conclude what its interior figurative motions may be: For, although the interior and exterior actions of a composed figure be different, yet the exterior may partly give a hint or information of the interior: I say, "partly"; because it is impossible that one finite particular creature, should have a perfect knowledge or perception of all the interior and exterior actions of another particular creature: For example, our sensitive perception patterns out an animal, a mineral, a vegetable, etc.; we perceive they have the figure of flesh, stone, wood, etc. but yet we do not know what is the cause of their being such figures: for, the interior figurative motions of these creatures, being not subject to the perception of our exterior senses, cannot exactly be known: Nevertheless, although our exterior senses have no perception thereof, yet their own parts which are concerned in it, as also their adjoining or neighbouring parts may: For example, a man knows he has a digestion in his body, which being an interior action, he cannot know, by his exterior senses, how it is made; but those parts of the body where the digestion is performed, may know it; nay, they must of necessity do so,[110] because they are concerned in it,

[109] Cavendish has summarized and rejected three "transmission" theories of sensory perception: the dioptrical writers' view that images are communicated via the reflection of light, the mechanical view that perception is the impact and resistance of corporeal particles, and the scholastic view that perception arises due to the emission of species; cf. John Norris, *Essay on the Ideal or Intelligible World*, vol. II, pp. 368ff.
[110] A constraint on causation commonly held in the seventeenth century: The cause must know how to bring about the effect. See, e.g., Malebranche, *The Search After Truth*, bk VI, pt II, ch. 3.

as being their proper employment. The same may be said of all other particular parts and actions in an animal body, which are like several workmen employed in the building of a house: for, although they do all work and labour to one and the same end, that is, the building of the house; and every one may have some inspection or perception of what his neighbour doth; yet each having his peculiar task and employment, has also its proper and peculiar knowledge how to perform his own work: for, a joiner knows best how to finish and perfect what he has to do; and so does a mason, carpenter, tiler, glazier, stone-cutter, smith, etc. And thus it is with all composed figures or creatures; which proves, that perception has only a respect to exterior parts or objects; whenas self-knowledge is an interior, inherent, innate, and, as it were, a fixt being; for it is the ground and fountain of all other particular knowledges and perceptions, even as self-motion is the cause and principle of all other particular actions; and although self-knowledge can be without perception, yet perception cannot be without self-knowledge; for it has its being from self-knowledge, as an effect from its cause; and as one and the same cause may produce numerous effects, so from one self-knowledge proceed numerous perceptions, which do vary infinitely, according to the various changes of corporeal self-motion. In short, self-knowledge is the fundamental cause of perception; but self-motion the occasional cause. Just like matter and self-motion, are the causes of all natural figures; for, though perception could not be without self-knowledge, yet were there no self-motion, there would be no variety of figures, and consequently, not exterior objects to be perceived.

Q. 13. *How is it possible, that several figures can be patterned out by one act of perception? for example, how can a man, when he sees a statue or a stone, pattern out both the exterior shape of the statue, the matter which the statue is made of, and its colour, and all this by one and the same act?*

I answer, First it is to be observed, that matter, colour, figure, magnitude, etc. are all but one thing, and therefore they may easily be patterned out by one act of perception at one and the same time. Next, I say, that no sense is made by one single part, but every sense consists of several parts, and therefore the perception of one sense may very well pattern out several objects at once. For example, I see an embroidered bed; my eye patterns out both the velvet, gold, silver, silk, colour, and the workmanship, nay, superficially the figure of the whole bed, and all this by one act and at one and the same time. But it is to be observed, that one object may have several proprieties, which are not all subject to the perception of one sense; as for example, the smell of an odoriferous body, and its colour, are not subject to the same sense; neither is the hardness or softness, roughness or smoothness of its parts, subject to the sense of smelling or seeing, but each is perceived by such a sense as is proper for such a sort of perception. Nevertheless, these different perceptions do not make them to be different bodies; for even one and the same attribute or propriety of a body may be patterned out by several senses; for example, magnitude or shape of body may be patterned out both by sight and touch; which proves, that there is a near affinity or alliance betwixt the several senses; and that touch is, as it were a general sense, which may imitate some other sensitive perceptions. The truth is, it is as easy for several senses to pattern out the several proprieties of one body, as it is for several painters to draw the several parts of one figure; as for example, of a burning candle, one may draw the wax or tallow, another the wick, another the flame: The like for the perceptions of several senses: Sight may pattern out the figure and light of a candle; touch may pattern out its weight, hardness or smoothness; the nose may pattern out its smell; the ears may pattern out its sparkling noise, etc. All which does evidently prove, that perception cannot be made by pressure and reaction; or else a fire-coal, by the perception of sight, would burn out the eyes, because it would by pressure, inflame its next adjoining parts, and these again the next, until it came to the eye. Besides, it proves that all objects are material; for, were light, colour, figure, heat, cold, etc. immaterial, they would never be patterned out by corporeal motions: for, no painter is able to copy out, or draw an immaterial mode or motion; neither could immaterial motions make pressure, nor be subject to reaction. Lastly, it proves, that perception is an effect of knowledge in the sentient, and not in the external object; or else there would be but one knowledge in all parts, and not several knowledges in several parts; whereof sense and reason inform us otherwise, viz. that particular figures have variety of knowledges, according to the difference and variety of their corporeal figurative motions.

But then some will say, that the actions of matter would be more infinite than the parts. I answer, There can be neither more nor less in infinite: for, infinite can be but infinite; but since parts, figures, changes of motion, and perceptions, are one and the same; and since

division and composition, are the chief actions of nature, it does necessarily follow, that, as the actions vary, so do also their parts and particular
perceptions.

*Q. 14.   How is it possible that any perception of outward objects, can be
made by patterning, since patterning doth follow perception? for, how can
anyone pattern out that which he has no perception of?*

I answer: Natural actions are not like artificial; for art is but gross and
dull in comparison to nature: and, although I allege the comparison of a
painter, yet is it but to make my meaning more intelligible to weaker
capacities: for, though a painter must see or know first what he intends to
draw or copy out; yet the natural perception of exterior objects is not
altogether after the same manner; but, in those perceptions which are
made by patterning, the action of patterning, and the perception, are one
and the same: for, as self-knowledge is the ground of perception, so
self-motion is the action of perception, without which, no perception
could be; and therefore perception and self-action are one and the same.
But I desire that it may well be observed what I have mentioned
heretofore, to wit, that although there is but one self-knowledge, and one
self-motion in nature, yet they being material, are divisible: and therefore, as from one infinite cause, there may flow infinite effects, and one
infinite whole may be divided into infinite parts; so, from one infinite
self-knowledge, and self-motion, there may proceed infinite particular
actions and perceptions.

But some, perhaps, may ask, (1) Why those particular knowledges and
perceptions are not all alike, as being all but effects of one cause? To
which I answer, that if the actions or motions of nature were all alike, all
parts would have the like knowledges and perceptions; but the actions
being different, how can it be otherwise, but the perceptions must be
different also? for, since every perception is a particular self-action, then
as the actions of nature vary, and as parts do divide and compose, so are
likewise their perceptions.

(2) It may be objected, that if the perception of the exterior senses in
animals, be made by the way of patterning, then when a part of the body
feels pain, the rational motions, by patterning out the same, would be
pained, or sick.

I answer: This does no more follow, than that the eye patterning out

the exterior figure of water, fire, earth, etc. should become of the same
nature: for, the original is one thing, and the copy another: the picture of
a house of stone, is not made of natural stone, nor is the picture of a tree,
a natural tree; for if it were so, painters would do more than chemists by
fire and furnace; but by reason there is a very close conjunction between
the rational and sensitive perceptive motions, so that when the sensitive
motions of the body, pattern out some exterior object, the rational most
commonly do the same. That which we call pain or sickness in the body,
when patterned out by the mind, is called trouble, or grief: for as there
are degrees in their purity, subtlety and activity, so their perceptions are
also different. But it is well to be observed, that although some parts are
ignorant of others, when they work not to one and the same perception;
yet, sometimes there is a more general knowledge of a disease, pain, or
soreness: For example, a man may have an inflammation or soreness in
one part of his arm or leg, and all the rest of the parts of that limb, may be
ignorant thereof; but if the inflammation, soreness or pain, extend
throughout the whole arm or leg, then all the parts of that limb are
generally sensible of it.

(3) It may be objected, that if the rational perceptive motions take
patterns from the sensitive, then reason can never judge of things as
naturally they are, but only of their copies, as they are patterned out by
the sensitive motions.

[I answer, My meaning is, that sometimes the rational takes patterns
from the sensitive, and other times the sensitive from the rational; but
both, for the most part, act together, and, as it were, in the same instant of
time, and in communion, in patterning one object, only the copies are not
the same; for one copy is of the rational, the other of the sensitive
perception: so that there is a double perception of one and the same object;
the one rational, the other sensitive. For instance, when I see an object, I
have also a thought of that object; and that thought is a copy of the object,
made of the rational part of matter, but not the sensitive pattern; so that
there is a great difference betwixt the rational perception and the sensitive. For a second instance, the sensitive perception of light in the eye, is
one thing; the rational perception or thought of light, is another; which I
mention, to express in some manner the nature of perception rational;
though at the same time I understand, there are infinite perceptions
rational, as well as infinite perceptions sensitive: wherefore I cannot say,
that all rational perceptions are like to human thoughts, otherwise, than in

respect of purity; for we may perceive in ourselves a greater purity and subtlety of the rational, than of the sensitive.][111]

But then some may say, if the rational part has liberty to move as it will, then it may perceive without sense; that is, reason may make perceptions of outward objects in the organs of the senses, when the senses make none; as for example, the rational motions in the eye may perceive light, when the sensitive do not; and sound in the ear, when the sensitive do not.

To which I answer; It is probable, that the rational do many times move to other perceptions than the sensitive; as I have often declared; but if their actions be orderly and regular, then most commonly they move to one and the same perception; but reason being the purer and freer part, has a more subtle perception than sense, for there is great difference between sense and reason, concerning the subtlety of their actions; sense does perceive, as it were, in part, whenas reason perceives generally, and in whole; for if there be an object which is to be patterned out with all its proprieties, the colour of it is perceived only by sight; the smell of it is perceived by the nose, its sound is perceived by the ear, its taste is perceived by the tongue, and its hardness or softness, coldness or heat, dryness or moisture, is perceived by touch; so that every sense in particular, patterns out that object which is proper for it; and each has but so much knowledge of the said object as it patterns out; for the sight knows nothing of its taste, nor the taste of its touch, nor the touch of its smell; and so forth: But the mind patterns out all those figures together, so that they are but as one object to it, without division: which proves, that the rational perception, being more general, is also more perfect than the sensitive; and the reason is, because it is more free, and not encumbered with the burdens of other [parts]:[112] Wherefore the rational can

[111] Lacking in 1666, which instead contains:

I answer, first, that reason is not so necessitated, as to have no other perception than what sense presents; for reason is the instructor and informer of sense, as an architect or surveyor is in the exstruction of a house. Next, I say, that in the act of perception, reason doth not only perceive the copies of the senses, but it perceives with the sense also the original; for surely the rational part of matter, being intermixed with the sensitive, must perceive as well the original, as sense doth; for it is not so involved within the sensitive, that it cannot peep out, as a jack-in-the-box; but both being closely intermixed, one makes perceptions as well as the other, as being both perceptive; and by reason the rational part makes the same perception as the sensitive doth, it seemeth as if the rational did take copies from the sensitive; which although it doth, yet this doth not hinder it from making a perception also of the original.

[112] As in 1666; 1668: part.

judge better of objects than the sensitive, as being more knowing; and knows more, because it has a more general perception; and hath a more general perception, because it is more subtle and active; and is more subtle and active, because it is free, and not necessitated to labour on, or with any other parts.

But some may say, How is it possible, that the rational part being so closely intermixed with the sensitive and the inanimate, can move by itself, and not be a labourer, as well as the sensitive?

I answer: The reason is, because the rational part is more [pure][113] and finer than the sensitive, or any other part of matter; which purity and fineness makes that it is so subtle and active, and consequently, not necessitated to labour with, or on other parts.

Again: Some may ask, whether those intermixed parts continue always together in their particulars? as for example, whether the same rational parts keep constantly to the same sensitive and inanimate parts, as they're commixed?

I answer: Nature is in a perpetual motion, and her parts are parts of her own self-moving body; wherefore they must of necessity divide and compose; but if they divide and compose, they cannot keep constantly to the same parts. Nevertheless, although particular parts are divisible from each other, yet the triumvirate of nature, that is, the three chief degrees or parts of matter, to wit, rational, sensitive and inanimate, which belong to the constitution of nature, cannot be separated or divided from each other in general; so that rational matter may be divided from sensitive and inanimate, and these again from the rational, but they must of necessity continue in this commixture as long as nature lasts. In short, rational, sensitive and inanimate matter are divisible in their particulars; that is, such a particular part of inanimate matter is not bound to such a particular part of sensitive or rational matter, etc. But they are indivisible in general, that is, from each other; for wheresoever is body, there is also a commixture of these three degrees of matter.

(4) Some may say, How is it possible, that reason can be above sense; and that the rational perception is more subtle and knowing than the sensitive; since in my *Philosophical Opinions*, I have declared that the sensitive perception doth inform the rational: or that reason perceives by the information of the senses?

[113] As in 1666; 1668: purer.

To which I answer: My meaning is not, that reason has no other perception, but by the information of the senses; for surely the rational perception is more subtle, piercing and penetrating, or inspective, than the sensitive, and therefore more intelligent and knowing: But when I say, that sense informs reason, I speak only of such perceptions where the rational figurative motions take patterns from the sensitive, and do not work voluntarily, or by rote.

Besides, it is to be observed, that in the mentioned book, I compare thoughts, which are the actions of the rational figurative motions, to the sensitive touch; so that, touch is like a thought in sense, and thought like a touch in reason: But there is great difference in their purity; for, though the actions of touch and thought are much after the same manner, yet the different degrees of sense and reason, or of animate, sensitive and rational matter, cause great difference between them; and as all sensitive perception is a kind of touch, so all rational perception is a kind of thoughtfulness: But mistake me not, when I say, thought is like touch; for I do not mean, that the rational perception is caused by the conjunction or joining of one part to another, or that it is an exterior touch, but an interior knowledge; for all self-knowledge is a kind of thoughtfulness, and that thought is a rational touch, as touch is a sensitive thought; for the exterior perceptions of reason resemble the interior actions or knowledge of sense. Neither do I mean, that the perception of touch is made by pressure and reaction, no more than the perception of sight, hearing, or the like; but the patterns of outward objects being actions of the body sentient, are, as it were, a self-touch, or self-feeling, both in the sensitive and rational perceptions. Indeed that subtle and learned philosopher, who will persuade us that perception is made by pressure and reaction, makes perception only a phantasm: For, says he, "reaction makes a phantasm, and that is perception."[114] [Yet there may be different thoughts; for all rational perceptions are not like human thoughts, no more than all the sensitive perceptions [are][115] like the exterior perceptions of an animal sensitive perception.][116]

(5) Some perhaps will say, that if the perception of the exterior animal senses be made by patterning, then that animal which hath two, or more eyes, by patterning out an exterior object, will have a double or treble perception of it, according to the number of its eyes.

---

[114] Hobbes, *Elements of Philosophy*, IV, ch. 25, § 3 (*EW*, I, 392); altered and condensed.
[115] 1668: is.   [116] Lacking in 1666.

I answer: that when the corporeal motions in each eye, move irregularly; as for example, when one eye moves this, and the other another way, or when the eyes look asquint; then they do not pattern out the object directly as they ought; but when the eyes move regularly, then they pattern out one and the same object alike, as being fixt but upon one point; and the proof thereof is, if there be two eyes, we may observe that both have their perceptions apart, as well as jointly; because those parts that are in the middle of each eye, do not make, at the same time, the same perceptions with those that are the side or extreme parts thereof, but their perceptions are different from each other: For example, the eyes of a man, or some other animal, pattern out a tree which stands in a direct line opposite to them; but, if there be meadows or hedges on each side of the tree, then the extreme or side parts of each eye pattern out those meadows or hedges; for one eye's perception, is not the other eye's perception; which makes them perceive differently, when otherwise they would perceive both alike. But if a thousand eyes do perceive one object just alike, then they are but as one eye, and make but one perception; for like as many parts do work or act to one and the same design; so do several corporeal motions in one eye, pattern out one object; the only difference is, that, as I said, every eye is ignorant of each other's perception.

But, you'll say, There are so many copies made, as there are objects.

I answer, It is true: But though there are many composed parts which join in the making of one particular perception; yet, if they move all alike, the perception is but one and the same: for, put the case there were a hundred thousand copies of one original; if they be all alike each other, so as not to have the least difference betwixt them; then they are all but as one picture of one original; but if they be not alike each other, then they are different pictures, because they represent different faces. And thus for a matched pair of eyes in one creature; if they move at the same point of time, directly to one and the same parts, in the same design of patterning out one and the same object; it seems but as one act of one part, and as one perception of one object.

Q. 15. How comes it, that some parts, for all they are perceptive, can yet be so ignorant of each other, that in one composed figure, as for example, in the finger of a man's hand, they are ignorant of each other; whenas other parts do make perceptions of one another, at a great distance, and when other parts are between?

I answer: This question is easily resolved, if we do but consider, that the difference of perception depends upon the difference of the corporeal figurative motions; for if the parts be not the same, the perceptions must needs be different; nay, there may infinite several perceptions be made by one and the same parts, if matter be eternal, and perpetually moving. And hence it follows, that some parts may make perceptions of distant parts, and not of neighbouring parts; and others again, may make perceptions of neighbouring or adjoining parts, and not of those that are distant: As for example, in the animal perception, taste and touch are only perceptions of adjoining objects, whenas sight and hearing do perceive at a distance; for if an object be immediately joined to the optic sense, it quite blinds it. Wherefore it is well to be observed, that there are several kinds and sorts of perceptions, as well as of other composed figures: As for example, there are animals, vegetables, minerals, and elements; and these comprehend each several particular kinds of animals, vegetables, minerals, etc. Again, these particular kinds are divided into several sorts, and each of them contains so many particulars; nay, each particular has so many different parts, of which it consists, and each part has its different particular motions. The same may be said of perceptions: For as the several compositions of several parts are, so are they: not that the bare composition of the parts and figures is the cause of perception; but the self-knowing and self-moving parts compose themselves into such or such figures; and as there are proprieties belonging to such compositions, so to such composed perceptions; so that the composed parts at the end of a finger, may not have the same perceptions with the middle parts of the same finger.

But some may say, If there be such ignorance between the parts of a composed figure, how comes it, that many times the pain of one particular part, will cause a general distemper throughout all the body?

I answer; There may be a general perception of the irregularities of such particular composed parts in the other parts of the body, although they are not irregular themselves; for if they had the same compositions, and the same irregularities as the distempered parts, they would have the same effects; that is, pain, sickness, or numbness, etc. within themselves: But, to have a perception of the irregularities of other parts, and, to be irregular themselves, are different things. [A painter may make an exact copy of a monster, which monster was not composed regular.][117] Nevertheless, some parts moving irregularly, may occasion other parts to do the same. But it is well to be observed, that adjoining parts do not always imitate each other, neither do some parts make perceptions of foreign objects so readily as others do; as for example, a man plays upon a fiddle, or some other instrument, and there are hundreds, or more to hear him; it happens oft, that those at a farther distance do make a perfecter perception of that sound, than those which are near; and oftentimes, those that are in the middle, as between those that are nearest, and those that are furthest off, may make a perfecter perception than all they; for, though all parts are in a perpetual motion, yet all parts are not bound to move after one and the same way; but some move slower, some quicker, some livelier, some duller; and some parts do move so irregularly, as they will not make perceptions of some objects, whenas they make perceptions of others; and some will make perfect perceptions of one and the same objects at some times, and not at other times: As, for example, some men will hear, see, smell, taste, etc. more perfectly at some, than at other times. And thus, to repeat what I said before, the several kinds, sorts and particulars of perceptions, must well be considered; as also, that the variety of nature proceeds but from one cause, which is self-knowing and self-moving matter.

Q. 16.   Why a man's hand, or any other part of his body, has not the like perception as the eye, the ear, or the nose, etc. because [there][118] are sensitive and rational motions in all the parts of his body?

I answer: The reason why the same perception that is within the eye, cannot be in the hand, or in any other part of a man's body, is, that the parts of the hand are composed into another sort of figure than the eyes, ears, nose, etc. are; and the sensitive motions make perceptions according to the compositions of their parts; and if the parts of the hand should be divided and composed with other parts, into another figure; (as for

---

[117] Lacking in 1666.   [118] As in 1666; 1668: they.

example, into the figure of an eye, or ear, or nose) then they would have the perception of seeing, hearing and smelling; for perceptions are according to the composition of parts, and the changes of nature's self-motions.

But then some will say, perhaps, that an artificial eye, or ear, will have the same perceptions, etc. being of the same figure.

I answer: that if its interior nature, and the composition of its parts were just the same as its exterior figure; as for example, if any artificial eye, or ear, were of animal flesh, and the like, it would have the like perception, otherways not.

Q. 17. How do we perceive light, fire, air, etc.?

I answer: By their exterior figures, as we do other objects: As for example, my eye patterns out the exterior figure of light, and my touch patterns out the exterior figure of heat, etc.

But then, you will say, If the eye did pattern out the figure of light, it would become light itself; and if touch did pattern out the figure of heat, it would become fire.

I answer: No more than when a painter draws fire or light, the copy should be a natural fire or light. For there is difference betwixt the copy and the original: and it is to be observed, that in the perception of sense, especially of sight, there must be a certain distance betwixt the object, and the sentient parts; for the further those are from each other, the weaker is the perception, by reason no corporeal figurative motion is infinite, but finite; and therefore it can but have such a degree of power, strength, or activity, as belongs to such a figurative action, or such a part or degree of matter. But as for fire and light, it is a certain and evident proof, that some perceptions, at least those of the exterior animal senses, are made by patterning; for, though the nature of fire and of light (for anything we know) be ascending, yet if fire be made in such a manner, that several may stand about, underneath, and above it; yet they all have the perception of the heat of fire, in what place soever, provided they stand within a limited or determinate compass of it: I say, of the heat which is the effect of fire; for that is only patterned out, and not the substance of the flame or fire itself: But on the contrary, if the heat of the fire did actually and really spread itself out to all the places nominated, as well downwards, upwards and sideways; then certainly it would be wasted in a little time, and leave its cause, which is the fire, heatless. Besides, that there are copies and originals, and that some perceptions are made by patterning, is evident by the appearance of one candle in several distances, which several appearances can be nothing else but several copies of that candle made by those parts that take patterns from the original; which makes me also believe, that after the same manner, many stars which we take for originals, may be but so many copies or patterns of one star, made by the figurative motions of those parts where they appear.

Q. 18. Whether the optic perception is made in the eye, or brain, or in both?

I answer: The Perception of sight, when awake, is made on the outside of the eye, but in sleep on the inside; and as for some sorts of thoughts or conceptions, which are the actions of reason, they are, to my apprehension, made in the inner part of the head, although I am not able to determine properly what part it is; for all the body is perceptive, and has sense and reason, and not only the head; the only difference is, that the several actions of several parts, cause several sorts of perceptions; and the rational parts being the most active, and purest, and moving within themselves, can make more figures in the same compass or magnitude, and in a much shorter time than the sensitive, which being burdened with the inanimate parts, cannot act so agilely and freely: Nevertheless, some of the sensitive actions are much agiler and nimbler than others, as we may perceive in several sorts of productions. But the rational parts being joined with the sensitive in the exterior parts of a figure, do, for the most part, work together with the same; otherwise, when they move by themselves in thoughts, conceptions, remembrance, and the like; they are more inward, as within the head; for there are perceptions of interior parts, as well as of exterior; I mean, within a composed figure, by reason all parts are perceptive: Neither does this prove, that if there be so many perceptions in one composed figure, there must be numerous several perceptions of one object in that same figure; for every part knows its own work, or else there would be a confusion in nature's actions: Neither are all perceptions alike, but as I said, according as the several actions are, so are the perceptions.

*Q. 19.   What is the reason, that the nearer a stick or finger is held
against a concave glass, the more does the pattern of it, made by the glass,
appear to issue out of the glass, and meet with the object that is
without it?*

I answer: It is not that something really issues out of the glass; but as in a
plain looking glass, the further the object goes from it, the more does its
copy or image seem to be within the glass: So in the same manner does
the length of the stick, which is the measure of the object, or distance that
moves: For, as to a man that rides in a coach, or sails upon water, the
shore, trees, hedges, meadows and fields, seem to move; whenas yet, it is
the man that moves from them; so it is with the figure in a looking glass:
Wherefore it is only a mistake in the animal sense; to take the motion of
one, for the motion of the other.

*Q. 20.   Whether a part or figure repeated by the same motions, be the same
part or figure as the former, or only like the former? as also, whether an
action repeated, be the same with the former?*

I answer: that if the parts, figures and actions be the same, they will
always remain the same, although they be dissolved and repeated millions of times; as for example, if you make a figure of wax, and dissolve it,
and make that figure again, just as it was before, and of the same parts,
and by the same action, it will be the very same figure; but if you alter
either the parts, or the figure, it may be like the former figure, but not the
very same. The like for action; if one and the same action be repeated
without any alteration, it is nothing else but a repetition of the corporeal
figurative motions; but if there be any alteration in it, it is not made by
the same figurative motions, and consequently, it is not the same action;
for though the self-moving parts be the same, yet the figurative motions
are not the same; not that those figurative motions are not in the same
parts, but not repeated in the same manner. Wherefore it is well to be
observed, that a repetition is of the same parts, figures and actions that
were before, but an alteration is not a repetition; for wheresoever is but
the least alteration, there can be no exact repetition.

Q. 21.   Whether there may be a remembrance in sense, as well as there is in reason?

I answer, Yes: for remembrance is nothing else but a repetition of the same figure, made by the same corporeal figurative motions; and as there is a rational remembrance, which is a repetition of the same figures, made by the rational, corporeal figurative motions; so there is also a sensitive remembrance, that is, a repetition of the same figures, made by the sensitive, corporeal, figurative motions: For example, I see an object; the sensitive motions in the eye, pattern out the figure of that object; but as soon as the object is removed, the perception is altered. It may be, I see the same object again in a dream, or in a frenzy, or the like distemper; and then the same figure is repeated which was made first by the sensitive motions of the figure of the object, when it was really present; which is a sensitive remembrance, whether the repetition be made after a pattern, or by rote, although it is more proper to say, that remembrance is only a repetition of such figures as are made by rote, than of those that are made after a pattern; for a repetition of those figures that are made after a pattern, is rather a present perception of a present object; whenas remembrance is of objects that are absent.

Q. 22.   Whether the rational parts, can quit some parts and join to others?

I answer: Our sense and reason perceives they do; or else there would be no motion, no separation, composition, dilatation, contraction, digestion, production, transformation, infancy, youth, age, nor no action in the world whatsoever: And by this it is also evident, that (as I said before) particular, rational and sensitive parts, are not bound to move always together, or to keep constantly to the same parts, no not in the action of perception; for though they most commonly work together when they move regularly; yet many times they do not: As for example, the sensitive do not always make perceptions of exterior objects, but many times make figures by rote; as it is manifest in madmen, and such as are in high fevers and the like distempers, which see or hear, taste or smell such or such objects when none are present; and the rational parts being regular, do perceive both the sensitive figures made by rote, and that there are no such exterior objects really present; also the rational parts make figures by rote, and without any outward pattern; but such voluntary figures cannot properly be named perceptions, by reason perceptions are occasioned by outward objects; but they are rather voluntary conceptions.

Q. 23.   If it be so, that parts can divide themselves from some parts, and join to other parts: Why may not the soul do the same, and change its vehicles, that is, leave such, and take other vehicles?

I answer: Concerning the natural soul of man, which is part of nature, and consists of the purest and subtlest degree of matter, which is the rational, it is without question, that is divisible and compoundable, because it is material, and therefore subject to changes and transmutations; But as for the supernatural soul, because she is spiritual, and consequently indivisible, as having no parts, and therefore not the propriety of a body which is to have figurative actions, it cannot be said of her, that she is subject to compositions, divisions, transmutations, etc. However, put the case the supernatural soul should have those proprieties of a body, although no body herself; yet there could be but one infinite soul in one infinite body; and as the body did divide, so the soul must of necessity do also; otherwise one soul would have many bodies, and some bodies would be soulless; which would cause a horrid confusion between souls and bodies. Wherefore in my opinion, Pythagoras' doctrine concerning the transmigration of souls, or that one soul can take several bodies, is as absurd, as that one body can quit one place, and acquire another, and so have more places than bodies; which if it were thus, we might with as much probability affirm, that many bodies could be in one place, and in the resurrection of bodies there would certainly arise a great dispute between several bodies for one soul, and between several souls for one body, especially if one body was particularly beloved of more than one soul; all which will breed such a war between souls and bodies, souls and souls, and bodies and bodies, that it would put all the world into a confusion; and therefore my opinion is, that nature is but one only infinite body, which being self-moving, is divisible and compoundable, and consists of infinite parts of several degrees; which are so intermixt, that in general they cannot be separated from each other, or from the body of nature, and subsist single and by themselves. Neither can it be otherwise, unless nature had several bodies; but though she has infinite parts, yet has she but one infinite body; for parts and body are but one corporeal, self-moving, self-living, and self-knowing nature; And as for the degrees of animate and inanimate matter, they are also but parts of that one body of nature, and the various and infinite knowledges, perceptions, lives, etc. considered in general, are nothing else but the life, knowledge, and perception of the infinite body of nature. And from hence it follows, that one man may have numerous souls, as well as he has numerous parts and particles; which as long as the whole figure of man lasts, their functions and actions are according to the nature of that figure; but when the figure of man dissolves (which dissolution is nothing else but a change of those motions that were proper to the nature of its figure) then all the parts of that figure, if they be joined and composed with other parts and figures, become not soulless, or lifeless; but, because they consist all of a commixture of animate and inanimate matter, they retain life and soul: only the actions of that life and soul are according to the nature of those figures which the parts of the animal body did change into. Thus, as I have mentioned in my *Philosophical Letters*,[y] no creature can challenge a particular life and soul to itself, but every creature may have by the dividing and composing nature of this self-moving matter, more or fewer natural souls and lives.

And thus much of knowledge and perception; which since it is not only the ground of natural philosophy, but a subject of a difficult nature, I have insisted somewhat longer upon it than I have done upon any other, and endeavoured to clear it as well as I could; so that now, I hope, all that I have declared hitherto, will be sufficient to give the ingenious reader a true information of my opinion thereof, and a satisfactory answer to any other scruples that should happen to puzzle his brain. I'll add no more at this present, but conclude with a brief repetition of those few notes concerning the principles, which by that small portion of reason and judgment that nature has allowed me, I have endeavoured to declare and prove in my works of natural philosophy.

1. There is but one matter, and infinite parts; one self-motion, and infinite actions; one self-knowledge, and infinite particular knowledges and perceptions.

2. All parts of nature are living, knowing, and perceptive, because all are self-moving; for self-motion is the cause of all particular effects, figures, actions, varieties, changes, lives, knowledges, perceptions, etc. in

[y] Preface.

nature, and makes the only difference between animate and inanimate matter.

3. The chief and general actions of nature, are division and composition of parts, both which are done but by one act; for at the same time, when parts separate themselves from such parts, they join to other parts; and this is the cause there can be no vacuum, nor single parts in nature.

4. Every particular part or figure is infinitely divided and composed from, and with other parts.

5. The infinite divisions and compositions hinder, that nature cannot run into extremes in her particulars, but keep the parts and actions of nature in an equal balance.

6. The inanimate part of matter has life, sense, and self-knowledge, as well as the animate; but being not moving in itself, or its own nature, it has not such a perceptive sense and self-knowledge, nor such an active life as the animate hath.

7. The parts of inanimate matter alter according to their commixture with the animate, and so do their particular self-knowledges.

8. As parts alter by the changes of motions, so do particular perceptions.

9. Though all perceptions are figurative actions, yet no particular creature can undoubtedly affirm, that all are made by patterning or imitation; by reason as the parts and actions of nature are infinite, so are also particular perceptions; and being infinite, they cannot be known by any particular creature.

10. There are, besides exterior perceptions, voluntary actions, both of sense and reason, not made by imitation, but freely and by rote; and these may be called conceptions, rather than perceptions.

11. Those are much in the wrong, who believe, that man can know no more than what his five senses do inform him; for, the rational part, which is the purest, subtlest, most active, and inspective part of nature, does inform itself of things which the sensitive cannot; as for example, how was the new world and the antipodes found out? for they were neither seen, nor heard of, nor tasted, nor smelled, nor touched. Truly our reason does many times perceive that which our senses cannot; and some things our senses cannot perceive until reason informs them; for there are many inventions which owe their rise and beginning only to reason. [Reason doth inform the sense of the one part; not but sense hath some knowledge in the inanimate part, but not so much as the

rational]¹¹⁹ It is not sense, but reason that knows or perceives, there is something beyond itself, and beyond nature, which is the only, eternal, and omnipotent God, and there can be no higher conception than this: for what is beyond it, is supernatural, and belongs to supernatural creatures; as for example, those divine souls which God has given to men, above their rational material souls: but as for the wicked souls, they come not from God, but are irregularities of nature, which God certainly will punish, as a master does the evil actions of his servant.

12. Art is but a natural creature or effect, and not a creator of anything.

13. Colour, magnitude, figure, place, time, gravity, levity, density, rarity, compositions, divisions, alterations, etc. are all one and the same with self-moving matter, and nothing else but the various actions of nature; which actions can no more be separated from body, than body can from matter, or parts from their whole; for, all that is natural, is corporeal: and therefore the distinction into substances and accidents, is to no purpose; since there cannot really be, no not imagined, such a thing as an incorporeal or substanceless motion or action in nature.

But some perhaps will say, If every part and particle of nature has magnitude, colour, figure, place, etc. how is it possible that they can be one and the same with body, since they are subject to several perceptions?

To which I answer, The several perceptions do not make them to be several bodies, but they are patterned out or perceived as several proprieties or attributes of one body, or as several effects of one cause; for though there is but one cause in nature, which is self-moving matter; yet that only cause must of necessity have several effects or proprieties, as figure, colour, place, magnitude, etc. And if I may without offence make a comparison between the creator and a creature, God is but one in his essence, as one infinite and eternal God, and yet has several divine attributes; and though the parts of nature cannot comprehend, conceive, or perceive God, yet they may conceive somewhat of his several attributes, after several manners or ways: In the like manner, although there is but one matter, yet that matter may be perceived after several manners or ways, it being impossible, that matter, or any part or particle of matter, although it were single, should be without those several mentioned proprieties; for, can anyone conceive or imagine a body

¹¹⁹ Lacking in 1666.

without figure, magnitude, place or colour, were it as little as an atom? and since there are no natural figures or creatures but consist of parts, those composed figures may have a different magnitude, place, colour, etc. from their parts and particles, were they single; but being self-moving, those figures may alter by self-motion: for it is as impossible for a body to be without parts, as for parts to be without body; but if matter were not self-moving, there would neither be alterations, perceptions, nor any natural actions, although there might be a fixt self-knowledge in nature's parts. And thus it is no wonder, how there can be several perceptions of one figure, by reason there's no figure but is composed of parts; and as we can conceive a whole and its parts, which yet are one and the same thing, several ways; (for a whole we conceive as a composition of parts, and parts we conceive as a division of the whole) so we may figure, place, magnitude, etc. And as we cannot conceive nor perceive motion without body; so neither can we conceive those mentioned proprieties without body, or body without them, they being nothing else but the corporeal, figurative actions of nature.

II Further Observations upon Experimental Philosophy, Reflecting withal upon some Principal Subjects in Contemplative Philosophy

I Ancient Learning Ought Not to be Exploded, nor the Experimental Part of Philosophy Preferred Before the Speculative

In this present age those are thought the greatest wits that rail most against the ancient philosophers, especially Aristotle, who is beaten by all; but whether he deserves such punishment, others may judge. In my opinion, he was a very subtle philosopher, and an ingenious man; It is true, he was subject to errors, as well as other men are, (for there is no creature so perfect but may err, nay, not nature herself; but God only who is omnipotent) but if all that err should be accounted fools, and destitute of regular reason, then those deserve it most, who think themselves wiser than they are, and upon that account few in this age would escape this censure. But concerning the opinions of ancient philosophers, condemned by many of our modern writers, I for my particular, do very much admire them; for although there is no absolute perfection in them, yet if we do but rightly consider them, we shall find, that in many things, they come nearer to truth than many of our moderns; for surely the ancients had as good and regular rational and sensitive perceptions, and as profitable arts and sciences as we have; and the world was governed as well, and they lived as happily in ancient times, as we do now, nay more. As for example; How well was the world governed, and how did it flourish in Augustus' time? how many proud and stately buildings and palaces could ancient Rome show to the world, when she was in her flower? The cedars, gold, and many other curiosities which Solomon used in the structure of that magnificent temple, (the like whereof our age cannot show) were as safely fetched and brought to him out of foreign places, as those commodities which we have out of other countries either by sea or land: Besides, I doubt not but they had as profitable and useful arts and knowledges, and as skillful and ingenious artists as our age can boast of; if not the very same, yet the like, and perhaps better, which by the injury of time have been lost, to our great disadvantage; it may be they had no microscopes nor telescopes, but I think they were the happier for the want of them, employing their time in more profitable studies: What learned and witty people the Egyptians were, is sufficiently known out of ancient histories, which may inform us of many more. But I perceive the knowledge of several ages and times, is like the increase and decrease of the moon; for in some ages "art and learning" flourishes better than in others, and therefore it is not only an injury, but a sign of ill nature, to exclaim against ancient learning, and call it pedantry; for if the ancients had not been, I question whether we should have arrived to that knowledge we boast of at this present; for they did break the ice, and showed us the way in many things, for which we ought to be thankful, rather than reward them with scorn. Neither ought artists, in my opinion, to condemn contemplative philosophy, nay, not to prefer the experimental part before her; for all that artists have, they are beholden for it to the conceptions of the ingenious student, except some few arts which ascribe their original to chance; and therefore speculation must need go before practice; for how shall a man practise, if he does not know what or which way to practise? Reason must direct first how sense ought to work; and so much as the rational knowledge is more noble than the sensitive, so much is the speculative part of philosophy more noble than the mechanical. But our age being more for deluding experiments than rational arguments, which some call a "tedious babble,"[120] doth prefer sense before reason; and trusts more to the deceiving sight of their eyes, and deluding glasses, than to the perception of clear and regular reason: nay, many will not admit of rational arguments; but the bare authority of an experimental philosopher is sufficient to them to decide all controversies, and to pronounce the truth without

[120] Probably a reference to Glanvill, *Scepsis Scientifica*, "To the Royal Society," unpaginated; and p. 117.

any appeal to reason; as if they only had the infallible truth of nature, and engrossed all knowledge to themselves. Thus reason must stoop to sense, and the conceptor to the artist, which will be the way to bring in ignorance, instead of advancing knowledge; for when the light of reason begins to be eclipsed, darkness of understanding must needs follow.

II   Whether Artificial Effects May Be Called Natural, and in What Sense

In my former discourses I have declared, that art produces hermaphroditical effects, that is, such as are partly natural, and partly artificial; but the question is, whether those hermaphroditical effects may not be called natural effects as well as others; or, whether they be effects quite different and distinct from natural? My answer is, When I call artificial effects hermaphroditical, or such as are not natural; I do not speak of nature in general, as if they were something else besides nature; for art itself is natural, and an effect of nature, and cannot produce anything that is beyond, or not within nature: wherefore artificial effects can no more be excluded from nature, than any ordinary effect or creature of nature. But when I say they are not natural, I understand the particular nature of every creature, according to its own kind or species; for as there is infinite nature, which may be called general nature, or nature in general, which includes and comprehends all the effects and creatures that lie within her, and belong to her, as being parts of her own self-moving body; so there are also particular natures in every creature, which are the innate, proper and inherent interior and substantial forms and figures of every creature, according to their own kind or species, by which each creature or part of nature is discerned or distinguished from the other; as for example, although an animal and a vegetable be fellow creatures, and both natural, because material; yet their interior particular natures are not the same, because they are not of the same kind, but each has its own particular nature quite different from the other; and these particular natures are nothing else but a change of corporeal figurative motions, which make this diversity of figures; for, were the same interior and natural motions found in an animal as are in a vegetable, an animal would be a vegetable, and a vegetable an animal, without any difference; and after this rate there would be no variety at all in nature; but self-motion acting diversely and variously, not only in every kind and species, but in every particular creature and part of nature, causeth that wonderful variety which appears everywhere, even to our admiration in all parts of nature. But to return to artificial effects; it is known that nature has her own ways in her actions, and that there are constant productions in every kind and sort of natural creatures, which nature observes in the propagation and increase of them; whose general manner and way is always the same; (I say, general, because there are many variations in the particular motions belonging to the production of every particular creature.) For example, all mankind is produced after one and the same manner or way, to wit, by the copulation of two persons of each sex; and so are other sorts of creatures produced other ways: also a perfect creature is produced in the same shape, and has the same interior and exterior figure as is proper to it, according to the nature of its kind and species to which it belongs; and this is properly called a natural production: But when the figurative motions in particular productions do not move after this ordinary way, as in the productions of monsters, it is called a preternatural or irregular production, proceeding from the irregularity of motions; not preternatural in respect to general nature, but in respect to the proper and particular nature of the figure. And in this regard I call artificial effects hermaphroditical, that is, partly natural, and partly artificial: Natural, because art cannot produce anything without natural matter, nor without the assistance of natural motions; but artificial, because it works not after the way of natural productions: for art is like an emulating ape, and will produce such figures as nature produces, but it doth not, nor cannot go the same way to work as nature doth; for nature's ways are more subtle and mysterious, than that they can be known by art, or any one particular creature, much less be traced; and this is the true construction of my sense, concerning natural and artificial productions; whereby it is manifest that I am not of the opinion of that experimental writer who thinks it no improbability, to say, that all natural effects may be called artificial, nay, that nature herself may be called the "art of God";[121] for art is as much inferior to nature, as a part is inferior to the whole, and all artificial effects are irregular in comparison to natural; wherefore to say, God or nature works artificially, would be as much as to say, they work irregularly.

---

[121] Power, *Experimental Philosophy*, pp. 192–93.

III Of Natural Matter and Motion

I am of that learned author's mind, who counts those but "narrow souls, and not worthy the name of philosophers, that think any body can be too great, or too vast, as also too little, in its natural dimensions; and that nature is stinted at an atom, and brought to a *non-plus* of her subdivisions";[122] for truly, if there cannot be extremes in infinite, there can also be none in nature, and consequently there can neither be smallest nor biggest, strongest nor weakest, hardest nor softest, swiftest nor slowest, etc. in nature; by reason nature is infinite in her actions, as well as in her parts, and has no set bounds or limits: And therefore the corpuscularian or atomical writers, which do reduce the parts of nature to one certain and proportioned atom, beyond which they imagine nature cannot go, because their brain or particular finite reason cannot reach further, are much deceived in their arguments, and commit a fallacy in concluding the finiteness and limitation of nature from the narrowness of their rational conceptions. Nevertheless, although nature's actions and parts are infinite, considered in general, yet my opinion is, that nature never doth actually run into infinite in her particular actions and parts; for as there are infinite divisions, so there are also infinite compositions in nature; and as there are infinite degrees of hardness, slowness and thickness, so there are also infinite degrees of softness, swiftness, thinness, etc. so that every particular motion or action of nature is balanced and poised by its opposite, which hinders a running into infinite in nature's particulars, and causes a variety of natural figures; for although infinite matter in itself, and its own essence, is simple and "homogeneous," as the learned call it, or of the same kind and nature, and consequently is at peace with itself; yet there is a perpetual opposition and war between the parts of nature, where one sometimes gets the better of the other, and overpowers it either by force or sleight, and is the occasion of its dissolution into some other figure; but there's no part so powerful as to reduce anything into nothing, or to destroy it totally from being matter: nay, not nature herself has such a power, but God alone, who as he has made nature, so he may destroy her: for, although nature has an infinite power, yet she is not omnipotent, but her power is a natural infinite power, whenas omnipotency is an attribute only belonging to

---

[122] Power, *Experimental Philosophy*, Preface, unpaginated; altered and condensed.

God; neither hath she a divine, but a natural infinite knowledge; by which it is evident, that I do not ascribe divine attributes to nature, which were to make her a God; nor detract from nature that which properly belongs to her; for, nature being infinite in body and parts, it would be absurd to confine her to a finite power and knowledge. By parts, I understand not only the infinite figures and sizes, but also the infinite actions of nature: and I am of Descartes' opinion, that the parts of matter may be made bigger or less by addition or subtraction of other parts; but I cannot yield to him when he says, that motion may be swifter and slower by addition given to the movent by other contiguous bodies more swiftly moving, or by subduction of it by bodies slower moved, and that motion may be transferred out of one body into another;[123] for motion cannot be conceived, much less subsist without matter; and if motion should be transferred or added to some other body, matter must be added or transferred also: Neither doth the addition of some parts of matter add always exterior local motion to the body it is joined to, but they retain the motion proper to their own figure and nature: As for example, if a stone be added to an animal, it will rather hinder than help its exterior motions. But I must refer the reader to my other philosophical works, in which I have discoursed more of this subject.

IV   Nature Cannot Be Known by Any of Her Parts

I am not of Pliny's opinion, "that nature in her whole power is never more wholly seen, than in her smallest works":[124] For, how can nature be seen in a part, whenas infinite cannot be known neither in nor by any part, much less a small part? Nay, were nature a great finite body, it could not be perceived entirely in and by a small or minute part, no more than a human eye can see all this world, celestial and terrestrial, at once. It is true, reason being joined to sense, may make a better discovery, than if they were separated; but as the human optic sense, although assisted by art, is not capable to perceive the exterior, much less the interior parts of the greatest, so neither of the smallest creatures; for art (as I mentioned before) many times deludes, rather than informs, making hermaphroditi-cal figures; and nature has more variety and curiosity in the several

---

[123] A reference to the summary of Descartes' views in Power, *Experimental Philosophy*, Preface, unpaginated.
[124] Pliny the Elder (23/24–79 AD), *Historia Naturalis* [Natural History], bk XI, § 1.

forms, and figurative corporeal motions of one of the smallest creatures, than the most observing and clearest optic sense can perceive. But mistake me not, I do not say that arts are not profitable, but that they are not truly and thoroughly intelligent or knowing of all nature's works; for several arts are like several other creatures, which have their particular natures, faculties and proprieties, beyond which they cannot go, and one creature is not able to comprehend or know all other creatures, no not any one single creature perfectly; which if so, then none can inform what it doth not know. Nay, not only one particular creature is not able to know it, but not one particular kind or sort of creatures; as for example, all mankind that ever have lived, or are at present living in this world, could never find out the truth of nature, even in the least of her parts, nay, not in themselves: For what man is he that knows the figurative corporeal motions, which make him to be such a creature as man, or that make any part of him? And what man or art can inform us truly of the figurative motions that make the nature of blood, flesh, bones, etc. or can give a reason why the heart is triangular, and the head spherical, and so for every differently shaped part of his body? I will not say, but that man may guess at it, but not infallibly know it by any art; wherefore reason will more truly discover so much of nature as is discoverable to one kind or sort of creatures, than art can do; for art must attend reason as the chief mistress of information, which in time may make her a more prudent and profitable servant than she is; for in this age she is become rather vain than profitable, striving to act beyond her power, as I do undertake to write beyond my experience; for which, it is probable, artists will condemn me; but if I err, I ask their pardon, and pray them to consider the nature of our sex, which makes us, for the most part, obstinate and willful in our opinions, and most commonly impertinently foolish: And if the art of "micrography" can but find out the figurative corporeal motions that make or cause us to be thus, it will be an art of great fame; for by that artists may come to discover more hidden causes and effects; but yet I doubt they will hardly find out the interior nature of our sex, by the exterior form of their faces or countenances, although very curious, and full of variety of several beauties; nay, I dare on the contrary say, had a young beautiful lady such a face as the microscope expresses, she would not only have no lovers, but be rather a monster of art, than a picture of nature, and have an aversion, at least a dislike to her own exterior figure and shape; and per chance, if a louse or flea, or such like insect, should look through a microscope, it would be as much affrighted with its own exterior figure, as a young beautiful lady when she appears ill-favoured by art. I do not say this, as if optic glasses could not present the true figure of an original; for if they do not exceed the compass of natural dimensions, they may; but when they endeavour to go beyond them, and do more than nature has done, they rather present monstrous, than truly natural figures. Wherefore those, in my opinion, are the best artists, that keep nearest to nature's rules, and endeavour not to know more than what is possible for a finite part or creature to know: for surely there is no better way to be rightly and truly informed of nature's works, than by studying nature's corporeal figurative motions, by the means of which study, they will practise arts (as far as art is able to be practised) more easily and successfully than they will do without it. But to conclude this discourse, some parts of nature are more endued with regular reason than others, which is the cause that some creatures of one and the same sort or kind, as for example, mankind, are more wise and ingenious than others; and therefore it is not art, but regular sense and reason that makes some more knowing, and some more wise and ingenious than others; and the irregular motions of sense and reason that make some more ignorant or more extravagant in their opinions, than others.

V Art Cannot Introduce New Forms in Nature

Some account it a great honour, "that the indulgent creator, although he gives not to natural creatures the power to produce one atom of matter, yet allows them the power to introduce so many forms which philosophers teach to be nobler than matter, and to work such changes amongst creatures, that if Adam was now alive, and should survey the great variety of man's production, that are to be found in the shops of artificers, the laboratories of chemists, and other well-furnished magazines of art, he would admire to see what a new world it were."[125] Where, first, I do not understand how man, or any other creature, should have the power of making or introducing new forms, if those forms were not already in nature; for no creature by any art whatsoever, is able to produce a new form, no more than he can make an atom of new matter,

---

[125] Robert Boyle, *Some Considerations touching the Usefulness of Experimental Natural Philosophy* (1663); slight alterations, especially to the beginning of the quotation (*WRB*, II, 14).

by reason the power lies in nature, and the God of nature, not in any of her creatures; and if art may or can work changes amongst some fellow creatures, they are but natural, by reason nature is in a perpetual motion, and in some parts in a perpetual transformation. Next, as for the question, Whether forms be more noble than the matter? my opinion is, that this can with no more ground of truth be affirmed, than that the effect is nobler than the cause;[126] and if any creature should have power to make forms, which are more noble than matter itself; then certainly that creature would be above nature, and a creator rather than a creature. Besides, form cannot be created without matter, nor matter without form; for form is no thing subsisting by itself without matter; but matter and form make but one body; and therefore he that introduces a new form, must also introduce a new matter; and though art changes forms, yet it cannot be said to introduce a new form; for forms are and have been eternally in nature, as well as matter, so that nothing is created anew, which never was in nature before. It is true, if Adam were alive now, he might see more variety, but not more truth; for there are no more kinds and sorts of natural creatures, than there were at his time, though never more metamorphosed, or rather I may say disfigured, [unnatural][127] and hermaphroditical issues than there are now; which if they should make a new world by the architecture of art, it would be a very monstrous one: But I am sure art will never do it; for the world is still as it was, and new discoveries by arts, or the deaths and births of creatures will not make a new world, nor destroy the old, no more than the dissolving and composing of several parts will make new matter; for although nature delights in variety, yet she is constant in her groundworks; and it is a great error in man to study more the exterior faces and countenances of things, than their interior natural figurative motions, which error must undoubtedly cause great mistakes, insomuch as man's rules will be false, compared to the true principles of nature; for it is a false maxim to believe, that if some creatures have power over others, they have also power over nature: it might as well be believed, that a wicked man, or the devil, hath power over God: for, although one part may have power over another, yet not over nature, no more than one man can have power over all mankind. One man or creature may overpower another so much, as to

---

[126] Cf. Francisco Suárez, *Disputationes metaphyicae* [Metaphysical Disputations] (Salamanca, 1597), disp. XXVI, § 1, 2 and 5–6; and Descartes, *Meditations* (AT, VII, 40–41; CSM, II, 28).
[127] As in 1666; 1668: unnaturally.

make him quit his natural form or figure, that is, to die and be dissolved, and so to turn into another figure or creature; but he cannot overpower all creatures; nay, if he could, and did, yet he would not be an absolute destroyer and creator, but only some weak and simple transformer, or rather some artificial disfigurer and misformer, which cannot alter the world, though he may disorder it: But surely, as there was always such a perpetual motion in nature, which did and doth still produce and dissolve other creatures, which production and dissolution is named "birth" and "death"; so there is also a motion which produces and dissolves arts; and this is the ordinary action and work of nature, which continues still, and only varies in the several ways or modes of dissolving and composing.

VI   Whether There Be Any Prime or Principal Figure in Nature; and of the True Principles of Nature

Some are of opinion, that the prime or principal figures of nature, are "globes" or "globular figures," as being the most perfect;[128] but I cannot conceive why a globular or spherical figure should be thought more perfect than another; for another figure may be as perfect in its kind, as a round figure in its kind: For example, we cannot say a bird is a more perfect figure than a beast, or a beast a more perfect figure than a fish, or worms; neither can we say man is a more perfect figure than any of the rest of the animals: the like of vegetables, minerals and elements; for every several sort has as perfect a figure as another, according to the nature and propriety of its own kind or sort. But put the case man's figure were more perfect than any other, yet we could not say that it is the principle out of which all other figures are made, as some do conceive that all other figures are produced from the globular or spherical; for there is no such thing as most or least perfect, because there is no most nor least in nature. Others are of opinion, that the principle of all natural creatures, is salt;[129] and that when the world dissolves, it must

---

[128] Boyle, in *Origin of Forms and Qualities according to the Corpuscular Philosophy* . . . (1666), discusses the "*globuli caelestes*, or such a *materia subtilis*, as the Cartesians employ to explicate most of the phenomena of nature" (*WRB*, III, 7); see fn. 47.

[129] A position held by numerous early chemists, e.g., Nicholas Le Févre, *A Compleat Body of Chemistry* (London, 1664); and Joseph Duchesne [Quercetanus], *The Practise of Chymicall and Hermeticall Physicke*, tr. Thomas Timme (London, 1605). It was also the view of William Cavendish; see *Opinions* (1663), pp. 459ff.

dissolve into salt, as into its first principle; but I never heard it determined yet, whether it be fixt or volatile salt: Others again are of opinion, that the first principle of all creatures is water;[130] which if so, then seeing that all things must return into their first principle, it will be a great hindrance to the conflagration of the world; for there will be so much water produced, as may chance to quench out the fire. But if infinite nature has infinite parts, and those infinite parts are of infinite figures, then surely they cannot be confined to one figure: Sense and reason proves, that nature is full of variety, to wit, of corporeal figurative motions, which as they do not ascribe their original to one particular, so neither do they end in one particular figure or creature. But some will wonder that I deny any part or creature of nature should have a supremacy above the rest, or be called prime or principal, whenas yet I do say that reason is the prime part of nature. To which I answer: that when I say, no creature in nature can be called prime or principal, I understand natural effects, that is, natural composed parts or creatures: as for example, all those finite and particular creatures that are composed of life, soul and body, that is, of the animate both rational and sensitive, and the inanimate parts of matter, and none of those composed creatures I mean, has any superiority or supremacy above the rest, so as to be the principle of all other composed creatures, as some do conceive water, others fire,[131] others all the four elements to be simple bodies, and the principles of all other natural creatures,[132] and some do make globous bodies the perfectest figures of all others;[133] for all these being but effects, and finite particulars, can be no principles of their fellow creatures, or of infinite nature. But when I say that reason, or the rational part of matter is the prime part of nature, I speak of the principles of nature, out of which all other creatures are made or produced, which principle is but one, viz. matter, which makes all effects or creatures of nature to be material; for all the effects must be according to their principle; but this matter being of two degrees, viz. animate and inanimate, the animate is nothing but self-motion; (I call it animate matter, by reason I cannot believe, as some do, that motion is immaterial, there being nothing belonging to nature which is not material, and therefore

---

[130] E.g., Thales and Van Helmont.
[131] Aristotle attributed this position to the early Pythagorean Hippasus of Metapontium and to Heraclitus of Ephesus (fl. *c.* 500 BC); see 984a7; *CWA*, II, 1556.
[132] I.e., Aristotle and his scholastic followers.
[133] I.e., Descartes and the Cartesians. See fn. 47.

corporeal self-motion, or animate matter is to me one and the same) and this animate matter is again subdivided into two degrees, to wit, the rational and sensitive; the rational is the soul, the sensitive the life, and the inanimate the body of infinite nature; all which, being so intermixed and composed, as no separation can be made of one from the other, but do all constitute one infinite and self-moving body of nature, and are found even in the smallest particles thereof, (if smallest might be said) they are justly named the principles of nature, whereof the rational animate matter, or corporeal self-motion, is the chief designer and surveyor, as being the most active, subtle and penetrating part, and the sensitive the workman: but the inanimate part of matter being thoroughly intermixed with this animate self-moving matter, or rather with this corporeal self-motion, although it have no motion in itself, that is, in its own nature; yet by virtue of the commixture with the animate, is moving, as well as moved; for it is well to be observed, that although I make a distinction betwixt animate and inanimate, rational and sensitive matter, yet I do not say that they are three distinct and several matters; for as they do make but one body of nature, so they are also but one matter: but, as I mentioned before, when I speak of self-motion, I name it animate matter, to avoid the mistake, lest self-motion might be taken for immaterial; for my opinion is, that they are all but one matter, and one material body of nature. And this is the difference between the cause or principle, and the effects of nature, from the neglect of which, comes the mistake of so many authors, to wit, that they ascribe to the effects what properly belongs to the cause, making those figures which are composed of the aforesaid animate and inanimate parts of matter, and are no more but effects, the principles of all other creatures; which mistake causes many confusions in several men's brains, and their writings. But it may be, they will account it paradoxical or absurd, that I say infinite matter consists of two parts, viz. animate and inanimate, and that the animate again is of two degrees, rational and sensitive, by reason the number of two is finite, and a finite number cannot make one infinite whole; which whole being infinite in bulk, must of necessity also consist of infinite parts. To which I answer, My meaning is not, that infinite nature is made up of two finite parts, but that she consists out of a commixture of animate and inanimate matter, which although they be of two degrees or parts, (call them what you will) yet they are not separated parts, but make one infinite body, like as life, soul and body, make but one man: for, animate matter is (as I said before) nothing else but self-motion; which self-motion joined with inanimate matter, makes but one self-moving body, which body by the same self-motion is divided into infinite figures or parts, not separated from each other, or from the body of nature, but all cohering in one piece, as several members of one body, and only distinguished by their several figures; every part whereof has animate and inanimate matter, as well as the whole body: nay, that every part has not only sensitive, but also rational matter, is evident, not only by the bare motion in every part of nature, which cannot be without sense, for wheresoever is motion, there's sense; but also by the regular, harmonious, and well-ordered actions of nature, which clearly demonstrates, that there must needs be reason as well as sense, in every part and particle of nature; for there can be no order, method or harmony, especially such as appears in the actions of nature, without there be reason to cause that order and harmony. And thus motion argues sense, and the well-ordered motion argues reason in nature, and in every part and particle thereof, without which nature could not subsist, but would be as a dull, indigested and unformed heap and chaos. Besides, it argues that there is also knowledge in nature, and all her parts; for wheresoever is sense and reason, there is also sensitive and rational knowledge, it being most improbable that such an exactly ordered and harmonious consort of all the infinitely various actions of nature should be without any knowledge, moving and acting, producing, transforming, composing, dissolving, etc. and not knowing how, whither, or why to move; and nature being infinite in her own substance, as well as in her parts; there in bulk, here in number; her knowledge in general must of necessity be infinite too, but in her particulars it cannot but be finite and particular; and this knowledge differs according to the nature of each figure or creature; for I do not mean that this sense and knowledge I speak of, is only an animal sense and knowledge, as some have misinterpreted; for animal sense and knowledge is but particular, and belongs only to that sort of creatures which are animals; but I mean such sense and knowledge as is proper to the nature of each figure: so that animal creatures have animal sense and knowledge; vegetables, a vegetative sense and knowledge; minerals, a mineral sense and knowledge; and so of the rest of all kinds and sorts of creatures. And this is my opinion of the principles of nature, which I submit to the examination of the ingenious and impartial reader to consider, whether it contains not as much probability as the opinion of those whose principles are either whirl-pools,[134] insensible *minima*,[135] *gas*, *blas* and *archeus*,[136] dusty atoms, thrusting backwards and forwards, which they call reaction, and the like, or of those that make artificial experiments the ground and foundation of the knowledge of nature, and prefer art before reason: for, my principles and grounds are sense and reason; and if they cannot hold, I know not what will; for where sense and reason has no admittance, there nothing can be in order, but confusion must needs take place.

VII Whether Nature be self-moving

There are some who cannot believe, "that any man has yet made out, how matter can move itself"; but are of opinion, "that few bodies move but by something else, no not animals, whose spirits move the nerves, the nerves again the muscles, and so forth the whole body."[137] But if this were so, then certainly there must either be something else that moves the spirits, or they must move of themselves; and if the spirits move of themselves, and be material, then a material substance or body may move of itself; but if immaterial, I cannot conceive why a material substance should not be self-moving as well as an immaterial. But if their meaning be, that the spirits do not move of themselves, but that the soul moves them, and God moves the soul; then it must either be done by an

---

[134] A reference to Descartes' theory of the vortical motion of celestial particles; see *Principles of Philosophy*, III, § 30 (AT, VIII B, 92; CSM, I, 253–54).

[135] In the scholastic particle theory that pitted itself against the atomism of Democritus and others, *minima naturalia* are the smallest corpuscles in which the form is preserved when a body is divided. Unlike the indivisible, unchanging, mechanically describable "atoms," *minima* are naturally divisible, characterized by the qualities of the bodies which they comprise, and they can act on each so as to produce internal qualitative changes. See, e.g., Aristotle, *Physics*, I, ch. 4; *On Generation and Corruption*, I, ch. 10. The mechanical philosophers drew on this doctrine to create eclectic particulate theories of matter.

[136] Key concepts in Van Helmont's vitalist philosophy of nature. The *archeus* or "designer," is a vital and knowing spirit, which uses the seminal ideas in its imagination as the blueprint for the formation of individuals; it governs the "fixed *archei*," which control the specific parts or organs of the individual. This spirit acts on matter by means of its watery vehicle, *gas*, which is the material manifestation of spirit, seen when we apply fire to a solid body and unleash its spiritual core. On "blas," see fn. 85.

[137] Robert Boyle, *Some Considerations touching the Usefulness of Experimental Natural Philosophy*: "Nor has any man, that I know, satisfactorily made out how matter can move itself: and indeed, in the bodies, which we here below converse withal, we scarce find that anything is moved but by something else; and even in these motions of animals, that seem spontaneous, the will or appetite doth not produce the motion of the animal, but guide and determine that of the spirits, which by the nerves move the muscles; and so the whole body, as may appear by the weariness and unwieldiness of animals, when by much motion the spirits are spent" (*WRB*, II, 42).

all-powerful command, or by an immediate action of God: The latter of which is not probable, to wit, that God should be the immediate motion of all things himself; for God is an immovable and immutable essence: Wherefore it follows, that it is only done by an omnipotent command, will, and decree of God; and if so, why might not infinite matter be decreed to move of itself, as well as a spirit, or the immaterial soul? But I perceive man has a great spleen against self-moving corporeal nature, although himself is part of her, and the reason is his ambition; for he would fain be supreme, and above all other creatures, as more towards a divine nature: he would be a God, if arguments could make him such, at least God-like, as is evident by his fall, which came merely from an ambitious mind of being like God. The truth is, some opinions in philosophy, are like the opinions in several religions, which endeavour-ing to avoid each other, most commonly do meet each other; like men in a wood, parting from one another in opposite ways, oftentimes do meet again; or like ships which travel toward east and west, must of necessity meet each other; for as the learned Dr. Donne says, the furthest east is west, and the furthest west is east;[138] in the same manner do the Epicur-ean, and some of our modern philosophers meet; for those endeavour to prove matter to be somewhat like a God, and these endeavour to prove man to be something like God, at least that part of man which they say is immaterial; so that their several opinions make as great a noise to little purpose, as the dogs barking or howling at the moon: for, God the author of nature, and nature the servant of God, do order all things and actions of nature, the one by his immutable will, and all powerful-command; the other by executing this will and command: The one by an incomprehen-sible, divine and supernatural power; the other in a natural manner and way: for God's will is obeyed by nature's self-motion; which self-motion God can as easily give and impart to corporeal nature, as to an immaterial spirit; but nature being as much divisible, as she is compoundable, is the cause of several opinions, as well as of several other creatures; for nature is fuller of variety, than men of arguments; which variety is the cause there are so many extravagant and irregular opinions in the world; and I observe, that most of the great and famous, especially our modern authors, endeavour to deduce the knowledge of causes from their effects, and not effects from their causes, and think to find out nature by art, not

---

138 The reference is to John Donne's poem, "Upon the Annunciation and Passion falling upon one day. 1608": "As in plain maps, the furthest west is east."

art by nature: whereas, in my opinion, reason must first consider the cause, and then sense may better perceive the effects: Reason must judge, sense execute: for reason is the prime part of nature, as being the corporeal soul or mind of nature. But some are so much in love with art, as they endeavour to prove not only nature, but also divinity, which is the knowledge of God, by art; thus preferring art before nature, whenas art is but nature's foolish changeling child; and the reason is, that some parts of nature, as some men, not knowing all other parts, believe there is no reason, and but little sense in any part of nature, but themselves; nay, that it is irreligious to say that there is, not considering that God is able to give sense and reason to infinite nature, as well as to a finite part. But those are rather irreligious, that believe God's power is confined, or that it is not infinite.

VIII   Of Animal Spirits

I am not of the opinion of those that place the cause of all sense and motion, in the animal spirits, which they call "the purest and most ethereal particles of all bodies in the world whatsoever, and the very top and perfection of all nature's operations."[139] For animal spirits, in my opinion, are no more than other effects of nature, only they are not so gross as some, but are parts of a most pure, refined and rare sort of inanimate matter, which being intermixed with the parts of animate matter, and enlivened by them, become very subtle and active; I will not say that they are of the highest and last degree of inanimate matter, nearest to the animate, (as they do say, they have the nearest alliance to spiritualities, which in my opinion, is as much as to say, they are almost nothing) or of the first degree of sensitive matter, there being no such thing as first and last in nature, but that they are only such pure and rare parts of inanimate matter, as are not subject to the exterior perception of human sense; for example, as the matter of respiration, or the like: for as there are infinite parts of inanimate matter, so there are also infinite degrees of strength, weakness, purity, impurity, hardness, softness, density, rarity, swiftness, slowness, knowledge, ignorance, etc. as also, several sorts and degrees of complexions, statures, constitutions, humours, wits, understanding, judgment, life, death, and the like; all which

---

[139] Power, *Experimental Philosophy*, p. 71; the parts of the quotation before and after the comma are transposed and condensed.

degrees, although they be in, and of the infinite body of nature, yet properly they belong to particular creatures, and have only a regard to the several parts of nature, which being infinite in number, are also of infinite degrees, according to the infinite changes of self-motion, and the propriety and nature of each figure; wherefore that opinion which makes animal spirits the prime or principal motion of all things, and the chief agent in nature's three kingdoms, mineral, animal and vegetative, reduces infinite nature to a finite principle; whereas anyone that enjoys but so much of human sense and reason, as to have the least perception or insight into natural things, may easily conceive that the infinite effects of nature cannot proceed from a finite particular cause; nay, I am firmly persuaded, that they who believe any finite part to be the cause and principle of infinite self-moving nature, do, in my opinion, not only sin against nature, but against God the author of nature, who out of his infinite bounty gave nature the power of self-motion. But if anyone desire to know, what's then the true cause and principle of all nature's creatures and figures: I answer, In my opinion, it is not a spirit or immaterial substance, but matter; but yet not the inanimate part of matter, but the animate; which being of two degrees, rational and sensitive, both of them are the infinite life and soul of the infinite body of nature; and this animate matter is also the cause of all infinite works, changes, figures and parts of nature, as I have declared above more at large. Now as great a difference as there is between animate and inanimate, body and soul, part and whole, finite and infinite, so great a difference there is also between the animal spirits, and the prime agent or movent of nature, which is animate matter, or (which is all one thing) corporeal self-motion; and as it would be paradoxical, to make inanimate matter to be the cause of animate, or a part to be the cause of the whole, whose part it is, or a finite to be the cause of infinite; so paradoxical would it also be to make animal spirits the "top and perfection of all nature's operations": nay, so far are they from being the prime movent of other bodies, as they are but moved themselves; for, to repeat what I mentioned in the beginning, animal spirits are only some sorts of rare and pure inanimate matter, which being thoroughly intermixt with the animate parts of matter, are more active than some sorts of more dense and grosser parts of inanimate matter: I say some; for I do believe that some of the most solid bodies are as active as the most rare and fluid parts of matter, if not exteriorly, yet interiorly; and therefore we cannot say,

that rare and fluid parts are more active than fixt and solid; or that fixt
and solid are less active than fluid bodies, because all parts are self-
moving. But if I was to argue with those that are so much for animal
spirits, I would ask them, first, Whether animal spirits be self-moving? If
they say they are, I am of their opinion, and do infer thence, that if animal
spirits, which are but a small part of nature, have self-motion, much
more has nature herself: But if not, I would ask, What gives them that
motion they have? If they say nature, then nature must be self-moving.
Perchance they'll say, God moves nature: It is true, God is the first
author of motion, as well as he is of nature; but I cannot believe that God
should be the prime actual movent of all natural creatures, and put all
things into local motion, like as one wheel in a clock turns all the rest: for,
God's power is sufficient enough to rule and govern all things by an
absolute will and command, or by a "Let it be done"; and to impart
self-motion to nature, to move according to his order and decree,
although in a natural way. Next, I would ask Whether any dead creature
have such animal spirits? If they affirm it, I am of their mind: If not, then
I would ask, What causes, in dead bodies, that dissolution which we see?
Thirdly, I would ask, Whether those animal spirits be annihilated and
generated anew? If they answer, Not, I am of their opinion: but if they
say, they are annihilated and generated anew; then I would fain know
who is their generator and annihilator? for nothing can generate and
annihilate itself. And if they say, God: I answer, It is not probable that
God should have made anything imperfect, especially in the production
of nature; for if there be things created anew, which never were before in
nature, it argues that nature was not perfect at first, because of a new
addition of so many creatures; or if anything could be annihilated in
nature, it would likewise argue an imperfection in nature, viz. that nature
was perfecter before those things were annihilated. And thus it would
infer, as if God had not power either to have made nature perfect at first,
or that God wanted work, and was forced to create and annihilate every
moment; for certainly, the work of creation and annihilation, is a divine
action, and belongs only to God. Lastly, concerning the functions and
offices which the animal spirits perform in animal, or at least human
bodies, by their several motions and migrations from the brain through
the spinal marrow, nerves, tendons, fibers, into all the parts of the body,
and their return to the brain; I have declared my opinion thereof twelve
years since, in my work of *Poetical Fancies*, which then came out the first

time; and I thought it not unfit to insert here, out of the same book, these following lines, both that my meaning may be the better understood, and that they may witness I have been of that opinion so many years ago.

The Reason Why Thoughts Are Made in the Head[z]

Each sinew is a small and slender string,
Which all the senses to the body bring:
And they like pipes or gutters hollow be,
Where animal spirits run continually:
Though small, yet they such matter do contain
As in the skull doth lie, which we call brain.
Which makes, if anyone do strike the heel,
That sense we quickly in the brain do feel:
It is not sympathy, but all one thing,
Which causes us to think, and pain doth bring:
For had the heel such quantity of brain
As doth the head and skull therein contain,
Then would such thoughts as in the brain dwell high,
Descend into our heels, and there they'd lie:
In sinews small, brain scattered lies about,
It wants both room and quantity, no doubt;
For did a sinew so much brain but hold,
Or had so large a skin it to infold
As has the skull, then might the toe or knee,
Had they an optic nerve, both hear and see.
Had sinews room fancy therein to breed,
Copies of verse might from the heel proceed.

And Again, of the Motion of Blood[a]

Some by their industry and learning found
That all the blood like to the sea turns round;
From two great arteries it doth begin,
Runs through all veins, and so comes back again.
The muscles, like the tides, do ebb and flow,
According as the several spirits go.
The sinews, as small pipes, come from the head,
And they are all about the body spread,

---

[z] Poem. Impres. 2, p. 52. [A somewhat altered version of "The Reason Why the Thoughts are Only in the Head," published in the first edition of *Poems*, p. 42.]

[a] Pag. 53. [A somewhat altered version of "The Motion of the Blood," in the first edition of *Poems*, pp. 42–43.]

Through which the animal spirits are convey'd
To every member, as the pipes are laid;
And from those sinew-pipes each sense doth take
Of those pure spirits, as they us do make.

IX   Of the Doctrine of the Sceptics concerning the Knowledge of Nature

When sceptics endeavour to prove, that not anything in nature can be truly and thoroughly known; they are, in my opinion, in the right way, as far as their meaning is, that not any particular creature can know the infinite parts of nature; for nature having both a divisible and compoundable sense and reason, causes ignorance, as well as knowledge, amongst particulars: But if their opinion be, that there is no true knowledge at all found amongst the parts of nature, then surely their doctrine is not only unprofitable, but dangerous, as endeavouring to overthrow all useful and profitable knowledge. The truth is, that nature being not only divisible, but also compoundable in her parts, it cannot be absolutely affirmed that there is either a total ignorance, or a universal knowledge in nature, so as one finite part should know perfectly all other parts of nature: but as there is an ignorance amongst particulars, caused by the division of nature's parts, so there is also a knowledge amongst them, caused by the composition and union of her parts. Neither can any ignorance be attributed to infinite nature, by reason she being a body comprehending so many parts of her own in a firm bond, and indissoluble union, so as no part can separate itself from her, must of necessity have also an infinite wisdom and knowledge to govern her infinite parts. And therefore it is best, in my judgment, for sceptics and dogmatists to agree in their different opinions; and whereas now they express their wit by division, to show their wisdom by composition; for thus they will make an harmonious consort and union in the truth of nature, where otherwise their disagreement will cause perpetual quarrels and disputes both in divinity and philosophy, to the prejudice and ruin of church and schools; which disagreement proceeds merely from self-love: For every man being a part of nature, which is self-loving as well as self-moving, would fain be, at least appear wiser than his fellow creatures. But the omnipotent creator has ordered nature so wisely, as to divide not only her power, but also her wisdom into parts, which is the reason that she is not omnipotent, being divisible and compoundable, whenas God can neither be divided nor composed, but is one simple, individual and incomprehensible being, without any composition of parts, for God is not material.

X   Of Natural Sense and Reason

Those authors which confess, "that vulgar reason is no better than a more refined imagination; and that both reason, fancy, and the senses, are influenced by the body's temperament, and like the index of a clock, are moved by the inward springs and wheels of the corporeal machine";[140] seem in my opinion, to confirm, that natural sense and reason is corporeal, although they do it in an obscure way, and with intricate arguments. But truly, do what they can, yet they must prove reason by reason; for irrational discourse cannot make proofs and arguments to evince the truth of nature: But first, it must be proved what sense and reason is; whether divine or natural, corporeal or immaterial. Those that believe natural sense and reason to be immaterial, are, in my opinion, in a great error, because nature is purely corporeal, as I have declared before: And those which affirm, that our understanding, will and reason, are in some manner like to God's, shall never gain my assent; for if there be so great a difference between God's understanding, will and decree, and between nature's, as no comparison at all can be made betwixt them; much more is there between a part of nature, viz. Man, and the omnipotent and incomprehensible God; for there is an infinite difference between divine attributes, and natural properties; wherefore to similize our reason, will, understanding, faculties, passions and figures, etc. to God, is too high a presumption, and in some manner a blasphemy. Nevertheless, although our natural reason and faculties are not like to divine attributes, yet our natural rational perceptions are not always delusions; and therefore it is certain, that nature's knowing parts, both sensitive and rational, do believe a God, that is, some being above nature: But many writers

---

[140] Glanvill, *Scepsis Scientifica*: " Now the fancies of the most, like the index of a clock, are moved but by the inward springs and wheels of the corporal machine; which even on the most sublimed intellectuals is dangerously influential. And yet this sits at the helm of the world's belief; and vulgar *reason* is no better than a more *refined imagination*. So then the senses, fancy, and what we call reason itself, being thus influenced by the body's temperament, and little better than indications of it; it cannot be otherwise, but that this love of ourselves should strongly incline us in our most abstracted dijudications" (pp. 91–92).

endeavour rather to make divisions in religion, than promote the honour and worship of God by a mutual and united agreement, which I confess is an irregularity and imperfection in some parts of nature; and argues, that nature is not so perfect, but she has some faults and infirmities, otherwise she would be a God, which she is not.

XI   Of a General Knowledge and Worship of God, Given Him by all Natural Creatures

It is not the sight of the beauteous frame of this world (as some do conceive) that makes men believe and admire God; but the knowledge of the existence of God is natural, and there's no part of nature but believes a God: for certainly, were there not any optic sense in nature, yet God would be the God of nature, and be worshipped and adored by her creatures, which are her parts; for it is irreligious to say, God should want admiration and adoration, for want of an eye, or any other of the animal or human organs; surely nature has more ways than five, to express and declare God's omnipotency. It is infinite sense and reason that doth worship and adore God; and the several perceptions of this sense and reason, know there is a God that ought to be worshipped and adored; and not only ears, or eyes, or the like exterior organs of man. Neither is it man alone, but all creatures, that do acknowledge God: for, although God cannot be perfectly known what he is in his essence; yet he may be known inasmuch as nature can know of him. But since nature is divisible in her parts, each part has but a particular knowledge of God, which is the cause of several religions, and several opinions in those religions; and nature being also compoundable, it causes a conformity and union of those opinions and religions in the fundamental knowledge, which is the existence of God. Wherefore that which makes a general and united knowledge of the existence of God, is, that nature is entire in herself, as having but one body, and therefore all her parts which are of that body, have also one knowledge of God: for, though the parts be different in the worship of God, yet they have not a different belief of the existence of God; not that God can be perfectly known either by nature, or any of her parts; for God is incomprehensible, and above nature: but inasmuch as can be known, to wit, his being; and that he is all-powerful, and that not anything can be compared or likened to him; for he is beyond all draught and likeness, as being an eternal, infinite, omnipotent, incorporeal, individual, immovable being. And thus it is not one part or creature viewing another, that causes either the knowledge or admiration of God, but the soul and life of nature, which are her sensitive and rational parts; and nature being the eternal servant and worshipper of God, God hath been also eternally worshipped and adored: for, surely God's adoration and worship has no beginning in time; neither could God be worshipped and adored by himself, so as that one part of him should adore and worship another; for God is an individual and simple being, not composed of parts; and therefore, as it is impossible for me to believe that there is no general worship and adoration of God; so it is impossible also to believe that God has not been adored and worshipped from all eternity, and that nature is not eternal; for although God is the cause of nature, and nature the effect of God, yet she may be eternal however, there being nothing impossible to be effected by God; but he, as an eternal cause, is able to produce an eternal effect; for, although it is against the rules of logic, yet it is not above the power of God.

XII   Of a Particular Worship of God, Given Him by Those That Are His Chosen and Elect People

Natural philosophy is the chief of all sorts of knowledges; for she is a guide, not only to other sciences, and all sorts of arts, but even to divine knowledge itself; for she teaches, that there is a being above nature, which is God the Author and Master of nature, whom all creatures know and adore. But to adore God after a particular manner, according to his special will and command, requires his particular grace, and divine instructions, in a supernatural manner or way, which none but the chosen creatures of God do know, at least believe; nor none but the sacred church ought to explain and interpret: And the proof, that all men are not of the number of those elect and chosen people of God is, that there can be but one true religion, and that yet there are so many several and different opinions in that religion; wherefore the truth can only be found in some, which are those that serve God truly, according to his special will and command, both in believing and acting that which he has been pleased to reveal and command in his holy word: And I pray God, of his infinite mercy, to give me grace, that I may be one of them, which I doubt not but I shall, as long as I follow the instruction of our blessed church, in which I have been educated. It is true, many persons are much troubled concerning free will and predestination, complaining, that the Christian church is so divided about this article, as they will never agree in one united belief concerning that point; which is the cause of the trouble of so many consciences, nay, in some even to despair. But I do verily believe, that if man do but love God from his soul, and with all his power, and pray for his saving graces, and offend not any creature when offences can or may be avoided, and follow the only instructions of the sacred church, not endeavouring to interpret the word of God after his own fancy and vain imagination, but praying zealously, believing undoubtedly, and living virtuously and piously, he can hardly fall into despair, unless he be disposed and inclined towards it through the irregularities of nature, so as he cannot avoid it. But I most humbly thank the omnipotent God, that my conscience is in peace and tranquility, beseeching him of his mercy to give to all men the like.

XIII   Of the Knowledge of Man

Some philosophical writers discourse much concerning the knowledge of man, and the ignorance of all other creatures; but I have sufficiently expressed my opinion hereof, not only in this, but in my other philosophical works, to wit, that I believe other creatures have as much knowledge as man, and man as much in his kind, as any other particular creature in its kind; but their knowledges being different, by reason of their different natures and figures, it causes an ignorance of each other's knowledge; nay, the knowledge of other creatures, many times gives information to man: As for example, the Egyptians are informed how high the river Nile will rise by the crocodile's building her nest higher or lower; which shows, that those creatures foresee or foreknow more than man can do: Also, many birds foreknow the rising of a tempest, and shelter themselves before it comes; the like examples might be given of several other sorts of animals, whose knowledge proceeds either from some sensitive perceptions, or from rational observations, or from both; and if there be such a difference in the rational and sensitive knowledge of one kind of creatures, to wit, animals; much more in all other kinds, as vegetables, minerals, elements, and so in all nature's works: Wherefore he that will say, there is no knowledge but in man, at least in animal kind; doth, in my opinion, say more than ever he will be able to prove; nay, the contrary is so evident, as it is without all dispute: But man, out of self-love, and conceited pride, because he thinks himself the chief of all creatures, and that all the world is made for his sake; doth also imagine that all other creatures are ignorant, dull, stupid, senseless and irrational; and he only wise, knowing and understanding. And upon this ground some believe, that man is bound and decreed to pray to God for all other creatures, as being not capable to pray for themselves; like as a minister is bound to pray for his flock. But really, if the pastor should only pray, and his sheep not, but they did continue in their sins, I doubt his prayers would be of little effect, and therefore it is well if their prayers and petitions be joined together. The like may be said of all other creatures; for the single knowledge and devotion of mankind, cannot benefit other creatures, if they be ignorant, and not capable to know, admire, adore and worship God themselves. And thus no man, with all the force of logic, will ever be able to prove, that he is either the chief above all other creatures, or that he only knows and worships God, and no natural creature else; for it is without dispute, that other creatures, in their kinds, are as knowing and wise, as man in his kind.

XIV   A Natural Philosopher Cannot Be an Atheist

I wonder how some of our learned writers can imagine, that those who study reason and philosophy, should make them "their vouchers of licentious practices, and their secret scorn of religion, and should account it a piece of wit and gallantry to be an atheist; and of atheism, to be a philosopher";[141] considering that reason and philosophy is the only way that brings and leads us to the natural knowledge of God: for, it would be as much absurdity to say, reason and philosophy induce atheism, as to say, reason is not reason; for, reason is the most knowing and wisest part of nature; and the chief knowledge of nature, is to know there is a God: Wherefore those that do argue in such a manner, argue without reason; and by calling others weak heads and fools, prove themselves irrational. But I perceive their supposition is built upon a false ground; for they are of opinion, that "the exploding of immaterial substances, and the unbounded prerogative of matter, must needs infer atheism":[142] which whether it do not show a weaker head than those

---

[141] Glanvill, *Scepsis Scientifica*, Preface, unpaginated; slightly altered and condensed.
[142] Ibid.: "And what the confident exploding of all immaterial substances, the unbounded prerogatives are bestowed upon matter, and the consequent assertions, signify, you need not be informed

have that believe no immaterial substances in nature, rational men may judge: for by this it is evident, that they make immaterial substances to be gods, by reason they conclude, that he who believes no immaterial substance in nature, is an atheist: And thus by proving others atheists, they commit blasphemy themselves; for he that makes a God of a creature, sins as much, if not more than he who believes no God at all. And as for the unbounded prerogative of matter, I see no reason why men should exclaim against it; for why should immaterial substances have more prerogative than material? Truly, I may upon the same ground conclude the prerogative of matter, as well as they do the prerogative of spirits; for both are but creatures, and in that case, one has no more prerogative than the other; for God could make a material being to move itself, as well as a material nothing. Nevertheless, although matter is self-moving, yet it has not a God-like omnipotent power, nor any divine attributes; but an infinite natural power, that is, a power to produce infinite effects in her own self, by infinite changes of motions: Neither doth it argue that nature is above God, or at least God-like; for I do not say, that nature has her self-moving power of herself, or by chance, but that it comes from God the Author of Nature; which proves that God must needs be above nature, although nature is infinite and eternal; for these proprieties do not derogate anything from the attributes of God, by reason nature is naturally infinite, which is infinite in quantity and parts; but God is a spiritual, supernatural and incomprehensible infinite: And as for the eternity of nature, it is more probable to regular reason, than that nature should have any beginning; for all beginning supposes time; but in God is no time, and therefore neither beginning nor ending, neither in himself, nor in his actions; for if God be from all eternity, his actions are so too, the chief of which is the production or creation of nature. Thus natural reason may conceive that nature is the eternal servant of God; but how it was produced from all eternity, no particular or finite creature is able to imagine, by reason that not only God, but also nature is infinite; and a finite creature can have no idea or conception of infinite.

. . . [T]hose that would be genteelly learned and ingenious, need not purchase it, at the dear rate of being atheists." (unpaginated)

XV   Of the Rational Soul of Man

Of all the opinions concerning the natural soul, of man, I like that best which affirms the soul to be a self-moving substance; but yet I will add a *material* self-moving substance; for the soul of man is part of the soul of nature, and the soul of nature is material: I mean only the natural, not the divine soul of man, which I leave to the Church. And this natural soul, otherwise called reason, is nothing else but corporeal natural self-motion, or a particle of the purest, most subtle and active part of matter, which I call animate; which animate matter is the life and soul of nature, and consequently of man, and all other creatures; for we cannot in reason conceive that man should be the only creature that partakes of this soul of nature, and that all the rest of nature's parts, or most of them, should be soulless or (which is all one) irrational, although they are commonly called, nay, believed to be such. Truly, if all other creatures cannot be denied to be material, they can neither be accounted irrational, insensible, or inanimate, by reason there is no part, nay, not the smallest particle in nature, our reason is able to conceive, which is not composed of animate matter, as well as of inanimate; of life and soul, as well as of body; and therefore no particular creature can claim a prerogative in this case before another; for there is a thorough mixture of animate and inanimate matter in nature, and all her parts. But some may object, that if there be sense and reason in every part of nature, it must be in all parts alike; and then a stone, or any other the like creature, may have reason, or a rational soul, as well as man. To which I answer: I do not deny that a stone has reason, or doth partake of the rational soul of nature, as well as man doth, because it is part of the same matter man consists of; but yet it has not animal or human sense and reason, because it is not of animal kind; but being a mineral, it has mineral sense and reason; for it is to be observed, that as animate self-moving matter moves not one and the same way in all creatures, so there can neither be the same way of knowledge and understanding, which is sense and reason, in all creatures alike; but nature being various, not only in her parts, but in her actions, it causes a variety also amongst her creatures; and hence come so many kinds, sorts and particulars of natural creatures, quite different from each other; though not in the general and universal principle of nature, which is self-moving matter, (for in this they agree all) yet in their particular interior natures, figures and proprieties. Thus, although there be sense and reason, which is not only motion, but a regular and well-ordered self-motion, apparent in the wonderful and various productions, generations, transformations, dissolutions, compositions, and other actions of nature, in all nature's parts and particles; yet by reason of the variety of this self-motion, whose ways and modes do differ according to the nature of each particular figure, no figure or creature can have the same sense and reason, that is, the same natural motions which another has; and therefore no stone can be said to feel pain as an animal doth, or be called blind, because it has no eyes; for this kind of sense, as seeing, hearing, tasting, touching and smelling, is proper only to an animal figure, and not to a stone, which is a mineral; so that those which frame an argument from the want of animal sense and sensitive organs, to the defect of all sense and motion; as for example, that a stone would withdraw itself from the carts going over it, or a piece of iron from the hammering of a smith, conclude, in my opinion, very much against the artificial rules of logic; and although I understand none of them, yet I question not but I shall make a better argument by the rules of natural logic: But that this difference of sense and reason, is not altogether impossible, or at least improbable to our understanding, I will explain by another instance. We see so many several creatures in their several kinds, to wit, elements, vegetables, minerals, and animals, which are the chief distinctions of those kinds of creatures as are subject to our sensitive perceptions; and in all those, what variety and difference do we find both in their exterior figures, and in their interior natures? Truly such as most of both ancient and modern philosophers have imagined some of them, viz. the elements, to be simple bodies, and the principles of all other creatures; nay, those several creatures do not only differ so much from each other in their general kinds, but there is no less difference perceived in their particular kinds: For example, concerning elements, what difference is there not between heavy and contracting earth, and between light and dilating air? between flowing water, and ascending fire? So as it would be an endless labour to consider all the different natures of those creatures only that are subject to our exterior senses. And yet who dares deny that they all consist of matter, or are material? Thus we see that infinite matter is not like a piece of clay, out of which no figure can be made, but it must be clayey; for natural matter has no such narrow bounds, and is not forced to make all creatures alike; for, though gold and stone are both material, nay, of the same kind, to wit, minerals, yet one is not the other, nor like the other. And if this be true of matter, why may not the same be said of self-motion, which is sense and reason? Wherefore, in all probability of truth, there is sense and reason in a mineral, as well as in an animal, and in a vegetable as well as in an element, although there is as great a difference between the manner and way of their sensitive and rational perceptions, as there is between both their exterior and interior figures and natures. Nay, there is a difference of sense and reason even in the parts of one and the same creature, and consequently of sensitive and rational perception or knowledge: for, as I have declared heretofore more at large, every sensitive organ in man hath its peculiar way of knowledge and perception; for the eye doth not know what the ear knows, nor the ear what the nose knows, etc. all which is the cause of a general ignorance between nature's parts; and the chief cause of all this difference, is the variety of self-motion; for, if natural motion were in all creatures alike, all sense and reason would be alike too; and if there were no degrees of matter, all the figures of creatures would be alike, either all hard, or all soft; all dense, or all rare and fluid, etc. and yet neither this variety of motion causes an absence of motion, or of sense and reason, nor the variety of figures an absence of matter, but only a difference between the parts of nature, all being, nevertheless, self-moving, sensible and rational, as well as material; for wheresoever is natural matter, there is also self-motion, and consequently, sense and reason. By this we may see how easy it is to conceive the actions of nature, and to resolve all the phenomena or appearances upon this ground; and I cannot admire enough, how so many eminent and learned philosophers have been, and are still puzzled about the natural rational soul of man. Some will have her to be a "light"; some an "entelechy," or they know not what; some the "quintessence of the four elements"; some composed of "earth and water"; some of "fire," some of "blood," some an "hot complexion," some an "heated and dispersed air," some an "immaterial spirit," and some "nothing."[143] All which opinions seem the more strange, the wiser their authors are accounted; for if they did proceed from some ignorant persons, it would not be so much taken notice of; but coming from great philosophers, who pretend to have searched the depth of nature, and

---

[143] This list of views is taken from Glanvill, *Scepsis Scientifica*, pp. 13–14, which identifies the proponents of the doctrines respectively as: Heraclides, Aristotle, Zeno, Hesiod and Anaximander, Parmenides (earth and fire), Empedocles, Galen, Varro, Hippocrates, and Crates and Dicaearchus.

disclosed her secrets, it causes great admiration in anybody, and may well serve for an argument to confirm the variety and difference of sensitive and rational knowledge, and the ignorance amongst natural parts; for if creatures of the same particular kind, as men, have so many different perceptions, what may there be in all nature? But infinite nature is wise, and will not have, that one part of hers should know more than its particular nature requires; and she taking delight in variety, orders her works accordingly.

XVI Whether Animal Parts Separated from their Bodies, Have Life

Some do question, Whether those parts that are separated from animal bodies, do retain life? But my opinion is, that all parts of nature have life, each according to the propriety of its figure, and that all parts of an animal have animal life and motion, as long as they continue parts of the animal body; but if they be separated from the body to which they did belong, although they retain life, yet they do not retain animal life, because their natural motions are changed to some other figure when they are separated; so that the parts which before had animal life and motion, have then such a kind of life and motion, as is proper and natural to the figure into which they are changed or transformed. But some separated parts of some creatures, retain longer the life of that composed figure whose parts they were, than others, according as the dissolving and transforming motions are slower or quicker: As for example, in some vegetables, some trees, if their boughs, arms or branches be lopt or cut from a lively stock, those boughs or branches will many times remain lively, according to the nature of the figure whose parts they were, for a good while; nay, if they be set or planted, they will grow into the same figure as the stock was; or if joined into another stock, they will be partly of the nature of the stock which they did proceed from, and partly of the nature of the stock into which they were engrafted: But yet I do not perceive that animal kind can do the like; for I make a question, whether a man's arm, if cut off from his body, and set to another man's body, would grow, and keep its natural form and figure, so as to continue an arm, and to receive nourishment from that body it is joined to? Nevertheless, I will not eagerly contradict it, considering that nature is very different and various both in her productions and nourishments, nay, so various, as will puzzle, if not confound the wisest part or creature of nature to find them out.

XVII   Of the Spleen

Concerning the spleen of an animal creature, whether it may artificially be cut out, and the body closed up again, without destruction of the animal figure, as some do probably conceive, I am not so good an artist as to give a solid judgment thereof; only this I can say, that not all the parts of an animal body are equally necessary for life; but some are convenient, more than necessary: Neither do I perfectly know whether the spleen be one of the prime or principal vital parts; for although all parts have life, yet some in some particular creatures are so necessary for the preservation of life, as they cannot be spared; whereas others have no such relation to the life of an animal, but it may subsist without them. And thus, although some parts may be separated for some time, yet they cannot continue so, without a total dissolution of the animal figure; but both the severed, and the remaining parts change from their nature, if not at all times suddenly, yet at last. And as for the spleen, although the separation should not be so great a loss, as the pain in losing it, yet some persons will rather lose their lives with ease, than endure great pain to save them. But the question is, If a man was willing to endure the pain, whether he would not die of the wound? for no creature can assure another of its life in such a case; neither can anyone be assured of his own: for there is no assurance in the case of life and death, I mean such a life as is proper to such a creature; for properly there is no such thing in nature, as death; but what is named death, is only a change from the dissolution of some certain figure, to the composition of another.

XVIII   Of Anatomy

I am not of the opinion of those who believe that anatomists could gain much more by dissecting of living, than of dead bodies, by reason the corporeal figurative motions that maintain life, and nourish every part of the body, are not at all perceptible by any exterior optic sense, unless it be more perceiving and subtler than the human optic sense is; for although the exterior grosser parts be visible, yet the interior corporeal motions in those parts, are not visible; wherefore the dissecting of a living creature can no more inform one of the natural motions of that figure, than one can by the observing of an egg, be it never so exact, perceive the corporeal figurative motions that produce or make the figure of a chicken. Neither can artificial optic glasses give any advantage to it; for nature is so subtle, obscure and various, as not any sort or kind of creatures can trace or know her ways: I will not say, but her parts may, in their several perceptions, know as much as can be known, for some parts may know and be known of others, and so the infinite body may have an infinite information and knowledge; but no particular creature, no, not one kind or sort of creatures can have a perfect knowledge of another particular creature; but it must content itself with an imperfect knowledge, which is a knowledge in parts. Wherefore it is as improbable for human sight to perceive the interior corporeal figurative motions of the parts of an animal body, by anatomy, as it is for a micrographer to know the interior parts of a figure, by viewing the exterior; for there are numerous corporeal figures or figurative motions of one particular creature, which lie one within another; and most commonly the interior are quite different from the exterior: As for example, the outward parts of a man's body are not like his inward parts; for his brain, stomach, liver, lungs, spleen, midriff, heart, guts, etc. are of different figures, and one part is not another part, no, not of the like nature or constitution; neither hath a man a face on the inside of his head, and so of the rest of his parts; for every part has besides its exterior, interior figures and motions, which are not perceptible by our exterior senses. Nevertheless, there is some remedy to supply this ignorance of the senses, by the perception of reason; for where sense fails, reason many times informs, it being a more clear and subtle perception than sense is: I say, many times, because reason cannot be always assured of knowing the truth: for, particular reason may sometimes be deceived as well as sense; but when the perceptions both of sense and reason agree, then the information is more true. I mean regular sense and reason, not irregular, which causes mistakes, and gives false informations; also the presentation of the objects ought to be true, and without delusion.

XIX   Of Preserving the Figures of Animal Creatures

I am absolutely of the opinion of those who believe natural philosophy may promote not only anatomy, but all other arts; for else they would not be worth the taking of pains to learn them, by reason the rational perceptions are beyond the sensitive. I am also of opinion, that there may be an art to preserve the exterior shapes of some animal bodies, but not their interior forms; for although their exterior shapes, even after the dissolution of the animal figure, may be somewhat like the shapes and figures of their bodies, when they had the life of an animal, yet they being transformed into some other creatures by the alteration of their interior figurative motions, can no ways keep the same interior figure which they had when they were living animals. Concerning the preserving of blood by the means of spirit of wine, as some do probably believe; my opinion is, that spirit of wine, otherwise called "hot-water," if taken in great quantity, will rather dry up or putrefy the blood, than preserve it; nay, not only the blood, but also the more solid parts of an animal body, insomuch as it will cause a total dissolution of the animal figure; and some animal creatures that have blood, will be dissolved in wine, which yet is not so strong as extracts or spirit of wine: But blood mingled with spirit of wine, may perhaps retain somewhat of the colour of blood, although the nature and propriety of blood be quite altered. As for the instance of preserving dead fish or flesh from putrefying and stinking, alleged by some, we see that ordinary salt will do the same with less cost; and as spirits of wine, or hot-waters, may, like salt, preserve some dead bodies from corruption, so may they, by making too much or frequent use of them, also cause living bodies to corrupt and dissolve sooner than otherwise they would do. But chemists are so much for extracts, that by their frequent use and application, they often extract human life out of human bodies, instead of preserving it.

XX   Of Chemistry, and Chemical Principles

It is sufficiently known, and I have partly made mention above, what a stir natural philosophers do keep concerning the principles of nature, and natural beings, and how different their opinions are. The schools, following Aristotle, are for the four elements, which they believe to be simple bodies, as having no mixture in themselves, and therefore fittest to be principles of all other mixt or compounded bodies;[144] but my reason cannot apprehend what they mean by "simple bodies"; I confess that

---

[144] On Aristotle, see *On the Heavens*, III and IV; cf. Digby, *Two Treatises*, The First Treatise, ch. 4.

some bodies are more mixt than others; that is, they consist of more differing parts, such as the learned call "heterogeneous": As for example, animals consist of flesh, blood, skin, bones, muscles, nerves, tendons, gristles, and the like, all which are parts of different figures: Other bodies, again, are composed of such parts as are of the same nature, which the learned call "homogeneous"; as for example, water, air, etc. whose parts have no different figures, but are all alike each other, at least, to our perception; besides, there are bodies which are more rare and subtle than others, according to the degrees of their natural figurative motions, and the composition of their parts: Nevertheless, I see no reason why those "homogeneous" bodies should be called simple, and all others mixt, or composed of them; much less why they should be principles of all other natural bodies; for they derive their origin from matter, as well as the rest; so that it is only the different composure of their parts, that makes a difference between them, proceeding from the variety of self-motion, which is the cause of all different figures in nature; for, as several workmen join in the building of one house, and several men in the framing of one government; so do several parts in the making or forming of one composed figure.

But they'll say, It is not the likeness of parts that makes the four elements to be principles of natural things, but because there are no natural bodies besides the mentioned elements that are not composed of them, as is evident in the dissolution of their parts: for example, a piece of green wood that is burning in a chimney, we may readily discern the four elements in its dissolution, out of which it is composed; for the *fire* discovers itself in the flame, the smoke turns into *air*, the *water* hisses and boils at the ends of the wood, and the ashes are nothing but the element of *earth*: But if they have no better arguments to prove their principles, they shall not readily gain my consent; for I see no reason why wood should be composed of the four elements, because it burns, smokes, hisses, and turns into ashes; fire is none of its natural ingredients, but a different figure, which being mixt with the parts of the wood, is an occasion that the wood turns into ashes: Neither is water a principle of wood; for water is as much a figure by itself, as wood or fire is, which being got into the parts of the wood, and mixt with the same, is expelled by the fire, as by its opposite; but if it be a piece of dry, and not of green wood, where is then the water that boils out? Surely dry wood hath no less principles, than green wood; and as for smoke, it proves no more that it is the element of air in wood, than that wood is the element of fire; for wood, as experience witnesses, may last in water, where it is kept from the air; and smoke is rather an effect of moisture, occasioned into such a figure by the commixture of fire.

Others, as Helmont, who derives his opinion from Thales, and others of the ancient philosophers, are only for the element of water; affirming, that that is the sole principle, out of which all natural things consist; for, say they, the chaos whereof all things were made, was nothing else but water, which first settled into slime, and then condensed into solid earth; nay, some endeavour to prove by chemical experiments, that they have disposed water according to their chemical way, so that it is visibly turned into earth, which earth produces animals, vegetables, and minerals. But put the case it were so, yet this doth not prove water to be the only principle of all natural beings; for first, we cannot think that animals, vegetables and minerals are the only kinds of creatures in nature, and that there are no more but them; for nature being infinitely various, may have infinite world, and so infinite sorts of creatures: Next I say, that the change of water into earth, and of this again into vegetables, minerals, and animals, proves no more but what our senses perceive every day, to wit, that there is a perpetual change and alteration in all natural parts, caused by corporeal self-motion, by which rare bodies change into dense, and dense into rare; water into slime, slime into earth, earth into animals, vegetables and minerals; and those again into earth, earth into slime, slime into water, and so forth: But I wonder why rational men should only rest upon water, and go no further, since daily experience informs them, that water is changed into vapour, and vapour into air; for if water be resolvable into other bodies, it cannot be a prime cause, and consequently no principle of nature; wherefore they had better, in my opinion, to make air the principle of all things. It is true, water may produce many creatures, as I said before, by a composition with other, or change of its own parts; but yet I dare say, it doth kill or destroy as many, nay more than it produces; witness vegetables and others, which husbandmen and planters have best experience of; and though some animals live in water as their proper elements; yet to most it is destructive, I mean, as for their particular natures; nay, if men do but dwell in a moist place, or near marsh grounds, or have too much watery humours in their bodies, they'll sooner die than they would do in a dry place. But, put the case water were a principle of natural things, yet it must have motion, or else it would never be able to change into so many figures; and this motion must either be naturally inherent in the substance of water, or it must proceed from some exterior agent; if from an exterior agent, then this agent must either be material, or immaterial: Also, if all motion in nature did proceed from pressure of parts upon parts, then those parts which press others, must either have motion inherent in themselves; or if they be moved by others, we must at last proceed to something which has motion in itself, and is not moved by another, but moves all things; and if we allow this, why may not we allow self-motion in all things? For, if one part of matter has self-motion, it cannot be denied of all the rest; but if immaterial, it must either be God himself, or created supernatural spirits: As for God, he being immovable, and beyond all natural motion, cannot actually move matter; neither is it religious, to say, God is the soul of nature; for God is no part of nature, as the soul is of the body; and immaterial spirits, being supernatural, cannot have natural attributes or actions, such as is corporeal natural motion. Wherefore it remains, that matter must be naturally self-moving, and consequently all parts of nature, all being material; so that not only water, earth, fire and air, but all other natural bodies whatsoever, have natural self-motion inherent in themselves; by which it is evident, that there can be no other principle in nature, but this self-moving matter, and that all the rest are but effects of this only cause.

Some are of opinion, that the three catholic or universal principles of nature, are matter, motion and rest;[145] and others, with Epicurus, that they are magnitude, figure and weight; but although matter and motion, or rather self-moving matter, be the only principle of nature; yet they are mistaken in dividing them from each other, and adding rest to the number of them: for matter and motion are but one thing, and cannot make different principles; and so is figure, weight and magnitude. It is true, matter might subsist without motion, but not motion without matter: for, there is no such thing as an immaterial motion, but motion must necessarily be of something: Also, if there be a figure, it must of

---

[145] Robert Boyle, *Origin of Forms and Qualities*: "These two grand and most catholic principles of bodies, matter and motion, being thus established, it will follow, both that matter must be actually divided into parts, that being the genuine effect of variously determined motion, and that each of the primitive fragments, or other distinct and entire masses of matter, must have two attributes; its own magnitude, or rather size, and its own figure or shape . . . So that now we have found out, and must admit three essential properties of each entire or undivided, though insensible part of matter; namely, magnitude . . ., shape, and either motion or rest . . ." (*WRB*, III, 16).

necessity be a figure of something; the same may be said of magnitude and weight, there being no such thing as a mean between something and nothing, that is, between body and no body in nature. If motion were immaterial, it is beyond all human capacity to conceive how it could be abstracted from something; much more, how it could be a principle to produce a natural being; it might easier be believed, that matter was perishable or reducible into nothing, than that motion, figure and magnitude should be separable from matter, or be immaterial, as the opinion is of those who introduce a vacuum in nature: And as for rest, I wonder how that can be a principle of any production, change or alteration, which itself acts nothing.

Others are for atoms and insensible particles, consisting of different figures, and particular natures; not otherwise united but by a bare "apposition,"[146] as they call it; by which, although perhaps the composed body obtains new qualities, yet still the ingredients retain each their own nature; and in the destruction of the composed body, those that are of one sort, associate and return into fire, water, earth, etc. as they were before.[147] But whatever their opinion of atoms be, first, I have heretofore declared that there can be no such things as single bodies or atoms in nature: Next, if there were any such particles in composed bodies, yet they are but parts or effects of matter, and not principles of nature, or natural beings.

Lastly, chemists do constitute the principles of all natural bodies, salt, sulphur and mercury.[148] But although I am not averse from believing that those ingredients may be mixt with other parts of nature, in the composition of natural figures, and that (especially) salt may be extracted out of many creatures; yet that it should be the constitutive principle of all other natural parts or figures, seems no ways conformable to truth; for salt is no more than other effects of nature; and although some extractions may convert some substances into salt figures, and some into others, (for art, by the leave of her mistress, nature, doth oftentimes occasion an alteration of natural creatures into artificial) yet these extractions cannot inform us how those natural creatures are made, and of what ingredients they consist: For, they do not prove that the same

[146] I.e., the atoms are related by surface contact and juxtaposition.
[147] See fn. 135.
[148] These three chemical principles were called the *"tria prima."* Paracelsus had added salt to sulphur and mercury – the mineral principles responsible for the generation of metals, according to the medieval Islamic chemists.

creatures are composed of salt, or mixt with salt; but cause only those substances which they extract, to change into saline figures, like as others do convert them into chemical spirits; all which are but hermaphroditical effects, that is, between natural and artificial; just as a mule partakes both of the nature or figure of a horse, and of an ass: Nevertheless, as mules are very beneficial for use, so are many chemical effects, provided they be discreetly and seasonably used; for minerals are no less beneficial to the life and health of man, than vegetables, and vegetables may be as hurtful and destructive as minerals, by an unseasonable and unskillful application: Besides, there may be chemical extracts made of vegetables, as well as of minerals; but these are best used in the height or extremity of some diseases, like as cordial waters in fainting fits; and some chemical spirits are far beyond cordial waters, as fire is beyond smoke; which cannot but be dangerous, and unfit to be used, except it be to encounter opposite extremes. By extremes, I mean not the extremes of nature, but the height of a distemper, when it is grown so far, that it is upon point of destroying or dissolving a particular animal figure: for nature being infinite, has no extremes, neither in her substance, nor actions; for she has nothing that is opposite to matter, neither is there any such thing as "most" or "least" in nature, she being infinite, and all her actions are balanced by their opposites; as for example, there is no dilatation, but hath opposite to its contraction; no condensation but has its opposite, viz. rarefaction; no composition but hath its opposite, division; no gravity without levity; no grossness without purity; no animate without inanimate; no regularity without irregularity: All which produces a peaceable, orderly and wise government in nature's kingdoms, which wise artists ought to imitate.

But you may say, How is it possible that there can be a peaceable and orderly government, where there are so many contrary or opposite actions; for contraries make war, not peace?

I answer: Although the actions of nature are opposite, yet nature, in her own substance, is at peace, because she is one and the same, that is, one material body, and has nothing without herself, to oppose and cross her; neither is she subject to a general change, so as to alter her own substance from being matter, for she is infinite and eternal; but because she is self-moving, and full of variety of figures, this variety cannot be produced without variety of actions, no, not without opposition; which opposition is the cause that there can be no extremes in particulars; for it balances each action, so that it cannot run into infinite, which otherwise would breed a horrid confusion in nature.

And thus much of principles: Concerning the particulars of chemical preparations, I being not versed in that art, am not able to give my judgment thereof, neither do I understand their terms and expressions; as first, what chemists mean by "fixation";[149] for there's nothing in nature that can properly be called fixt, because nature, and all her parts, are perpetually self-moving; only nature cannot be altered from being material, nor from being dependent upon God.

Neither do I apprehend what some mean by the "unlocking of bodies,"[150] unless they understand by it, a separation of natural parts proper for artificial uses; neither can natural effects be separated by others, any otherwise but occasionally; so that some parts may be an occasion of such or such alterations in other parts. But I must say this, that according to human sense and reason, there is no part or particle in nature which is not alterable, by reason nature is in a perpetual motion, and full of variety. It is true, some bodies, as gold and mercury, seem to be unalterable from their particular natures; but this only appears thus to our senses, because their parts are more fixt and retentive than others, and no art has been found out as yet, which could alter their proper and particular figures, that is, unite and dissolve, or rather cause an alteration of their corporeal retentive motions, that bind them into so fixt and consistent a body; but all that is mixt with them, has hitherto been found too weak for the alteration of their inherent motions: Nevertheless, this doth not prove that they are not altogether unalterable; for, though art cannot do it, yet nature may: but it is an argument that they are not composed of straying atoms, or most minute particles; for, not to mention what I have often repeated before, that there cannot be such most minute bodies in nature; by reason nature knows of no extremes, it is altogether improbable, nay, impossible, that wandering corpuscles should be the cause of such fixt effects, and by their association, constitute such indissoluble masses or clusters, as some do conceive, which

---

[149] A process of reducing a volatile body to a permanent coporeal form, e.g., a process resulting in the coagulation of a liquid, such as mercury, into a solid state.

[150] A process of separating out the components in a body; freeing a body from being "fixed." See the discussion of "fixation" and "volatilization" in Power, *Experimental Philosophy*, "A Digression of the Animal Spirits."

they call "primary concretions";[151] for there is no such thing as a primary concretion or composition in nature; only there are several sorts and degrees of motions, and several sorts of compositions; and as no particular creature can know the strength of motion, so neither can it know the degrees of strength in particular natural bodies. Wherefore, although composition and division of parts are general motions, and some figures may be more composed than others, that is, consist of more or fewer parts than others; yet there is none that hath not a composition of parts. The truth is, there is nothing prime or principal amongst the effects of nature, but only the cause from which they are produced, which is self-moving matter, which is above particular effects: yet nature may have more ways than our particular reason can apprehend; and therefore it is not to be admired that camphor, and the like bodies, do yield differing effects, according to the different occasions that make them move thus or thus: for, though changes and alterations of particulars, may be occasioned by others, yet they move by their own corporeal figurative motions; as it [is][152] evident by the power of fire, which makes other bodies move or change their parts and figures, not by its own transforming motion, but only by giving an occasion to the inherent figurative motions of those bodies, which by imitating the motions of fire, change into such or such figures, by their own proper, innate and inherent motions; otherwise if the alteration of combustible bodies proceeded from fire, they would all have the like motions, which is contradicted by experience. I will not deny, but there is as much variety in occasioning, as there is in acting; for the imitation is according to the object, but the object is not the immediate agent, but only an occasional efficient; so that, according to my opinion, there is no such difference as the learned make between patient and agent, when they call the exterior occasional cause, as (for example) fire, "the agent"; and the combustible body, "the patient"; for they conceive that a body thrown into fire, acts nothing at all, but only in a passive way suffers the fire to act upon it, according to the degree of its own, to wit, the fire's strength, which sense and reason perceives otherwise: for, to pass by what I mentioned before, that those bodies on which they suppose fire doth work, change according, not the fire's, but their own inherent figurative motions: It is most

---

[151] Boyle, for example, refers to his *minima naturalia* as "primitive concretions or clusters." See *Origin of Forms and Qualities* (*WRB*, III, 30).

[152] As in 1666; lacking in 1668.

certain, that if nature, and all her parts, be self-moving, which regular reason cannot deny; and if self-motion be corporeal, then every part of nature must of necessity move by its own motion; for no body can impart motion to another body, without imparting substance also; and though particular motions in particular bodies, may change infinite ways, yet they cannot quit those bodies, so as to leave them void and destitute of all motion, because matter and motion are but one thing; and therefore, though fire be commixed with the parts of the fuel, yet the fuel alters by its own motion, and the fire doth but act occasionally; and so do chemical spirits or extracts, which may cause a separation, and alter some bodies as readily as fire doth; for they are a certain kind of fire, to wit, such as is called a dead or liquid fire; for a flaming fire, although it be fluid, yet it is not liquid: The same may be said of the "antimonial cup":[153] for, it is not probable to sense and reason, there should be certain invisible little bodies that pass out of the cup into the liquor, and cause such effects, no more than there are magnetical effluviums issuing out of the loadstone towards iron, there being many causes which neither impart nor lose anything in the production of their effects; but the liquor that is within the antimonial cup, does imitate the corporeal figurative motions of the cup, and so produces the same effects as are proper to antimony, upon other bodies or parts of nature. In the same manner does the blood-stone[154] stop bleeding, not by imparting invisible atoms or rays to the affected parts, (or else if it were long worn about one's body, it would be wasted, at least alter its proper figure and virtue) but by being imitated by the corporeal figurative motions of the distempered parts. Thus many other examples could be alleged to prove, that natural motions work such or such effects within their own parts, without receiving any from without; that is, by imitation, and not by reception of motion. By which it is evident, that properly there is no passive or suffering body in nature, except it be the inanimate part of matter, which in its own nature is moveless or destitute of motion, and is carried along with, and by the animate parts of matter: However, although inanimate matter has no motion inherent in itself, as it is inanimate; yet it is so closely mixt with the animate parts, that it cannot be considered without motion, much

---

[153] One form of the highly debated antimonial remedies advocated by Paracelsus; the cup, made of antimony, imparts an emetic quality to wine left in it.

[154] Certain precious stones speckled with red, especially heliotrope, were thought to have an occult power to stop bleeding.

less be separable from it; and therefore, although it acts not of itself, yet it acts by virtue of the animate parts of matter.

Next, I cannot conceive what some chemists mean, when they call those principles or elements, which, they say, composed bodies consist of, "distinct substances";[155] for, though they may be of different figures, yet they are not of different substances, because there is but one only substance in nature, which is matter, whose several actions cause all the variety in nature. But, if all the parts of natural bodies, should be called principles or elements, then there would be infinite principles in nature; which is impossible, because there can be no more but one principle, which is self-moving matter; and although several creatures, by the help of fire, may be reduced or dissolved into several different particles, yet those particles are not principles, much less simple bodies; or else we might say as well, that ashes are a principle of wood: Neither are they created anew, because they are of another form or figure than when composed into one concrete body: for, there's nothing that is material, which is not pre-existent in nature, no, nor figure, motion, or the like, all being material, although not always subject to our human sensitive perception: for, the variation of the corporeal figurative motions blindeth our particular senses, that we cannot perceive them, they being too subtle to be discerned either by art or human perception. The truth is, if we could see the corporeal figurative motions of natural creatures, and the association and division of all their parts, we should soon find out the causes which make them to be such or such particular natural effects; but nature is too wise to be so easily known by her particulars.

Wherefore, chemists need not think they can create anything anew; for they cannot challenge to themselves a divine power, neither can there be any such thing as a new creation in nature, no not of an atom: Nor can they annihilate anything, they will sooner waste their estates, than reduce the least particle of matter into nothing; and though they make waste of some parts of natural bodies, yet those are but changes into other figures, there being a perpetual inspiration and expiration, that is, composition and division of parts; but composition is not a new creation, nor division

---

[155] Descartes understood a scholastic form to be a substance, distinct from matter, which unites with the latter to compose a natural body; he rejected the existence of such forms, other than the human soul. Boyle also rejected substantial forms thus understood, but he retained the term "form," to mean "not a real substance distinct from matter, but only the matter itself of a natural body, considered with its peculiar manner of existence . . ." (*WRB*, III, 28). Cavendish follows Boyle in denying that the forms and figures of bodies are substances.

an annihilation; and though they produce new forms, as they imagine, yet those forms, though they be new to them, are not new in nature; for all that is material, has been existent in nature from all eternity; so that the combination of parts cannot produce anything that is not already in nature. Indeed, the generation of new figures seems to me much like the generation of new motions, which would put God to a perpetual creation, and argue that he was not able to make nature or matter perfect at first, or that he wanted employment. But, say they, It is not matter that is created anew, but only figures or forms. I answer: If anyone can show me a figure without matter, I shall be willing to believe it; but I am confident nature cannot do that, much less art, which is but a particular effect: for, as matter cannot be without figure, so neither can figure be without matter, no more than body without parts, or parts without body; and if so, no figure or form can be created without matter, there being no such thing as a substanceless form. Chemists should but consider their own particular persons, as, whether they were generated anew, or had been in nature before they were got of their parents; if they had not been pre-existent in nature, they would not be natural, but supernatural creatures, because they would not subsist of the same matter as other creatures do. Truly, matter being infinite, how some new material creatures could be created without some parts of this infinite matter, is not conceivable by human sense and reason; for infinite admits of no addition: but if there could be an addition, it would presuppose an annihilation; so that at the same time when one part is annihilating or perishing, another must succeed by a new creation, which is a mere paradox.

But that which puzzles me most is, how those substances, which they call "tria prima,"[156] and principles of natural things, can be generated anew: for, if the principles be generated anew, the effects must be so too; and since they, according to their supposition, are catholic or universal principles, all natural effects must have their origin from them, and be, like their principles, created continually anew; which, how it be possible, without the destruction of nature, is beyond my reason to conceive. Some endeavour to prove by their artificial experiments, that they have and can produce such things out of natural bodies, which never were pre-existent in them; as for example, glass out of vegetables, without any

---

[156] See fn. 148.

addition of foreign parts, only by the help of fire. To which I answer, that, in my opinion, the same glass was as much pre-existent in the matter of those vegetables, and the fire, and in the power of their corporeal figurative motions, as any other figure whatsoever; otherwise it would never have been produced: nay, not only glass, but millions of other figures might be obtained from those parts, they being subject to infinite changes: for the actions of self-moving matter are so infinitely various, that, according to the mixture or composition and division of parts, they can produce what figures they please; not by a new creation, but only a change or alteration of their own parts; and though some parts act not to the production of such or such figures; yet we cannot say that those figures are not in nature, or in the power of corporeal, figurative self-motion; we might as well say, that a man cannot go, when he sits; or has no motion when he sleeps; as believe, that it is not in the power of nature to produce such or such effects or actions, when they are not actually produced: for, as I said before, although nature be but one material substance, yet there are infinite mixtures of infinite parts, produced by infinite self-motion, infinite ways; insomuch, that seldom any two creatures, even those of one sort, do exactly resemble each other.

But some may say, How is it possible that figure, being all one with matter, can change, and matter remain still the same, without any change or alteration?

I answer: As well as an animal body can put itself into various and different postures, without any change of its interior animal figure: for, though figure cannot subsist without matter, nor matter without figure, generally considered; yet particular parts of matter are not bound to certain particular figures: Matter in its general nature, remains always the same, and cannot be changed from being matter, but by the power of self-motion, it may change from being such or such a particular figure: For example, wood is as much matter as stone, but it is not of the same figure, nor has it the same interior innate motions which stone hath, because it has not the like composition of parts as other creatures of other figures have; and though some figures be more constant or lasting than others, yet this does not prove that they are not subject to changes, as well as those that alter daily, nay, every moment; much less, that they are without motion; for all motions are not dividing or dissolving, but some are retentive, some composing, some attractive, some expulsive, some contractive, some dilative, and infinite other sorts of motions, as it is evident by the infinite variety which appears in the differing effects of nature: Nevertheless, it is no consequence, that, because the effects are different, they must also have different principles: For first, all effects of nature are material; which proves, they have but one principle, which is the only infinite matter. Next, they are all self-moving; which proves, that this material principle has self-motion; for without self-motion, there would be no variety or change of figures, it being the nature of self-motion to be perpetually acting.

Thus matter and self-motion being inseparably united in one infinite body, which is self-moving material nature, is the only cause of all the infinite effects that are produced in nature, and not the Aristotelian elements, or chemists' *tria prima*, which sense and reason perceives to be no more but effects; or else if we should call all those creatures "principles," which by the power of their own inherent motions, change into other figures, we shall be forced to make infinite principles, and so confound principles with effects; and after this manner, that which is now an effect, will become a principle; and what is now a principle, will become an effect; which will lead our sense and reason into a horrid confusion and labyrinth of ignorance.

Wherefore, I will neither follow the opinions of the ancient, nor of our moderns in this point, but search the truth of nature, by the light of regular reason: for, I perceive that most of our modern writings are not filled with new inventions of their own, but, like a lumber, stuffed with old commodities, botched and dressed up anew, contain nothing but what has been said in former ages. Nor am I of the opinion of our divine philosophers, who mince philosophy and divinity, faith and reason, together, and count it irreligious, if not blasphemy, to assert any other principles of nature, than what they (I will not say, by head and shoulders) draw out of the Scripture, especially out of Genesis, to evince the finiteness and beginning of nature; whenas Moses doth only describe the creation of this world, and not of infinite nature: But, as pure natural philosophers do not meddle with divinity, or things supernatural; so divines ought not to entrench upon natural philosophy.

Neither are chemists the only natural philosophers, because they are so much tied to the art of fire, and regulate or measure all the effects of nature according to their artificial experiments, which do delude, rather than inform their sense and reason; and although they pretend to a vast and greater knowledge than all the rest, yet they have not dived so deep into nature yet, as to perceive that she is full of sense and reason, which is life and knowledge; and in parts, orders parts proper to parts, which causes all the various motions, figures and changes in the infinite parts of nature. Indeed, no creature that has its reason regular, can almost believe, that such wise and orderly actions should be done either by chance, or by straying atoms, which cannot so constantly change and exchange parts, and mix and join so properly, and to such constant effects as are apparent in nature. And as for Galenists,[157] if they believe that some parts of nature cannot leave or pass by other parts, to join, meet, or encounter others, they are as much in an error as chemists, concerning the power of fire and furnace: for, it is most frequently observed thus amongst all sorts of animals; and if amongst animals, I know no reason but all other kinds and sorts of creatures may do the like; nay, both sense and reason inform us, they do; as appears by the several and proper actions of all sorts of drugs, as also of minerals and elements, and the like; so that none ought to wonder how it is possible that medicines that must pass through digestions in the body, should, neglecting all other parts, show themselves friendly only to the brain or kidneys, or the like parts; for, if there be sense and reason in nature, all things must act wisely and orderly, and not confusedly; and though art, like an emulating ape, strives to imitate nature, yet it is so far from producing natural figures, that at the best it rather produces monsters instead of natural effects;[158] for it is like the painter, who drew a rose instead of a lion: nevertheless, art is as active as any other natural creature, and doth never want employment; for it is like all other parts, in a perpetual self-motion; and although the interior actions of all other parts do not appear to our senses, yet they may be perceived by regular reason; for what sense wants, reason supplies, which oftner rectifies the straying and erring senses, than these do reason, as being more pure, subtle and free from labouring on the inanimate parts of matter, than sense is, as I have often declared; which proves, that reason is far beyond sense; and this appears also in chemistry, which yet is so much for sensitive experiments: for, when the effects do not readily follow according to our intentions, reason is fain to consider and enquire into the

---

[157] The followers of Galen; see fn. 4.
[158] A response to a quotation from Van Helmont, which Cavendish had previously cited in her *Phil. Letters*: "The art of chemistry is not only the chambermaid and emulating ape, but now and then the mistress of nature" (p. 362).

causes that hinder or obstruct the success of our designs. And if reason be above sense, then speculative philosophy ought to be preferred before the experimental, because there can no reason be given for anything without it. I will not say that all arts have their first origin from reason; for, what we name chance, does often present to the sensitive perception such things which the rational does afterwards take into consideration; but my meaning is, that, for the most part, reason leads and directs the ways of art; and I am of opinion, that contemplative philosophy is the best tutoress, and gives the surest instructions to art, and amongst the rest, to the art of chemistry, which no doubt is very profitable to man many several ways, and very sovereign in many desperate diseases, if discreetly and moderately used; but if chemical medicines should be so commonly applied as others, they would sooner kill than cure; and if Paracelsus was as frequently practised as Galen, it would be as bad as the plague: Wherefore chemical medicines are to be used as the extreme unction in desperate cases, and that with great moderation and discretion.

XXI   Of the Universal Medicine, and of Diseases

I am not of the opinion, that there can be a universal medicine for all diseases,[159] except it be proved that all kinds of diseases whatsoever, proceed from one cause; which I am sure can never be done, by reason there is as much variety in the causes of diseases, as in the diseases themselves. You may say: All diseases proceed but from irregular motions. I answer: These irregular motions are so numerous, different and various, that all the artists in nature are not able to rectify them. Nay, they might sooner make or create a new matter, than rectify the irregularities of nature more than nature herself is pleased to do; for though art may be an occasion of the changes of some parts or motions, of their compositions and divisions, imitations, and the like; like as a painter takes a copy from an original, yet it cannot alter infinite nature; for a man may build or pull down a house, but yet he cannot make the materials, although he may fit or prepare them for his use: so artists may dissolve and compose several parts several ways, but yet they cannot make the matter of those parts; and therefore, although they may observe the

---

[159] Cf. Van Helmont, *Oriatrike*, pp. 469ff.

effects, yet they cannot always give a true or probable reason why they are so, nor know the several particular causes which make them to be so: To see the effects, belongs to the perception of sense; but to judge of the cause, belongs only to reason; and since there is an ignorance as well as a perceptive knowledge in nature, no creature can absolutely know, or have a thorough perception of all things, but according as the corporeal figurative motions are, so are the perceptions; not only in one composed figure, but also in every part and particle of the same figure; for one and the same parts may make several perceptions in several creatures, according to their several figurative motions. But reason being above sense, is more inspective than sense; and although sense doth many times inform reason, yet reason being more subtle, piercing and active, doth oftner inform and rectify the senses when they are irregular; nay, some rational parts inform others, like as one man will inform another of his own voluntary conceptions, or of his exterior perceptions; and some sensitive parts will inform others, as one artist another; and although experimental philosophy is not to be rejected, yet the speculative is much better, by reason it guides, directs and governs the experimental: but, as knowledge and understanding is more clear, where both the rational and sensitive perception do join; so experimental and speculative philosophy do give the surest informations, when they are joined or united together.

But to return to the universal medicine; although I do not believe there is any, nor that all diseases are curable; yet my advice is, that no applications of remedies should be neglected in any disease whatsoever; because diseases cannot be so perfectly known, but that they may be mistaken; and so even the most experienced physician may many times be deceived, and mistake a curable disease for an incurable; wherefore trials should be made as long as life lasts. Of dropsies, cancers, kings-evils, and the like diseases, I believe some may be curable, especially if taken at the first beginning, and that without great difficulty, and in a short time; but such diseases which consist in the decay of the vital parts, I do verily believe them incurable: As for example, those dropsies, consumptions, dead-palsies, etc. which are caused either through the decay of the vital parts, or through want of radical substance: Neither do I think a natural blindness, dumbness, deafness, or lameness, curable; nor natural fools, or idiots. Nay, I fear, the best chemist will be puzzled to cure a settled or fixt gout, or the stone, in such bodies as are apt to breed it; for stones are produced several ways; and as their productions are different, so are they: Wherefore, although many do pretend to great things, yet were their cures so certain, they would be more frequent. I will not say, but many times they perform great cures; but, whether it be by chance, or out of a fundamental knowledge, I know not; but since they are so seldom performed, I think them to be rather casual cures. In my opinion, the surest way both in diseases and applications of remedies, is, to observe the corporeal, figurative motions of both, which are best and surest perceived by the rational perception, because the sensitive is more apt to be deluded.

XXII   Of Outward Remedies

Remedies, which are applied outwardly, may be very beneficial, by reason the bodies of animal creatures are full of pores, which serve to attract nourishment, or foreign matter into the body, and to vent super-fluities. Besides, the interior parts of those bodies, to which outward remedies are applied, may imitate the qualities or motions of the remedies, by the help of their own sensitive motions, and therefore the application of outward remedies, is not altogether to be rejected. But yet I do not believe that they do always, or in all persons, work the like effects; or that they are so sure and sovereign, as those that are taken inwardly. The truth is, as remedies properly and seasonably applied, can work good effects; so they may also produce ill effects, if they be used improperly and unseasonably; and therefore wise physicians and surgeons know by experience, as well as by learning and reason, what is best for their patients in all kind of distempers: Only this I will add concerning diseases, that in the productions of diseases, there must of necessity be a conjunction of the agent and patient, as is evident even in those diseases that are caused by conceit: for, if a man should hear of an infectious disease, and be apprehensive of it, both the discourse of him that tells it, and the mind of him that apprehends it, are agents or causes of that disease, in the body of the patient, and concur in the production of the disease; the difference is only, that the discourse may be called a "remoter cause"; and the rational motions, or the mind of the patient, a "nearer or immediate cause": for, as soon as the mind doth figure such a disease, the sensitive corporeal motions, immediately take the figure from the mind, and figure the disease in the substance or parts of the body of the patient; the rational proving the father, the sensitive the mother, both working by consent: Whereby we may also conclude, that diseases, as well as other sorts of creatures, are made by nature's corporeal figurative motions; and those parts that occasion others to alter their natural motions, are most predominant: for, although nature is free, and all her parts self-moving; yet not every part is free to move as it pleases, by reason some parts overpower others, either through number, strength, sleight, shape, opportunity, or the like advantages; and natural philosophy is the only study that teaches men to know the particular natures, figures and motions of the several composed parts of nature, and the rational perception is more intelligent than the sensitive.

XXIII   Of Several Sorts of Drink and Meat

Some physicians, when they discourse of several sorts of drinks and meats, do relate several wonderful cures which some drinks have effected: And truly, I am of opinion, that they may be both beneficial and hurtful, according as they are used properly, and temperately; or improperly, and excessively: but I find there are more several sorts for curiosity and luxury, than for health and necessity: Small ale or beer, is a sovereign remedy to quench drought; and one glass of wine proves a cordial; but many glasses may prove a kind of poison, putting men oftentimes into fevers, and the like diseases. And for diet drinks, I believe they are very good in some sorts of diseases; and so may tea, and coffee, and the water of birches, for anything I know; for I never had any experience of them; but I observe, that these latter drinks, tea, and coffee, are now become mode drinks, and their chief effects are to make good fellowship, rather than to perform great cures; for I can hardly believe, that such weak liquors can have such strong effects. Concerning several sorts of meats, I leave them to experienced physicians, for they know best what is fit for the bodies of their patients: Only about the preservation, or keeping of several sorts of meats from putrefaction, I will say this, that I have observed, that what will keep dead flesh and fish, as also vegetables, from putrefaction, will destroy living animals; for, if living animals should, like dead flesh, be picked up, and kept from air, they would soon be smothered to death; and so would fire, which yet is no animal. Neither can ladies and gentlewomen preserve their lives, as they do several sorts of fruit. Nevertheless, both this, and several other arts, are very necessary and profitable for the use of man, if they be but fitly and properly employed: but we may observe, that whenas other creatures have no more than what is necessary for their preservation, man troubles himself with things that are needless, nay, many times hurtful: Which is the cause there are so many unprofitable arts, which breed confusion, instead of proving beneficial and instructive.

XXIV   Of Fermentation

Fermentation, of which Helmont and his followers make such a stir, as it is enough to set all the world afermenting or working,[160] is nothing else but what is vulgarly called digestion; so that it is but a new term for an old action: And these digestions or fermentations, are as various and numerous as all other actions of nature, to wit, respiration, evacuation, dilatation, contraction, etc. for action and working are all one.

But there are good and ill fermentations; those are done by a sympathetical agreement of parts, but these by an antipathetical disagreement: Those tend to the preservation of the subject, these to its destruction: Those are regular, these irregular: So that there are numerous sorts of fermentations, not only in several sorts of creatures, but in several parts of one and the same creature: for, fermentation or digestion is according to the composition of the fermenting or digestive parts, and their motions.

XXV   Of the Plague

I have heard, that a gentleman in *Italy* fancied he had so good a microscope, that he could see atoms through it, and could also perceive the plague; which he affirmed to be a swarm of living animals, as little as atoms, which entered into men's bodies, through their mouths, nostrils, ears, etc.[161]

---

[160] For Van Helmont, fermentation is a universal process in which the first principle of matter, water, is disposed to receive seminal images of the variety of individual things. The undifferentiated water transmutates into the *gas* that is the essence of a particular individual. The process renders matter volatile and spiritual, and the ferment takes on the role of the *archeus* of the object. So, fermentation explains not only digestion, but the generation of animals, vegetables and minerals.

[161] Athanasius Kircher (1602–80) used the microscope to provide evidence for his theory that disease is caused by the animate "seeds" of "worms" insensible to the naked eye. See Kircher's *Scrutinium physico-medicum contagiosae luis, quae pestis dicitur* [A Physico-Medical Enquiry of the Contagious Plague, Which Is Called the Pest] (Rome, 1658).

To give my opinion hereof, I must confess, that there are no parts of nature, how little soever, which are not living and self-moving bodies; nay, every respiration is of living parts: and therefore the infection of the plague, made by the way of respiration, cannot but be of living parts; but, that these parts should be animal creatures, is very improbable to sense and reason; for if this were so, not only the plague, but all other infectious diseases would be produced the same way; and then fruit, or any other surfeiting meat, would prove living animals. But I am so far from believing that the plague should be living animals, as I do not believe it to be a swarm of living atoms flying up and down in the air; for if it were thus, then those atoms would not remain in one place, but infect all the places they passed through; whenas yet we observe, that the plague will often be but in one town or city of a kingdom, without spreading any further. Neither do I believe (as some others say) that it is always the heat of the sun, or air, that causes, or at least increases the plague; for there are winter-plagues, as well as summer-plagues; and many times the plague decreases in summer, when it is hot; and increases in winter, when it is cold: Besides, the air being generally hot, over all the country or kingdom, would not only cause the infection in one town or city, but in all other parts.

Therefore my opinion is, that as all other diseases are produced several manners or ways, so likewise the plague; and as they generally do all proceed from the irregularities of corporeal natural motions, so does also the plague. But since it is often observed, that all bodies are not infected, even in a great plague; it proves that the infection is made by imitation, and, as one and the same agent, cannot occasion the like effects in every patient; as for example, fire in several sorts of fuels, nay, in one and the same sort; as for example, in wood; for some wood takes fire sooner, and burns more clearly, and dissolves more suddenly than some other; so it is also with the plague, and with all other diseases that proceed from an outward infection: for, the exterior agent is not an immediate cause, but only an occasion that the patient has such or such motions: and as the imitating motions are stronger or weaker, quicker or slower; so is the breeding of the disease. I will not deny, but there may be such figurative, corporeal motions in the air or earth, which may cause infections amongst those animals that live within the compass thereof; and many times the air or earth may be infected by animals: But some particulars not being infected at all, though they be frequently with those that have the plague, it proves, that the figurative motions of their bodies do not imitate those motions that make the plague; whenas, if the air were filled with infectious atoms, none would escape; nay, they would not only enter into men, but beasts and birds, etc.

Concerning the spotted-plague, it proceeds from a general irregularity of dissolving motions, which cause a general gangrene of all the body; and to find a cure for this disease, is as difficult, as to find the philosophers' stone; for, though many pretend to cure it, yet none has as yet performed it; what may be done hereafter, I know not; but I doubt they will be more able to raise a man from the dead, or renew old age, and change it into youth, than do it.

As for other diseases, I refer the reader to my other works, especially my *Philosophical Opinions*; for my design is not now to make a physical treatise: and there they will find, of the disease called "ague," that its cause is the irregularity of the digestive or concoctive motions, and so of the rest; for in this present work I intended nothing else, but to make reflexions upon *experimental philosophy*, and to explain some other points in *natural philosophy*, for the better understanding of my own opinions; which, if I have done to the satisfaction of the reader, I have my aim, and desire no more.

XXVI   Of Respiration

Having made mention both in the foregoing discourse, and several other places of this book, of respiration, I'll add to the end of this part, a full declaration of my opinion thereof.

First, I believe that there are respirations in all creatures and parts of nature, performed by the several passages of their bodies, to receive foreign, and discharge some of their own parts. Next, I believe, that those respirations are of different sorts, according to the different sorts of creatures. Thirdly, as the respirations of natural parts and creatures, are various and different, so are also the pores or passages through which they respire; as for example, in man, and some other animals, the nostrils, ears, mouth, pores of the skin, are all of different figures: And such a difference may also be between the smaller pores of the skin, of the several parts of man, as between the pores of his breast, arms, legs, head, etc. also the grain or lines of a man's skin may be different, like as several figures of wrought silks or stuffs sold in mercers' shops; which if they did make several colours by the various refractions, inflexions, reflexions and positions of light, then certainly a naked man would appear of many several colours, according to the difference of his pores or grains of the skin, and the different position of light. But sense and reason does plainly observe, that the positions of light do not cause such effects; for, though every several man, for the most part, hath a peculiar complexion, feature, shape, humour, disposition, etc. different from each other; so that it is a miracle to see two men just like one another in all things: yet light alters not the natural colour of their bodies, no more than it can alter the natural figures and shapes of all other parts of their bodies; but what alteration soever is made, proceeds from the natural corporeal motions of the same body, and not from the various positions, refractions and reflexions of light; whose variety in nature, as it is infinite, so it produces also infinite figures, according to the infinite wisdom of nature, which orders all things orderly and wisely.

III Observations upon the Opinions of Some Ancient Philosophers

Although the indisposition of my body did in a manner dissuade me from studying and writing any more; yet the great desire I had to know the opinions of the ancient philosophers, and whether any came near my own, overcame me so much, that even to the prejudice of my own health, I gave myself to the perusing of the works of that learned author Mr. Stanley, wherein he describes the lives and opinions of the ancient philosophers;[162] in which I found so much difference betwixt their conceptions and my own, in natural philosophy, that were it allowable or usual for our sex, I might set up a sect or school for myself, without any prejudice to them: But I, being a woman, do fear they would soon cast me out of their schools; for, though the muses, graces and sciences are all of the female gender, yet they were more esteemed in former ages, than they are now; nay, could it be done handsomely, they would now turn them all from females into males: So great is grown the self-conceit of the masculine, and the disregard of the female sex.

But, to let that pass, the opinions of the ancient, though they are not exempt from errors no more than our moderns; yet are they to be commended, that their conceptions are their own, and the issue of their own wit and reason; whenas most of the opinions of our modern philosophers, are patched up with theirs; some whereof do altogether follow either Aristotle, Plato, Epicurus, Pythagoras, etc. others make a mixture of several of their opinions; and others again take some of their opinions, and dress them up new with some additions of their own; and what is worst,

---

[162] Thomas Stanley, *The History of Philosophy*; all future references will be to the 1687 edition, reprinted New York/London: Garland Publishing, 1978.

after all this, instead of thanks, they reward them with scorn, and rail at them; whenas, perhaps, without their pains and industry, our age would hardly have arrived to that knowledge it has done. To which ungrateful and unconscionable act, I can no ways give my consent, but admire and honour both the ancient, and all those that are real inventors of noble and profitable arts and sciences, before all those that are but botchers and brokers; and that I do in this following part, examine and mark some of their opinions as erroneous, is not out of a humour to revile or prejudice their wit, industry, ingenuity and learning, in the least; but only to show, by the difference of their opinions and mine, that mine are not borrowed from theirs, as also to make mine the more intelligible and clear; and, if possible, to find out the truth in natural philosophy; for which, were they alive, I question not but I should easily obtain their pardon.

I   Upon the Principles of Thales

Thales, according to historical relation, was the first that made disquisitions upon nature,[163] and so the first natural philosopher.[164] His chief points in philosophy are these:

> 1. He says, that water is the principle of all natural bodies.[165] 2. That nature is full of demons, and spiritual substances.[166] 3. That the soul is a self-moving nature,[167] and that it both moves itself, and the body.[168] 4. That there is but one world,[169] and that finite.[170] 5. That the world is animate, and God is the soul thereof, diffused through every part.[171] 6. That the world is contained in a place.[172] 7. That bodies are divisible into infinite.[173]

---

[163] Stanley, *The History of Philosophy*, vol. I, p. 5; Diogenes Laertius given as source. See the latter's *Lives and Opinions of Eminent Philosophers*.

[164] Ibid., p. 5 ; Tertullian, *Apologeticus* [Apology] given as source.

[165] Ibid., p. 5; discussion in pseudo-Plutarch, *De placitis philosophorum naturalibus* . . . [On the Physical Opinions of the Philosophers], I, 3 and Stobaeus, *Eclogae physicae et ethicae* [Physical and Ethical Eclogues], I, 13 cited. In modern editions, the first book of the *Eclogues*, which contains the physical eclogues, can be found in the first book of his *Anthologium* [Anthology].

[166] Ibid., p. 6; Stobaeus, Aristotle, *On the Soul*, I, ch. 8 and Cicero, *De legibus* [On the Laws], II given as sources.

[167] Ibid., p. 7; pseudo-Plutarch, *On the Physical Opinions of the Philosophers*, IV, 2 and Stobaeus given as sources.

[168] Ibid., p. 7; Stobaeus, *Physical and Ethical Eclogues*, I given as source.

[169] Ibid., p. 7; pseudo-Plutarch, *On the Physical Opinions of the Philosophers*, II, 1 given as source.

[170] Ibid., p. 7; discussion in Aristotle, *On the Heavens*, I, chs. 10 and 12 cited.

[171] Ibid., p. 7; Diogenes Laertius given as source.

[172] Ibid., p. 7; Diogenes Laertius given as source.

[173] Ibid., p. 8; pseudo-Plutarch, *On the Physical Opinions of the Philosophers*, I, 16 given as source.

Concerning the first, viz. that water is the principle of all natural things, Helmont doth embrace this opinion, as I have declared in my *Philosophical Letters*, and in the foregoing part of this book, and have given, withal, my reasons why water cannot be a principle of natural things, because it is no more but a natural effect: for, though humidity may be found in many parts or creatures of nature, yet this doth not prove that water is a principle of all natural bodies, no more than fire, earth, air, or any other creature of nature: And though most philosophers are of opinion that elements are simple bodies, and all the rest are composed of them, yet this is no ways probable to reason, because they consist of the same matter as other bodies do, and are all but effects of one cause or principle, which is infinite matter.

Next, that nature is full of demons, or spiritual substances, is against sense and reason; for what is incorporeal, is no part of nature: and upon this account, the soul cannot be immaterial, although he makes her to be a self-moving nature; for what has a natural motion, has also a natural body, because matter and motion are but one thing; neither can a spiritual substance move a corporeal, they being both of different natures.

As for the world, that there is but one, I do willingly grant it, if by the world he did mean nature; but then it cannot be finite. But Thales seems to contradict himself in this theorem, whenas he grants, that bodies are divisible in infinite: for, if there be infinite actions, as infinite divisions in nature, then surely the body of nature itself must be infinite.

Next, he says, that God is the soul of the world, which if so, God being infinite, he cannot have a finite body to animate it; for a finite body, and an infinite soul, do never agree together: but, that God should be the soul of the world, no regular reason can allow, because the soul of nature must be corporeal, as well as the body; for an incorporeal substance cannot be mixed with a corporeal. Next, the world, as the body of nature, being divisible, it would follow, that God, which is the soul, would be divisible also. Thirdly, every part of the world would be a part of God, as partaking of the same nature; for every part, if the soul be diffused through all the body, would be animate.

Lastly, concerning place, as, that the world is contained in a place; my opinion is, that place is nothing else but an affection of body, and in no ways different or separable from it; for wheresoever is body or matter, there is place also; so that place cannot be said to contain the world, or else it would be bigger than the world itself; for that which contains, must needs, in compass or extent, exceed that which it contains.

II   Some Few Observations on Plato's Doctrine

1. Plato says, that life is twofold, contemplative, and active; and that contemplation is an office of the intellect, but action an operation of the rational soul.[174]

To which I answer, first, that I know no other difference between intellect and reason, but that intellect is an effect, or rather an essential propriety of reason, if reason be the principle of nature; for the rational part is the most intelligent part of animate matter. Next, I say, that contemplation is as much an action, as any other action of nature, although it be not so gross as the action of the body; for it is only an action of the mind, which is more pure and subtle than either the sensitive or inanimate parts of matter are, and acts within itself, that is, in its own substance or degree of matter.

2. He says, that sense is a passion of the soul.[175]

I answer: There is as much difference between sense, and the soul, as there is between sense, and reason, or a sensitive life, and a rational soul; for the rational parts of matter, are not the sensitive, nor the sensitive the rational; a fool may have his sense regular, and his reason irregular; and therefore sense and reason are not one and the same, although they have an inseparable communion in the body or substance of nature.

3. He argues thus: That which moves in itself, as being the principle of motion in those things which are moved, is always moved, and consequently immortal, ungenerable and incorruptible: But, the soul is so. *Ergo*, etc.[176]

I answer: Natural matter being thus self-moving, is the same.

4. Form, says he, is joined to matter.[177]

I answer: Form and matter are but one thing; for it is impossible to separate matter from form, or form from matter; but what is not

---

[174] Cf. Stanley: "[T]he chief office of the contemplative consisteth in the knowledge of truth, as of the active, in the practice of those things which are dictated by reason" (Ibid., p. 181). Here and in what follows, Stanley claims that he is giving "the doctrine of Plato delivered by Alcinous." See *The Handbook of Platonism / Alcinous*, tr. John Dillon (Oxford: Clarendon Press, 1993).

[175] Ibid., p. 181.

[176] Ibid., p. 191; altered and condensed.

[177] Ibid., p. 185; Stanley writes of Plato's "first matter" *receiving* and *being subjected to* forms.

divisible, is not compoundable; and what cannot be separated, cannot be joined.

5. Qualities, says he, are incorporeal, because they are accidents.[178]

I answer: If qualities be incorporeal, they do not belong to nature: for, since the principle of nature is matter, all that is natural, must also be material or corporeal; and therefore all natural qualities or accidents must of necessity be corporeal, by reason quality can no more be divided from matter, than figure, magnitude, colour, place, and the like; all which are but one and the same with body, without any separation or abstraction.

6. What Plato affirms of that which never is, and never had a beginning, and of that which has a beginning, and not a being,[179] is more than he or anybody can rationally prove; for what never was, nor is, no man can know or imagine; because all what is known or imagined, has its real being, if not without, yet within the mind; and all thoughts have not only a being, but a material being in nature; nay, even the thought of the existence of a deity, although deity itself is immaterial.

7. I wonder so witty a philosopher as Plato, can believe, that matter in itself, as it is the principle of nature, is void of all form;[180] for he affirms himself, that whatsoever hath parts, hath also figure; but matter has parts, (by reason there can be no single part in nature, but wheresoever is body or matter, there are parts also) and therefore matter cannot be void of figure. But if by form, he mean the innate and inherent self-motion of matter, he contradicts himself: for, how can all things be made of matter, as their principle, if matter be destitute of self-motion? Wherefore infinite matter has not only self-motion, but also figure, though not a circumscribed or limited figure: Neither can it be proved, that nature, being infinite, is not qualitative, no more than she can be proved to have no parts, or to be finite. In short, it is impossible for my reason to believe, that matter should be capable of, and subject to all forms, and yet be void of all quality, form and species; for whatsoever has neither form, figure, nor quality, is no body, and therefore Plato's matter is immaterial, or incorporeal. If it were possible that there could be some converse or meeting between his and my soul, I would ask his soul how he would prove, that one and the same thing could exist, and not exist, at one and

---

[178] Ibid., p. 186; slightly altered and condensed.
[179] Ibid., p. 196; Cavendish's rendering of material in ch. 34.
[180] Ibid., p. 185; altered and condensed.

the same time; that is, how matter could be no matter, or something and nothing at the same time; and whence it came to be thus? For, though our reason does believe, that the omnipotent creator, can make something of nothing, and reduce something into nothing; yet no reason is able to comprehend how God could make a being which is neither something nor nothing; neither corporeal nor incorporeal. But Plato concludes, that matter is destitute of all form, because it is subject to change of forms and figures in its particulars, which is a very great mistake; for the changes of forms or figures, do not alter the nature of matter, but prove rather, that wheresoever there is form or figure, there is matter also; so that none can be without the other, at no time. A piece of wax may be transformed into millions of figures; but it can never be deprived of all figure; no more can matter.

8. Concerning ideas, Plato's opinion is, that they are principles of nature, and the eternal notions of God, perfect in themselves; or an external exemplar of things which are according to nature.[181] But I would ask him, What notions are, and whence they come? and, if they be pictures or patterns of all things in nature, What makes or causes them? He will say, They are the thoughts of God. But what creature in the universe is able to describe the thoughts or notions of God? For, though I do humbly acknowledge God to be the Author of Nature, and with the greatest reverence and fear, adore that infinite deity; yet I dare not attribute any notions or ideas to God, nor in any manner or way express him like our human condition; for I fear I should speak irreverently of that incomprehensible essence, which is above all finite capacity, reason, or idea.

Next, he says, that those ideas are not of things made by art, nor of singulars; nor of preternatural accidents, as diseases; nor of vile and abject things, nor of relatives. Which if so, I would enquire whence those effects do proceed? For if the eternal ideas, according to his opinion, are principles of all natural things, they must also be principles of the aforementioned effects, they being also natural: If they do not proceed from any principle, they must proceed from themselves; which cannot be, by reason they are effects of nature: but if they have another principle besides the eternal notions, or ideas; then there must be another power besides these, which power would oppose the divine power, or the power

---

[181] Ibid., p. 185; Cavendish's rendering of material in ch. 9.

God has endued nature withal. In short, if the ideas of God be the principle of nature, they must be a principle of all natural things; for that which is not universal, can never be a principle; which if so, then the ideas or notions of God would not only be the cause and principle of all goodness, but of all evil effects; and if there be more wicked or evil souls in the world than good ones, there would proceed more evil from God, than good; which is not only impossible, but impious to affirm. But perchance he will say, that the ideas of the aforementioned effects, are generated and annihilated. I answer: As for nature, she being eternal and infinite, is not subject to new generations and annihilations in her particulars; neither can principles be generated and annihilated: and as for supernatural or immaterial ideas, they being incorporeal, cannot be subject to a new generation, or annihilation; for what is supernatural, is not capable of natural affections, nor subject to a natural capacity any ways. In truth, Plato with his ideas in God, in the angelic mind, in the soul, etc. makes a greater stir than needs, and breeds more confusion in nature than she really knows of: for, nature is easy to be understood in her general principles, that regular sense and reason may conceive them without framing any such ideas or minds. He distinguishes also the idea or exemplar of an house, which the architect has in his mind, and, as his pattern, exactly strives to imitate, from the building or structure of the house itself, by this, that he calls that intelligible, but this material and sensible; whenas yet the form or pattern in the architect's mind, is as much material, as the builded house itself; the only difference is, that the exemplar, or figure in the mind, is formed of the rational matter only, which is the purest, finest, and subtlest degree, and the other is made of grosser materials.

9. The soul of the world he makes immaterial, but the body material: and hence he concludes the world to be eternal, because the soul is such which is not capable to be without body; and although it be incorporeal, yet its office is to rule and govern corporeal nature.[182] But concerning the soul of nature, I have sufficiently declared my opinion thereof in other places, to wit, that it is impossible she should be immaterial: for, if the body of nature be divisible and compoundable, the soul must be so too; but that which is not material, cannot admit of division nor composition: Wherefore the soul cannot be immaterial, or else some parts of the world

---

[182] Ibid., pp. 187–88; Cavendish's rendering of material from chs. 13–14.

would be destitute of a soul, which might deserve it as well as the rest; which would argue a partiality in the Creator. I wonder, wise men will attribute bodily affections to immaterial beings, whenas yet they are not able to conceive or comprehend them; by which they confound and disturb nature, which knows of no immaterials, but her essence is matter.

10. As for his ethics, where he speaks of beauty, strength, proportion, etc. I'll only say this,[183] that of all these there, are different sorts; for, there's the strength of the mind, and the strength of the body; and these are so various in their kinds and particulars, that they cannot be exactly defined: Also beauty, considering only that which is of the body, there are so many several sorts, consisting in features, shapes, and proportions of bodies, as it is impossible to describe properly what beauty is, and wherein it really consists: for, what appears beautiful to some, may seem ill-favoured to others; and what seems extraordinary fair or handsome to one, may have but an indifferent character of another; so that, in my opinion, there's no such thing as an universal beauty, which may gain a general applause of all, and be judged alike by everyone that views it; nay, not by all immortal souls, neither in body nor mind; for what one likes, another may dislike; what one loves, another may hate; what one counts good, another may proclaim bad; what one names just, another may call unjust. And as for temperance, which he joins to justice, what may be temperance to one, may be intemperance to another: for, no particular knows the just measures of nature; nay, even one and the same thing which one man loves today, he may chance to hate, or at least dislike, tomorrow; for nature is too various to be constant in her particulars, by reason of the perpetual alterations and changes they are subject to; which do all proceed from self-moving matter, and not from incorporeal ideas. Thus rational souls are changeable, which may be proved by the changes of their fancies, imaginations, thoughts, judgments, understandings, conceptions, passions, affections, and the like; all which are effects or actions of the rational soul; nay, not only natural rational souls, but even divine souls, if they were all good, none would be bad, nor vary as we find they do; and therefore I cannot believe that all souls can have the same likeness, being so different amongst themselves.

---

[183] Ibid., pp. 192–94; Cavendish is responding to chs. 27 and 28.

III   Upon the Doctrine of Pythagoras

1. The most learned of the Pythagoreans do assert, that things apparent to sense, cannot be said to be principles of the universe; for whatsoever consists of things apparent to sense, is compounded of things not apparent; and a principle must not consist of anything, but be that of which the thing consists.[184]

To which I answer: First, I cannot conceive what they mean by things apparent to sense; if they mean the sensitive organs of human creatures, they are mistaken; for there may be, and are really many things in nature, which are not apparent to human sense, and yet are not principles, but natural effects: Wherefore, not all things that are apparent to human sense, are principles of nature. Besides, there may be many other creatures which do far exceed men or animals in their sensitive perceptions; and if things be not subject to human sense, they may be subject to the sense of other creatures. But if by sense they mean the sensitive life of nature, they commit a far greater error; for there's nothing which is not subject, or has a participation of this universal sense in nature, as well as of reason. It is true, particular senses cannot perceive the infinite figurative motions of nature; neither can the subtlest sense have a perception of the interior, innate, figurative motions of any other creature: But I do not speak of particular senses; but of that infinite sense and reason, which is self-moving matter, and produces all the effects of nature.

But, you'll say, How can infinite be a principle of particular finites?

I answer: As well as the infinite God can be the author of nature, and all natural beings; which, though they be finite in their particular figures, yet their number is infinite.

2. Concerning the numbers of Pythagoras, which he makes so great a value of;[185] I confess, wheresoever are parts, and compositions and divisions of parts, there must also be number; but yet, as parts cannot be principles, so neither can numbers: for, self-moving matter, which is the only principle of nature, is infinite, and there are no more principles but this one. It is true, regular compositions and divisions are made by consent of parts, and presuppose number and harmony; but number and harmony cannot be the cause of any orderly productions, without

---

[184] Stanley, *The History of Philosophy*, vol. II, p. 548; slightly altered; Sextus Empiricus, *Adversus mathematicos*, IX [Against the Physicists, I] given as source.

[185] See ibid., pp. 523–30; 548–50.

sense and reason; for how should parts agree in their actions, if they did not know each other; or if they had no sense nor reason? Truly, there can be no motion without sense; nor no orderly motion, without reason; and though Epicurus' atoms might move by chance without reason, yet they could not move in a concord or harmony, not knowing what they are to do, or why, or whither they move; nay, if they had no sense, it is impossible they should have motion: and therefore, in my opinion, it is the rational and sensitive parts which by consent make number and harmony; and those that will deny this sensitive and rational self-moving matter, must deny the principles of motion, and of all constant successions of all sorts and kinds of creatures, nay, of all the variety that is in nature. Indeed, I am puzzled to understand learned men, what they mean by principles, by reason I see that they so frequently call those, principles, which are but effects of nature: Some count the "elements" principles; some, "numbers"; some, "ideas"; some, "atoms," and the like: And by their different opinions, they confirm, that there is as well discord and division, as there is concord and composition of the parts of nature; for, if this were not, there would be no contrary actions, and consequently, no variety of figures and motions.

3. Whatsoever is comprehended by man, says Pythagoras, is either body, or incorporeal: Amongst which incorporeals, he reckons also time.[186] But this opinion is contradicted by regular sense and reason; for no human, nor any other natural creature, is able to comprehend an incorporeal, itself being corporeal; and as for time, place, and the like, they are one and the same with body; which if so, how can they be incorporeal? Neither is it possible, that incorporeal beings should be principles of nature, because there is as much difference between corporeal and incorporeal, as there is between matter, and no matter; but how no matter can be a principle of material effects, is not conceivable: For God, though he be an immaterial essence, and yet the author of material nature, and all natural beings; yet he is not a natural, material principle, out of which all natural things consist, and are framed; but a supernatural, decreeing, ordering and commanding principle, which cannot be said of created incorporeals: for, though nature moves by the powerful decree of God, yet she cannot be governed by finite incorporeals, by reason they

---

[186] Ibid., p. 550; slightly altered and condensed; Sextus Empiricus, *Adversus mathematicos*, VII [Against the Logicians, 1] given as source.

being finite, have no power over a material infinite; neither can there be any other infinite spirit, but God himself.

4. Pythagoras' doctrine is, that the world, in its nature, is corruptible,[187] but the soul of the world is incorruptible;[188] and that without the heavens, there is an infinite vacuum, into which, and out of which the world repairs.[189] As for the corruptibility of the world, I cannot understand how the soul thereof can be incorruptible, and the world itself corruptible: for, if the world should be destroyed, what will become of the soul? I will not say, that the all-powerful God may not destroy it when he pleases; but the infiniteness and perpetual self-motion of nature, will not permit that nature should be corruptible in itself: for, God's power goes beyond the power of nature. But it seems, Pythagoras understands by the world, no more than his senses can reach; so that beyond the celestial orbs, he supposes to be an infinite vacuum; which is as much as to say, an infinite nothing: and my reason cannot apprehend how the world can breathe and respire into nothing, and out of nothing.

5. Neither am I able to conceive the truth of his assertion, that all lines are derived from points, and all numbers from unity,[190] and all figures from a circle:[191] for, there can be no such thing as a single point, a single unity, a single circle in nature, by reason nature is infinitely divisible and compoundable; neither can they be principles, because they are all but effects.

6. Concerning the soul, the Pythagoreans call her a self-moving number, and divide her into two parts, rational and irrational; and derive the beginning of the soul, from the heat of the brain.[192]

---

[187] Ibid., p. 550; slightly altered; pseudo-Plutarch, *On the Physical Opinions of the Philosophers*, ii, 4 given as source.

[188] Ibid., pp. 550–54; Cavendish's rendering of material in chs. 2, 5 and 10; pseudo-Plutarch, *On the Physical Opinions of the Philosophers*, ii, 4; iv, 7 and Diogenes Laertius given as sources.

[189] Ibid., p. 551; slightly altered; Aristotle, *Physics*, iii, ch. 4 and pseudo-Plutarch, *On the Physical Opinions of the Philosophers*, ii, 9 given as sources.

[190] Ibid., p. 550; Sextus Empiricus, *Adversus mathematicos*, ix [Against the Physicists, i] given as source.

[191] Ibid., p. 535; Proclus, *In primum Euclidis elementorum librum commentarii* [Commentaries on the First Book of Euclid's Elements], ii, definition 5 given as source. But Stanley states: "A superficies they compared to the number 3 for that is the first of all causes which are found in figures: for a circle, which is the principle of all round figures, occultly compriseth a triad in center, space, and circumference. But a triangle which is the first of all rectiline figures, is manifestly included in a ternary . . ."

[192] Ibid., p. 552; slighly altered and condensed; pseudo-Plutarch, *On the Physical Opinions of the Philosophers*, iv, 4; iv, 20 given as source.

The souls of animate creatures, as they call them, they allow to be rational, even those which others call irrational, to wit, those in all other animals besides man; but they act not according to reason, for want of speech.[193] The rational soul, say they, is immortal,[194] and a self-moving number; where, by number, they understand the mind,[195] which they call a "monad." These, and the like opinions, which Pythagoreans have of the soul, are able to puzzle Solomon's wit or understanding to make any conformity of truth of them; and I will not strictly examine them, but set down these few paradoxes.

1. I cannot apprehend how the same soul can be divided into substances of such differing, nay, contrary proprieties and natures, as to be rational and irrational, mortal and immortal.

2. How the heat of the brain can be the principle of the soul; since the soul is said to actuate, move and inform the body, and to be a principle of all bodily actions: Besides, all brains have not the like temperament, but some are hot, and some cold, and some hotter than others: Whence it will follow, that all animals are not endued with the like souls, but some souls must of necessity be weaker, and some stronger than others.

3. How irrational creatures can have a rational soul, and yet not act according to reason for want of speech: for, irrational creatures are called so, because they are thought to have no reason; and as for speech, it is an effect, and not a principle of reason; for, shall we think a dumb man irrational, because he cannot speak?

4. I cannot conceive how it is possible that the soul is a self-moving number, and yet but a "monad," or unity; for a unity, they say, is no number, but a principle of number: Nor, how the soul, being incorporeal, can walk in the air, like a body; for, incorporeal beings cannot have corporeal actions, no more than corporeal beings can have the actions of incorporeals. Wherefore I will leave those points to the examination of more learned persons than myself. And as for the Pythagorean transmigration of souls, I have declared my opinion thereof heretofore, in the "First Part."

---

[193] Ibid., p. 552; slighltly altered and condensed; pseudo-Plutarch, *On the Physical Opinion of the Philosophers*, IV, 20 given as source.

[194] Ibid., p. 553; Diogenes Laertius given as source.

[195] Ibid., p. 553; slightly altered; pseudo-Plutarch, *On the Physical Opinion of the Philosophers*, IV, 2 given as source.

IV Of Epicurus His Principles of Philosophy

1. Concerning the world, Epicurus is of opinion, that it is not eternal and incorruptible; but, that it was generated, and had a beginning, and shall also have an end, and perish: For, says he, "It is necessary that all compounded things be also dissipated, and resolved into those things of which they were compounded."[196] By the world, he understands a portion of the universe, that is, the circumference of heaven, containing the stars, the earth, and all things visible: For heaven he supposes to be the extreme, or utmost part of the world; and by the universe, he understands infinite nature, which consists of body, and vacuum; for he thinks, bodies could not move, were there no vacuum to move in.

Whereof, I do briefly declare my opinion, thus: If the universe, or nature itself, be infinite, eternal and incorruptible, all parts of nature, or the universe, must be so too; I mean, in themselves, as they are matter, or body: for, were it possible, that some of them could perish, or be annihilated; the universe would be imperfect, and consequently not infinite, as wanting some parts of its own body. It is true, particular natural figures may be infinitely changed, dissolved, transformed; but they can never be dissolved from being matter, or parts of nature; and if not, they cannot perish; no, not the figures of finite parts: for as matter cannot perish, so neither can figure, because matter and figure are but one thing; and though one part be transformed into millions of figures, yet all those figures do not perish in their changes and alterations, but continue still in nature, as being parts of nature, and therefore material. Thus, change, alteration, dissolution, division, composition, and all other species of motions, are no annihilation, or perishing; neither can it be proved, that parts dissolve more than they unite; because dissolution or division, and composition of parts, are but one act: for, whensoever parts separate themselves from some, they must of necessity join to others; which doth also prove, that there can be no vacuum in nature; for, if there were, there would be division without composition: besides, there would be no parts, but all parts would be several wholes, by reason they would subsist by themselves. Thus nature would not be one

---

[196] Stanley, *The History of Philosophy*, vol. III, p. 877. In volume I, "Noted," (unpaginated), Stanley acknowledges Gassendi as his main source for knowledge about Epicurus. See Gassendi, *De vita et moribus Epicuri* [On the Life and Precepts of Epicurus] (Lyon, 1647) and *Animadversiones in decimum librum Diogenis Laertii* [Animadversions on Book Ten of Diogenes Laertius] (Lyon, 1649).

infinite body, composed of infinite parts; but every part being a whole by itself, would make some kind of a finite world; and those parts which separate themselves from each other by the intervals of vacuum, would subsist precised from each other, as having no relation to one another, and so become wholes of parts; nay, if several of those entire and single bodies should join closely together, they would make such a gap of vacuum, as would cause a confusion and disturbance both amongst themselves, and in the universe. Wherefore sense and reason contradicts the opinion of vacuum; neither is there any necessity of introducing it, by reason of the motion of natural bodies; for they may move without vacuum better than within vacuum: Since all bodies are not of the like nature, that is, dense, close, or compact; but there are fluid bodies, as well as hard bodies; rare, as well as dense; subtle, as well as gross; because there is animate and inanimate matter in nature. But concerning the world, it seems, Epicurus doth not mean by the dissolution of the world, an absolute annihilation, but only a reduction into its former principles, which are atoms; however, if this be his meaning, he contradicts himself, when he affirms, that the universe, a portion of which the world is, was ever such as is now; and shall ever be thus: For if it shall continue so forever as it is now, how is it possible, that it should be reduced into atoms? He says also, "that the universe is immovable and immutable."[197] If he mean it to be immutable in its essence or nature, so that it cannot be changed from being material; and immovable, so that it cannot be moved, beyond or without itself; I am of his opinion: For nature being purely and wholly material, cannot be made immaterial, without its total destruction; and being infinite, has nothing without itself to move into: Otherwise, nature is not only a self-moving body, but also full of changes and varieties; I mean, within herself, and her particulars. As for his infinite worlds, I am not different from his opinion, if by worlds he means the parts of infinite nature; but my reason will not allow, that those infinite worlds do subsist by themselves, distinguished from each other by vacuum; for it is mere nonsense to say, the universe consists of body and vacuum; that is, of something, and nothing: for nothing cannot be a constitutive principle of anything, neither can it be measured, or have corporeal dimensions; for what is no body, can have no bodily affections or properties. God, by

---

[197] Ibid., p. 859; slightly altered; Eusebius, *Praeparatio evangelica* [Evangelical Preparation] given as source.

his omnipotency, may reduce the world into nothing; but this cannot be comprehended by natural reason.

2. The matter or principle of all natural beings, Epicurus makes atoms: For, says he, "There are simple, and compounded bodies in the universe; the simple bodies are the first matter, out of which the compounded bodies consist, and those are atoms; that is, bodies indivisible, immutable, and in themselves void of all mutation; consisting of several infinite figures; some bigger, and some less."[198] Which opinion appears very paradoxical to my reason; for if atoms be bodies, I do not see how they can be indivisible: by reason, wheresoever is body, there are also parts; so that divisibility is an essential propriety or attribute of matter or body. He counts it impossible, that one finite part should be capable of infinite divisions; but his vacuum makes him believe there are single finite parts, distinguished from each other by little spaces or intervals of vacuity, which in truth cannot be; but as soon as parts are divided from such or such parts, they immediately join to other parts; for division and composition, as I mentioned before, are done by one act; and one countervails the other. It is true, there are distinctions of parts in nature, or else there would be no variety; but these are not made by little intervals of vacuity, but by their own figures, interior as well as exterior, caused by self-motion, which make a difference between the infinite parts of nature. But put the case there were such atoms, out of which all things are made; yet no man that has his sense and reason, regular, can believe, they did move by chance, or at least without sense and reason, in the framing of the world, and all natural bodies; if he do but consider the wonderful order and harmony that is in nature, and all her parts. Indeed I admire so witty and great a philosopher as Epicurus, should be of such an extravagant opinion, as to divide composed bodies into animate and inanimate, and derive them all from one principle, namely, senseless and irrational atoms: For if his atoms, out of which all things consist, be self-moving, or have, as he says, some natural impulse within themselves, then certainly all bodies that are composed of them, must be the same. He places the diversity of them only in figure, weight, and magnitude, but not in motion, which he equally allows to all; nay,

---

[198] Ibid., pp. 861–63; Lucretius, *De rerum natura* [On the Nature of Things], II and IV, and Diogenes Laertius given as sources. This is Cavendish's rendering of material in chs. 4–7. Stanley notes that while the kinds of figure atoms can have are not infinite, there are an infinite number of atoms of each figure.

moreover, he says, that although they be of different figures, weight, and magnitude, yet they do all move equally swift; but if they have motion, they must of necessity have also sense, that is, life and knowledge; there being no such thing as a motion by chance in nature, because nature is full of reason as well as of sense, and wheresoever is reason, there can be no chance; Chance is only in respect to particulars, caused by their ignorance; for particulars being finite in themselves, can have no infinite or universal knowledge; and where there is no universal knowledge, there must of necessity be some ignorance. Thus ignorance, which proceeds from the division of parts, causes that which we call chance; but nature, being an infinite self-moving body, has also infinite knowledge; and therefore she knows of no chance: nor is this visible world, or any part of her, made by chance, or a casual concourse of senseless and irrational atoms; but by the all-powerful decree and command of God, out of that preexistent matter that was from all eternity, which is, infinite nature; for though the Scripture expresses the framing of this world, yet it doth not say, that nature herself was then created; but only that this world was put into such a frame and state, as it is now; and, who knows but there may have been many other worlds before, and of another figure than this is: nay, if nature be infinite, there must also be infinite worlds; for I take, with Epicurus, this world but for a part of the universe; and as there is self-motion in nature, so there are also perpetual changes of particulars, although God himself be immovable; for God acts by his all-powerful decree or command, and not after a natural way.

3. The soul of animals, says Epicurus, is corporeal, and a most tenuous and subtle body, made up of most subtle particles; in figure, smooth and round, not perceptible by any sense: and this subtle contexture of the soul, is mixed and compounded of four several natures; as, of something fiery, something aerial, something flatuous, and something that has no name; by means whereof it is endued with a sensitive faculty. And as for reason, that is likewise compounded of little bodies, but the smoothest and roundest of all, and of the quickest motion.[199] Thus he discourses of the soul, which, I confess, surpasses my understanding; for I shall never be able to conceive, how, senseless and irrational atoms can produce sense and reason, or a sensible and rational body, such as the soul is; although he affirms it to be possible: It is true, different effects may

---

[199] Ibid., pp. 884–85; Cavendish's rendering of material in ch. 9; Diogenes Laertius given as source.

proceed from one cause or principle; but there is no principle, which is senseless, can produce sensitive effects; nor no rational effects can flow from an irrational cause; neither can order, method, and harmony proceed from chance or confusion: and I cannot conceive, how atoms, moving by chance, should only make souls in animals, and not in other bodies; for if they move by chance, and not by knowledge and consent, they might, by their conjunction, as well chance to make souls in vegetables and minerals, as in animals.

4. Concerning perception, and, in particular, the perception of sight; Epicurus affirms, that it is performed by the gliding of some images of external objects into our eyes, to wit, that there are certain effluxions of atoms sent out from the surfaces of bodies, preserving the same position and order, as is found in the superficies of them, resembling them in all their lineaments; and those he calls images, which are perpetually flowing in an interrupted course: and when one image goes away, another immediately succeeds from the superficies of the object in a continued stream; and this entering into our eyes, and striking our sight, with a very swift motion, causes the perception of seeing.[200]

This strange opinion of his, is no less to be admired than the rest, and shows, that Epicurus was more blind in his reason, than perhaps in his eyesight: For, first, how can there be such a perpetual effluxion of atoms, from an external body, without lessening or weakening its bulk or substance, especially they being corporeal? Indeed, if a million of eyes or more, should look for a long time upon one object, it is impossible, but that object would be sensibly lessened or diminished, at least weakened, by the perpetual effluxions of so many millions of atoms: Now, how is it possible, that the eye can receive such an impress of so many atoms, without hurting or offending it in the least? Thirdly, since Epicurus makes vacuities in nature, how can the images pass so orderly through all those vacuities, especially if the object be of a considerable magnitude? For then all intermediate bodies that are between the sentient, and the sensible object, must remove, and make room for so many images to pass through. Fourthly, how is it possible, that, especially at a great distance, in an instant of time, and as soon as I cast my eye upon the object, so many atoms can effluviate with such a swiftness, as to enter so suddenly through the air into the eye; for all motion is progressive, and

---

[200] Ibid., pp. 887–88; Cavendish's rendering of material in chs. 11 and 12; Diogenes Laertius, Lucretius and Sextus Empiricus given as sources.

done in time? Fifthly, I would fain know, when those atoms are issued from the object, and entered into the eye, what doth at last become of them? Surely they cannot remain in the eye, or else the eye would never lose the sight of the object; and if they do not remain in the eye, they must either return to the object from whence they came, or join with other bodies, or be annihilated. Sixthly, I cannot imagine, but that, when we see several objects at one and the same time, those images proceeding from so many several objects, be they never so orderly in their motions, will make a horrid confusion; so that the eye will rather be confounded, than perceive anything exactly after this manner. Lastly, a man having two eyes; I desire to know, whether every eye has its own image to perceive; or, whether but one image enters into both: If every eye receives its own image, then a man having two eyes, may see double; and a great drone-fly, which experimental philosophers report to have 14,000 eyes, may receive so many images of one object; but if but one image enters into all those eyes, then the image must be divided into so many parts.

5. What Epicurus means by his divine nature, cannot be understood by a natural capacity: for, he says it is the same with corporeal nature; but yet not so much a body, as a certain thing like a body, as having nothing common to it with other bodies, that is, with transitory, generated, and perishable things.[201] But, in my opinion, God must either be corporeal, or incorporeal; if corporeal, he must be nature itself; for there's nothing corporeal, but what is natural; if incorporeal, he must be supernatural; for there is nothing between body, and no body; corporeal and incorporeal; natural, and supernatural: and therefore to say, God is of a corporeal nature, and yet not a body, but like a body, is contrary to all sense and reason. It is true, God hath actions, but they are not corporeal, but supernatural, and not comprehensible by a human or finite capacity: Neither is God naturally moving; for he has no local or natural motion, nor doth he trouble himself with making anything, but by his all-powerful decree and command he produces all things; and nature, which is his eternal servant, obeys his commands: Wherefore the actions of nature cannot be a disturbance to his incomprehensible felicity, no not to nature, which being self-moving, can do no otherwise, but take delight in acting; for her actions are free and easy, and not forced or constrained.

---

[201] Ibid., p. 859; very slightly altered.

6. Although he affirms, that God, or nature, considers man no more than other creatures; yet he endeavours to prove, that man is the best product of his atoms;[202] which to me seems strange, considering that all compositions of atoms come by chance, and that the principles of all creatures are alike. But truly, take away the supernatural or divine soul from man, and he is no better than other creatures are, because they are all composed of the same matter, and have all sense and reason, which produces all sorts of figures, in such order, method, and harmony, as the wisdom of nature requires, or as God has ordered it: for nature, although she be infinite and eternal, yet she depends upon the incomprehensible God, the Author of Nature, and his all-powerful commands, worshipping and adoring him in her infinite particulars; for, God being infinite, must also have an infinite worship; and if nature had no dependence on God, she would not be a servant, but God herself. Wherefore, Epicurus his atoms, having no dependence upon a divine power, must of necessity be Gods; nay, every atom must be a peculiar God, each being a single body, subsisting by itself; but they being senseless and irrational, would prove but weak Gods: Besides, his chance is but an uncertain God, and his vacuum an empty God; and if all natural effects were grounded upon such principles, nature would rather be a confused chaos, than an orderly and harmonical universe.

V   On Aristotle's Philosophical Principles

Having viewed four of the most eminent of the ancient philosophers, I will proceed now to Aristotle; who may justly be called the "Idol of the Schools"; for his doctrine is generally embraced with such reverence, as if truth itself had declared it. But I find he is no less exempt from errors, than all the rest, though more happy in fame. For fame doth all, and whose name she is pleased to record, that man shall live; when others, though of no less worth and merit, will be obscured, and buried in oblivion. I shall not give myself the trouble of examining all his principles; but, as I have done by the former, make my observations on some few points in his philosophy.

1. The sum of his doctrine concerning motion, and the first mover, is comprehended in these few theorems.

---

[202] Ibid., pp. 874; 875–76; Cavendish's rendering of material in chs. 3 and 5.

1. There are three sorts of motion; accretion and diminution, alteration and local motion. 2. Rest is a privation of motion. 3. All motion is finite; for it is done in time, which is finite. 4. There is no infinite quantity or magnitude in act, but only in power, and so no body can be actually infinite. 5. Whatsoever is moved, must necessarily be moved by another. 6. There is a first mover in nature, which is the cause and origin of all motions. 7. This first mover is infinite, eternal, indivisible and incorporeal. 8. Motion itself is eternal; because time, the measure of motion, is eternal.[203]

Concerning the first, I answer, that nature and all her parts are perpetually self-moving; and therefore it is needless to make three sorts of motions: we might say rather, there are infinite sorts of motions; but yet all is self-motion, and so is accretion, diminution, and alteration; for though our senses cannot perceive the motions of all bodies, how, and which way they move; yet it doth not follow from thence, that they are not moving: for solid composed bodies, such as minerals, may (though not to our human sense) be more active than some rarer and thinner bodies, as is evident in the loadstone and iron, and the needle. Nay, in several other bodies applied by art physically: for if nature be self-moving, as surely she is, then her parts must necessarily be in a continual action, there being no such thing as rest or quiescence in nature. Next, Aristotle seems to contradict himself, when he says, that all motion is finite, because it is done in time, and yet affirms, that both motion and time are eternal; for eternal is that which hath neither beginning, nor end; and if motion and time be thus, how can they be finite? [Thirdly] I deny, that whatsoever is body or quantitative, cannot be infinite in act, but is only infinite in power; for if it be probable, that there can be an eternal motion, and eternal time, which is infinite in act; why should it not also be probable, that there is an infinite quantity? For motion is the action of body, and it is absurd, in my opinion, to make body finite, and the action infinite. Truly, if Aristotle means the world to be finite, and yet eternal, I do not conceive how they can consist together; for, if the world be finite in quantity, he must allow an infinite vacuum beyond it; which if he doth, why may not he allow as well an infinite quantity? But he has no more ground to deny there is a quantity actually infinite, than he has ground to affirm that it is only

---

[203] Stanley, *The History of Philosophy*, vol. II, pp. 374–75; Cavendish's rendering of material in chs. 5 and 6; Aristotle, *Physics*, v, ch. 2; VI, chs. 7 and 2 ; VII, ch. 1; VIII, chs. 6, 7, 10 given as source.

infinite in power: for, if that which is in power, may be deduced into act, I see no reason, but the world, which is nature, may be said infinite in act, as well as in power. [Fourthly] I deny also his theorem, that whatsoever is moved, must necessarily be moved by another; for wheresoever is self-motion, there needs no exterior movent; but nature and all her parts have self-motion, therefore they stand in no need of an exterior movent. It is true, one part may occasion another by its outward impulse or force, to move thus or thus; but no part can move by any other's motion, but its own, which is an internal, and innate motion: so that every part and particle of nature, has the principle of motion within itself, as consisting all of a composition of animate or self-moving-matter; and if this be so, what need we to trouble ourselves about a first mover? In infinity and eternity there is neither first nor last, and therefore Aristotle cannot understand a first mover of time; and as for motion itself, if all parts move of themselves, as I said before, there is no necessity of an exterior or first mover. But I would fain know what he means by the action of the first mover, whether he be actually moving the world, or not? If he be actually moving, he must of necessity have natural motion in himself; but natural self-motion is corporeal; and a corporeal propriety cannot be attributed to an incorporeal substance: But if he be not actually moving, he must move nature by his powerful decree and command; and thus the first mover is none else but God, who may be called so, because he has endued nature with self-motion, and given it a principle of motion within itself, to move according as he has decreed and ordered it from all eternity: for God, being immovable and incorporeal, cannot actually move the universe, like the chief wheel in a watch. And as for his incorporeal intelligences, which are eternal and immovable, presiding over the motions of the inferior orbs, forty-seven in number; this is rather a poetical fancy, than a probability of truth, and deserves to be banished out of the sphere of natural philosophy; which enquires into nothing but what is conformable to the truth of nature: And though we are all but guessers, yet he that brings the most probable and rational arguments, does come nearer to truth, than those whose ground is only fancy without reason.

2. Heaven, says Aristotle, is void of generation and corruption, and consequently of accretion, diminution and alteration; for there are no contraries in it; nor has it levity, or gravity; neither are there more worlds

but one, and that is finite; for if there were more, the earth of one would move to the earth of the other, as being of one kind.[204] To which I answer: first, as for generation, dissolution, accretion, diminution and alteration of celestial bodies; it is more than a human creature is able to know: For, although we do not see the alterations of them, yet we cannot deny but they have natural motion: Now where motion is, there's also change and alteration. For, put the case the moon were such another body as this terrestrial globe we inhabit, we can only perceive its outward progressive motion; nevertheless it may contain as many different particulars, as this globe of the earth, which may have their particular motions, and be generated, dissolved, composed, divided and transformed, many, nay, infinite ways: The same may be said of the rest of the planets, and the fixed stars. And as for gravity, and levity, we do only perceive they are qualities of those parts that belong to this terrestrial globe; but we cannot judge of all bodies alike. We see air has neither gravity nor levity; for it neither ascends, nor descends: nay, this terrestrial globe itself, has neither gravity nor levity, for it is surrounded by the fluid air, and neither ascends nor descends. The truth is, there's no such thing as high and low, in nature; but only in reference to some parts; and therefore gravity and levity are not universal, and necessary attributes of all natural bodies. Next, concerning the multiplicity of worlds, that there can be no such thing, but that the earth of one would move towards the earth of the other: I answer, first, there's no necessity that all worlds must have a terrestrial globe; for nature hath more varieties of creatures, than elements, vegetables, minerals, and animals. Next, if it were so, yet I see no reason that one creature must necessarily move to another of the same kind: For, put the case, as I said before, the moon was such another terrestrial globe as this, yet we see they do not move one to another, but each remains in its own sphere or circle.

3. I admire Aristotle makes the principles of nature, "matter," "form" and "privation,"[205] and leaves out the chief, which is "motion"; for were there no motion, there would be no variety of figures: besides, matter and form are but one thing; for wheresoever is matter, there is also form or figure; but privation is a non-being, and therefore cannot be a principle of natural bodies.

[204] Ibid, p. 375; altered and condensed; Aristotle, *On the Heavens*, I, chs. 2, 3, 5, 7 given as source.
[205] Ibid., p. 373; altered and condensed; Aristotle, *Physics*, I, ch. 7 given as source.

4. There is no such thing as simple bodies in nature;[206] for if nature herself consists of a commixture of animate and inanimate matter, no part can be called simple, as having a composition of the same parts. Besides, no part can subsist single, or by itself: wherefore, the distinction into simple and mixt bodies, is needless; for elements are as much composed bodies, as other parts of nature. Neither do I understand the difference between perfect and imperfect mixt bodies;[207] for nature may compose, mix and divide parts as she pleaseth.

5. The primary qualities of the elements, as heat and cold, humidity and siccity, says Aristotle, are the cause of generation, when heat and cold overcome the matter.[208] I wonder he makes qualities to be no substances, or bodies, but "accidents," which is something between body, and no body; and yet places them above matter, and makes generation their effect. But, whatsoever he calls them, they are no more but effects of nature, and cannot be above their cause, which is matter: Neither is it probable, there are but eighteen passive qualities; he might have said, as well, there are but eighteen sorts of motions; for, natural effects go beyond all number, as being infinite.

6. Concerning the soul, Aristotle doth not believe, "that it moves by itself, but is only moved accidentally, according to the motion of the body."[209] But he doth not express from whence the motion of the soul proceeds, although he defines it to be "that by which we live, feel and understand."[210] "Neither," says he, "is there a soul diffused through the world; for there are inanimate bodies, as well as animate":[211] But sense and reason perceives the contrary, to wit, that there is no part of nature but is animate, that is, has a soul. "Sense," says he, "is not sensible of itself, nor of its organ, nor of any interior thing; for sense cannot move itself, but is a mutation in the organ, caused by some sensible object."[212] But the absurdity of this opinion I have declared heretofore: for, it is contrary to human reason to believe, first, that sense should be sensible of an outward object, and not of itself; or, (which is

[206] Ibid., p. 376; Cavendish's response to material in ch. 7; Aristotle, *On the Heavens*, III, ch. 3 given as source.
[207] Ibid., pp. 378–80; Cavendish's response to material in chs. 12–13; Aristotle, *Meteorology*, I, chs. 1–14; II, chs. 2–5, 8–9; III, chs. 2, 6; IV, chs. 1, 2, 3, 4, 6, 8 given as source.
[208] Ibid., p. 379; altered and condensed; Aristotle, *Meteorology*, IV, ch. 1 given as source.
[209] Ibid., pp. 380–81; altered and condensed; Aristotle, *On the Soul*, I, ch. 3 given as source.
[210] Ibid., p. 381; slightly altered; Aristotle, *On the Soul*, II, ch. 2 given as source.
[211] Ibid., p. 381; altered; Aristotle, *On the Soul*, I, ch. 5 given as source.
[212] Ibid., p. 381; altered and phrases transposed; Aristotle, *On the Soul*, II, ch. 5 given as source.

all one) have perception of exterior parts, and not self-knowledge. Next, that an external object should be the cause of sense, whenas sense and reason are the chief principles of nature, and the cause of all natural effects. Again, "sense," says he, "is in all animals, but fancy is not; for fancy is not sense: Fancy acts in him that sleeps, sense not."[213] To which I answer; first, fancy or imagination is a voluntary action of reason, or of the rational parts of matter; and if reason be in all animals, nay, in all creatures, fancy is there also. Next, it is evident that sense acts as much asleep as awake; the difference I have expressed elsewhere, viz. that the sensitive motions work inwardly in sleep, and outwardly awake. "The intellect," to Aristotle, "is that part of the soul by which it knows and understands, and is only proper to man; whenas sense is proper to animals: It is twofold, patient and agent; whereof this is immortal, eternal, not mixt with the body, but separable from it, and ever in action: The patient intellect is mortal, and yet void of corruptive passion, not mixt with the body, nor having any corporeal organs."[214] But these, and many other differences of intellects, which he rehearses, are more troublesome to the understanding, than beneficial for the knowledge of nature: And why should we puzzle ourselves with multiplicity of terms and distinctions, when there's no need of them? Truly, nature's actions are easy, and we may easily apprehend them without much ado. If nature be material, as it cannot be proved otherwise, sense and reason are material also; and therefore we need not to introduce an incorporeal mind or intellect. Besides, if sense and reason be a constitutive principle of nature, all parts of nature do partake of the same; nor hath man a prerogative before other creatures in that case only: the difference and variety of motions, makes different figures, and consequently different knowledges and perceptions; and all fancies, imaginations, judgment, memory, remembrance, and the like, are nothing else but the actions of reason, or of the rational parts of animate matter; so that there is no necessity to make a patient and agent intellect, much less to introduce incorporeal substances, to confound and disturb corporeal nature.

---

[213] Ibid., p. 382; altered and phrases transposed; Aristotle, *On the Soul*, III, ch. 3 given as source.
[214] Ibid., pp. 383–84; altered, condensed and phrases transposed; Aristotle, *On the Soul*, III, chs. 4–5 given as source.

VI   Of Skepticism, and Some Other Sects of the Ancients

There are several sorts of sceptics different from each other; for though almost every one of the ancient philosophers has his own opinions in natural philosophy and goes on his own grounds or principles, yet some come nearer each other, than others do: And though Heraclitus, Democritus, Protagoras, and others, seem to differ from the sceptics, yet their opinions are not so far asunder, but they may all be referred to the same sect.

Heraclitus is of opinion, that contraries are in the same things; and sceptics affirm, that contraries appear in the same thing;[215] but I believe they may be partly both in the right, and partly both in the wrong. If their opinion be, that there are, or appear contraries in nature, or in the essence of matter, they are both in the wrong: but, if they believe that matter has different and contrary actions, they are both in the right: for there are not only real, but also apparent or seeming contraries in nature, which are her irregularities; to wit, when the sensitive and rational parts of matter do not move exactly to the nature of their particulars: As for example, honey is sweet to those that are sound, and in health; but bitter to those that have the overflowing of the gall: where it is to be observed, that honey is not changed from its natural propriety, but the motions of the gall being irregular make a false copy: like as madmen, who think their flesh is stone; or those that apprehend a bird for a stone, a man for a tree, etc. Neither the flesh, nor stone, nor tree, are changed from their own particular natures; but the motions of human sense in the sentient, are irregular, and make false copies of true objects; which is the reason that an object seems often to be that, which really it is not. However, those irregularities are true corporeal motions; and thus, there are both real and seeming contraries in nature: but, as I mentioned before, they are not contrary matters, but only contrary actions.

Democritus says, that honey is neither bitter, nor sweet, by reason of its different appearance to differently affected persons.[216] But, if so, then he is like those that make neutral beings; which are between body, and no body: Which is a paradox to regular reason.

---

[215] Stanley, *The History of Philosophy*, vol. III, p. 789; altered; Sextus Empiricus, *Outlines of Pyrrhonism*, I, " Wherein Scepticism differs from . . . the Philosophy of Heraclitus" given as source.

[216] Ibid., p. 789; altered; Sextus Empiricus, *Outlines of Pyrrhonism*, I, "Wherein Scepticism differs from the Philosophy of Democritus" given as source.

The Cyrenaick sect affirms, that all bodies are of an incomprehensible nature.[217] But I am not of their opinion: for, although the interior, corporeal, figurative motions are not subject to every creature's perception, yet in nature they are not incomprehensible: As for example, the five senses in man, are both knowing and ignorant, not only of each other's perception, but of the several parts of exterior objects; for, the eye only perceives the exterior figure, magnitude and colour, and not the nose; the nose perceives its scent, but not its colour and magnitude; the ear perceives neither its magnitude, colour nor scent, but only its sound, and so forth. The like may be said of the infinite perceptive parts of nature, whereby they are both obscured and discovered to particulars, and so may be truly known in general, but not in particular, by any finite creature, or part of nature.

The Academics say, that some fancies are "credible," others "incredible"; and of those that are credible, some are "credible only," and some "credible and circumcurrent": As for example, a rope lying loosely in a dark room, a man receives a credible fancy from it, and runs away: Another considering it more exactly, and weighing the circumstances, as, that it moves not, that it is of such a colour, and the like; to him it appears a rope, according to the credible and circumcurrent fancy.[218] To which I answer; A mistake is an irregularity of sense, and sometimes of reason too: if sense be only mistaken, and not reason, reason rectifies sense; and if reason be only mistaken, and not sense, then sense rectifies reason; but when both sense and reason are mistaken, the irregularity doth either last longer, or changes into regularity, by the information of some other circumstances, and things which may rectify, sometimes, the irregular motions both of sense and reason; that is, the sensitive and rational motions of other parts, may rectify those irregularities.

I could make many more observations, not only upon the aforementioned, but several others of the ancient philosophers; but my design is not to refute their opinions, but, as I mentioned in the beginning, to show the difference between theirs, and my own: And by this we may see, that irregularities do not only appear in our present age, but have been also in times past; nay, ever since nature has been, or else there

---

[217] Ibid., p. 790; slightly altered; Sextus Empiricus, *Outlines of Pyrrhonism*, I, "Wherein Scepticism differs from the Cyrenaick Sect" given as source.

[218] Ibid., p. 791; slightly altered; Sextus Empiricus, *Outlines of Pyrrhonism*, I, "Wherein Scepticism differs from the Academick Philosophy" given as source.

would never have been such extravagant opinions concerning the truth of nature.

But the chief which I observe, is, that most of the ancient make a commixture of natural and supernatural; corporeal and incorporeal beings; and of animate and inanimate bodies. Some derive reason from fancy; and some introduce neutral beings, which are neither corporeal nor incorporeal, but between both; especially, they do make general principles of particular effects; and abstract quality, motion, accidents, figure, place, magnitude, etc. from matter, which causes so many confusions and differences in their opinions; nor can it be otherwise, because of the irregularities and divisions of nature's corporeal actions: and most of our moderns do either follow altogether the opinions of the ancient philosophers, putting them only into a new dress, or patch them up with some of their own, and so make a gallimaufry in natural philosophy.

Glossary

admire	to marvel or wonder at
allege	to quote or cite
antiperistasis	the opposition of contraries; the resistance brought about against any action
aqua fortis	nitric acid
aqua vitae	alcohol, especially of the first distillation
atmospherical pillars/ weather glasses	early thermometers; early barometers
by head and shoulders	violently or by force (figuratively used for things irreverently introduced in writing)
bo-peep	the child's game of alternately hiding and revealing one's face; peekaboo
bowl	a sphere or ball; a round solid body used in games such as nine-pins, skittles, bowling; a billiard ball
by rote	by the mere exercise of memory, without understanding; by custom or habit; with precision and by heart (Cavendish figuratively stretches the latter meaning when she describes dream images as produced "by rote" from the internal storehouse of memory. Mental content produced by rote is contrasted with content that requires an external occasional cause, e.g., occurrent sense perception.)

calorific	heat inducing
challenge	to lay claim to; demand as a right
Charles' Wain	seven bright stars in the constellation Ursa Major; also known as "the Plough"
circumcurrent	running around; considering all around
clarifaction	process of making a liquid free of impurities; act of clarifying
clayey	composed of, or of the nature of, clay
commodious/convenient	suitable; proper; fitting
conceit	an idea or thought; judgment; opinion
concoction	the ripening, maturing or perfecting of what is raw or coarse; the alteration of matter by moist heat; digestion
concretion	a compound body comprised of corporeal first principles
conventicle	a secret religious meeting of nonconformist sects or religious dissenters; a building used for these meetings
credible	deserving credit; of good repute; inclined to believe
decoction	an extraction of the principles of a substance by boiling it; reduction by evaporation in boiling; digestion; maturing or perfecting by heat
dilatation	process of dilating; expansion; widening out
disponent	disposing; inclining in a particular direction, or towards a specific end
distinguishment	a distinction
divine	a person, usually a cleric, skilled in theology
endue	endow; invest; to bring to a certain state or condition
equinoctial	a great circle on the celestial sphere in the same plane as the equator; the celestial circle
ergo	therefore (Latin)
except	to object; to leave out; to exclude; to excuse
exempt	debarred; excluded

existency	existence; a state or mode of being; a being; a substance
expense	an act of using up or consuming
exstruction	the action of building or piling up
fain	preferably; gladly; willingly; glad under the circumstances; desire; wish; obliged
frigorific	cold inducing; chilling
gownmen	members of the university
greensickness	Chlorosis: an iron-deficiency chiefly affecting girls at puberty, characterized by a greenish tint to the skin
ipse dixit	a dogmatic claim grounded solely in the authority of the speaker; from the Latin "he himself (the master) said it"
jennet	a Spanish saddle horse
joiner	a skilled carpenter, especially a cabinet-maker
kings-evils	a condition of the young with a disposition to acquire tuberculosis, and lymphatic and glandular swelling, which was held to be curable by the touch of the king or queen
kitling	the young of any animal; a kitten
lumber	a pawnbroker's shop
mechanics	the mechanical philosophers, e.g., Hobbes and Boyle, who held that all natural phenomena could be explained in terms of the configurations of material, impenetrable particles, and the changes in the particles' degrees of motion due to impact
mode	currently in style or in vogue; a property (e.g., shape) which cannot subsist by itself, but must inhere in a substance (e.g., body)
non plus	not more; no more (Latin)
non ultra	not beyond; none beyond (Latin)
otherways	otherwise
peculiar	distinct and particular; individual
periwig	a wig

philosophers' stone	in the alchemical tradition, the substance which can transform baser metals into gold
posset	hot, sweetened milk, curdled with wine or ale, and mixed with spices
precise	to particularize, to define precisely
propriety	property, especially an essential or distinctive quality; proper or particular characteristic
rarefaction	process of refining by decreasing something's solidity or density
remove	act of changing one's place; shifting a thing from one place to another
several	single; distinct
siccity	lack of moisture; dryness
spirituous	containing a volatile principle; having the nature of, or containing, alcohol
surfeiting meat	[not seventeenth-century usage; possibly one of the following] excess, leftover meat; putrid meat that causes "surfeit" or illness; vomited meat
tenter	a tenterhook; a hooked organ or part
that . . . this (sing.)/ those . . . these (pl.)	the former . . . the latter
this . . . that (sing.)/ these . . . those (pl.)	the latter . . . the former
transeunt causation	causation taking place between distinct entities, in contrast with immanent causation
trencher	a knife or slicing instrument; a platter of wood, metal or earthenware
turner	one who turns or crafts objects of wood, metal, etc. on a lathe; a potter
under the line	at the equator
virtuoso (sing.)/ virtuosi (pl.)	someone with a general interest in the arts and sciences, and who pursues scholarly investigations; a wit or *savant*; a scientist,

	especially a member of the Royal Society of London
vitriol	a sulfate of a metal, e.g. ferrous sulfate (green vitriol), copper sulfate (blue vitriol), etc.; early chemists used the term to indicate elemental salt
whenas	whereas; when
withal	besides; in addition; nevertheless; therewith; with
without	outside of, or exterior to; unless; except that

Index

Index

breeding, 66–8
Bréhier, Émile, xxi n. 16
butterfly, 29, 61–2

causation, xxix–xxx, xxxv
cause, xxx–xxxiv, 113–16, 141–2, 165, 176,
    178, 193, 203, 206, 209, 211, 236, 242, 271
    occasional, xxxiii, xxxiv, 19–20, 27, 28, 40,
    119, 121, 140, 155, 170–1, 176, 234, 269,
    primary or principal, xxxi, xxxiii, 116
Cavendish, Charles, xiii, xviii
Cavendish, Margaret
    Grounds of Natural Philosophy, xvii
    Observations upon Experimental Philosophy,
    xvii, xxxvi, 11, 13
    The Philosophical and Physical Opinions, xvi,
    xx, 13, 57, 94, 151, 181, 247
    Philosophicall Fancies, xiv, xvii, xx, xxi
    Philosophical Letters, xvi, xviii, 11, 13, 57,
    67, 74, 136, 191, 251
    Poems, and Fancies, xv, 212
    "To Naturall Philosophers", xvi
Cavendish, William, xiii
chance, 82, 129, 169, 240, 258, 263–5, 267
change, xxix, xxxii, xxxiv, 18, 132–4, 137, 166,
    261, 270
chaos, xxviii, 229
Charleton, Walter, xiii, xiv, xv, xviii, xxix n.
    25, 10 n. 8, 100 n. 77, 114 n. 82, 120 n. 86
Châtelet, (Gabrielle) Emilie de Breteuil,
    Marquise du, xxxvi
cheese, 67, 115, 170
chemistry/chemists, xxxvi, 91, 227–41
Christianity, xxiii, 218
Christina, Queen of Sweden, xii
Chrysippus, xxii
Cicero, Marcus Tullius, xxxi, 7 and n. 4
Cleomedes, xxii n. 18
Clucas, Stephen, xxi n. 15
Coffey, Peter, xxx n. 26
cold, 54–5, 58, 72, 84, 95–106, 111–16, 117,
    120–4, 177, 180, 271
colour, 37–8, 75–87, 88–90, 98, 146–8, 160, 162,
    169, 176–7, 180, 193–4, 248, 253, 274
    black, 75–8, 80, 84, 85, 86, 98
    white, 76–8, 84, 85, 86, 98
complexion, 76, 84–5
composition, 20, 29, 32, 35–6, 130, 132,
    139–40, 145, 156, 161–2, 167, 178, 181,
    189, 192–3, 199, 204, 225, 228, 232, 234,
    236, 255, 257, 261, 263, 270
comprehension, 17, 274
conception, 149–51, 158, 170, 187, 192, 256
concord, 34, 258

concretions, primary, 234 n. 151
    see also *minima naturalia*
condensation, 58, 72, 232
congelation, 107, 110–11, 113, 117, 123–4
contraction, 35, 106–7, 124–5, 172–3, 189, 232,
    245
Conway, Anne, x, xi, xii, xviii, xx
corruption, 123, 259, 269
Crates, 223 n. 143
creation, 36, 137, 173, 202, 212, 236–7, 241,
    254, 266
cylinder, xxxi, xxxiv
Cyrano de Bergerac, Savinien de, 4 n. 2
Cyrenaick sect, 274

darkness, 75–8
death, 81, 98, 120, 204, 225
decay, 151, 172
Dee, John, 87 and n. 59
Democritus, xiv, xviii, 273
density, 30, 125–6, 129, 193
Descartes, René, x; xii–xvi; xix; xxiii; xxiv n.
    22; xxix; xxxiii n. 29; xxxv; xxxvi; 10 nn.
    8, 9; 74–5 and n. 49; 86 n. 57; 106 n. 81;
    116 n. 85; 120 n. 86; 128; 146 n. 102; 153
    n. 105; 200; 236 n. 155
Dicaearchus, 223 n. 143
Digby, Kenelm, x, xiii, xv, xvii, xxi
digestion, 35, 139, 151–2, 162, 172, 175, 189,
    245
    see also fermentation
dilatation, 35, 124–5, 172–3, 189, 232, 245
diminution, 128, 268–70
Diogenes Laertius, 250 nn. 163, 171, 172; 259
    n. 188; 260 n. 194; 261 n. 196; 263 n. 198;
    264 n. 199; 265 n. 200; 271 n. 210
discourse, 14, 49
disease, 232, 241–3, 245–7, 254
dissolution, 69, 128, 139, 145, 167, 170, 172–3,
    191, 199, 204, 212, 225, 228, 261, 270
distance, 130–1, 168, 184
distempers, 20, 33, 232, 241
divinity, 214, 239
division, xxvi, 20, 32, 35–6, 132, 139–40, 145,
    156, 161–2, 178, 181, 192–3, 199, 232,
    234, 236–7, 255, 257, 259, 261, 263, 270
Donne, John, 209 and n. 138
dreams, 20, 33, 77, 171, 189
dropsy, 66, 242
dryness, 54–5, 58, 271
Duchesne, Joseph, 204 n. 129
Dumée, Jeanne, xi

ears, 151–2, 160, 173, 177, 180, 185–6, 223, 274

282

Cambridge texts in the history of philosophy

Titles published in the series thus far

Aristotle *Nicomachean Ethics* (edited by Roger Crisp)

Arnauld and Nicole *Logic or the Art of Thinking* (edited by Jill Vance Buroker)

Bacon *The New Organon* (edited by Lisa Jardine and Michael Silverthorne)

Boyle *A Free Enquiry into the Vulgarly Received Notion of Nature* (edited by Edward B. Davis and Michael Hunter)

Bruno *Cause, Principle and Unity* and *Essays on Magic* (edited by Richard Blackwell and Robert de Lucca with an introduction by Alfonso Ingegno)

Cavendish *Observations upon Experimental Philosophy* (edited by Eileen O'Neill)

Cicero *On Moral Ends* (edited by Julia Annas, translated by Raphael Woolf)

Clarke *A Demonstration of the Being and Attributes of God and Other Writings* (edited by Ezio Vailati)

Condillac *Essay on the Origin of Human Knowledge* (edited by Hans Aarsleff)

Conway *The Principles of the Most Ancient and Modern Philosophy* (edited by Allison P. Coudert and Taylor Corse)

Cudworth *A Treatise Concerning Eternal and Immutable Morality* with *A Treatise of Freewill* (edited by Sarah Hutton)

Descartes *Meditations on First Philosophy*, with selections from the *Objections and Replies* (edited by John Cottingham)

Descartes *The World and Other Writings* (edited by Stephen Gaukroger)

Fichte *Foundations of Natural Right* (edited by Frederick Neuhouser, translated by Michael Baur)

Hobbes and Bramhall on Liberty and Necessity (edited by Vere Chappell)

Humboldt *On Language* (edited by Michael Losonsky, translated by Peter Heath)

Kant *Critique of Practical Reason* (edited by Mary Gregor with an introduction by Andrews Reath)

Kant *Groundwork of the Metaphysics of Morals* (edited by Mary Gregor with an introduction by Christine M. Korsgaard)

Kant *The Metaphysics of Morals* (edited by Mary Gregor with an introduction by Roger Sullivan)

Kant *Prolegomena to Any Future Metaphysics* (edited by Gary Hatfield)

Kant *Religion within the Boundaries of Mere Reason and Other Writings* (edited by Allen Wood and George di Giovanni with an introduction by Robert Merrihew Adams)

La Mettrie *Machine Man and Other Writings* (edited by Ann Thomson)

Leibniz *New Essays on Human Understanding* (edited by Peter Remnant and Jonathan Bennett)

Malebranche *Dialogues on Metaphysics and on Religion* (edited by Nicholas Jolley and David Scott)

Malebranche *The Search after Truth* (edited by Thomas M. Lennon and Paul J. Olscamp)

Melanchthon *Orations on Philosophy and Education* (edited by Sachiko Kusukawa, translated by Christine Salazar)

Mendelssohn *Philosophical Writings* (edited by Daniel O. Dahlstrom)

Nietzsche *The Birth of Tragedy and Other Writings* (edited by Raymond Geuss and Ronald Speirs)

Nietzsche *Daybreak* (edited by Maudemarie Clark and Brian Leiter, translated by R. J. Hollingdale)

Nietzsche *Human, All Too Human* (translated by R. J. Hollingdale with an introduction by Richard Schacht)

Nietzsche *Untimely Meditations* (edited by Daniel Breazeale, translated by R. J. Hollingdale)

Schleiermacher *Hermeneutics and Criticism* (edited by Andrew Bowie)

Schleiermacher *On Religion: Speeches to its Cultured Despisers* (edited by Richard Crouter)

Schopenhauer *Prize Essay on the Freedom of the Will* (edited by Günter Zöller)

Sextus Empiricus *Outlines of Scepticism* (edited by Julia Annas and Jonathan Barnes)

Shaftesbury *Characteristics of Men, Manners, Opinions, Times* (edited by Lawrence Klein)

Voltaire *Treatise on Tolerance and Other Writings* (edited by Simon Harvey)

CPSIA information can be obtained at www.ICGtesting.com
Printed in the USA
LVOW10s1933030816

498924LV00002B/179/P